UNLEASHING INDIA
ON WORLD MARKETS

UNLEASHING INDIA ON WORLD MARKETS

Raghu Nandan

Response Books
A division of Sage Publications
New Delhi / Thousand Oaks / London

First published in 2001 by

Response Books
A division of Sage Publications India Pvt Ltd
32 M–Block Market, Greater Kailash–I
New Delhi 110 048

Sage Publications Inc	Sage Publications Ltd
2455 Teller Road	6 Bonhill Street
Thousand Oaks, California 91320	London EC2A 4PU

Published by Tejeshwar Singh for Response Books, typeset in 10.3 pts Cheltham by Line Arts Phototypesetters, Pondicherry and printed at Chaman Enterprises, Delhi.

Library of Congress Cataloging-in-Publication Data
Nandan, Raghu.
   Unleashing India on world markets/Raghu Nandan.
      p. cm.
   Includes bibliographical references and index.
   1. India—Commerce. 2. Exports—India. I. Title.
   HF3786.5 .N26 2001   382'.6'0954—dc21   2001020226

ISBN: 0–7619–9530–7 (US-Hb)   81–7829–007–3 (India-Hb)
       0–7619–9531–5 (US-Pb)   81–7829–008–1 (India-Pb)

Production Team: Sangeeta Goswami, R.A.M. Brown and Santosh Rawat

DEDICATION

I dedicate this book to the person who gets my vote as the

INDIAN OF THE CENTURY

Throughout this book, the reader will detect a strong undercurrent of a single thought. We, Indians, are not good at working with each other. We tend not to build strong commercial, professional, political or cultural institutions. Rather, we are good at splitting them, as each of us wants to be the boss.

This is nothing new or recent. Recorded history shows that we have always been so. This notwithstanding, the fact remains that we have always had a tradition of excellence running parallel to our divisive nature. We have had far more talented, dedicated and brilliant people than most other nations. Look at the exquisitely carved temples and other structures our ancestors have left behind. Every inch speaks volumes about our work ethic and our attitude towards quality consciousness. Nobody supervised the craftsmen, but, say, my ancestor detected a tiny fault in a stone he had been working on for months. I know for certain that he would not patch it up and put it in. He would, instead, throw it away and start the carving all over again!

The tragedy of my nation is that at a time when some of my ancestors were dedicating their lifetimes building unmatched structures, certain other of my ancestors were busy fighting with each other, breaking up the kingdoms into ever smaller bits and pieces, or joining hands with the invaders.

Today, even with all our massive intellectual capital and resources, we are going around the world with a begging bowl.

I am proud to mention an exception.

There is one Indian who has shown that if we cooperate with each other, we can build a massive, world beating organisation. Unlike most other Indian commercial organisations which are single generation success stories, splitting up as soon as the old man dies, this organisation is built on a strong foundation of a truly cooperative spirit and is structured to grow and never split.

He is the man who has forced us into building a model institution of economic democracy. He showed us how it was possible, by working with each other, to turn India from a deficit to a surplus nation in milk production.

I dedicate this book to
DR VERGHESE KURIEN

Words are not adequate here as I am on my knees before the Almighty praying for many more Indians like him.

CONTENTS

PREAMBLE

What this book is and is not

Ideas I stand for are not mine. I have borrowed from Socrates, I have copied them from Chesterfield, I have stolen from Jesus. And I put them in a book. If you do not like these, whose would you rather use?

DALE CARNEGIE

India is a prisoner of its overseas trade. But see, the door is locked from within

I have often got into arguments with my friends in India who find this remark silly or even offensive. Are we not a sovereign independent nation? Well, never mind what we think of ourselves, the world indeed thinks poorly of us.

We are living on international handouts and are hampered in what we do as we do possess any clout. Even small nations do not look up to us. It all boils down to our economic strength on the world market, the strength of our foreign trade. We, the world's second largest nation, had, in 1950, only a 1.91 per cent share of the world trade. In 1998, this went down to a humiliating 0.07 per cent!

I am not proud of what we have done to our nation. My father's generation left us a nation that was comfortably well off. We were earning enough foreign exchange for our needs and had plenty of self respect. My generation has made a mess of things and we are now being forced to live on the above-mentioned handouts.

Why I wrote this book

I am keen to talk to the next generation to get them to wake up. In caliber, enlightenment and knowledge this generation is far ahead of mine. All that is needed is a change of attitude and we will unlock all doors and unleash India on world markets.

There are many questions about my country that have been bothering me. This book is the result of what I have seen of the developing world all my working life, and what I have seen of India through the eyes of the people of these nations coupled with my own probing into the mindset of the business community of my generation.

My various assignments have taught me a lot and this book is an attempt at sharing some of this knowledge with the next generation of my fellow Indians. Looking from the outside in, I think I have developed a slightly different perspective on our problems. Now, back to what motivated me to write this book. Well, three points mainly:

- Are we really interested in exporting? This may seem like an inane question but I will illustrate with an example. My experience of coming to India looking for skilled people, the know-how, and the equipment for my small- and medium-scale manufacturing projects in Africa, etc. left me very frustrated. In all my dealings with an entire spectrum of the Indian business community, I had the nagging feeling that they considered me more a nuisance rather than a prospective buyer. I failed to understand why our people considered exports an unmitigated headache. I feel very strongly about this and have done some plain-speaking about some of my personal experiences in Chapter 1.
- The second point concerns my interaction with MBA and PGDM students in various institutions all over the country where I am invited as a guest lecturer and sometimes as an external examiner. I find that students, almost without exception, are looking forward to a career with an MNC. If not, they would like to get a job with what they call a 'lala' company, work here for a while and then start something of their own. To me, this is a serious indictment and condemnation of our entire corporate sector. I feel very strongly about this, too, and have done a lot of probing into the mindset of our business leaders. (Chapter 2.3).
- The third point concerns the benefits of a nation organising itself. The British conquest of the world enormously benefited the common man back home in England enabling the nation to grow more powerful, while the Spanish and Portuguese conquests did no such thing as it was only the noblemen who benefited from these conquests. The reason is simply because the British people worked together to build strong commercial and trade institutions while the Spaniards etc. worked on the principle of each man for himself. (Chapter 2.5) In recent times, I have seen with my own eyes how the ethnic Chinese, who are only a small minority in most Asian nations, command enormous economic clout through their abilities of mutual networking and of uniting against everybody else. It is tragic but true that though overseas

Indians often form the largest ethnic group in many countries, we are known more for our internal rifts and bickering. Take tiny Fiji. We are the largest ethnic group, but have over 180 associations that are always at loggerheads!

The point I am trying to make is that while the overseas Chinese are getting stronger, the overseas Indians are losing ground wherever they are. The overseas Chinese are increasingly going into China and contributing to the massive growth of the economy there by getting products made for their own markets with their know-how. By contrast, no overseas Indian can come to India to get anything made for his own market as Indians, even our big traders, do not have captive markets anywhere. True, we do make investments in India but these are purely on the basis of 'best-rate-of-return'. I have found overseas Indians going as readily to Pakistan if the return is better. I know many Indians in the Silicon Valley who have made huge investments in computer hardware in Taiwan. I feel very strongly about this, too, and talk about it in Chapters 3.4, 4.4, 4.5 and 7.3. This is a problem that needs to be addressed.

The issues I seek to address

In the following paragraphs I present an extract of the various issues I seek to address in this book. These paragraphs are not a chapter-by-chapter summary, but rather an overview of the points I am making, because many chapters overlap in context.

It is silly blaming the government for everything

Blaming everything on the government using the excuse that India has been a protected market etc. is nonsense. We seem to be very fond of first blaming everything on the government and then, if that does not hold water, blaming the politicians and corruption. Lastly, we have always availed of the last resort of blaming the British!

True, our successive governments have implemented various policies of import substitution and protecting the domestic markets. I will look at these policies from two angles.

(a) One is that having a protected market, or a closed economy, by itself does not lead to any damage to the economy. Almost every emerging economy has tried to protect fledgling domestic producers. Further, no domestic market has been more jealously and rigorously protected than Japan's, Korea's and also, to some extent Taiwan's. When I go into the details, I will compare, with India, the various tariff and non-tariff barriers that, till recently, have been in place making imports of finished products into these countries next to impossible. Yet, the same protective policy that is said to have destroyed the Indian economy, has lead to mind-boggling development in these countries.

(b) The other is that, looking at our economic history, we have never been aggressive exporters, and import substitution as a strategy for industrial development is nothing new. It has always been present in the Indian mindset, even decades before independence. It was certainly not the brainchild of our founding fathers, though they are roundly blamed for it. Prof. Mahalanobis and possibly Pandit Nehru merely developed the centuries old Indian mindset into our first comprehensive master plan.

In this book, there is no discussion of government policies, or what the government should or should not be doing. I am concerned with only a managerial approach to the problem of our declining exports. I will discuss some export sectors, or missed opportunities, which have not the remotest connection with government policies, incentives or constraints.

The days of the small, one-man-exporter outfits are gone

The days when a briefcase carrying salesman could show samples and book export orders are gone. It has to be the large firms now, and it simply has to be a matter of national attitude. Neither governments nor small timers were the engines for the relentless and sometimes ruthless push into the overseas markets and growth in Japan and Korea.

Not only amongst the Asian Tigers, but in every successful nation it is the large firms that spearhead the drive into exports. In India, on the contrary, the attitude of our business leaders is killing our exports and our economy. I will discuss, in Chapter 2.3, that the majority of our country's largest corporations have no interest in exports. They export very little, but the value of their imports is so large that they account for the largest net outflow of foreign exchange!

Commercial and organisational infrastructure

This is the other main point of this book. In very simple words, this also means how we work with each other in the business and economic context. Without a solid, cohesive and dynamic commercial and organisational infrastructure we can forget about the export markets we already have, leave aside conquering new markets in the developing world.

I explain what these terms mean in the context of the dismal performance of our export sector, in Chapter 2.5, but I come to this point again and again in the course of the book.

The new economy of today is dominated by inter-company trade and person-to-person communication across the table. Countries no longer trade; people and businesses do. Networks, strong in commercial and organisational infrastructure, are at the core of the new global economy.

I will examine how the last 15 years have seen the phenomenal growth of Japanese, Korean, and Singapore Chinese export houses. These firms now have an extensive network of branches in all the major cities in India as well as all over Asia, Africa, the West Indies and South America, and have virtually changed the rules of the game. They are characterised by strong organisational infrastructure, rapidly taking the market for non-traditional exports away from Indian export houses. (Chapter 4)

When it comes to the very essential network of branches we need all over the world, forget our large business houses, even the large export houses have almost no professionally managed network outside India. 'I have my son in New York and my cousin in Frankfurt' seems to be just about it.

Killing our markets with 'Guanxi'

It is true that the Chinese also have only small, family-owned firms, but the Chinese overseas are a network of networks. Their's are small and family-owned businesses which stay singularly apart, but which work together when the need arises. When there is a crisis or a great opportunity presents itself, they close ranks and cooperate. This is called 'Guanxi'.

These small, family-owned firms excel at integrating design talent, manufacturing capacity, production management expertise, marketing and packaging skills, and financing to produce products nobody can compete with.

All the key players among the ethnic Chinese know each other. They are intensely competitive among themselves, but rigidly exclude outsiders, especially those not of the same family, village or clan.

The family businesses of the Chinese overseas are networks, of companies and other enterprises, of clans and villages. An outstanding characteristic of the ethnic Chinese network is that no one is in charge. The marketplace is in charge.

Individual ethnic Chinese networks of companies are completely decentralised from the whole; yet they are extraordinarily efficient parts of the whole.

How, what and where to sell

What I have tried to convey above, and the approach I am taking in this book, is that we need not worry about trying to export what the Japanese, the Europeans or the Americans are exporting. We do not have the stuff these people are selling.

Our strategy should be to sell lower technology items to the Japanese, the Europeans and the Americans. And more important, try to sell even lower technology products to the huge market in the developing world which we have so far completely ignored.

For this, our only competition is Taiwan, Korea and China. For China, read the overseas Chinese living in Singapore, Hong Kong and all over Asia.

If we are going to fight them, it is important for us to know these nations. I have devoted a lot of this book in taking a hard look at them. How they think and work, how they organise themselves and most important, how we can trade with them—what I call the Asian renaissance. (Chapter 4)

Hurdles or bottlenecks

The first and most damaging one is, of course, the fact that every Indian is in it for himself and there is no cohesive effort at presenting a solid front to the competition. (Chapters 1.4 and 1.5)

The second is the fact that India has a very poor capacity for producing the tools and moulds which are the lifeblood of most manufacturing units. This is, indeed, tragic because we have a fantastic pool of highly trained and skilled mould makers who earn more than their share of respect overseas. Tata Precision Industries in Singapore is a very well respected name in the high tech mould-and-tool-making world of Singapore and is staffed predominantly by Indians. Yet, back home, most of the plastic and engineering units import their requirement. (Chapter 3.2)

Third, our NRIs or overseas Indians. It is sad that I am mentioning our overseas Indians as a bottleneck, but it is true. In most of the developing world, which is the target market for our goods, the NRIs and overseas Indians are professionals and traders who have money but no clout and have no captive markets to offer. Their success depends upon the success of the host countries. But when an Indian exporter ventures into a country, if there are local people of Indian origin, that is the first contact point. And there the matter ends, as this precludes direct contact and dealings with other ethnic people in the particular country. Particularly in countries like South Africa, Kenya, Thailand, Malaysia and Singapore, the local Indian generally does not have the capacity, or the organisation or even the inclination to develop the market for a new product. He will, at best, import what he needs for his own setup. But the real tragedy is that he will never say so. He will never, ever, introduce a visitor to a suitable local party and stand back.

Fourth, our attitude towards homework before and after an overseas exposure. The executive, or more often, the son of the big boss, just does not seem to find the time to read about the countries to be visited, to educate oneself on the customs and the business climate, and to prepare for the competition likely to be encountered. He is busy getting brochures and pricelists ready. There is always a lot to do before the trip. And after the trip, there is a new set of hurdles: the propensity to hoard knowledge, the unwillingness to put on record what has been learnt during the trip, and the lack of incentives to share the information. People are generally not willing to share knowledge in terms of what could be valuable to others within the company.

Fifth, I will seek to establish a connection between the overwhelming shoddiness of goods produced in India and our way of life. I feel it is possible that shoddiness has become a habit with us and is seriously damaging our export prospects. To us, 'quality' does not include 'finish'. It is my firm belief that firms that have a tradition of stringent quality control for all their products at all times demonstrate better export performance than those that produce some items specially for export. To me a label saying 'Export Quality' is an advertisement that the rest of the goods produced are shoddy. Like a hotel advertising 'clean sheets and towels in the deluxe rooms'.

Sixth, in view of liberalisation, our business leaders are increasingly turning to purchasing readymade know-how and technology and are moving away from investments in R&D. In many places in this book, I have said that the lack of innovativeness in our industry is one of the major hurdles for our exports.

By lack of innovativeness I certainly do not mean that we have any shortage of clever, original ideas, but 'Short cuts' has almost become our definition of innovativeness. Go to a roadside mechanic and he will somehow get your old Buick going again by repairing the carburettor with a piece of string. Enter an Air-India aircraft and the first thing that hits you in the face is the use of sticky tape as the ubiquitous repair tool everywhere. Even the tape which is used is carelessly torn and slapped on shoddily. Is that, to us in modern India, innovativeness? I seek to establish that our attitude towards innovativeness, i.e. of somehow getting things done, is landing us in trouble. We are losing the export markets we already have to highly innovative producers of consumer goods.

What this book is not

As a very general yardstick, I have tried to complement rather than compete with what an average MBA or PGDM student in India is likely to have read. There are any number of excellent text books, guides and books presenting data by Indian and foreign authors on the subject of export promotion and marketing. Therefore, I do not go into the details of export documentation, procedures, custom and other formalities.

Apart from the published material, the Federation of Indian Export Organisations has a number of excellent institutions affiliated to it where an entire gamut of courses are offered. These go into all manners of detail on how one should start an export house, how one should go looking for a market, what the export formalities are, how one can go about getting the finance and the various exports incentives available in India, etc.

I see no point in repeating ground that has already been covered.

I have also tried to avoid a discussion of the problems of our more traditional items of export because these have been the subject of endless debate and numerous papers have been published on it. I do not, therefore, write in detail about textiles, leather goods, bicycles and bicycle parts, engineering goods, agricultural produce, non-processed industrial raw materials, and so on.

Again, I have not prepared long tables of analysis and graphs of our published import and export statistics. Events in our country are taking place so rapidly that, except for the purpose of proving a point, these become quickly outdated. There are a few exceptions and I have used published data and statistics only when essential to the context, or to indicate a trend.

As I said above, I have tried to avoid too much discussion of government policies or of what the government should or should not be doing. True, I am detailing some of the strong points of our past and present economic policy but only to compare the effects of these with that of similar policies in other countries.

I am looking at the problem of our dismal export performance from a managerial angle. I do not believe we can get away by simply blaming all our problems on the government.

PART ONE

Indian Managerial Attitudes

*If you want your company to work like a family,
keep your family out of your company.*

1
A collection of short stories

You say you are competitive in price and quality?
Good. That is only the first step.

1.1   *The developing world*
                                    wants to import from india

Let's start with some stories

During a management seminar for senior executives of Indian business houses, I gave examples of some practical problems faced by
importers in other countries, particularly the developing countries in
Africa, Asia and South America, when wanting to import from India.

Though the seminar addressed some general aspects of the structural weakness of the Indian economy, I gave three examples which
illustrated that it was not an accident that India was losing the
export markets, particularly in the developing countries, nor was it
accidental that the very aggressive export houses from the East
Asian countries, Taiwan, Korea, Malaysia and Singapore, were gob-
bling up these markets.

At the end, when the seminar was thrown open for discussion,
I was shocked by the highly emotional response from some of
the participants. It seems I had exposed a sensitive nerve. I was
amazed that many of our senior executives were not aware of the
true status of India in the world market, and were actually offended
when this was spelled out. This lead to some heated debate and the
seminar developed in a most unexpected direction. We will talk
about this in the next chapter.

Now to illustrate the problem, some personal experiences. The
first example concerned an opportunity that came up when I was
on an assignment in Malawi (Central Africa). This was some years
ago.

Malawi wants help to make photo albums

Malawi is one of the better-governed countries in Africa, and the
only black African country that always had good relations with
South Africa. As a result, it had plenty of aid and assistance from
South Africa, and the average Malawian had a somewhat better
standard of living.

I seek to establish that there are three main problems with our export effort.
First is the very low priority accorded by our commercial sectors to anything to
do with exports.
Second, the level at which we are conducting our export marketing—small individual exporters, mainly concerned with benefiting from the incentives. We
shall discuss this in Chapters 5.1 and 5.6.
Third, the poor backup these people get from the industrial, trading, and service sectors. These sectors, in India, are almost all entirely small, individual
or family-owned-and-managed firms. Each operates in isolation. There is no
cohesive effort. True, there are the big business houses, but they are all
inward looking and not the least interested in exports. More on this in Chapters 2.3 and 2.5.

I was the team leader on an assignment funded by the Industrial
Development Fund of the Commonwealth Secretariat, London. A
Malawian entrepreneur had put in a request for technical assistance
to manufacture the full range of photo albums. This was a project in
the small-scale sector and the entrepreneur was looking for an overseas source of know-how to help him set up the project. He was
keen on a transfer of technology, the supply of equipment, a long-
term contract for supply of raw materials, and help in selling the output to other African countries. The overseas party was not required
to invest, as the necessary funds had been arranged.

Since the Malawian entrepreneur was a person of Indian origin,
(his family had moved to Malawi three generations ago) and since
India is a member of the Commonwealth fund, on my suggestion,
the concerned industrial development people of Malawi wrote to
the Indian High Commission there. They suggested that we write to
a few large Indian firms, export houses and export promotion agencies. There was no reply. I wrote reminders explaining that this was
not a simple, one-time export order but a proposal for a technical
joint venture which would be a source of continuing revenue for a
suitable firm in India for many years.

There was still no reply. We got a routine note from one of the
Export Promotion agencies that the inquiry would be circulated to
the members. That was that.

I came to India. I saw many superb Indian-made albums in various shops. Most of these had only a brand name and no address.

The first hurdle was to find out who made these. The shopkeeper, of course, was of no help. We did not have any yellow pages in those days and the trade directories were hopelessly outdated. I had to spend a back-breaking week before I could locate, near Delhi, a firm that was producing a full range of excellent albums. They had developed the technology indigenously—no joint venture, no technical collaboration and no overseas help. This was a family-owned partnership firm, entirely managed by two brothers and a cousin, with no professional senior staff or executives. They said that they were not registered anywhere so naturally none of the government agencies knew about them. The quality of the product was reasonable and suited the Malawian firm's requirements.

I travelled to Delhi and was very well received by one of the partners. We discussed the proposal in detail. However, I got a very polite no. The firm was just not interested.

They explained that they had a management problem. They gave me an example. They said that they supplied the albums all over India. The cost of transport was sometimes much greater than the cost of the albums. Yet, they had never considered having a subsidiary factory in the South or anywhere else. They did not have anybody to spare to be sent to the South. 'We cannot even have another factory in our own country, how can we get involved in a project overseas?' They were also not keen to make an initial offer for exports. Too many complications, too many formalities and, besides, there were some family problems to sort out first.

I was devastated. I went back to Malaysia, (I was based there at the time,) and casually mentioned this problem to some friends over drinks and dinner. The next day, I was shocked to get a call from my counterpart in Malawi. The local rep of a Korean firm was sitting with him to discuss the project! One of my friends at the dinner, it seems, was connected with a Korean firm in Malaysia and the message had been flashed overnight!

I can cite hundreds of examples like this from all over the country. There is a certain person making disposable plastic cups and plates in Pondicherry. He has a good market in Delhi and Punjab. The items are light but bulky and so the cost of transport is much greater than the cost of the items. He has never considered setting up another unit in the North. Why? 'I have only one son and he is in the computer line'.

HERE IS SOME HOMEWORK FOR YOU:

When participants sign up for my seminars, I sometimes give them a small assignment to complete before they come to the venue. I suggest the reader try this too.

The assignment goes something like this. The idea is to put yourself in the place of a buyer from, say, Kenya, who comes to India for a short visit, say two weeks, to locate and negotiate with suppliers of specific items.

Give yourself the same two weeks to do this.

First task. Look around in your bathroom and kitchen and note the brands on commonly used non-electrical items. Items like taps, the sink, the tub or the pots and pans. Your assignment is to locate the manufacturer. Remember, you are not looking for any manufacturer of, say, bathroom taps. You need to locate the firm that makes the particular brand of taps you saw. Feel free to use any means you have—phones, friends, shopkeepers, trade directories, whatever.

Second task. Pretend you are from Nairobi and are interested in importing stainless steel kitchen sinks from India. Give yourself two weeks to get an export offer. Remember, any dealer in India, even someone dealing in bicycles, will tell you that he can export kitchen sinks! Your task is to get FOB (Free On Board) and CIF (Cost, Insurance and Freight) quotations. Again, feel free to use any means you have.

You will get a first-hand idea of the frustrations an overseas buyer faces when visiting India to look for products.

A small manufacturer tries to export bicycle seats.

The second example illustrated one of the very common problems faced by foreign importers when dealing with small manufacturers who try to do their own exports. It should be remembered that the bulk of India's export in manufactured goods is through this channel, i.e. individual foreign importers dealing with individual manufacturers/exporters here. Exports via large organised firms which have their own network of branches overseas is very minimal. I am not talking about the exports of commodities and other low value-added bulk items.

Here again, it will be seen that the problem is the very poorly organised small, family-owned firm where the owner has to allocate his time between taking his sick mother to the hospital, looking after the purchases, production and sales, and the huge amount of paperwork involved with exports. For small export orders, it is obviously not worthwhile to engage a professional to handle all the paperwork. The problem I am highlighting here results from the common practice of avoiding record keeping. For fear of the tax-man, firms try to have as little information on paper as can be helped, making it impossible for the owner-manager to keep track of inventory.

This story repeats itself all over India and is typical of one man trying to do everything.

I was living in Malaysia when I had a visitor from Delhi who was a friend of a friend. He was keen to export bicycle seats. I took him to a Chinese friend who was importing the items from Taiwan and Hong Kong. He was shown two brands, Ajanta and Ellora. The quality and the price were about the same. The main difference was the very attractively designed brand emblems in embossed brass fixed to every piece. My friend liked the look of the products and the price and decided to place an order for a fairly large consignment on two conditions. One, he would not extend the letter of credit (L/C) beyond the stipulated three months delivery period as this would add to the cost, and two, the supplier was free to choose any of the two brands he showed, but the brand must be mentioned in the L/C and could not be changed after the order was placed. The supplier agreed to supply the Ajanta brand and accepted the order.

I was quite impressed with the way the exporter presented himself and his products and so was not prepared for a frantic telex (this was before the days of the fax) I got a couple of weeks after the L/C expired. It said that the consignment was already at Bombay port, but could not be shipped as the L/C had expired. It asked for the L/C to please be extended by another three months. If the consignment was already at the port, why three months?

Anyway, I persuaded my friend to extend the L/C by bearing part of the cost.

This was met by silence for another two months. We received no response to our telexes. Then, suddenly, I again got a very interesting and unexpected telex. I was told that the entire consignment at the Bombay port had been stolen! However, to keep up the good-will, they were willing to re-supply the whole order and bear the loss, but the Ajanta brand was not available and I was requested to modify the L/C for Ellora!

Anybody but a fool could have seen through the ploy. As I confirmed later, the 'consignment at Bombay' was just a bluff. The exporter could not get the consignment ready till the first L/C had already expired. Then, on getting everything ready, he found that he did not have any stock of the embossed emblems for Ajanta. The lead time for delivery of the new emblems was six months, so the fellow had no choice but to supply the other brand and cook up a clever story of theft.

This not only destroyed this fellow's chances of ever getting any business from Malaysia again, he also destroyed his country's goodwill because my Chinese friend openly ridiculed India and Indians.

I would say that the brilliance of thought and inventiveness shown by the fellow after the event should have been redirected to working more productively!

I cannot say that the fellow was a crook or a cheat or even a bad businessman. I came to Delhi and met him and after all these years he still remains a good friend. He simply had too much on his hands. As I said, this story repeats itself all over India and is typical of one man trying to do everything.

Europe needs our pressure cookers

The commercial attaché of the Indian Embassy in Germany was on a visit to Frankfurt and I met him at a dinner hosted by a local businessman. A leading German entrepreneur who owned a number of wholesale outlets all over Europe was with us at the same table.

He apologised for 'talking shop' at a social function, but wanted to know if the Indian Embassy could intervene in a small problem he was having with a well-respected industrial group in India.

It seems he had been shown some samples of excellently made pressure cookers. The prices were very attractive and he immediately placed a small order. The goods arrived and were sold in no time at all. During the next year or so, he placed larger and larger orders and was able to corner a fair share of the market. Suddenly, the firm in India decided to discontinue the business!

I was coming to India so I brought a letter from the Indian Embassy and went personally to meet the party. I was told a story that must have been repeated countless times all over the country. The explanation was simple. They had now developed an excellent market in India and were not able to feed the demand. Exports were an option only while they still had spare capacity. A secondary reason was to garner the authenticated goodwill of having an 'export quality' product.

The other side of the story

If one informally sits down and talks to Indian business houses, a powerful reason emerges why, even with relative prices and incentives favouring the export market, a producer would not wish to sell more than a certain proportion of his output on that market.

The reason is risk aversion. A producer would attempt to spread the risks and uncertainties attendant on each market by selling to both. What are these uncertainties in the export markets? A number of them: the possibility of adverse movements in the relative price due to such factors as shifts in exchange rates, changes in domestic or international prices, demands or input availability, and changes in foreign government policy which could cause such shifts. Given the past record of many governments, particularly in the developing world, wariness on this score is not unreasonable.

This leaves our export producers faced with the real risk of suddenly getting no orders. In practice, markets are indeed imperfect, and even if a producer is willing to sell at 'the' international price, he may not be able to do so. Random events in the international market, as mentioned above, may upset trade. These are by no means unusual. Major markets in Iran and Iraq, and later in Nigeria, disappeared suddenly with the outbreak of war and the fall in oil prices. In 1975, India's bicycle chain exports met with unusually severe competition from Taiwan, which had apparently received large consignments of cheap Japanese steel for this purpose. In the following year, Taiwanese exports were constrained in some markets on charges of dumping, and Indian business revived!'

So, back to the beginning

At the start of this chapter, I mentioned the highly emotional response from some of the participants, as it seems I had exposed a sensitive nerve. I said that I found it amazing that many of our senior executives were not aware of the fact that India, the second largest nation in the world, had only a 0.7 per cent share of the world trade and that this was also declining. Now, let's go to the next chapter and address this in some detail.

1.2   Contract manufacture of automotive components

Don't run my country down

As I said in the closing paragraph of the earlier chapter, when the seminar was thrown open for discussion, the very first person who spoke accused me very respectfully but firmly of running my country down. He pointed to the large number of outstandingly successful enterprises in India and said that I was using stray examples which were not typical and served no purpose.

I felt the best thing to do at this stage was to let the participants debate this amongst themselves, with me and the other faculty members remaining observers. I will mention here that this was a management seminar organised by one of the leading management schools in the country and the participants were all mature, experienced people who held senior executive positions in large organisations in India.

A lot of very interesting thoughts emerged. At times the debate did, indeed, get emotional, but one thing was clear. The students did not really know how the organisational infrastructure of the bulk of our industrial, trading, and service sectors compared with that of the outside world. Nobody really understood the practical aspects of how the country was geared to exports.

I decided to give them a practical demonstration.

✓ I felt the best way of getting the point across to the students was to get them actually involved in some of the problems of exports from India. At the same time, they would see, first hand, how modern manufacturing works in India and compare this with the same in other parts of the world.

An interesting assignment

I explained that I was visiting India on an assignment for a large British firm who were planning on a few manufacturing subsidiaries in

India. I told the students that I would look forward to three or four of them forming a task force to assist me and, of course, would give them a share in my fee. The students were experienced executives and were from different parts of the country so we would easily be able to cover the major cities for the survey. Once everybody had the data ready, we would meet and circulate our findings to all the other participants of the seminar for their information and record.

The assignment was unusual in two aspects. One was the unusual marketing strategy the British firm wanted to try out. They had modern manufacturing facilities in UK, Malaysia and Brazil, producing a wide range of automobile and industrial spare parts which found a good replacement or spare parts market in Africa, East Asia and South America. The problem was that their brand was somewhat upmarket and a little expensive. They had a reasonable market share but could not penetrate the cheaper and lower-quality end of the market which was also substantial. So what they planned to do was to produce a lower range of their items in India under a different brand and encourage the sale of these through a different sales network, in covert competition to their own higher end products.

The second unusual aspect was that the British firm wanted to manage the operations in India on the lines of what they were already doing elsewhere. They had only small liaison offices in Malaysia and Brazil, and managed the whole operation from the home office in the UK through professional firms in those countries.

In other words, they wanted to get different items custom-made by different specialist suppliers in different parts of India, but wanted to manage and control the operation from a remote location.

This was unusual for the automobile sector in India but is nothing new internationally. Japanese and Korean manufacturers get components made all over the world, exactly as they want them, without having their own establishments in those countries.

Before going on with a further discussion of my project, it would be a good idea to have a look at and try to understand the global auto components buyer. What will make it of particular interest to the professional reader is that this applies equally to the electrical, electronic and household appliances industries.

The world over, auto majors and their components suppliers have moved away from vertical integration. They no longer make everything themselves. They have been outsourcing and contracting out most of the manufacturing operations including finished components and sub-assemblies for quite some time now. This applies equally to the electrical, electronic and household appliances industries.

Indeed, there are multinationals who are already getting some products made in India, but India's share in this opportunity is only a fraction of that of countries such as Malaysia, Singapore, Thailand and China.

I will seek to establish that the reasons are that the buyers undertake a lot of trouble investigating and evaluating the suppliers. They not only look at the breakdown of capital structure, costs, and the overall feasibility, but also manufacturing skill and technology levels, and the level and skill of the staff. The local economic scenario, material, labour, capital, interest costs, currency fluctuations, etc., besides how the vendor chooses to address these advantages or disadvantages does matter since he will always be weighed against other suppliers elsewhere in the world.

The world auto components market

Three aspects:

1. Dependability of the vendor on all fronts is a critical factor. I mentioned earlier that nowhere in the world these days do the big auto companies make everything themselves. They outsource and contract out the supplies of even finished components and sub-assemblies. This has been going on for quite some time now. The management of external resources has thus become more and more critical to their business process. This trend has been further fine-tuned to a system of operating with integrated single suppliers who can design and engineer systems and offer solutions for new designs and models. This naturally places a lot of demands on the supplier and the dependability of the vendor becomes an important aspect.

2. There is immense competitive pressure to reduce costs even with shorter and shorter production runs. The reason for this is that auto component manufacturers all over the world have recognised that exports are imperative for sustained growth and

for beating domestic demand swings. So, in order to make inroads into the global market, they invest a lot of time and money in understanding the needs of the global buyer and how he operates. They understand that the buyer operates in an environment where there is constant pressure to reduce costs and improve the efficiency of the supply chain.

3. The days when the customer merely asked you for a sample and a quote are gone. The overseas buyer puts your set-up under a microscope first. Whether a vendor or a subcontractor will be in a position to maintain his competitive price over a period of time is very important to a buyer. The short-term strategy of small firms offering prices that are way below cost simply to get the business is disastrous as the firm will be forced to fold up. Further, small firms tend to have an overly optimistic attitude on the resources which are going to be available to them. 'Let me get this order and then I will surely be able to manage the finance.'

These are the reasons why buyers go through a lot of trouble investigating and evaluating suppliers. Their very survival depends upon it.

One can see how the fiercely competitive nature of the global automobile industry, applying constant pressure down the line on vendors and subcontractors, pares down costs. Through constant research, this leads to better usage of materials, improved efficiency of manufacture and application of better technology. Consequently, all suppliers are expected to have their own ongoing cost reduction programmes.

Amazing and drastic changes no one would have expected even a few years back are taking place every other day the world over with component manufacturers realigning themselves and revamping their managerial, technical, R&D, and even financial set-ups.

I will be illustrating this with an example I mentioned earlier where my seminar participants and other team members got a first-hand look at what the world needs and what India can offer.

The reasons for the remarkable success the Asian Tigers have achieved in developing and marketing their capacities and working with the large auto makers would become evident. The business leaders of these nations have managed to understand the mindset of the buyers.

Buyers definitely feel more at ease in the company of a leader or one who is clearly headed in that direction, hence the importance of clear business objectives and plans, mission statements and a vision. The buyer likes to look at the roadmap that the vendor has charted for himself for the future. Needless to say, vendors must have a clear understanding of the dynamics of their business in order to position themselves strategically in the fast-changing scenario. Any vendor's capability and enthusiasm to identify and systematically implement excellence in manufacturing practices is taken note of by the buyer.

In the final analysis, it is always safe to keep in mind the fact that the global buyer will deal with a supplier only when and as long as he can maintain his competitive advantage.

Modern manufacturing and India

The tasks the British firm gave us, and our success or failure at these, went something like this.

1. Locate the contract manufacturers

The British firm wanted us to locate at least three or more manufacturing units in different parts of India having suitable facilities to manufacture the items on contract. Rather than have their capacity committed to a large unit, they wanted to use a few small units spread out in different parts of the country. It was obvious that additional inputs of technology, finance and quality-control procedures would be needed. These would be made available from the UK as well as from optional foreign equity participation.

This made sense. Though the consumers were in small, less developed countries, they wanted what they wanted immediately and not after six months, and they wanted the product made precisely as per their requirements. So, the single-order, small-volume, quick-response nature of the business ruled out the larger firms which were more tuned to large volumes, a slow response time and mass production techniques.

As has been discussed above, it was essential that the units be professionally managed with proper organisational infrastructure, and have a track record of manufacturing products to international standards. This meant lean manufacturing techniques, just-in-time production, minimum inventory, and quick response time to the very frequent design changes.

Result   Surprisingly, there was no problem in this. We found quite a few suitable manufacturing firms in almost all parts of India, who had remarkably efficient and state-of-the-art set-ups and were keen to take up production.

However, as the dependability of the vendor on all fronts is a critical factor, the firms fully cooperated with us when we attempted to make an audit of their past operations to see whether they can be relied upon to keep their commitments. Here, we came up against an unexpected problem. There were almost no records. For fear of the taxman, the firms had maintained almost no past records. All details of transactions, except for the engineering drawings and specs, had been destroyed.

2. Response time-lag

The next point related to the fact that if an order for a completely new item is received, the contracting unit should be able to respond quickly by locating all sorts of new downstream vendors and suppliers of a vast range of plastic components, electrical parts and packaging materials.

Result   This became a problem particularly because much of the manufacturing capacity in India is away from the big towns. For a manufacturer in a small town, it is next to impossible to find out in a short period of time who can supply a particular new item. Networking information, up-to-date trade directories, telephone yellow pages and trade associations leave a lot to be desired. With the advent of the internet, this is fast changing, but it is only the very large firms which have a presence on the net. It will be a long time before one can locate here the bulk of our small-scale vendors.

3. Supply of tooling

We were asked to locate a few sophisticated and professionally-managed tool rooms in different parts of the country, preferably in proximity to the manufacturing units, for the quick design and production of tools, dies, moulds and jigs for new items. The lead time for the supply of the moulds, for instance, should be days rather than months, but, most important, the delivery schedules must be rigorously adhered to.

Result This also became a problem. There are any number of excellent tool- and mould-makers in India who can make quite complicated tools and moulds to very close tolerances, but these are all small, disorganised, and one-man-show set-ups. They can never guarantee sharp deliveries. We will be discussing this point, which constitutes a major hurdle in the way of our exports, in Part 3 of this book.

4. Locate export houses

We had to locate some professionally-managed export houses who could undertake to develop and service the markets in Africa and the East Asian countries. True, the British firm had a well-established presence in these countries, but the idea was to export the products from India in pseudo competition to the UK firm. So the products had to be marketed by an Indian export house. We were told to look for an established export house that had its own marketing expertise and an extensive network of branches or associated firms in the selected countries. They should have had a track record of the export of manufactured goods, preferably engineering items, to these markets.

We were clearly told that a briefcase-carrying salesman visiting the export markets and collecting orders was not feasible.

Result This posed another problem. India has a number of individually-managed export houses. Though many of these even have multi-million dollar turnovers, they did not serve the purpose. We could not find a single export house which had any sort of a set-up in Africa or East Asia, or any experience of these markets. The concept of developing and servicing the export markets in developing countries by having a presence there was, we found, quite alien to Indian thinking. Our marketing technique is still very much that of a briefcase-carrying salesman visiting the export markets and collecting orders.

5. Locate management firms

We were setting up contract manufacturing facilities in various locations, and the entire operation was to be supervised and controlled by a small liaison office in Delhi or Bombay assisted in the day to day aspects by an Indian management consultancy and accountancy firm. This concept is nothing new. Many multinationals get components made all over the world without having their own establishments in those countries.

My British clients needed the services of well organised and established professionals in different fields, particularly in accountancy, management and legal firms. It was obvious that the British firm did not wish to deal with dozens of different managerial and service organisations all over India. It made sense to deal with, say, a single large accountancy and management consultancy firm which had its own networks. Also a large legal firm, and so on. This is how things are done in developed nations and this is also how things are progressively being done in East Asian countries.

In short, we had to look for, say, a legal firm which had offices or networks in Bombay, Madras, Calcutta, Bangalore, Hyderabad, etc. as well as in smaller towns to assist in local laws, regulations and procedures, as well as represent the UK firm in meetings as observers. Here we were asked specifically to look for Indian firms, as they would presumably know their own country best. Same for a management firm.

Result This too was a problem. We came up against the possibility of all sorts of problems and delays because all the professional and management firms that fit the bill were located in the big cities. Yes, they had friends and associates who could be asked to do our work in the smaller towns, but that was hardly the same thing. We could not locate any professional service firm that really had an all-India presence. There are quite a few MNCs in the accountancy, managerial and legal fields who fit the requirements, but these were not Indian and had been ruled out.

To make a long story short, the British firm could not come to India and went to Thailand instead. For the UK firm, coming to India would have meant a major commitment in organisational infrastructure. They had to come here and set up an organisation to do everything in-house. This they were not prepared to do. They could have joined hands with an Indian firm who were already good at what they were planning to do, but finding such a firm was not possible.

These shortcomings of our structural organisation are what this book is all about. I discuss this in some further detail in Chapters 2.5 and 2.6.

There is a market for us, out there

Not only the Indian auto component industry, but the electrical, electronic and household appliances industries too now have the opportunity, like never before, to internationalise their operations and spread their wares across the globe. This is because the entry of global majors gives us access to their worldwide manufacturing operations and to their international component suppliers too. One good way to tap this vast potential is to network with global buyers and be aware of not only their requirements for components but also the specialised services which will enable one to find a niche in this market.

Here, a big problem faced by Indian companies is the lack of strong vendor–buyer linkups. This is a problem for both the vendors and the buyers. I will show in a moment that this is a major constraint in improving the efficiency of Indian industry.

Buyers in the Indian industry have a long tradition of dealing with vendors at an arm's length. Purchasing the same component from a number of vendors is a standard practice, essential because the vendors have no organisational credibility. No manufacturer can afford to put 'all his eggs in one basket'.

This approach has resulted in vendors confining themselves to becoming mere manufacturers of sub-assemblies/components and following only the designs and specifications supplied by the purchaser. This is particularly true in the automobile, electronic and domestic appliance industries which have the greatest growth potential. While some of their vendors have built up good manufacturing capabilities, they have completely neglected design and development.

To make matters worse, the purchasing companies themselves have lacked strong-enough design and process engineering capabilities to be able to advise their vendors on how to either improve produce performance or to lower costs and improve reliability. It is true that till recent times, companies did not have much of an incentive to improve their efficiency and lower costs as the one-sided relationship between vendors and the purchaser was markedly skewed in favour of the latter.

The bottom line is that there are few vendors who are interested in independently taking up design and development of new components/sub-assemblies to enhance performance and reduce costs. This completely rules out the modern approach, where the product development team provides the supplier with only the specifications of what the component has to do. The detailed design, within certain cost targets, is then left to the supplier.

I have said above that this is a problem for both vendors and buyers, and is a major constraint in improving the efficiency of the Indian industry. Because, for Indian companies, this means having to develop products almost completely on one's own.

This has an adverse impact on two fronts. One is the time taken to develop new products as well as the attendant cost increases. The other adverse impact of developing and manufacturing components in-house is that it reduces flexibility, increases investments and reduces the potential benefits of the economies of specialisation and scale that can be availed of with specialised vendors.

Automotive Network Exchange

One of the answers for companies that want to become leaner and nimbler is to seek other means of improving the way they buy their components and raw materials. The internet is providing a huge boost to the process. By using the internet, or various private internet systems based on it, companies can deal more directly with their suppliers to improve deliveries, stock levels, designs and lead times. Even better, they can use the networks to get lower prices by holding electronic auctions for the supply of basic components.

Leading the way is a system known as Automotive Network Exchange, which America's Big Three car companies started as a pilot scheme in mid-1999 and were due to put into operation with most of their suppliers in the summer of 2000. They then plan to extend it to Europe. Any company wishing to sell to the Big Three will then have to get online and be ready to settle down to do some serious electronic bargaining. Other industries have happily taken up the idea. Boeing already runs its spares business through extranet. General Electric has one of the largest such systems in the whole of manufacturing for dealing with its suppliers.

All this should produce huge benefits. It will make it easier and swifter for assembly line companies and their suppliers to work in partnership. Engineering designs on the web will save time and money by cutting out a whole series of meetings and consultations. By turning car parts into commodities that can be bought and sold at auctions, the web will help open the market, and make for keener competition and lower prices. The old ways of buying and selling were time-consuming and expensive. The new way opens the door to the mass customisation that lean producers now dream of.

None of this will make a byte's worth of difference, of course, unless our Indian manufacturers are nimble enough to seize the opportunities technology is offering them. The essential thing is for everybody in a company to understand how a business runs itself successfully. Management by edict and procedures is out. That is just a way for bosses to tell subordinates what to do. In the new century, manufacturing needs to be a process in which the only objective is to meet customer needs. The process should also ensure that the assorted kinds of workers feel involved in the task, and that they are able to make use of an array of facts and data supplied on electronic platters.

So how does a company get this way? By organising production around customers, not the other way round. For the developed world, this can sometimes mean moving halfway across the world. Not only do companies have to chase cheap labour for the simpler parts of their new global supply chains; they also have to bow to the customers' demand that they provide product and service on the customers' doorstep.

This is the future that Indian companies in the spare parts and components field must look forward to.

1.3   *Export toys from India? Huh? You must be joking!*

Innovative gimmicks

Let's not talk only of toys. There are hundreds of very simple, but highly innovative, plastic and wooden products currently being sold in the US and all over the western world. These are cheap, well designed, elegant and very popular. They could be plastic toys, soft toys, games, gimmicks, kitchen and garden items, hobby and craft items, and so on.

In the West, the market for these items is growing exponentially. The reason is the increasing spending power of the consumers. People want to live better, their children expect better toys and their wives, better gadgets in the kitchen. This has created a massive new opportunity. Also, the shortage of skilled workers such as carpenters and masons means that people have to do everything themselves. So, the above list is enlarged to include items catering to the 'Do it yourself' trade, which is one of the fastest growing market segments.

These items are widely advertised and sold all over the western world, almost all 'Made in China'. For 'Made in China', read either 'Made in Hong Kong' which is also China or made in China by the overseas Chinese.

India has never been able to make and export such simple items. It has no share of this fantastic market and is not likely to have it either.

It is not that we do not have the technology. We are producing a number of far more complex and sophisticated plastic products, mostly without any foreign technical inputs, at prices comparable with world prices. So what, then, is wrong?

The reasons are very complex, and are what this book is all about. In particular, we have to look at the very concept of innovativeness and the way new products are marketed in the world.

Note:

In order to understand some aspects of the highly complex reasons for not being able to manufacture and export the items I mention here, I will be looking at the very concept of innovativeness from three angles.

First, I will take a stray example, and discuss how Hong Kong can earn huge profits from a simple innovative idea. India cannot even consider manufacturing it, though the prices here are lower. This is discussed here.

Second, in the following chapter, I will introduce you to Guanxi, the Chinese concept of networking or integration of an entire spectrum of activities from design talent, manufacturing capacity, production management expertise, marketing and packaging skills, and financing, without which the development of innovative items is not possible. Guanxi is also discussed in Chapters 4.4 and 4.5. In chapter 6.4, I will give an example of how Guanxi caused us to lose a simple but highly profitable project to Thailand.

Third, we shall be looking at our own innovation in industrial and consumer products in chapter 3.3. This is a major bottleneck for exports. Indeed, India has an exemplary track record of innovation in the entire spectrum of items from pharmaceuticals to computer software. We have a long tradition of innovation. The roadside mechanic managing to repair a complex carburettor with a piece of string is also innovation. We are very good at this sort of thing.

We will be taking a hard look at this, because, except for some stray examples, our innovations have not been able to win any world markets.

We are talking about a completely new range of immensely profitable products which did not exist a decade ago. These are all quick-turnover, high-volume, and low-lifecycle-cost items. The western market has a voracious appetite for these items which come and go in a matter of months, sell in huge numbers and cost very little. Every day there is a new item on the market.

A simple example

To explain the highly complex reasons and to establish the groundwork for this book, we will take a simple example and discuss all operations from start to finish. We will see what happens if we want to make this item in India, and how it would be made in Hong Kong. We will look at financial inputs and at profitability.

These, and many such items, formed the foundation of Hong Kong's massive economic base. It has now moved away, however, from being a manufacturing-based economy to being a highly sophisticated service-based economy.

We will be talking about Hong Kong in greater detail when, in the following section, we take a hard look at how small, family-owned firms in Hong Kong work with each other and excel at integrating design talent, manufacturing capacity, production management expertise, marketing and packaging skills, and financing to produce products nobody can compete with.

Here we will take a quick look at ourselves and see why India cannot make and export these items.

I am using a simple item to explain, step by step, how Hong Kong makes these items and illustrate what is wrong with the way we run our businesses. The item itself does not matter. I am using this random item for the purposes of illustration only.

During a trip to the US, I was very impressed with a simple car washing gimmick that was being advertised on TV. I can only call it a gimmick as it was nothing but an ordinary garden sprinkler, where the water pressure rotates the head through which the water exits, sprinkling it all around.

This device, wholly made of plastic, is simply a three ft length of a half-inch pipe, with a rotating brush. One end connects to a water hose. In the middle is a tap or valve to shut off or control the water pressure. At the other end is an attachment, something like the sprinkler mentioned above, that has a brush through which the water exits. The pressure of the water makes the brush rotate, so you scrub the car while washing it. The brush head is hollow and with a cap which you can fill with liquid detergent so that you can soap and scrub the car at the same time. There are two brush attachments. One made of felt for washing the body of the car, and the other made of bristles for the tyres. Simple.

This is a beautifully finished, custom-designed item which retails for US$ 20. The ex-factory price is US$ 5, approximately Rs 225.

Development stages

Now, let's see how these items are developed from an idea in somebody's head to the time it reaches the customer, and also compare how this item would get made in India with how Hong Kong would go about making it.

The stages any new innovative item, such as the above, will go through are:

- an idea in somebody's head
- a quick survey to see if there is a market
- production of the advertising leaflet or brochure
- the engineering design on paper
- design and production of the moulds, tools and jigs etc.
- development of the prototypes
- test marketing
- mass production of the item
- advertising and promotion
- distribution to the point of sales
- information and public relations backup
- after-sales service, if needed

Before going on to how I tried to get the item made here, a short comment on the first matter of difference between Hong Kong and India in the context of the above.

In India, there are excellent firms capable of all the operations listed above. But each firm works in isolation. No single firm has the resources or the organisational infrastructure to undertake all the essential tasks. So, if the idea appeals to someone, this project would have to be promoted, undertaken and financed by a single organisation. Work would need be farmed out to other firms but strictly against money paid up front. Indian firms rarely form consortiums or networks.

In Hong Kong, it would be the joint effort of a number of independent specialist firms working together as a network. Small independent firms invariably form instant consortiums, flooding the world with hundreds of items.

The Chinese concept of Gunaxi, of independent firms networking together and integrating their technical, marketing and financial resources as a common effort is a remarkable concept and merits further discussion. This is discussed in the next section and also in Chapters 4.4 and 4.5 of this book.

I do the rounds in India

So, back to how I tried to get the item made here.

I have a sample of the car washing device with me and I have shown this item to a number of medium and large plastic goods manufacturers in India. The standard response is that there should be no problem. The price and quality can be easily matched. Not only that, we can get the exact quality made in India at about Rs. 180—25 per cent cheaper. Excellent. Let's go and flood the market!

The first problem. The design and production of the moulds and the tooling would be expensive, would need a very substantial cash advance and would require a lead time of at least six months. I am shocked when I am told that I might be better off importing the moulds. Come on, somebody has get to be joking! India short of capacity to make moulds? Indian technicians are highly respected and keenly sought after the world over as mould makers. So what is the problem in our own country? Let's leave this for the moment as we will be discussing it later in this book. (Chapter 3.2).

Another more serious problem. Who will promote the item? Who will pay for the initial production lot? No plastic manufacturer was willing to take up the manufacture and sale of this item on their own. Manufacture, yes. Pay me, went the refrain, and I will make it for you, but this item has almost no market in India. How many will be willing to pay Rs 800 (which would be the retail price) for a car washing device when we do not wash our own cars? Sorry, they said, but we are talking about a product which only has an export market. Nobody here has the set-up to invest in promoting this sort of an item for the overseas market.

Hey, wait on. What sort of money are we talking about? Well, to justify the cost of the moulds and the tooling for the custom design, and the set-up time for the machines, the initial order must be, I was told, for at least a hundred thousand pieces. If you twist my arm real hard, I may agree to an initial run of 50,000 pieces. This is the minimum and very tight. Quotation: Rs. 180 each. 50,000 pieces @ Rs 180 is Rs nine million!

This much money up front just to get it made. Selling and promotion all extra! The idea is dead even before it is born!

Remember, this is a speculative proposal. For my test survey, I had a sample to show the manufacturers. But in actual practice, an item like this is an idea born in somebody's head and if I were to just describe the item to our manufacturers, I would merely be wasting my time.

As is the case with all innovative items, we have no idea if the item will ultimately sell. If it does, indeed, succeed, an order of two or three hundred thousand pieces is nothing for the huge American market. But shelling out such a huge amount of money on a mere idea is just not on. Plus, as I said, there remains the cost of packaging, shipping, marketing, sales promotion, and so on.

How does Hong Kong do it?

How does Hong Kong manage to make these items? The trick lies in the networking of disparate capacities. It lies in how small specialist firms integrate their design talent, management expertise, marketing and packaging skills. The entire spectrum of economic activities is carried out mostly by small, family-owned firms, but these are very intensely efficient entities and work very closely with each other as a strong cohesive group. Their businesses stay singularly apart, but they work together all the time. When a crisis arises or an opportunity presents itself, they close ranks and cooperate.

The word 'small' has to be understood in context as many of them employ hundreds of engineers and have dozens of factories.

The family businesses of the Chinese overseas are networks, of companies and other enterprises, of clans and villages. An outstanding characteristic of the ethnic Chinese network is that no one is in charge. The marketplace is in charge.

There are firms in Hong Kong who specialise in producing items of the sort we mentioned. There are executives who do nothing but look around for new ideas. Once an idea has been identified, it is passed around at the weekly meeting of the research, design, production and marketing units. People participating in these meetings are mostly from different firms. They have got together for this project, but will compete in the case of another project. If the idea is approved, everybody makes sure they understand what is involved. The mould maker and the design engineer are involved from the start, helping in maximising the use of components where the moulds are already available. Everybody makes an investment in terms of his own work, and reaps the rewards accordingly.

The idea is then sent to a design firm where a computer simulation model is produced. I have seen incredibly beautiful pamphlets, with computer generated colour photographs of the item and a demonstration of how it will work, printed and sent to the market for test marketing. This is even without a single item having been produced.

The marketing organisation at the other end, say in the US, which may be a different firm but is part of the integrated set-up, takes up the test marketing and, if the results are positive, the sales and distribution.

Marketing innovative products

Before going on, it will be a good idea to take a quick look at how the market for these items in the western world works. There is tons of literature on the subject of marketing to the western world but I will mention here only two aspects relevant to the marketing of toys, gift items, and other innovative consumer items.

There is no way of selling these in the US, except by extensive (and expensive) advertising on the TV, over the radio, in newspapers or by direct mail. Or, by a combination of these. But the common factor is that if the item catches the customer's fancy, he wants it immediately. The days when the customer would make a note of the item and wait till he got to the nearest town to look for it, are gone.

He wants to get on the phone and order it by mail order or, call an 800 number and get the name of the outlet near his home where he can see a demo and buy it.

An 800 number is a special phone number in the US that enables a customer to make a collect call. It is a phone number preceded by the three digits 800, say 800–12345. The company advertises this to enable a customer to call the company from any part of the US, day or night, and not pay for the call. For a nationwide marketing organisation, having an 800 number is an essential requirement.

This 800 number is useful in many ways. If I am interested in a particular type of Microwave oven and want to know where I can get a demo, I call the telephone enquiry, ask for the company by name and get their 800 Number. I call the number and immediately get details about the nearest dealer, whether the dealer has stocks, whether there are any special offers coming up, etc.

The only Indian organisation I am aware of which has an 800 number in the US is Air-India.

The other aspect to understand is the gift marketing system in the US. This is the system of 'wish list registration' in store chains nation-wide.

Say, my son is getting married. In India, the couple would get 15 toasters, 22 electric irons, and maybe half a dozen rice cookers, plus an assortment of items which are of no use except to pass on as wedding gifts to others. There is nothing one can do about this.

In the US, my son and his future wife went to a branch of a nation-wide store chain. There they selected the items they needed and entered the list in the store gift list computer with their names. They did this in two different stores. They mentioned the names of the two stores on their wedding card. Their friends could then go to any of the store's branches, in any part of the US, enter the couple's names and see the items they had selected. Depending upon the budget, the person could buy the gift and it would get deleted from the list. This way, the couple get what they need and no useless gifts pile up in their home. This works well for occasions such as birthdays, weddings and anniversaries.

A final word

Talking of Hong Kong again, it can be seen that the reason for the outstanding success of the small manufacturers in the export market is the degree of integration and networking the Chinese firms have with each other. This does not suggest, even remotely, that the Chinese firms are all honest, ethical or fair to each other. But they have, over a period of time, realised that working together means money for everybody.

Now, imagine an Indian firm attempting to make and export an innovative product. It would have to be good at and have the money for the long value-added chain of services, design, promotion and overseas marketing. There are many firms which could, of course, have a reasonable degree of success in designing and making the product, but they would get the participation of no other Indian commercial house.

There is not a single Indian export house or specialist marketing firm in the US that an Indian firm can approach for this sort of project in a participatory manner. What a tragedy.

Hey! don't forget the money!

Yes, I almost forgot. Well, we saw above that the first production order of the device I was using as an example would have to be in the range of 50,000 pieces, with a total outlay of about US$ 200,000. If there are a few specialist firms networking together, this initial outlay is reduced considerably. If the device fails, there may be a small loss but a breakeven can often be achieved.

The cost of the tooling and the initial development costs are amortised in the first lot. But, if the device works, the normal production run can be anything up to a million pieces. The returns are mind-boggling.

1.4   *The art of integration*

Story of the mechanic and the doctor

In the last chapter, we saw how small, independent, family-owned firms in Hong Kong work with each other. Independent, family-owned firms specialising in the different fields of design, manufacturing, marketing and financing build instant networks whenever an opportunity arises to produce items nobody can compete with. This is true not only of the Hong Kong Chinese, but also of all overseas Chinese.

In this section I seek to establish that a complete lack of such integration and networking in the entire commercial sector in India leads to our customers, particularly our overseas buyers, feeling highly frustrated.

It is very much outside the scope of this book to discuss the business ethics of the overseas Chinese or of anybody else for that matter. We shall be talking about the art of integration of diverse capabilities only in the context of how the Chinese are able to produce and market items which we cannot.

This is best illustrated by a common saying in Malaysia.

✓ *While driving in the Malaysian countryside, if you have an accident and are hurt, you should pray that the nearest doctor is an Indian. But, if your car is damaged, you should hope that the nearest mechanic is a Chinese.*

Before going on, a word on the ethnic composition of Malaysia. There is a lot more on Malaysia in Chapter 7.3, but in brief, the nation consists mainly of people of three racial origins: the Malays who trace their origin to the Arabs, the Chinese and the Indians. They are all local citizens but are categorised as Malaysian–Indian, Malaysian–Chinese, and so on.

Indians, mainly South Indians, were brought in by the British as indentured labour. Sikhs were brought in for the police force, and the others followed as traders. Today, Indians, about 10 per cent of the population, are overwhelmingly in the working class and are into small-time trading. Some have done well and have educated their children to be professionals such as doctors, accountants and lawyers. There are very few architects or engineers however. Indians do well only in professions where one can look forward to being self employed.

The Chinese, by contrast, are almost everywhere and are the work engines of the economy. The Malays, with government encouragement, are fast catching up. The Indians are losing ground everywhere. But that is another story altogether.

Back to the story I started with. The reason one would wish for the nearest doctor to be an Indian is that our people make the best doctors anywhere in the world. They are considerate, take a genuine interest in their patients and can be woken up at any time of the night. Apart, of course, from being clever. The point to be noted here is that the doctor will be working purely as an individual, but that is all that you need for emergency treatment.

On the other hand, if your car is damaged, you may need a body repair workshop, an electric wireman, an aircon mechanic, or all of them. If you take it to a small-town Indian mechanic, he will do the repair work he is good at and direct you to other mechanics as needed. If he needs any spare parts, he will invariably not have the required stock and you will have to wait till he gets it from the nearest source. The other mechanics would also be small independent workshops. Each will do his own job and keep at arm's length any other problem you may be facing. Everyone makes it clear that he is an individual and minds his own business. You will pay him and the others separately.

However, if you find a Chinese mechanic, no matter what his particular skill, he will not only be better organised, but you will find an instant network of other Chinese mechanics participating in the repair of your car. 'Participating' is the correct term as you will be surprised to find that other mechanics have been informed and are immediately available to work on your car. They would belong to independent workshops, maybe even some distance away, but will work as an instant consortium. Before you know it, the spare parts are on their way. Though the first point of contact will not automatically assume the role of the leader, you will be amazed to see that all your work gets done with an incredible degree of efficiency without anyone taking on the role of leader or boss. Each is clearly his own boss, but works as a part of a unique team to seize the opportunity that has arisen. You can pay your first point of contact by credit card or cash for all the work done.

At the end of the day one finds that though there are plenty of excellent Indian car mechanics in Malaysia and Singapore, they remain small, with the business dying out with the old man. The children have nothing to inherit unless they become mechanics too. Even then, there is work for only one son. The Chinese mechanics do much better, are more expensive yet have better business, and can afford to build their businesses into small organised set-ups. Most can afford to have a good inventory of spare parts. Often, the whole family is involved. An educated daughter may be working as a secretary during the day, but she will be in the shop in the evening helping out.

Learning from your neighbours

A point to be noted in the above is that I was not talking about Indians in India. I was talking about Indians who have lived in Malaysia/ Singapore for generations. People who, in many cases, have never even been to India but who, in attitude, thought and behaviour, are exactly the same as the folks at home.

I cannot stop wondering why our people do not watch and learn from their next door Chinese neighbours considering they have grown up with them, lived all their lives with them and seen how they do business. My description of how the car mechanic in Malaysia runs his business could well have been the description of a fellow running his in Bhagalpur.

Greeting cards in Pondicherry

Here I would mention another example of our not bothering to observe how others do things. This again, as I said above, leads to our customers, particularly our overseas buyers, feeling highly frustrated and going elsewhere for business.

In India, Pondicherry and the nearby Auroville are probably the only places where a number of non-missionary, non-religious, foreigners have settled down and made India their home. These people have established a number of small enterprises such as screen printing, bakeries and confectioneries, handicrafts, decorative candle-making, greeting card production, and furniture production in order to make a living. These enterprises exist side by side with similar units run by locals.

The contrast of how a foreigner runs a unit and how an Indian next door runs a similar unit is shocking and is there for everyone to see. The former are excellently organised, and clean and tidy, with everything in place. Workers invariably wear clean uniforms, are better paid and more committed to their jobs. Everybody knows what is going on and if you call when the boss is away, you will get a decent response and maybe even the information you need. Though the prices are invariably higher, the business is obviously better. It is indeed a pleasure doing business with them. I do not think they advertise or engage in any export promotion, but somehow they seem to have an excellent export market.

The local-run units are smaller and shockingly shoddy. Inventory, cartons, boxes and worker tiffin boxes are all over the floor. Nobody but the owner knows what is going on. There is a phobia against keeping any sort of record. The owner has to send someone to check how much of a particular item is in stock. It is almost as if the owner is not even aware that there is a customer out there who can go elsewhere. Invariably, if the boss is away, and a customer calls, he is treated with apathy, ignorance or, worse, rudeness. In the larger units, when a customer calls, he is instantly assaulted with policies and procedures that make it difficult to do business. I have personal experience of this.

Some years ago, I was in India for a holiday from Singapore and was in Pondicherry. I decided to have some special greeting cards produced in a hurry. I knew the cost would be a fraction of what it would cost me back home in Singapore. The work involved some digital photography, computer graphic design, screen printing and a special way of folding the cards. I knew that there were plenty of local people who could do the various jobs. I went to a well-established local printer and took great pains to explain what I wanted done. The owner listened and took the sketches I gave him, but I could see that he had made no detailed notes.

I suggested that I talk directly to the various people who would do the different jobs so that they understood exactly what I wanted. The owner refused to have me talk directly to any of the other firms, insisting on doing the explanations himself: 'No problem, Sir, I will handle it.' I was sure that I was heading into a nightmare. Sure enough, when the initial proofs came, they were such a disaster that I walked out disgusted.

I was running out of time when I was introduced to a French lady running a screen printing workshop in Auroville, about 5 km away. She had one look at the job and quickly had the concerned people in to talk to me. Everybody made sure they understood what I wanted and I had a fantastic job done. The cost, of course, was higher but I got the results I wanted.

Indeed, the small local firms do realise that local and overseas customers are going away frustrated. The point I am making is that the local businesses have success stories right next door, but they make no effort to learn.

Increasingly, overseas customers are demanding, and receiving, customised solutions tailored to their specific needs. The customer today does not want the ready-to-sell product. He knows exactly what he wants and if he cannot be offered this, we can not only forget about exports, we can also look forward to losing our home markets to outsiders who are increasingly coming here to do business. The new customers are individuals, with distinct needs, requirements, and concerns. The generic customer is gone, and so are generic solutions and the 'one size fits all' sales process. The best of all worlds is that in which we are versatile enough—as organisations, as individual businesses and as instant consortiums—to match export requirements with the right products and processes. This can only be achieved by different businesses coming together and working as one.

I am trying my best to establish that the only viable, sustainable future business model is one of collaboration. The competitive dynamics and the global economic system today are simply too complex for any single player to possess all the core competencies needed for the marketplace. The future will require instant alliances, often with companies that were formerly competitors. Today, collaboration and competition coexist in relation to market requirements. You may compete in the morning, for example, with a company that you may collaborate with in the afternoon.

Networking and subcontracting

The above examples also illustrate the sharp contrast between networking or integration and subcontracting. What the local printer did was subcontract out the work and act as the principal contractor. In networking, there is often no boss.

An important aspect of networking is the mentality or the attitude of the people involved. All the parties need to demonstrate patience, and possess the motivation, the training as well as the tools for conflict resolution. How do we agree to disagree? How do we agree to solve our problems together? For example, do we agree to trust each other's intentions regarding the unwritten partnership, no matter the depth of the disagreement?

I can guarantee that there will be problems. There will be big problems and little ones. Customers will be upset with you for what someone else has done. It helps if the customer is aware of the composition of the instant consortium and is working directly with the components.

Networking and teamwork

Just as there is a difference between networking or integration and subcontracting, as I illustrated in the above examples, there is also a vast difference between networking and teamwork. Teamwork is as essential to the success of an Indian enterprise venturing into the export market as networking. Maybe even more so. A word of explanation first. Teamwork simply means a group of people working together as one body, for example, a sports team, a debating team or a sales team on a special task. They are all people working as one and under one leader. Networking is nothing like this. In the concept I have explained above, there is generally no leader. Almost like the internet where there is no one central computer.

In this connection, it is important to understand how complex business relationships have become. Till recently, business, especially selling, was normally conducted through one-to-one relationships. Increasingly today, partnership builders (whether they are salespersons or senior management) will require to possess skills in facilitating, coaching, leading, and mentoring teams of people. To be a master at creating partnerships, one needs to be an expert at bringing together people with all sorts of opinions, ideas, and motivations, from across the organization, to create teams. Cross-functional, cross-organisational teams are at the core of partnering relationships between organisations.

Business, in the future, will be done by teams networking together. Teams are where the relationships will be created and where problem solving will take place. Teams are also where partnerships will be truly forged. Networking is where the benefits of super specialisation can be spread out.

I would certainly say that the most vital skill in the future for everyone in the workplace will be the ability to work on teams. This has major implications for all of us.

The future of doing business with important customers will require that we discard the old model of the Lone Ranger salesperson and replace it with a diverse, committed group of people working closely together to serve and retain customers. Some of those people will be salespersons, some product specialists, and some executives. Some may not even be in the same company. They will all be united by the overriding mission of working together to meet the needs of customers.

Chinese, western and Indian models

I will expand the above examples to contrast the business models of the western nations, the Chinese, and the Indians at home in India. As I said above, it is very much outside the scope of this book to discuss the business ethics of the overseas Chinese or of anybody else. I am using these business models to highlight how others can do things which we cannot.

The car repair workshops, or the small, screen printing shop that I mentioned cannot exist anywhere in the western world or even in modern Japan as workshops here mean, and are, large corporate units. There is no question of the presence of small roadside mechanics. By extension, the same is true of their economies. They consist of mostly large, organised corporate units, with very little contributed by the so-called backyard units.

As the above example has shown, and as I said in the earlier section, the Chinese concept of independent firms networking together and integrating their technical, marketing and financial resources is a remarkable concept and is in a great measure responsible for the outstanding success of the Chinese business houses all over Asia. This applies as much to the car mechanics as to the entire spectrum of economic activities. The trick lies in the networking of disparate capacities. Very much like small firms in India, the bulk of the economic activity is carried out mostly by these small, family-owned firms, that are very intensely efficient entities and which can, when needed, work very closely with each other, almost as a single, strong, and cohesive unit. That is the first aspect where Indian firms fail.

The second aspect of the failure of Indian firms is that though Chinese businesses stay singularly apart, when an opportunity presents itself, they close ranks and cooperate. Indian firms are much like the small roadside car repair workshops in Malaysia: small, independent units, each working on their own and happy to remain small and isolated as, to the Indian mindset, growth requires the giving up or sharing of absolute control.

I have said this in many places in this book and I repeat that the only viable, sustainable future business model for us in India is one of collaboration which means teamwork, networking and integration. The future is one of alliances.

1.5   *Strategies for future competitiveness*

Stuff that dreams are made of

> 'It is always a good thing to build castles in the air. But then, go ahead and build foundations of rock underneath.'
>
> In this section I will build some castles in the air. In the rest of the book I will see if we can build foundations of rock underneath.

Every citizen of every nation has dreams of what his nation should be. These dreams become more focused if a citizen has been away from home for some years. I have lived and worked outside India, mostly in the developing and newly emerging nations of Africa, West Indies and Asia and have seen how many of these so-called developing nations, nations that only yesterday were begging us for professionals, have rapidly overtaken India in economic development. The quality of life the citizens of these countries now take for granted is what an average Indian can only dream of.

I have also seen India through the eyes of the people of these nations.

So, I think I have developed a slightly different perspective on our problems. My dreams consist mainly of our people having better jobs and a better life. The only way we can do this is by becoming more competitive. Sorry, I did not put that quite right. I dream of us becoming more aggressively ruthless in competing with everybody.

My vision—A competitive, knowledge economy

To realise my dream, we require a quantum jump in capabilities while managing our cost competitiveness.

My vision, or rather my dream, is for my country to become an advanced and globally competitive knowledge economy within the next decade, with manufacturing and services as its twin engines of growth. This strategy will help to diversify our dependence beyond any single industry, sector or market, thereby reducing vulnerability and providing a broader economic base.

Manufacturing should become an integral component of India's new outward-looking economy, with capabilities not only in production but in the entire manufacturing value chain, from research and development and design to marketing and sales. We are very weak in this area and unless our manufacturing capacity is upgraded from the mostly small- and medium-scale sectors, we can make no progress.

Having said that, it should be noted that manufacturing can never be the base for India's growing economy if India remains purely production oriented. Instead, it should position itself as a critical hub where MNCs and our own firms use India as a base to manufacture high-tech high-value-added products and provide manufacturing related services to companies here as well as in the region. We have to move upstream in the value chain to doing R&D and design, as well as downstream to encompass logistics, marketing and sales, including encouraging overseas firms to have their regional operational headquarters here.

We should aim towards being a knowledge economy where the basis for competitiveness will be intellectual capital and the capability to absorb, process and apply knowledge. This can only be done in the larger corporate sectors and not in small-scale units. We already possess strong technological capability but are missing a vibrant entrepreneurial culture that thrives on creativity, nimbleness and good business sense. On the one hand, our entrepreneurs are mostly inward looking and intensely individualistic. They tend not to organise themselves into larger institutions. On the other, it has taken our government a long time to wake up to the immense potential of information technology. The increasing ease of production, distribution and maintenance of goods and services around the world is changing organisational structures.

Knowledge is becoming the key in a world dominated by information and technology. Given that technology will continue to pervade both the industrial and social arenas, the ability to develop, manage and apply information and technology will be critical. This applies to both manufacturing and service activities in the Indian economy.

Again, though our workforce is already cost-competitive, with world-class capabilities in business management and technology, we are extremely poorly motivated and fare badly as compared to nearby Asian countries in productivity, innovation and international market development. We have to do something about instilling a greater sense of pride, professionalism and commitment in our workforce, plus work harder to attract, motivate and retain staff in growing organisations.

One of the ways of doing this as also to develop into a knowledge economy, is to actively be an open cosmopolitan society, attractive to global talent and connected with other global knowledge nodes. At the moment, we only export talent and have almost a hostile atti-tude towards importing global talent. How, then, are we to develop a critical mass of Indians who will be risk-taking entrepreneurs, innovators and organisation builders? It is only by working together with global talent within the domestic environment that our tal-ented youngsters will be able to move India ahead in the Informa-tion Age.

Whether we like it or not, foreign MNCs have already had a con-siderable contribution to make to India's economic growth. We must continue to attract them and root them here. Indeed, while MNCs will remain a crucial component of our economy, we should also strengthen our already successful partnerships with them, be-cause these will help build domestic capabilities and forge strategic links with other regions. This is the only way the more promising of our local enterprises could be nurtured into world-class companies.

It is only when we have our own stable of world-class companies with core competencies which can compete effectively in the global economy, that we will increase the depth of our corporate profile and broaden the economic base for more sustained and resilient growth.

The challenges

As I said above, the external environment is evolving rapidly. Mas-sive changes in trade, investment, technology, employment, finance and even ideology are taking place at a mind-boggling pace. Rapid technological improvements and globalisation, which have expanded the trading of services across national borders and great distances without being hampered by the physical movement of people or goods, have dramatically altered production and consumption patterns. Most countries now recognise the benefits, or rather the inevitability of economic liberalisation, which has boosted international trade and cross-border investments. WTO membership, for whatever it is worth, currently exceeds 130 countries and is still growing. China and the former USSR have also moved towards a market economy.

New opportunities in the services, in manufacturing and in trade will continue to emerge. This will be driven by further services liberalisation, increasing affluence and the advent of e-commerce.

The external economic environment, which is changing so rapidly, is posing significant challenges for India. Let's talk about this. Overcoming these challenges is a very significant part of my dream.

The first challenge is for India to become competitive amidst intensifying competition and technological leapfrogging. Here we do not have a level playing field as we have to overcome a massive negative bias within the country against anything global. Our corporate leaders just do not have a global mindset. Also, we face keen competition from both developed and newly developing countries. The former benefit from a stronger indigenous technological base, a higher skilled workforce and a long tradition of world trade, while the latter are endowed with highly dynamic and better-organised commercial sectors.

To stay competitive, India has to find, develop and market sustainable 'niches' where we can start providing attractive, total cost-capability business packages. I am not talking here about the very low value-added work we are already doing in the software sector. To continue to participate and benefit from the growth all around us in Asia, we need to develop world-class capabilities to position India as a strategic partner for MNCs and other investors.

The second challenge is the shortage of talent and entrepreneurs. On the face of it, this seems silly. Shortage of talent and entrepreneurs? Surely, I must be joking! What I mean is that we need people with good business acumen and an enterprising spirit to turn business opportunities into *long-term* profits. We need to continue to develop, attract and retain talent, including foreign talent. The implications for the workforce of the future are immense. Internationally mobile capital and labour is now traversing the world in search of the best returns. More complex and demanding systems call for more innovative workers. New work processes and skill sets will be required.

The third challenge is the need for a paradigm shift in our mindset. Our dependence mentality—that of looking to the government to solve our problems and make decisions for us—and our aversion to risk-taking and change, has to be corrected. We need to adapt and initiate change or else become obsolete in a rapidly evolving world.

The fourth challenge is to manage our economic restructuring. We should be able to distinguish the tiny but very much more productive internationally-oriented sectors from the less productive, domestically-oriented sectors. The latter consist of an entire spectrum of enterprises from the very small village units to the large business houses. It is critical to manage this dual nature of the India economy. We must continue to encourage the restructuring and upgrading of internationally-oriented sectors.

As knowledge is now becoming obsolete quicker, the fifth challenge is the need to equip our workforce with critical enabling skills through continuous education and re-training so that we can re-invent ourselves continually. This will help to ensure the employability of displaced workers, address the aging population issue, and enhance our value-adding role in the world. Our dependence on foreign managerial skills in MNCs also has to be managed carefully in view of the consequent resource demands made by expatriates in terms of accommodation, transport, children's education, etc.

It is true that these global trends pose significant challenges but they also offer tremendous opportunities for the long-term survival and prosperity of a large economy such as India's which is in the process of opening up. Our future growth will depend on our ability to enhance existing strengths and leverage on new opportunities. India needs to position itself to ride on these trends.

Social fabric of competitiveness

I think the phrase 'social fabric of competitiveness' was invented in Singapore, because I have often heard it used there in all sorts of situations. It is probably one of the ways the government makes sure the citizens are aware of their responsibility in keeping Singapore intensely competitive. It is an admirable attempt to make people recognise that economic competitiveness, and the ability to respond successfully to global forces, has a strong social dimension.

Of course, it is understood that the social fabric, the relationships between different groups in society, has an important effect on competitiveness. In India, the sharp divisiveness of society has had an effect on our competitiveness in the face of globalisation. The Marwaris and the Bengalis find it difficult to work with each other in Bengal, the Brahmins and the lower castes in the South, the Hindus and the Muslims in UP, and so on. It is impossible to think of, say, a lower-caste-owned organisation in Chennai where the Brahmin staff work sincerely and with complete dedication.

While there are as many theories about the competitiveness of nations and of economies as there are economists and social scientists, the underlying fact remains undisputed. The agency which drives this competitiveness resides in individuals and organisations. To be competitive in the face of changes requires two things.

- First, an intelligence function, or the ability to recognise that there is indeed a problem, that new solutions are needed, and the ability to come up with new solutions. The agency which performs the intelligence function resides in the individual and involves entrepreneurship.
- And second, an implementation function or the ability to follow through and implement the solution. This would reside in commercial organisations in terms of their ability to make innovations in products, production, marketing and distribution.

In India, we have enough of the first kind, but every individual acts on his own and the implementation function is lost.

That was my dream!

Well that was my dream. That was me, building castles in the air. Now, I go on to the rest of the book, where we will talk about putting foundations of rock underneath.

Exports and our economy

*It is amazing that the Indian bureaucrat and the Indian
businessman are citizens of the same country.*

A Singapore businessman
talking to a trade delegation
from India, 1980

2.1

All the fuss over exchange rates

*The primary task of a nation is to defend its currency.
And this can only be done by the private business, aided
wherever needed by the government.*

Nobusuke Kishi.
First Prime Minister of Post-war Japan.

We see the result of this thinking in the modern-day rise of Japan. From being a lowly, humiliated nation it is now a major power. Though the strength of a nation's currency is dependent on a number of complex factors, the foundation is a strong export economy. Unless a nation earns more foreign exchange than it spends, no amount of economic jugglery by the government is going to help. This is true of all successful economies: their business communities are strongly committed to exports.

Patriotic Indians

One of my management gurus said that merely singing about the past greatness of a nation does not make a citizen patriotic. In this highly competitive modern world, we have to see where we stand in comparison with others. Nobody can deny us our existent strengths. We need, though, to take a hard look at the areas where we are weak and try to do something about these.

While I do not think I am different from the average Indian, one of the aspects I feel very strongly about is our attitude to our foreign exchange position and to the rate of exchange of the rupee in the international market.

I am neither an economist nor do I know much about international finance, exchange rate mechanisms and other impressive sounding jargon like the purchase power parity, etc. But I do know one thing. The world treats us as a very weak nation. And, to me, this is because of the weakness of our overseas trade and our currency.

> Many years ago, I visited a very large trading house in Japan. I saw the following embossed in golden letters in the main foyer.
>
> ### 'ANY NATION THAT SPENDS MORE FOREIGN EXCHANGE THAN IT EARNS IS A PARASITE'.
>
> I am told that this was subsequently removed as clients from the developing world found it offensive.
>
> This was the credo of the Japanese after the war, and we see the results today.

When I saw this, I felt intensely humiliated.

But this was nothing like what I felt when we had our nuclear test. I was in the US when I saw and heard TV journalists and commentators comment on the world's second largest nation. I heard leaders of tiny but successful nations humiliate us. We had to face the ultimate shame of being told not to expect any more handouts.

And, all of this because we did something which they have done many times over? Many nations have performed hundreds of nuclear tests and there has been nary a peep from any of these self-appointed guardians of the world's well being. I do not know whether the test was the right thing to do or not, but I certainly do know that it was purely an internal matter.

So what happened? Our Prime Minister had to personally beg for mercy when sanctions were imposed, our credit rating plummeted, and our currency nosedived with it.

• Here I am, standing in front of my fellow Indians, asking a simple question. Are we an independent sovereign nation?

I remember how when the Prime Minister of Malaysia lambasts world leaders, they listen. The reason? His nation has a solid export base and he does not need handouts from anybody, the IMF included. The leaders of other nations lend him a ear because they need his trade. I also remember the time the Prime Minister of Singapore, a tiny but hugely successful nation, came to India and he was asked by our journalists to tell us how to run our country! And our media lapped it up, putting it on the front pages. Remember how the American leaders apologised to China for having bombed its embassy building by mistake in Bosnia? Of course, America needs the trade with China.

To me, it all boils down to the strength of our economy, of our foreign exchange and our exports. If we are going around with a begging bowl, we will naturally have to put away thoughts of sovereignty and national pride in our pockets.

Are we really interested?

I have often tried to speak on the subject of our dismal export effort in various seminars and in guest lectures to business school students in various universities in South India. I do not succeed because I am invariably asked to suggest more than one topic for my talk, and any topic other than exports is selected.

I try to talk about this topic casually when I meet friends.

My feeling is that it is not a subject our people are really interested in. How are we concerned with exports, foreign exchange and the value of the rupee in our everyday life? We anyway have problems galore not to be bothered by these faraway aspects.

Indeed, one finds that most people believe the media hype about our comfortable foreign exchange reserves and are convinced that there is no problem.

It is almost an axiom that we cannot start solving a problem if we do not first recognise that there is, indeed, a problem. Only then can we go on to the stages of diagnosis and treatment. In India, when one talks about the subject of declining exports, the need to earn more foreign exchange, the problems of the balance of trade and the sharply declining value of the rupee, most people show no interest.

However, even when sometimes this topic does get discussed, as at seminars and conferences of the various chambers of commerce, trade and industrial associations, the large number of export promotion bodies and, of course, in academia and the business schools, it is always in a peripheral manner.

In India, one finds that nobody wants to talk about:

- How and why we are losing our export markets to immensely better-organised Asian and Western firms
- Why China, with its abysmal standard of living for its people, attracts many times the foreign investment that we do
- Why we still think that we can go on exporting traditional products to traditional markets. And so on

Instead, the topic is invariably how the government is doing everything wrong, with everybody roundly condemning all government policies since the time of independence. The unanimous verdict is that there is only one way of improving our exports. More duty drawbacks, more incentives, many more handouts and quicker processing of paperwork.

Our standing in the world market

Before going on to a discussion of the problems of our dismal exports and with our international trade, here is something interesting for you.

Try your hand at some educated guesswork.

(See Appendix 1 AND 2 for the answers and discussion)

TEST NO. 1. Having said a lot of things about how the world treats India, it is high time we took a hard look at where we stand in the world in terms of competitiveness. Here, I would point the interested reader to a very interesting study which is carried out every year by the International Institute for Management Development, Lausanne, Switzerland. It publishes the World Competitiveness Yearbook (WCY) every year which is available on the net. This is frequently updated. See the WCY pages on the IMD site: www.imd. ch/wcy

---

Question 1. Of the 45 nations analysed in **1980**, where do you think India stood?

        a) Number 25 from the top?
        b) Number 38 from the top?
        c) Number 40 from the top?
        d) Number 44 from the top?

Of the 49 nations analysed in **1999**, where do you think India stood?

        a) Number 25 from the top?
        b) Number 40 from the top?
        c) Number 43 from the top?
        d) Number 48 from the top?

TEST NO. 2. The United Nations publishes an annual International Trade Statistics Yearbook, which is by far the most comprehensive compilation of data on international trade. Before answering the following questions, remember that India is the world's second largest nation and, in our own opinion, we are second to none in brains.

Question 2. What was India's share of the world trade in **1950**?

    a) 22.82%
    b) 5.68%
    c) 1.91%
    d) 0.07%

In **1998**, what was our share in the world trade?

    a) 22.82%
    b) 5.68%
    c) 1.91%
    d) 0.07%

Our comfortable foreign exchange reserves

One of the reasons there is no panic about our dismal export performance is because our foreign exchange reserves are said to be at a healthy level.

Of course, there are as many estimates of what constitutes a healthy level as there are economic pundits. I am not going to detail the long list of statistics as discussions on these are available to the interested reader in our newspapers and newsmagazines and, in any case, are beyond the scope of this book. I am enclosing a few references as recommended reading on the subject in the bibliography.

What I am going to talk about here is how I think we ended up with this healthy situation without any tangible increase in our exports.

We need to look at the remittances of our overseas workers. These are shown by the Reserve Bank as private transfer receipts in the balance of payments account. These have increased at an annual rate of over 20 per cent since 1990–91 compared to the annual rate of increase of less than 8 per cent in earnings from all merchandise exports. As a result, private transfer receipts as a proportion of merchandise exports have gone up from 11 per cent in 1990–91 to 30 per cent in various NRI deposit schemes.

These deposits constituted almost two-thirds of our foreign exchange reserves, as at March-end 1999.

Remittances are not national earnings

Here again, and hard core economists may not agree, when my children, for example, send me money or park their savings in my savings account, I cannot claim these as my earnings. I may be fully justified in feeling proud that my children care for me and in feeling rich, but only in emotional terms. My going around proclaiming my wealth will only sound hollow. So also with the remittances our people are sending back home. India managed to give them a good education but gave them no employment prospects, so they went knocking on the doors of other nations for their livelihood. The fact that these deposits constitute almost two-thirds of our foreign exchange reserves, may be a matter of emotional pride but it is a matter of economic shame. The situation is inducing in us a sense of very dangerous complacency, and in the eyes of the world we remain a weak nation.

Balance of payments

This is one more term that I cannot fully comprehend. I have at least a hundred articles in my scrapbook where outstandingly brilliant gurus tell me that the BOP position is not worrisome. Well, it must not be if they so state.

The small print tells me that our trade gap is increasing. This is the gap between what we export and what we import. This will continue to increase because we are importing more and more and our exports are not able to keep pace. Our experts, however, tell us not to worry as we have our inwards remittances i.e., our children's support, and our software exports, which are a sugar-coated version of cheap manpower export, and as foreign aid and investment keeps on flowing into India.

True, in the wake of our nuclear adventure, Moody's downgraded our credit rating to below investment grade but we also have the resounding success of the Resurgent India Bonds.

Well, well, well. Where other nations take pride in their capacity to earn money, we are happy that we have no problems borrowing it.

I am sorry if I sound bitter. I am looking at my nation from a particular angle and see that we, the second largest nation, have only a 0.07 per cent share of the world trade and stand a measly 43 out of 49 nations in terms of competitiveness. The experts are all looking at a completely different picture and telling me not to worry. They keep assuring me that everything is hunky-dory, that our BOP is OK and that we have comfortable reserves. In the meantime, the world could go on humiliating us.

Devaluation for exports

The demand for more and more devaluation is tragic but it exists. Whenever the rupee goes down our exporters jump for joy.

Economists tell us this is a standard mechanism, often applied to stimulate export growth. A typical exporter in an open economy always prefers a drop in the nominal exchange rate, simply because it enhances his export earnings in terms of the local currency. He gets more rupees for the same dollar earning. This result is well known but it does not help our exports. It is not at all certain that a nominal rupee devaluation is reflected in an overall increased export performance.

> I will be addressing this point repeatedly in this book that our dismal export performance has very little to do with prices. We have many items which are very competitive in price and quality, and I have discussed an example in Chapter 6.4.
>
> If we were to offer, say, our manufactured goods at half the price, there would still be no buyers. The reasons why no new opportunities are coming our way and why we are, indeed, losing much of our overseas trade are too complex to be addressed in a couple of paragraphs.
>
> This is what the whole book is about.

The spurt in export growth rate, in rupee terms, immediately after two successive devaluation exercises since 1991 and our so-called liberalisation saga, did not last very long. The average annual growth rate of exports, in rupee terms, which was 15.7 per cent during

1992–96, came down sharply to 1.5 per cent in 1997–98. This lead to a rise in expectation as regards the further devaluation of the rupee. Although the rupee has continuously depreciated with respect to the dollar since September 1997, exports have not responded to the falling rupee commensurately. On the contrary, in recent times some principal, low value-added export items like agriculture and allied products, leather and leather goods, plastic and linoleum products, transport equipments and electronic goods have registered negative growth rates.

I have read some analysts attribute the recent drop in export growth rates to the remarkable depreciation in South-East Asian currencies and also to the debacle in these economies.

This is unmitigated rubbish. The South-East Asian crisis has undoubtedly caused a fall in demand for Indian export items, but only in those markets. This market was never substantial in any case. And, as far as the currency depreciation in these economies is concerned, India does not compete with those nations in most export markets. It should also be borne in mind that Indian exporters have received several export-related incentive schemes, quite unprecedented before 1991.

Official and unofficial exports

In developing countries like India where foreign exchange markets are subject to stringent rules and regulations, the quantum of actual exports may not undergo much change following devaluation. The official statistics often tend to overestimate the actual impact of currency depreciation or devaluation.

The impact of the devaluation of the rupee on export earnings in India is usually studied based on the official data provided by the Reserve Bank of India and other official agencies. There are two other sources, namely, the International Trade Statistics Yearbook published by the United Nations and the Direction of Trade Statistics published by the International Monetary Fund, which provide trade figures of both the exporting and the corresponding importing country.

However, huge discrepancies exist between our export and the corresponding importing country's import figures. True, these are partly explained in terms of the so-called 'transport costs' or the difference between the CIF and FOB values, but the discrepancies are too large to be solely explained in terms of freight and insurance costs.

I would point the reader to an excellently researched paper on 'Currency Devaluation and Exports' by Sugata Marjit and Byasdeb Dasgupta published in the *Economic and Political Weekly* dated April 29, 2000.

Overseas trade data, especially those of developing countries like India, are of immense importance because these are the basis on which our economic policy is formulated. The reliability of trade statistics over domestic economic data is attributed to several factors. Primarily, foreign trade is supposedly a well-defined area in which goods move under the nose of custom officials. Goods are supposedly counted and/or measured systematically for such purposes as the imposition of tariffs, subsidies and other regulations. In developing economies, where foreign exchange is scarce, particular attention is paid to the overseas trade sector, the single largest source of the demand for and the supply of foreign exchange. Also, the records kept by both trading partners, which can be compared side by side, present a check on accuracy.

Still there remain doubts regarding the quality of Indian overseas trade data. In the Indian case, Sugata Marjit and Byasdeb Dasgupta observed huge differences between India's official export figures and the corresponding importing country's import figures. For the period 1951–96, India's official export figures were always underdeclared barring a few exceptions. The devaluation/depreciation of the rupee narrowed the gap between our official export data and the corresponding importing country's import data for some years. It is, therefore, interesting to study the impact of exchange rate devaluation on the official and the actual export growth rates.

Every strictly-controlled foreign exchange market generally sustains an overvalued exchange rate. One gets more rupees for the dollar in black than officially. Due to the existence of this black market in foreign exchange, a huge number of illegal transactions take place as the local currency value of the foreign currency reflects a black market premium. So the actual exports are far higher than what is shown in official statistics.

✓ It is important to note that this technique of under-invoicing places the exporter completely at the mercy of the buyer. The buyer pays some part of the money through the bank and the rest in cash. There is no documentary proof that the buyer owes this money and cases of default, particularly involving overseas Indian traders, are legion.

The Export Credit Corporation of India has identified as many as 2000 'negative buyers' mostly from the developed countries, who have a consistent track record of bad dealings with Indian exporters. Most of the negative buyers identified were traders of Indian origin settled in countries like the US, UK and Germany. The reader would note that I have a full chapter (3.4) where I discuss how I consider our NRIs a bottleneck to our exports.

It is interesting to note that, with devaluation, the official exchange rate tends to converge temporarily to its market value and the under-invoicing of exports declines for a short period of time. The officially reported statistics dub this as an actual spurt in export earnings. The optimism demonstrated immediately after the devaluation in the official trade statistics is short-lived as exports fall back on the trend growth line which may be determined by several factors other than the exchange rate.

However, there may be a different implication of devaluation on the partner country's import statistics assuming, of course, that developed country partners possess better monitoring capabilities and hence partners' import data are subject to less adulteration than our export data.

Devaluation, by reducing the black market premium, increases the officially reported export sales, which is often dubbed devaluation-lead-growth in actual exports.

Exports in a time warp

The industrial economy of this country is undergoing dramatic, fundamental and enduring changes, and we are gradually moving in the direction of becoming, partly, a service economy too. However, one area of the economy that seems to have got itself tied up in a time warp is the export sector.

Published export figures show a niggardly two to three per cent growth, this after recording double digit growth in the years immediately after liberalisation. These figures do not reflect the ups and downs of a business cycle but the malaise that has struck deep roots in the sector that was supposed to take India into the global market with a bang. The fluctuating fortunes evident from one year to another suggest a structural problem in the export effort that continues to place reliance on traditional items and markets.

I have been looking at the published export statistics and cannot understand one thing. We all know that Indian IT companies are making waves in the global and national market with their high value addition, variously estimated to be in the range of Rs 180,000 million. None of this, however, is reflected in India's exports. The items that do figure are the same ones that figured as star exporters in the 1980s namely, textiles, gems and jewellery, light engineering, marine products, hides and skins, leather and bulk drugs. All of these are low-value-addition items; some have relatively high import intensities and others face, by their very nature, non-tariff barriers, such as environmental concerns in the case of leather. And, most of all, these items face competition from other developing countries with better export management skills.

Indeed, firms from Korea, Taiwan and Singapore are here in India exporting our products to their captive markets all over the world.

The problems that beset India's exports are in the nature of an affliction that has to be excised, but not by the government. There have been five medium-term export promotion policies in the past six years and the most distinguishing feature of all of these has been the lack of strategies for altering the export basket to take into account India's new core competencies and advantages.

But why blame policy or their authors at the commerce ministry for treading the beaten path? It is surely the export promotion councils, the agencies and experts, not to mention the producers and the exporters themselves, who should be organising themselves into strong cohesive export fronts.

Only if this issue is addressed will India gain a clear advantage in exports. India is also losing its competitive advantage in most areas of traditional exports. For instance,

✓ The share of leather goods in the total exports to the US has dipped from 3.76 per cent in 1992–93 to 1.37 per cent in 1998–99.
✓ The share of readymade garments including accessories has remained at approximately 15 per cent
✓ Exports of textiles excluding readymade garments have fallen from 12.06 per cent to 10.44 per cent in the same period
✓ On the other hand, software exports have increased their share from around 21 per cent in 1992–93 to 64 per cent in 1998–99

Belatedly, there have been a few major policy reforms in the software sector to boost its export capacity. But there is an urgent need to recognise IT services other than software that can provide this country with a unique chance to acquire a new competitive edge. Teleworking and remote processing are big business for the developing countries and entrepreneurs are grabbing a major share of the business. It is time the country recognised the great potential that the new businesses in the IT industry possess, not only to alter the character of the services industry but also to help India's forex reserve grow by leaps and bounds. India has the potential to grab a major chunk of the new business. Recognising that reality would help India's new exports thrust.

I would also point the reader to the Eximbank Study: 'Economic Growth Is Linked To Export Growth.' It is a very interesting and relevant document and there is an extract posted on their web page.

The Exim Bank's latest occasional paper on 'Exports in India's Growth Process' examines the instrumental role of international trade in general and that of exports in particular in the Indian growth process in the light of the experience of other developing countries. The study has been carried out with the help of the Indian Council for Research on International Economic Relations (ICRIER), New Delhi, and is available from the Bank.

The objectives of the study were to:

1. Analyse the combination of rapid export growth and rapid economic growth, and policy-related indicators that have been associated with this phenomenon.
2. Analyse what the changes over time have been in terms of the share of industrial exports to total exports including what the rapidity of the inter-temporal changes in the internal composition of industrial exports has been.
3. Find out what the major changes in the structure of comparative advantage have been over time.

The study focuses not only on India but also on those countries which compete with India in third country markets. The study covers nine other countries namely, the People's Republic of China, Malaysia, Indonesia, the Philippines, Thailand, the Republic of Korea, Taiwan, Bangladesh and Pakistan, in addition to India. The study reconfirms the fact that globalisation is a two-way interactive process in which the internal mainsprings of the growth process such as competent governance, technological and organisational innovations, improvements in the quality of human resources, and stable macroeconomic management are reinforced by interacting with the world through international trade. The basic point emphasised is that international trading opportunities cannot benefit a given country in the absence of favourable internal factors relating to the society, polity and economy.

A comparison between India and China with respect to export performance reveals that the Indian process of opening up has been considerably slower than that of China over the recent period 1980–96 and that the aggressive participation in international trade undertaken by China since the late 1970s has contributed towards a much faster rate of economic growth.

The conclusion on the basis of the above findings clearly indicates that there is no plausible reason why India should not accelerate the pace of export-orientation in its efforts to achieve and maintain a seven-per-cent-plus growth rate in real GDP. In fact, India is much more favourably placed to benefit from interacting with the global economy than many other low-income countries. India has a democratic polity, a well-established legal system, an independent judiciary, a diversified industrial structure and plenty of innovative entrepreneurship.

It is true that a reallocation of resources away from inefficient import-substitution-oriented activities and toward export-oriented activities would involve major structural adjustments, which are bound to be painful. Safety nets are absolutely essential to alleviate and minimise the pains of adjustment. And, as these pains are necessary to put the economy on a higher growth path, our society and polity will have to evolve credible mechanisms of cost sharing and conflict resolution. This is the challenge we face.

2.2   *Protectionism: A curse? Huh?*

First, about minding your language

As I said in the preamble, I have worked all my working life in many developing countries as a specialist in the field of industrial development, and this book is based on what I have seen of the developing world, and what I have seen of India through the eyes of the people of these nations.

I would come to India with overseas businessmen, looking for expertise, equipment and raw materials for small- and medium-scale manufacturing projects in Africa, etc. I would also go to many other Asian and European nations for the same purpose. So, I think I am one of the few Indians who has first-hand experience of how outsiders view our businessmen, and also how the same outsiders compare us with people of other developing nations.

One of my Singaporean Chinese colleagues, who is married to a lady of Tamil origin, and who has been to India many times with me had a very interesting comment to make. While in India, there were numerous occasions when he interacted informally with educated people, businessmen and professionals over lunches, cocktails and dinners.

He said:

'It seems that by far the most popular topic of conversation anywhere is criticism of everything your government has done in the past. A very close second topic in popularity is the discussion of the corruption of the politicians. However, there are situations where these two topics do not work. In such cases there is always the damage the British did to India.'

Of course, my friend could not know that we are the loudest in running our country down, especially when talking to outsiders. In comparison, one would never find the Japanese or people of any other Asian nation talking in such a loose manner about their own nation. True, everybody has opinions about their government and politicians, but they are usually careful about what they say in the presence of foreigners, particularly with people who are prospective customers.

Also, nobody criticizes the personal habits of one's competitors. This is in extremely poor taste and puts the customer immediately on the defensive.

Here's another thing. I have had countless experiences of an employee of a company we are visiting trying to meet us privately to say, 'Forget about this firm. My brother-in-law's uncle can give you a better deal!'

> The reader may well question the connection all this has with the subject of this book.
>
> Well, two things. First, we should be aware of the highly damaging effect our loud criticism of everything Indian has on foreign businessmen and visitors. No businessman comes to India looking for what to buy. He already knows what he wants. He invariably comes here to evaluate and compare what we have to offer with the offers he already has from elsewhere.
>
> The other thing foreign visitors notice is that our businessmen spend more time running their competitors down than in selling themselves and their products.

This is the other observation my friend made. He said that every Indian he met had a unique and brilliant slant on how and why India was in such a mess. Moreover, no matter who a visiting businessman meets, the person claims to be uniquely and exceptionally well-connected with the current ruling circles and offers himself as the only person who can get the job done.

The massive and concerted effort we make in running our country down frightens him. We are clearly telling him to go elsewhere.

Protectionism

Our businessmen have had to work with the Indian political and bureaucratic system. They have lived with it, understood it, learned to manipulate it and, of course, acquired a stake in it. The most successful have learned to manipulate the rules and the bureaucrats in charge, investing heavily to that end. They have learnt that more important than obtaining an industrial license is preventing others from doing so.

India has carried the flag for protection in the Third World because protection has meant less competition and safer profits. Businessmen may be waking up to what this approach has done to the economy as a whole, but they cannot be blamed for fearing that they themselves will lose out if real reform ever happens. Such fears partly reflect a lack of self-confidence, because Indian businessmen are fully convinced that they cannot compete as equals in the world economy.

Although the private corporate sector in India had always been accorded an important role in the industrialisation of the country, until recently its function was complementary to the public sector. The growth of the private corporate sector had to take place within the limits laid down by government regulations.

Many Indian companies, despite all the obstacles, have already proved that we have huge economic strengths and that our comparative advantage in cheap and well-trained labour could make us a global source for manufactured goods. Everything one sees in a humming centre of business such as Mumbai tells you that India would thrive on greater competition, astonishing itself and the rest of the world.

Protectionism: A curse?

We need to look at the subject of various policies: on import substitution, on protecting the domestic markets and on enabling big business houses to enjoy monopolies, which our successive governments have implemented, from three angles.

1. Having a protected market, or a closed economy, by itself does not lead to any damage to the economy. Almost every emerging economy has tried to protect fledgling domestic producers. Further, no domestic market has been more jealously and rigorously protected than Japan's, Korea's and also, to some extent, Taiwan's. When I go into the details, I will compare, with India, the various tariff and non-tariff barriers that, till recently, have been in

place making imports of finished products into these countries next to impossible. Yet, the same protective policy that is said to have destroyed the Indian economy, has lead to mind-boggling development in these countries.

2. In Chapter 3.3, when discussing our innovativeness, I will show that in 1945, the US was the only industrialised nation untouched by the devastation of two World Wars. American business had no competition. The world was borrowing money from them to buy their products, and they could set prices and standards based solely on what they felt like. So what did they do? Did they sit back and enjoy the monopolies they had like our big business houses did in the heyday of the License Raj? Everybody knows the answer to this. They went out and made alliances, set up subsidiaries, went into franchising in a big way and made sure the world remained their backyard.

3. As mentioned earlier, if we look at our economic history, import substitution as a strategy for industrial development has always existed, much before independence. All the industries set up by our pioneering business houses after the first World War were purely for import substitution. This can be taken as another manifestation of the fact that we have always been an inward-looking people. I will offer a very startling example of this at the end of this chapter.

As regards the first point, the answer is to be probably found in the nature of Japanese (and, to some extent, Korean) society. People here exhibit a far keener commitment than most other nations to the place where they work, to their company, to their government and to their nation. This loyalty gives each such organisation great strength. We will be discussing this in greater detail in Chapter 4.

On the other point of our inward-looking mindset, it is probably true that history drove us almost irresistibly to the course we chosè after 1947. The country's heritage at Independence was an intense suspicion of foreigners, trade and capitalism. Moreover, it seemed that a tried-and-tested alternative to rapacious western liberalism was at hand, this being the Soviet model. From 1947 onwards, an ever-proliferating bureaucracy planned the economy's future in extraordinary detail, using ideas and methods exclusively borrowed from the Soviet Union. So, we pursued self-sufficiency.

That pursuit has been our undoing.

A declared goal of this approach was to separate India from the world economy. This was done by replacing imports with domestic production, by discouraging foreign investment, and in many other ways. Nehru and his followers cannot be blamed for being of the view that interaction with the rest of the world would inevitably lead to dependence. This was the most fashionable ideology at that time. If our country was not to be exploited, it would have to go its own way.

✓ Why talk of our founding fathers, India's colonial past still shapes the attitudes of much of our educated middle class. This is hardly surprising, because that past has indeed been extraordinary. At the time of the Great Mutiny of 1857, 250 million Indians were, in effect, the subjects of the 1,700 shareholders of the East India Company, a commercial undertaking. This company protected its interests with a private army that was, at that time the best organised and the largest military force in the world, consisting wholly of Indians.

The principal author of the second plan was P.C. Mahalanobis, a cabinet adviser. His ideas blended Fabian socialism with values that had been propounded by Mahatma Gandhi—notably, disclaim for consumer goods and revulsion at the idea of 'luxuries'. India, said the Nehru–Mahalanobis blueprint, would transform itself from an agricultural economy into an industrial one. Investment would be channeled into the production of capital goods. Imports would be turned away with tariffs, quotas outright bans. There would be no need for exports. Consumer goods would stay in short supply, so people would save. These savings would then provide the resources for more investment.

Why has Indian development gone so tragically wrong? There are number of books on the subject, nobody has a simple answer and of course, every expert puts the blame squarely and completely on our economic policies.

So, what next?

Yet few of India's troubles are as intractable as Indians, especially, suppose them to be. Of all its miseries, the greatest by far is the country's economic failure, which is as broad and deep as the poverty that it sustains. If India could put its economy right, many of its other difficulties would immediately seem less overpowering; they would at least begin to seem treatable. Undeniably, political stability and human progress in India depend on greater economic success. That is exactly why so many Indians smile with resignation at the hopelessness of their case.

They are wrong. Nowhere else, not even in communist China or in the countries that constituted the former Soviet Union, is the gap between what might have been achieved and what has been achieved as great as it is in India. The country is rich in the resources that matter most for economic advance—not physical resources (which it also has) but human resources. Indians are capable of punishingly hard work; are, remarkably for people so poor, thrifty; are entrepreneurial; and are ambitious and materialistic. When Indians have ignored the Hindu injunction never to cross the 'black sea' and travel abroad, they have prospered within a generation. Only at home are there so many imprisoned, in their hundreds of million, in a sink of despair and degradation.

In many respects India has achieved a high degree of self-reliance, befitting its place in the world. We found the resources we needed for growth at home, in high domestic savings, so we avoided the foreign debts that have crippled Latin America. We conducted a responsible macroeconomic policy, avoiding over-borrowing and keeping the inflation rate low (by third-world standards). We have reduced the incidence of poverty and made great progress in advancing other measures of welfare: literacy rates have improved and infant mortality rates, declined.

The changes India need are not far short of a revolution. The main prescription for policy is easy enough: India must be opened up to the rest of the world; the state must withdraw from micro-managing the economy and concentrate instead on building the social and physical infrastructure that the country lacks. The private sector should stop wasting its time trying to remain small and learn to build strong cohesive organisations and multinational commercial institutions.

If this happened, predicting the result would be equally straight-forward. India's remarkable people would undoubtedly thrive. We will have nothing to fear from competition or from the uncertainties of an unplanned world.

2.3 *Let's look at our big fellows*

India's biggest importers

If India has to get back its export business, it is the big business houses who have to lead the push. It is a tragedy that these business houses, who have some of the best brains in the world, with many even having excellent managerial set-ups, have only short-term policies and prefer an easy and immediate profit in the domestic market. They do not tend to be interested in the long-term push into the export markets.

Big business in every successful country spearheads the nation's exports, and foreign exchange earning drives. In India, far from earning any foreign exchange, big business gets the priority in spending it.

If we are looking for evidence, we can turn to the issue of *Business Today* dated August 22, 1998. A detailed analysis on page 71 of the issue lists the export performance of 50 of the largest manufacturing companies, ranked as per their 1997–98 sales. It shows that *'the majority of country's largest corporations export so little that the value of their imports is far greater, making them net negative exporters.'*

As per the published statistics for the year 1997–98, 50 of our largest firms, all put together, earned only Rs 800,000 million in foreign exchange, but spent a massive Rs 6,900,000 million, a drain of Rs 6,000,000 million in foreign exchange per year. And this, by the very people who should have been earning it.

The attitude of our business leaders is what is killing our exports and our economy.

Indian business houses can, of course, get their act together, form consortia and have offices in all major cities of the world. But the first meeting of any consortium will come to an abrupt end with 'why should my nephew be posted to Dar es Salaam when your son is being sent to New York?'

A hard look at the structure of our big business houses throws up another very disturbing aspect. The vast majority of our big business houses are single generation success stories. Another analysis in the 1998 annual issue of *Business Today* shows that almost all the large business houses have split, again and again. Many well-known houses have just split and died out.

Coming back to the main topic of foreign exchange: what are our big business houses really thinking?

Talk to any senior executive of a large business house or listen to the speeches at chambers of commerce functions. Yes, they all say, we should export. Yes, we do accept that we have almost always had a negative trade balance, but there is no need to panic. There is no crisis. We are setting up a committee to look into what the government should do. Meanwhile, our inward remittances are substantial and we manage to get loans and aid.

So, that is it.

The big boys, the leading lights of our commerce require the foreign exchange in order to import things they need to make profits, but they are not prepared to earn it. They are happy so long as somebody else is earning this money for them. They are happy that our boys and girls, our children, go abroad, slog and grind away in all sorts of conditions, and send their hard-earned money home.

So, when a Japanese trading house humiliates our nation by putting up the credo mentioned in Chapter 2.1, would our 50 big business houses stand up and be counted?

Now on to the future

For a look at the future, let's look at the immediate past.

The 1990s have been very significant for the larger Indian business houses. The process of liberalisation started in 1991 continues in fits and starts. As seen from the manifestos of the ruling and opposition parties there seems to be no doubt that economic reforms will continue, no matter who comes to power and when. I have already addressed the issue of the increasing presence of the MNCs.

I get the impression that the larger business houses are indeed realising that they have to first become domestically and then globally competitive in terms of positioning their products and services on par with world-class organisations. The industry, the consumer as well as the service set-ups have started witnessing a major shift in customer preferences from conventional products to new products and services.

This, I think, will also decide the fate of many Indian organisations.

This scenario is going to make it very difficult for most of our big boys who are not used to world-class competition.

Do not worry, our big boys will not be big for long

From the various changes that are taking place, it will be clear that an organisation which can cater only to a highly protected domestic market and which cannot compete with organisations of world-class excellence will not be able to exist. Look at any successful economy of the world.

> ✓ Note: I am using the word 'successful' and not 'open'. Nations like Japan and Korea are outstandingly successful but have never been open.

In these economies, there are only two types of organisations which exist.

1. Organisations which export a minimum of 70 per cent to 80 per cent of their products, or,
2. Organisations which can offer 70 per cent to 80 per cent of their products to substitute imported products at world-class prices and quality.

> I will repeat. '...substitute imported products at world-class prices and quality'. Our big businesses have made import substitution their high-price-poor-quality religion.
>
> Indeed, there are many Indian organisations which do want to become global but have never acquired global skills because they have been comfortable with the local style of management.
>
> The Indian organisational immune system, which attempts to kill anything that is strange and new, can rarely be switched off.

It is going to be very difficult for such organisations to exist, considering various points of view. Let us look at some of the global and local parameters which are going to be very critical in the next decade.

First, the pace of growth of Indian organisations and the aggressiveness of global organisations do not match and will not for a long time to come. For example, Hindustan Motors came into existence in the 1950s and Hyundai, in Korea, in the 1970s, both under extremely protective regimes. India, however, offered a huge domestic market. In 1997, the total production of Hindustan Motors was about two hundred thousand cars while Hyundai sold 2.5 million! This is just one example of how multinational organisations grow, given the type of environment that is going to be ushered in. The global market which, of course, includes the Indian market, will offer an immense opportunity for such large-scale growth. Our big boys who do not want to grow at such a pace for whatever reason cannot survive.

The second important aspect is our attitude towards the introduction of new products. I am addressing this in considerable detail in Chapter 3.3, but we have seen how much of original research our industry indulged in and how many new models, say, our automobile industry has offered in the past 50 years. Compare this with the number of models Maruti has introduced since 1985. Ford, Samsung and Hyundai, which only came into India very recently have already introduced a number of new models. The World Competitiveness Yearbook (Appendix 1 and 2) shows that in terms of introducing new products, India is ranked 47 among 48 countries. The global market will demand new products at a faster pace. If our big boys are not going to take it as a challenge for whatever reason, they will have to leave the field.

The next parameter is the availability of professional input in the managing of organisations. There can only be two types of organisations:

1. Professionally-managed organisations, and
2. Organisations with some professionals!

In the former, functional responsibilities are assigned to professionals and the top management plays the role of a facilitator, encouraging professionals to display their talents. Responsibility and commensurate authority are passed on and risk-taking is encouraged. This is non-existent in the larger Indian-owned firms. True, there are outstanding exceptions and they are encouragingly proving that if we get down to it, we can do anything.

In the organisations with some professionals, the top management, invariably the owners and their family members, consider themselves much more competent than the professionals in the firm. This may really be so in some cases. However, if an organisation is to grow aggressively, the top management should believe in and implement the decentralisation of authority and responsibility. Due to the non-competitive environment in which Indian managers have been brought up they are not used to taking risks and making critical decisions. And managers who are willing to take the risk and shoulder the responsibility feel stifled if their potential is not used fully. Indeed, this is resulting in the migration to MNCs not only of these managers, but also of our youth, with our budding MBAs seeking jobs only with MNCs.

In my opinion, the most critical aspect here is the Jurassic profile of the Indian educational institutes which become the source of future manpower supply to various levels of the Indian organisation. While organisations are talking about globalisation, economic reforms, competitiveness, quality systems, productivity measures, etc., these issues are not reflected in the curriculum at schools and colleges. In terms of concept and technology orientation, our institutions do not match the expectations of the new marketplace. A lot of effort is spent mastering the machine, the technology or resources such as money and material. Very little effort is made to inform students on future job requirements with reference to the emerging competitiveness.

2.4   *Welcome the new East India Co.*

Here come the outsiders

Years ago the East India Co. exposed the structural weakness of our society which led to the loss of our nation. Well, to some extent, it is happening again. This time around, it is the structural weakness of our commercial and professional sectors which is the concern.

Hardly a day goes by without one of our political or business leaders voicing concern about the almost unrestricted entry of Multinational Companies (MNCs) into the Indian market.

There are dramatic changes taking place in the Indian market due to the entry of the MNCs. Dramatic but tragic, because we are not making the MNCs work for us. We are learning nothing from them. We are not even working with them as equals. We are ending up working for them. Just like we did for the British.

The real tragedy is that many of these new conquerors are from the East, from countries such as Korea, Taiwan and Singapore, who, till only recently, were begging us for skilled professionals. These nations have harnessed the energy of MNCs to get where they are today.

You may well ask what all of this has to do with this book. Should n't we be talking about our exports instead?

I will establish that though our nation is once again fighting a losing battle against conquerors, the real worry, however, is our rapidly declining exports. We have to learn to fight the MNCs at home because it is they who are taking away our markets overseas.

In this chapter, I will present an overview of the situation and in the following chapter, I will seek to establish that the problem is purely managerial. We need to take a hard look at how we organise ourselves and run our businesses.

First, what do we mean by a multinational company in India? There are as many definitions as there are politicians, and everybody twists the definition around to suit their arguments.

There have been number of partly foreign-owned firms doing business in India for decades. Phillips, Glaxo, ITC, Hindustan Lever, Colgate, Cadburys—the list goes on and on. Are these MNCs?

Is an MNC an outsider, in India to do business? But who is an out-sider? Say a company called Goodfolks Enterprises, which has oper-ations and branches in many countries, comes to India. If it is owned by a Mr Raghu Nandan of the US, it is considered an NRI company and we will lay a red carpet and offer it all sorts of incen-tives. But if it is owned by a Mr John Smith it will be considered an MNC, and our politicians and businessmen will start making a noise, forgetting the fact that ownership can change hands overnight.

In both cases, the company is foreign-owned and the same set of laws should be applicable to both.

We can look at this in another way.

An outsider is an outsider always

If the entry of MNCs is simply the case of outsiders coming to India for business purposes, this has been the story for generations. Almost every state in India has 'outsiders' who always remain so. A Marwari or a Punjabi in Bengal, Assam or Orissa is an outsider and always remains one. If this point is in any doubt then consider this. A third generation local Marwari, born, educated and brought up in Bengal, can never be the chief minister. So also, a Punjabi in Tamil Nadu. And so on.

The point is not the presence of MNCs as outsiders. We have always had outsiders. The point is how much the locals learn from them.

Did the Bengalis learn from the Punjabis who were doing busi-ness next door? By extension, the same is true of us learning from multinationals. Just as there have been thousands of Bengalis who have worked all their life for Marwaris but learnt nothing of their business acumen, we now have thousands of young Indian profes-sionals working for the MNCs but have seen no upgradation of our business attitudes or styles.

Four Asian countries, variously designated the four dragons, the four tigers, or the newly industrialising economies have become the focus of attention in the modern world. These four countries, South Korea, Malaysia, Taiwan and Singapore, despite varied back-grounds, have followed an aggressive policy towards the inflow of foreign direct investments, i.e. the entry of MNCs.

All these four economies developed due to their policy of export promotion, though they have travelled different paths. (Chapter 4.1)

All of them used MNCs as learning grounds and have now started developing their own brands in the international market. These economies are examples of the change in position from being a recipient of technology to being able to forge an alliance in development. The multinationals of these nations are becoming more proactive in their approach to international business, and have an increasingly strong presence in India. These multinationals have adapted the management styles of the West, and so are management and investment companies, not tied to specific products. Their procedure is to identify opportunities, recruit managers, borrow the money and then buy the technology through a joint venture.

Scared of MNCs? We are not alone

Before going into what these MNCs are doing here, it should be mentioned that India is not the only country where the local people are worried about the entry of MNCs. There are many countries, in many different parts of the world, with different economic systems at varying stages of development, who are all headed in the same direction. There are, of course, different national circumstances which explain the detailed strategies and timing of the individual initiatives, but virtually all countries, whatever their prior policies or philosophies, have liberalised their trade (and usually investment) regimes. Even hard core closed economies like Japan and Korea are opening up, albeit reluctantly.

The reason is that there has been a rapid increase in global interdependence. A very big chunk of international trade is trade not between countries but within the different national units of multinationals. And, even trade is no longer merely in goods and commodities. The services sector is growing very fast and this sector does not recognise any boundaries.

Success in today's global economy requires that countries compete effectively in international markets rather than simply at home. This is true no matter how large the domestic market. The list includes some of the world's most self-contained economies including Brazil and virtually all of Latin America, which embraced import substitution doctrines as recently as two decades ago. The list of countries that have joined the competitive liberalisation race also includes, perhaps most notably, the United States, which maintained extensive quotas on autos, machine tools, steel and numerous other products less than 15 years ago.

The most stunning reversal of all comes from many of the former command economies of the Communist world, ranging from China through to Central Europe to parts of the former Soviet Union and now Vietnam.

It follows that economic success in today's world requires countries to compete aggressively for the footloose international investment which brings with it efficiency in the distribution of global production and thus jobs, profits and technology.

Most countries offer direct incentives to foreign investors but an open trade and investment regime is even more critical for this purpose. Mexico was, for example, traditionally a very closed economy (and extremely wary of embracing its northern neighbour) but decided to liberalise when it became convinced that doing so was essential to avoid losing out in the global competition for capital.

If the whole world is opening up, why not India? Why not, indeed. Let's look at the dramatic changes taking place in the world due to the entry of the MNCs.

MNCs are there, all over the world

Beware: multinational companies are on the rampage, destroying jobs, turning the wage structure topsy turvy and generally wrecking local economies! Or so critics of globalisation make it out to be. A cool look at the numbers, however, tells a different story, as is clear from a cross-country study published in 1998 by the World Bank. This was the first document to take a detailed look at the contribution of foreign firms to national economies.

To be fair, the critics are right about one thing: multinationals are becoming increasingly important. Foreign firms account for a growing share of production and employment in most developed economies. In 1996, for example, the latest year for which comparative figures were available, foreign firms produced 15.8 per cent of the manufacturing output in America, up from 13.2 per cent in 1989 and 8.8 per cent in 1985. They accounted for 11.4 per cent of jobs in manufacturing, up from 10.8 per cent in 1989. Britain, Canada and

Sweden display a similar trend. In Ireland, foreign firms account for whopping 66 per cent of the output and 47 per cent of the employment.

Some countries have been able to keep out the multinationals. In the world's second-biggest economy, Japan, foreign firms scarcely figure: they employ a mere 0.8 per cent of workers.

The report goes into a discussion on whether the growth in importance of the foreign firms in national economies is a bad thing.

The facts suggest not.

Fact one: Foreign firms pay their workers more than the national average, and the gap is widening. In America, for example, foreign firms paid 4 per cent more than domestic ones in 1989; in 1996 they paid 6 per cent more.

Fact two: In most countries, foreign firms are creating jobs faster than are their domestic counterparts. In America, the workforce of foreign firms rose by 1.4 per cent a year between 1989 and 1996, compared with an annual rise of 0.8 per cent in domestic ones. In both Britain and France, employment at foreign firms increased by 1.7 per cent a year; at domestic ones it fell by 2.7 per cent.

Fact three: Foreign firms spend heavily on research and development (R&D) in the countries where they invest. In 1996, they accounted for 12 per cent of America's R&D spending, 19 per cent of France's and a remarkable 40 per cent of Britain's. Indeed, in some countries foreign firms spend more of their turnover on R&D than domestic ones do. In Britain, for example, foreign firms spent 2 per cent of their turnover on R&D; domestic firms only 1.5 per cent.

Fact four: Foreign firms tend to export more than domestic ones. In 1996, foreign firms in Ireland exported 89 per cent of their output, domestic ones only 34 per cent. The gap was 64 per cent: 37 per cent in the Netherlands, 35.2 per cent: 33.6 per cent in France and 13.1 per cent: 10.6 per cent in Japan. The big exception is America, where domestic firms exported 15.3 per cent of their output, foreign ones only 10.7 per cent.

These benefits of foreign investment are even bigger in Europe's poorer economies. Take the case of Turkey. Wages in foreign firms here are 124 per cent above the average; the workforce in these firms has risen by 11.5 per cent a year compared with 0.6 per cent in domestic ones; and the R&D spending of these firms is twice as high as in domestic firms.

It is clear that we are in the midst of a revolution. It is a revolution that is shaking the very foundations of business. But this revolution is not just about the kind of large-scale change that you watch on the evening news. It is more dramatic. This revolution will forever change the basic and most primal connection of business—the relationship between buyer and seller.

During this revolution, those organizations and individuals who can create new relationships with customers will find themselves with an unimagined competitive advantage. Those who don't will lose.

Our youth is telling us something

It is very much outside the scope of this book to delve into the arguments raging through India about the benefits or otherwise of the entry of MNCs. I know from my personal experience of interacting with budding MBAs all over India that the overwhelming preference is for a job with an MNC. Our youth is making it clear that only if one does not find a job with an MNC should one take a job with an Indian company and, that too, for a few years, before starting off something on one's own.

There is this hype about multinationals, probably on the strength of their higher pay packets and the superlative learning climate they provide. Global companies get the pick of fresh engineers and management graduates.

Thereafter, our youth is aware of the constant investments in training that multinationals make. It is not just an ability to send employees on external programmes overseas, but environmental learning which comes from working with a relatively brilliant peer group. This is because the rigorous selection process, free from the cousin-of-the boss syndrome, ensures that the innate capability in the executives selected is better than that in domestic firms.

Having acquired a taste for multinationals, or having seen your classmates working in these companies, the decision to join an Indian or a 'lala' company is by no means an easy one.

Our managers need to wake up

I seek to establish that the problem is purely managerial. We need to take a hard look at how we organise ourselves and how we run our businesses.

We have been defeated not only in the consumer market but everywhere. Some examples:

- On the domestic front, let's look at the professional services sector. Immensely better-organised professional MNCs, legal, accountancy, management consultancy, architectural and consulting engineering firms are coming in and appropriating the cream of the business. Increasingly, the large multilateral-funded projects are going to them because of their outstanding international credentials. Our brilliant but poorly organised one-man-shows are no match for these world-class firms. Forget about international credentials, most well-established professional firms in Delhi are not even known in the South. Indeed, our small firms happily set up joint ventures with the MNCs or work as subcontractors.
- After having built half of the Middle East, one would have thought that our construction sector would have acquired all the modern high-tech skills required. Instead, we find that the best high-tech construction and infrastructure building jobs at home are going to MNCs. Observe any massive overseas-funded hotel, resort, condominium, road or bridge project. Quite likely you will find an MNC executing it. Yet, till only a decade ago, it was an exclusively Indian domain. I have met and spoken to many of our respected names in the construction industry. They are really worried. As I said above, if MNCs are able to penetrate our market so easily, how can we compete with the same fellows for international contracts?
- We are rapidly losing our best brains to the MNCs. The top output of MBA and other professional institutions, as well as highly experienced managers, prefer jobs with MNCs.
- The last 15 years has seen the phenomenal growth of Japanese, Korean, and Singapore Chinese export houses. These firms now have an extensive network of branches in all the major cities in

India as well as all over Asia, Africa, West Indies and South America. They are rapidly taking the market for non-traditional exports away from Indian export houses who have absolutely no network outside India.

- The tragedy extends to overseas Indians settled in Africa and South-East Asia. The last 15 years has also seen the phenomenal growth of large Japanese, Korean, and Chinese trading firms who have set up well-managed supermarkets and departmental stores in the big cities in the regions mentioned above in partnership with local people. They are edging out the small businesses, the grocery and sundry shops owned by overseas Indians, who are being forced to sell out and return to India.
- In the fast moving consumer goods (FMCG) market, it is astonishing that respected Indian firms like the Tatas, Shaw Wallace, Calcutta Chemicals, Lakme, and Godrej have found it to their strategic advantage to sell off their consumer brands and consumer divisions to MNCs. Shops in small towns and villages all over India are increasingly full of soaps, toothpastes and sundries formerly made by Indian firms but now marketed by MNCs.

Fast moving consumer goods

So, let's take a hard look at the FMCG market.

From a professional manager's point of view, nobody can deny the massive changes taking place, and all for the better. The entire professional management scene in India has had and got a massive overhaul and boost. But what was the problem with the well-established Indian household names selling toothpaste and soaps to the Indian villages and small towns? What are these MNCs bringing in that we did not already have? What exactly is new about them?

✓ There is no Indian brand equity in brands such as Walls or Maggi. Nobody outside of the well-heeled and well-travelled urban elite knows that these are foreign brands. These are all new and unknown brands to consumers in the smaller towns in India. There have always been number of such foreign-sounding brand names in India.

✓ The large majority of the new entrants are not bringing in any remarkable new technology. The technology they are bringing in was always within reach of the larger Indian business houses. Indian-made ice cream, spectacle frames, breakfast foods or soups were already using the technology the MNCs now use.

✓ The new ventures are not managed by foreigners. Hardly any expatriates are being brought in. All the new firms are managed, from top to bottom, by Indians. The Indian managers were always there, their considerable skills already available to our Indian business houses.

✓ Even in the professional fields, our small one-man-show legal, accountancy, management consultancy, architectural and consulting engineering firms set up joint ventures with large professional firms and find that they end up providing the real brainpower.

True, there are a number of MNC failures too, but that is not the point. The point is that these newcomers are rapidly eroding the market share of well-established Indian firms. What is so unique about them?

I will be attempting to answer this in the following chapter, but here let me go back to what I said above about MNCs in professional areas. All over the western world, one finds large accountancy, legal, architectural and consulting practices. These sometimes have hundreds of partners, and many of these firms are now strong multinationals. Recently, large professional firms from the newly emerging Asian Tigers have entered the scene.

Many of these firms are now in India too. Indian architects, accountants and engineers are held in very high regard, and are eminently successful all over the world, but mainly as small individual practitioners. The practice dies out with the individual. True, many multinationals such as Price Waterhouse Coopers have a number of Indians as partners. This does not, however, make them Indian firms; it only goes to prove the point.

The way we work

The point is that Indians do not work well with each other; we are, as a rule, intensely individualistic people. We perform best when we are our own bosses, and tend not to build large economic institutions. Of course, we are brilliant, hard working and loyal, but only when working for or with non-Indians.

One last point. Can we not turn to our NRIs for help? Nobody is clear about what contribution the NRIs can and should make to the Indian economy. Indeed, overseas Indians make considerable contributions to the economies of other countries, but Indian businessmen and traders overseas almost never grow into large organisations. They remain petty one-family outfits, some with a multi-million dollar turnover, splitting as soon as the old man dies. The employment opportunities they offer to their own people are only at the unskilled clerical or menial levels. Their children, who qualify as trained professional managers, financial executives, etc., are either self employed or rise to senior executive positions in the service of non-Indians.

It is no use comparing the NRIs with the overseas Chinese and what they are doing in China. The overseas Chinese are the engines of the outstanding success of the Asian Tigers. They are corporate leaders who have developed and command massive organisational infrastructure and, by doing so, effectively control the economies of many Asian countries. They are now helping develop China's economy by using it as a base to feed their own substantial markets. The NRIs are professionals and traders who control nothing. Their success depends upon the success of the West. They can only bring in funds and professional skills to India. They have no captive markets to offer.

Even insofar as NRI funds are concerned, there is no nationalistic attitude. The NRI money and skills will go where it always has, anyplace it is secure and offers a better rate of return. In pragmatic terms, how and why should India be the country of their choice?

The above indeed points to an urgent need for a change in the mindset of those engaged in commercial and professional activities. We need to build strong and resilient growth-oriented organisational infrastructure in all walks of commerce and, perhaps, even in politics.

Working for MNCs

The feedback I have been receiving from MBAs who have been working in MNCs for some years is interesting. They feel that excessive control by the parent company can be a bother. Though multinationals talk about concepts like think global, act local, it often boils down to meaning 'let the globals think and the locals act'. Due to this extreme centralisation, our people here never feel a sense of ownership for the brand. I know many past MBA students who had the capacity to make for good operations persons, but in the jobs they had there was not much they were doing in terms of thinking, as the firm's strategy was decided overseas.

This, of course, is not strictly true of all global companies. Some multinationals, particularly those from the West, do have a more democratic approach for managing their worldwide subsidiaries. A point to be noted here is that there is no question of Japanese or Korean companies in India letting local staff even fully understand what is going on, leave aside giving them a chance at higher level decision making.

Multinationals from the West do indeed offer a good lifestyle with a reasonable amount of security. You interact with a bright bunch of people, both professionally and personally. That certainly provides you with a certain degree of learning and maturity. Rewards, in this instance, are not purely intangibles like job satisfaction but visibles like remuneration. In the end, what happens is that multinational employees get a premium attached, so most Indian companies have to shell out handsome packages to wean them away.

Extensive training is another hallmark of multinationals. Multinationals regularly motivate employees by the constant upgradation of their skills through training and job rotation. They impart a lot of in-house as well as external training. This is one aspect missing in Indian firms. In the first 10–15 years of your career, training is externally induced. As you move along you do get into the self-learning mode. You move from an explicit to a tacit learning stage. In the initial period, stimuli are given to you, but later you search for your own.

While multinationals impart exemplary training for use in that particular company or business, one area they miss out on is the managing of uncertainty.

For ambitious professionals, the future growth in a local company is an issue. There are fewer avenues. The option is to grow with the organisation, in terms of both new businesses and geographies. As long as Indian companies can create fresh challenges to satisfy their spirits, it may well be just the beginning.

Post-Reform strategies

There are a number of excellently researched papers by our leading economists and corporate gurus on how the Indian corporate sector has utilised a variety of strategies in the post-reform period to cope with the increasing competitive pressures. Everybody tells us that with the maturing of the Indian oligopolies, the attitudes are changing and that the Indian corporate sector is vigorously restructuring itself.

If one looks deeper, the restructuring is mainly defensive. It is geared towards consolidation in a few chosen areas to correct the inefficiencies created by over-diversification in the pre-reform era, rather than going forward to launch a concerted attack on world markets.

* MNCs have actively participated in the merger and acquisition process to gain market entry or to strengthen their presence. In very simple language, Indian firms eagerly sell out and move away from anything the MNCs take an interest in.
* The reliance of the Indian corporate sector on foreign technology purchase has increased. More and more technology flows are now tied in with equity. This means overseas firms will sell you the technology if you sell them a share of your company.
* In house technology generation has taken a backseat, because the purchase of foreign technology is easy and generates quick results.
* True, our firms are making efforts to improve manufacturing capability. This is being done through building alliances as well as through initiatives within the firm. Quality upgradation seems to be an important priority. These efforts at improving manufacturing capability may still prove to be inadequate to meet the competitive challenges because the alliances are mainly with foreign firms.
* It is also true that export-based growth strategies are being adopted by some of the corporate biggies, but such strategies are not widespread; export orientation increased appreciably in the early years of reform but have seen a major collapse since 1997–98.

Overall, our exposure to the international market is till inadequate to put Indian firms on the world map.

2.5 *Organisational infrastructure*

Big words!

Before explaining what I think these big words mean, let me first mention why I am talking about this concept in the first place. In the last chapter, I gave an overview of the situation regarding the entry of the MNCs when I had written:

✓ I will establish that though our nation is once again fighting a losing battle against conquerors, the real worry, however, is our rapidly declining exports. We have to learn to fight the MNCs at home because it is they who are taking away our markets overseas.

In other words, we need to take a hard look at how we work and how we do business. We need to understand how this is different from the way MNCs work.

In this chapter I will seek to establish that the problem is purely managerial. The MNCs are not only better but very differently organised. We will be taking a hard look at how we organise ourselves.

It is my conviction that central to the issue of improving India's export performance is a basic management concept known as 'growth-based organisational infrastructure'. I can also say this in simple words. 'If we do not learn to work together and build organisations, we can forget about exports'.

Some questions that arise are: What is so different about the way MNCs are organised? What is this vastly different attitude Indian businessmen and entrepreneurs have towards running a business, a commercial organisation or an institution? How is it that they are succeeding where we are failing?

We will address this issue in some detail here and I will be illustrating it with examples.

Some definitions

First, let us try and understand what is meant by organisational infrastructure.

This book makes a strong distinction between just running a successful business and building an organisation. We will not be dealing with how to set up and run a successful business, as there are number of excellent books and publications on the subject. What is crucial is that we learn how to build effective organisations in India, organisations that grow and do not split. Management gurus in India are very fond of saying that we need 'professionally'-managed organisations and not 'family'-managed firms. I do not agree. I can give a number of examples of purely family-managed firms in Hong Kong and Singapore which are superbly managed and highly growth oriented.

BASIC (OR ECONOMIC) INFRASTRUCTURE is defined and explained in text books on economics as what an economy needs to grow on and consists of everything from a network of roads and transport systems, to communications, to an efficient banking and postal system, etc.

ORGANISATIONAL INFRASTRUCTURE is the basic building block of any commercial activity. This infrastructure is what an organisation, an institution, a company or a commercial house builds on. This is how a corporate entity grows, nationwide and then worldwide.

Everybody has their own definition of the factors that make an organisation. In very simple terms, every commercial activity, be it a simple street corner bakery, a hair cutting saloon, or a consumer goods retailer, has some sort of an organisational infrastructure. There is the owner or his manager, and there is a clear line of authority downwards, even though there may be only one or two employees.

Here, as I said above, a distinction needs to be made between

✓ running a successful enterprise
✓ just organising something
✓ building an organisation.

Organising, in this sense, is needed even in situations which do not involve building an organisation. For example, in the case of a community effort in cleaning up a neighbourhood, a national effort for flood relief or, to take a classic example, of devotees constructing a temple. Matters such as the allocation of tasks, the delegation of authority and the putting in place of systems for control are involved whenever the efforts of large numbers of people have to be coordinated in carrying out a common task.

Building an organisation, however, involves things besides structures and methods of working. Above all, it involves binding people together with a sense of belonging and a sense of common purpose continuing over time, and cementing the whole together with some shared values and ideals. It is a process of social architecture, of institution building. It is no coincidence that so many of the world's great business corporations—IBM, Marks and Spencer, 3M, Honda, Daihatsu, Volvo and the like—have grown because they paid special attention to organisation building. For these companies, the creation of a human organisation aspiring to certain ideals has been a key objective. For them, organising in the narrower sense, say with an immediate, short term profit motive, is of no significance.

Let's take a break here

Since what we have been discussing has been rather technical, we deserve a break! Let's have some fun. I have devised a simple interactive session for MBA students which illustrates what we have been talking about.

Here is how the session goes. I ask students to refer to the country index of a world atlas and choose the names of a hundred nations at random. Then we list them in order of size, and keep two dozen of the largest. So, we end up with 24 not-too-small nations selected at random. I call out the names and the students decide whether the nation is economically successful or not. The nations doing reasonably well go into the first list and the ones not doing too well go into a second list. Arranged alphabetically, this may be, for example, a typical selection:

LIST NO. 1	LIST NO. 2
BARBADOS	ARGENTINA
CYPRUS	BANGLADESH
ENGLAND	BRAZIL
FRANCE	INDONESIA
MALAYSIA	KENYA
MALDIVES	MALAWI

MALTA	NIGERIA
MAURITIUS	PAKISTAN
NEW ZEALAND	PAPUA NEW GUINEA
SINGAPORE	PORTUGAL
THAILAND	THE PHILIPPINES
USA	TURKEY

Now for something surprising. We have a perfectly random listing of nations that have done well and those that have not. It is almost like magic that nations in each list have a lot of characteristics in common. And, it is equally surprising that there is nothing in common between the two lists. Nations that do well behave in a certain way, with the reverse also holding true.

This is, for example, what happens in a classroom. Students who do well always have a few things such as talent, hard work and discipline in common. This group, again, has hardly anything in common with those who do not perform well.

The same goes for nations. I then ask students to start listing out the common characteristics. This is the feedback I get.

POLITICAL CLIMATE. The students could immediately see that the outstanding characteristic of the nations in the first list is that they have stable political systems. They have only a handful of political parties, strong political discipline and very little internal bickering and dissidence, with almost no splitting of parties and no party hopping. I can almost say with certainty that when there is strong political discipline, the nation does well.

Very unlike the second list where the political climate leaves a lot to be desired, mirroring the economy.

BUSINESS ATTITUDES. Again, nations in the first list tend to build strong business institutions which are mostly professionally managed and have, in recent times, looked outward to doing business in other regions. A common characteristic of these nations is that they have given birth to many world-class companies. Even small nations like Malta and Cyprus have home-grown firms which have bases and business interests in other countries. In other words, if people work well together, the nation invariably does well.

By strong contrast, the nations in the second list have a tradition of small businesses run by individuals. People do not work well with each other and run small, poorly-organised set-ups which sometimes make a lot of money but invariably do not grow into organisations. The business generally dies out with the old man. The better-run businesses in these countries are generally those run by MNCs.

EXPORT ORIENTATION. It is almost an extension of the above that the nations in the first list share a common characteristic of being strongly export oriented. Their commercial sectors possess the organisational backup to go out and compete with others on their home turf.

All the nations in the second list have negative trade balances. Indigenous business houses are busy fighting amongst themselves and are not bothered about competing with anybody else.

LIFE AND LIVING STANDARDS. Visiting any of the nations on the second list, one is overwhelmed by a feeling of shabbiness and shoddiness everywhere one looks—roads, buildings, shopfronts, buses and taxis. Everything one sees is ramshackle and awfully maintained. So is the reputation of the goods produced in these nations.

This is in sharp contrast to the neat and elegant way people in the nations on the first list live. Somehow the very attitude to life is different and this clearly shows up in the quality of goods produced.

Different nations, different attitudes

The point I am trying to make here is that when nations do well, there are certain basic reasons for it. Economists and social scientists have published tons of literature analysing the success (and failure!) of individual nations, but the overwhelming evidence I have seen during my work in developing nations all over the world points to a simple fact.

✓ It is only if the people of a nation have a tendency to work together and build strong business, political and social institutions that the nation progresses. It is merely a question of attitude.

The people in the second list share the common characteristic of being intensely individualistic working on the principle of everybody for themselves alone. The result is there to see. Businesses remains small and petty, though sometimes with a multi-million turnover!

For an organisation to grow, there has to be a distinct organisational structure, lines of authority, allocation of responsibility, division of labour, a system, discipline, accounting, record keeping and available statistics, besides esprit de corps, cooperation and 'team play'. With everybody working for themselves and themselves alone this, of course, cannot happen.

I know I have indulged in a fair bit of generalisation here. When we look at different countries, and attempt to compare the parts played by the factors I mention above, we find that their relative importance changes immensely from nation to nation. We begin to realise that it is not merely the art of organising that requires knowledge of aims, processes, men and conditions as well as of the principles of organisation. And while it is true that businessmen and entrepreneurs of different nations have vastly different attitudes to how they wish their organisations to be managed, the common feature remains undisputed. Businessmen and entrepreneurs succeed not when they work as individuals but when they work as and build cohesive organisations.

This has also nothing to do with whether an organisation is family-managed or not. As an example, in the West, only professionally-managed firms grow into large organisations. But in the East, purely family-managed Chinese firms exhibit all the signs of professionally-managed firms and grow.

Make plenty of money or grow into an organisation

In most cases in India, none of the above factors are visible. The organisational infrastructure is simply profit motivated. The entire commercial activity is aimed at tangible profit in the short term, and the only effort made is to maximise this profit. Invariably, the profit is ploughed back into the business only to an extent that it results in immediate extra profit.

There is no thought being given to the set-up growing as an organisation. The owner designs the managerial set-up more for absolute control and power rather than with growth-inducing strategies in mind. The attitude is: 'I want the firm to grow only to an extent that I can keep everything under my own control.' If the activity is profitable, the surplus is withdrawn for secure investment in real estate, etc. The owner has palatial houses and lives in five-star comfort but the factory and offices are shabby and ill maintained.

This is one of the points I often raise when talking to MBA students. I ask them the meaning of success in life. To most of them, the meaning of success is simply making a lot of money. I have not met anybody who is determined to work from the beginning towards growing into an organisation.

An interesting example. In the early 1960s, I was very fond of eating out at a restaurant called Moti Mahal in Old Delhi. The place was shabby and reasonably dirty but the food, especially the Tandoori Chicken, was superb. Recently, I went there again and the place has all but closed down. I was told that the old man had died, leaving an enormous fortune to his children who, however, had no interest in the business. Across the world, in the US, I have been following the fortunes of another outfit famous for its chicken. The old man also died, leaving only a reasonable fortune for his children, but the organisation he founded now has worldwide presence—Kentucky Fried Chicken. In the Indian example, the business died with the old man and the money went soon after. In the American example, the massive organisational infrastructure he built keeps on growing.

I think I have got my point across. It really depends on what you want to leave behind, money or an organisation.

That was then, this is now

This may have been acceptable in the past, when India was isolated and insulated from the rest of the world. Also, the employment structure in India consisted mainly of small- and medium-sized family-owned enterprises, which did not really offer much scope for professional employment or organisation building.

Now, however, the economic and commercial scenario is changing with the entry of the very much better-organised MNCs.

To illustrate the point, let's look at the organisational infrastructure of some Indian firms in the fast moving consumer goods (FMCG) sector and compare these with MNCs in the same field.

There are indeed many excellent local companies in the business of selling common household items like toothpastes, soaps and detergents. Companies like Godrej and Balsara in Bombay, Dabur in Calcutta, etc.

However, their nationwide presence is trifling as compared to that of multinational companies such as Hindustan Lever, Colgate–

Palmolive and Procter & Gamble. These MNCs have an extensive network of branches and distributors in even the smallest of towns in the remotest parts of the nation. Their organisational infrastructure is massive. The Indian firms I mentioned above are indeed excellently managed but their set-ups are markedly different and very much more regional.

The organisational infrastructure of the MNCs is such that they not only have a vast network of dealers and stockists all over the country, but also have dozens of contract manufacturers in many small towns. I am not sure how many of us know that MNCs farm out most of their manufacturing to contract manufacturers. These are small local firms who produce finished goods for the MNC from the raw material, packing material, printed cartons, labels, collapsible tubes, etc. supplied by them. These supplies are also generally sourced within short distances from the contract manufacturer. The contract manufacturers and the packing material suppliers are often set up with technical and financial assistance from the MNC. The quality of goods produced is rigidly monitored by the MNC.

It is clear that this requires immense logistical support, and indicates the type of organisational infrastructure the firms have.

One cannot say that our indigenous firms lack managerial or organisational skills. Far from it. We have some of the best brains in the world. But our attitude towards building organisational infrastructure is miles away from that needed to grow nationwide, leave aside world-class, companies.

Compare Coke/Pepsi with the Thumsup gang

Another example. When we threw Coke out of India, they left behind an excellent production and distribution network. It should have been a simple matter for an Indian organisation to step in and continue to develop the market under a new brand name.

Instead, what we got were a number of small soft drink manufacturers all over India. Their profile:

✓ They were all small, individual-owned, regional companies.
✓ Without exception, they were poorly managed.
✓ Their contribution to the national economy was non-existent.
✓ They were small companies, so generally paid no taxes.

✓ They offered only low-level menial employment opportunities because the family or the owners did everything themselves.

✓ There were absolutely no employment opportunities for, say, qualified MBAs.

✓ Quality standards were, again, quite non-existent.

✓ None of them had any infrastructure to feed the market beyond, say, 100 miles from their location.

Parle was a very big company in Bombay but Parle had no presence in Bengal, Bihar, Orissa or Tamil Nadu.

In contrast we now see Coke and Pepsi all over India. As one of my MBA students pointed out after a rural project visit, 'You get Coke and Pepsi in villages where you do not even have clean drinking water!'

Profile:

✓ The organisational infrastructure of Coke and Pepsi ensures that a bottle of coke in Pondicherry would be identical to the one you will buy in Assam. Or in Singapore, for that matter.

✓ These firms have excellent employment opportunities for all sorts of professionals at all levels, up to the top management.

✓ The Indian treasury gets good taxes.

✓ The firms have massive budgets to enable them to participate in India's economic and cultural life, by sponsoring sporting, cultural and academic events.

Why stop with one example?

I can go on and compare the tomato sauce or the fruit juice cordial market. Before Nestlé came onto the scene, there were excellent Indian firms manufacturing products of almost the same quality. But it is only Nestlé that has been able to establish a strong nationwide presence, and hardly a day goes by without their introducing a new product. And remember, most of the success is to be attributed to Indian managerial talent that has always been available to our Indian companies.

The other classic example is one which has been worked to death by every journalist in India. Hindustan Motors vs Hyundai vs Maruti etc.

What the Indian media does not mention is that Hindustan Motors was working under no more a protectionist regime than were the Japanese or the Koreans. But the Japanese and, later on, the Koreans took advantage of the rigorous protection in the domestic market to develop into world-class players. The Indians just concentrated on making quick money for themselves, for their dealers and for their political masters.

True, there are number of MNC failures too, but that is not the point. The point is that these MNCs are rapidly eroding the market share of well-established Indian firms.

Quick! press the rewind button

Before going further, I am going to press the rewind button and go back a long time in history.

An unusual way of understanding the term 'organisational infrastructure', and grasping one of the reasons why our economy has not done well, is to go way back into history. Let's look at the how and the why of the British coming to India and, subsequently, taking over almost the whole world.

I will seek to establish that the strong and well-established corporate organisational infrastructure they had at home was the foundation on which the British empire grew.

Also, I will compare the way the British set up colonies with the way the Spanish and, to a lesser extent, the Portuguese did. I will show that the common man back home in England benefited immensely from this whereas the common people in Spain or Portugal did not.

THE BRITISH CONQUEST. The British came and conquered India mainly because of our own weaknesses and faults. That is, however, not the aspect I am concerned with. If one looks at the British conquest from a British point of view, and from a purely managerial and organisational point of view, one cannot help but be amazed at the infrastructure and commercial organisation the British possessed even in the seventeenth century. They had to have such a base back home to have been able to successfully establish such a large trading empire in India.

They could not possibly have set up their trading and, subsequently, their political empire if they did not have a well-established banking and financial system, a legal system, postal services, company laws and regulations, and a few large, efficiently-managed private companies in every field of enterprise. Remember, this is the early seventeenth century we are talking about.

One should notice that the Englishman who came here did not come as an individual. He was a team member, an integral part of the British empire. And everything the British did in India was to the benefit of England as a nation and not for the benefit of any individual. The individuals who came here were not particularly clever, rather the reverse, but they had the skill of setting us Indians against each other and making us work for them. It is indeed, a credit to their style of management that the Indians who fought for them were much better soldiers than those who fought for the local princes.

They ended up having the whole world working for them to the benefit of England. There was a mind-boggling rise in the standard of living of the common people of Britain.

There was never an armed invasion by the British. They came here only as traders.

✓ *Their success is entirely due to the massive amount of organisational backup back home.*

THE PORTUGUESE were here as much as two hundred years earlier, having defeated the combined Gujarati–Calicut fleet in February 1509 at Diu. The Portuguese had immensely superior naval firepower, and this victory can be said to be the beginning of European colonialism in the subcontinent.

With the discovery by the Portuguese of the sea-route to India at the close of the fifteenth century, movement in the Indian Ocean was strictly controlled. There are ample records to show that from the first decade of the sixteenth century, the Portuguese, under the presumption of having the right to supremacy over the Indian Ocean, insisted on 'passes' for all ships plying in it. After occupying Malacca, in the Malay peninsula, they enforced the system of passes with greater strictness. They established their fortresses and settlements on the Eastern and Western coasts of India and detailed patrolling vessels to stop and confiscate ships not provided with their passes.

✓ *But the point is that the people of Portugal, the common man, hardly benefited from all of this.*

The Portuguese had better naval and military capabilities, and they controlled the sea-trade routes to a great extent, but the advantages were purely militaristic and non-civil.

The Portuguese lacked the discipline, and the technological and economic infrastructure back home to really benefit from all this. They controlled the sea-trade routes but, very unlike the British, had nothing much to trade in. They had no manufactured products to export and no marketing networks to sell what they could import from the East.

Every commander who came here was in the business for himself and there was absolutely no rise in the standard of living for the people back home. The new colonies they set up were small and were quickly lost to the more enterprising British, and other North Europeans.

THE SPANISH. The same was true of the Spanish, and to a much greater extent. They were very much more powerful on the seas and conquered a much greater part of the world, but Spain was and remained a poor and backward nation.

One-man-show vs organised corporate effort

So we come back to modern times and I go back to what I said above about MNCs in professional areas.

In the professional services sector, even though Indian architects, accountants and engineers are held in very high regard, and are eminently successful, they operate only as small individual practitioners. The practice never spreads out from the home base and invariably dies out with the individual.

By contrast, one finds large accountancy, legal, architectural and consulting practices all over the western world. These sometimes have hundreds of partners and many are now strong multinationals. Recently, large professional firms from the newly emerging Asian Tigers have joined the bandwagon. Many of these firms are now in India. Our brilliant but poorly organised one-man-shows are no match for these world-class firms.

Business culture

We have been talking about the attitudes people of various nations have towards running their businesses. We can look at this in a more academic context. We can say that, based on these attitudes, specific business cultures develop within individual businesses and industries of various nations. Our management gurus have been talking about business culture for a long time, without discussing what our business culture is doing insofar as our competitiveness in world markets is concerned.

What is a business culture? A detailed discussion of this topic would be beyond the scope of this book. Cultures can exist across a society or in elements within it—families, religious groups, regions, or any other social institution. However, it does also exist in economic organisations such as industries or businesses, and this is relevant to what we are talking about.

Any business culture will have its own special features. The origins of a corporate culture might reasonably be expected to lie in the past and present entrepreneurial leadership of the company, the type of employees it recruits, the way in which work is organised, the technology used, and the competitive environment within which it operates. The characteristics of a culture will be found in the relations between individuals and between them and the organisation seen through various dimensions, such as the exercise of power, the forms of communication, symbols, and rituals, the degree of commitment that the organisation and the individual offer one another, the capacity to accept dissent, the ways in which new individuals are integrated, and the existence of shared attitudes and objectives.

The strength and distinctiveness of the value system through which these various dimensions are shared will vary from nation to nation, as will be the extent to which members of the organisation are committed to it.

I have provided a number of illustrations in this chapter explaining in simple language how business culture has implications on the efficiency of the organisation in the short run, and its strategy in the long run. Efficiency can be seen in terms of cost, innovation and competitiveness. Strategy may be seen in terms of the explicit plans that emerge from the organisation's controlling group, or the direction taken as an implicit consequence of a particular culture.

Business culture and MNCs

When an organisation is functioning only in the domestic environment, its business culture can be recognised by practices, forms of communication, and physical symbols to which meaning is attached. These are the outward signs of a culture rooted in the minds of its participants, created by shared experiences and routine exchanges of technological or organisational requirements. These then get reinforced by group pressures and the influence of those with power. This business culture then becomes imprinted on the organisation and its members develop a strong resistance to change or manipulation.

To a great extent this gives meaning and validity to the action of individuals and they become committed to it. For this reason, attempts to impose a business culture of one organisation or nation on another may prove superficial and often operates against organizational interests.

I remember an example of this. Many years ago, Malaysia had a new Prime Minister in Dr Mahathir Mohammad. The first thing he did was to deflect the immense influence western business houses held over local business culture.

He saw the deep imprint that western business culture was having on individuals and organisations, creating an inertia that prevented the necessary adjustments when the nation's political structure, environment and objectives were changing. It was clear that such a strong culture was proving dangerous for organisations facing change, by reinforcing individuals' capacities to continue to act contrary to organisational needs and its members continuing to work in contrary directions.

Prolonged dissonance between culture and organisational needs was reducing efficiency and even leading to organisational collapse in some cases.

So, Dr Mahathir Mohammad initiated a policy of 'Looking East' and encouraged the import of the more Asian business cultures of Japan, Korea, etc.

Of course, organisations did initially contain overlapping or conflicting cultures. Modern businesses are complex organisations undertaking different activities in a variety of locations. Malaysia was developing into an open economy and there were a number of cases where the corporation was the product of a merger between firms with distinct histories and cultures.

The result was that few organisations, especially businesses, had memberships that shared a single culture. Technology, organisation and experience helped in shaping a new business culture which was a variant of the original corporate cultures.

MNCs in India

In India, the Malaysian example cannot work. There is no powerful central leadership, and we do not have any history of a strong business culture. The conflicts of imported business cultures and our individualistic styles of functioning can threaten organisational efficiency and survival. Individuals or particular sections in an organisation may pursue goals that differ from the rest of the organisations. The benefits of a clearly identified business culture for communication, cooperation and motivation are lost.

It is true that a successful business culture will not save a firm from the consequences of a business situation that is disastrous, though it will certainly help it to adapt and respond more effectively. Conversely, firms with a powerful market position generating substantial profits may survive with apparently inappropriate cultures, though they may be less able to cope with change and their survival may be temporary.

2.6 *World-class companies*

Let's put things in context first

I do not need to be reminded that this is not a book on marketing or international management. We are talking about exports. So, what has a full chapter on world-class companies got to do with this book?

Well, everything.

- First, the MNCs responsible for such dramatic changes in our economy were all world-class companies first before they became MNCs.
- Second, many Japanese, Korean and now Singaporean export houses are setting up base in India. These firms, all world-class companies, are earning huge profits by exporting Indian products to their own markets all over the world. Indian export houses have no share of this fast developing market.
- Third, for India to enter and compete in the world market, we need to build a pool of world-class local companies.

I have been saying repeatedly that for India's export performance to improve, our larger business houses have to play a leading role. It is tragic that much of India's economic growth in the recent past has largely been driven by multinationals. If, in the list of MNCs, we include partly foreign-owned firms like Philips, ITC, Hindustan Lever, Colgate, Glaxo and Cadburys, which have been here for a long time, we can certainly say that MNCs have provided a considerable contribution to India's economic growth. For the immediate future too, foreign MNCs will continue to be an integral part of the Indian economy. For us to maintain and build on our self reliance and competitiveness, we need to build our own world-class companies. This will increase the depth of our corporate profile and broaden the base for sustained growth.

What are world-class companies?

While there are as many definitions of what a world class company is as there are economists and management pundits, I do not think there can be a universal definition of a world-class company.

It can generally be said a company that has become a MNC, must have been a world-class company at home first. You must be a front-runner in your respective field, subscribing to state-of-the-art management and technological practices in keeping with environmental changes at home. Only then can you hope to enjoy global and diversified operations, and garner the top market share in your respective business area.

Today, size is no longer synonymous with being world-class, as new manufacturing techniques and computerised production allow small factories to produce customised goods at mass-produced prices. The emphasis has shifted from size to efficiency, dynamism, agility and a reputation for timeliness. A world-class company today is one that can meet the highest standards anywhere in order to command resources and operate beyond borders.

World-class companies are significant contributors to domestic economic growth. The Scandinavian countries provide an interesting example. Unlike India, these countries have limited manpower and domestic markets. Nonetheless, they have companies that are world leaders in their respective high-technology fields and are key pillars of their economies. Nokia of Finland, for example, is the world's second largest producer of mobile telephones and Ericsson of Sweden, the third.

I would say that any Indian firm with a strong entrepreneurial base can develop into a world-class company if it continues to build its core competencies and is seriously interested in competing in the international market. On a very rough basis, I can list out several key capabilities which are necessary for our companies to grow into world-class companies:

1. SKILLED MANPOWER RESOURCE. Apart from having highly trained workers, the management must be entrepreneurial, with an international perspective in order to be able to track and capitalise on the latest business trends in the region and around the world;

2. RESEARCH AND DEVELOPMENT. Firms must possess the ability to develop proprietary R&D in order to maintain their competitive edge;

3. ADEQUATE CAPITAL and financing. Local companies with sound expansion plans must have easy access to funding. This is especially important for high technology start-ups, which are normally deemed to be more risky by investors;

4. MARKET NETWORKS for access to regional markets. Apart from good distribution channels, firms must also have market intelligence to meet customised market needs.

An essential feature of being a world-class company is that it should be able to engage relevant smaller firms as your partners in rendering supporting services for your operations. With this partnership, the expertise and knowledge gained by the bigger companies will filter down to the smaller firms and, in due course, allow them to gain their own foreign market experience and a foothold in the region.

Need for indigenous world-class companies

As I said above, if, in the list of MNCs we include partly foreign-owned firms which have been here for a long time, we can certainly say that MNCs have provided a considerable contribution to India's economic growth. We have attracted these world-class players by offering them a cost-effective workforce, good supporting physical infrastructure and an emerging pro-business environment and the second largest domestic market in the world. As compared to many other developing nations, we are politically stable and efficient.

However, as an infrastructure-scarce country which has a long way to go before we can reach a near-developed state in terms of our economy, this MNC-driven growth is not good for us in the long term. Indian companies now face intense competition, both in the domestic market and in an increasingly borderless world. In this context, as I said above, we need to build a stable of our own world-class companies with core competencies, which can compete effectively in the global economy.

There are two key roles that our home-grown world-class companies or indigenous MNCs should play.

• First, they should be leaders in the development of indigenous technological capabilities.
• Second, they should spearhead our investments overseas to help grow our external wings.

Our ability to deploy relevant technology and manage our resources efficiently will help to ensure our competitive edge. These competitive elements will be more and more important in the next chapter of our economic growth. We must spare no effort to upgrade the operating environment so as both to continue to attract world-class MNCs and to root them here and nurture the growth of our own firms.

The world out there

We read everyday in the Indian media about how rapidly the external environment is evolving. Journalists and academicians try to explain the important changes in trade, investment, technology, employment, finance and even ideology taking place all over the world. Rapid technological improvements and globalisation have had a dramatic effect on production and consumption patterns, particularly in the developing world.

So, let's take a quick look at the key global trends and the opportunities and challenges they pose to India in the immediate future. An in-depth understanding of these critical driving forces and uncertainties in the global environment is essential for our business houses to develop an attitude which will enable them to grow into world-class companies.

For the last two decades, the world's economy has been going through two great changes.

The first change is that a lot of industrial production has moved from the US, Western Europe and Japan to developing countries in Latin America, and South-East Asia. One can take the example of the exodus of low-cost production of items such as textiles, clothing, shoes, handbags, car seats, electrical wiring, plastic toys, and cheap electronic devices from the rich world over the past two decades.

Already many western and Japanese companies have more employees (and customers) in poor countries than in rich ones.

The second great change, an important aspect for India to note and take advantage of, is that in the rich countries as well as in countries like Hong Kong and Singapore, the balance of economic activity is swinging from the manufacturing to the services sector.

This has resulted in the flourishing of global merchandise trade, driven by the pressure of trade liberalisation in most countries. Most countries also now recognise the benefits of economic liberalisation, boosting international trade and investments. The direct result of this has been that tariff barriers the world over have fallen, and India is following suit by demolishing the massive import restrictions which have been in place for a long time.

A household can use only so many cars and refrigerators and dishwashers in its members' lifetime. As countries get richer, a rising share of income is spent on holidays, health and education. Also, because people are busy, they want to hire others to clean their homes, launder their clothes, plan their holidays, entertain them and so on. Jobs traditionally thought of as part of 'manufacturing', such as the design and marketing of products, are now becoming service jobs. As the demand for such jobs increases, they tend to become better paid and more interesting as compared to the drudgery of factory work, much of which is, in any case, moving overseas.

In Asia, Hong Kong and Singapore now lead the world in terms of a strong growth in the service economy. In the US and Britain, the proportion of workers in manufacturing has shrunk since 1900 from around 40 per cent to a fraction of that. Even in Germany and Japan, which rebuilt so many factories after 1945, manufacturing's share of jobs is now well below 30 per cent. The effect of the shift is increased as manufacturing moves from rich countries to the developing ones, whose cheap labour gives them a sharp advantage in many of the repetitive tasks required by mass production.

The global and transnational trade in services is also growing in value and importance. The rapid growth in global services trading is the direct consequence of two factors.

✓ First, the global and regional liberalisation and deregulation mentioned above, leading to greater market access.
✓ And second, the technological innovations and improvements such as internet and electronic commerce which have eased the

manner in which services can be traded across national borders and great distances without there being any need for the physical movement of people or goods.

This, plus the unbundling and outsourcing by the manufacturing sector of previously in-house functions such as logistics and IT services has created vast new opportunities in the services trade which will continue to grow. This will be driven by further services liberalisation, increasing affluence and the further development of e-commerce.

The rapid technological improvements in information and communication networks has also been reflected in the massive improvement in all sorts of freight movement and transportation. While the volume of the goods handled has taken a quantum leap, the cost of air and sea transportation has fallen significantly. This has lead to the globalisation of production networks.

Three international business models

Companies are motivated to consider international activity when they realise that a market for their products and/or services extends beyond the geographic borders of their country. This expanded perception of the market carries with it the attraction of increased revenues and profits. Companies that expand into the international marketplace are categorised by management gurus into three classes.

Let's look at these very briefly.

1. The global exporters—the Japanese way

Exporters often find that success is dependent on the early expansion of export activities. Companies most often do this in one of two ways. They either increase the human element, by locating expatriate company representatives in the designated country to act as sales and marketing agents, or they add value to the product itself and make it more attractive to the export market by means of minor modifications or features to fit the overseas environment.

We call companies that engage in such value-enhancing modifications 'global exporters'. They often make extensive forays outside of their home countries to capture knowledge about market and customer requirements. They also study competitors' operations around the world to increase their management knowledge base. While they gather and analyse this market intelligence information they, however, still run most company operations from home.

As exporters begin to set their sights on globalisation, they are gradually forced to bow to local pressures and start deploying local manufacturing activity to support local sales presence. Eventually, perhaps reluctantly, they deploy product-development in selected locations. By doing so, they begin to take on the structural appearances of a multinational.

Global exporters tend to view the world more from a geographic rather than a business perspective. They do well at managing their company as a world business system. On the other hand, they are very reluctant to move any core activities outside of their home country.

Global exporters are highly integrated, work in multidisciplinary teams, and share a strong common culture. The home country is like a high-walled citadel, and they rely on the very strong control of and on directives from home-country headquarters. They also rely very heavily on their own nationals for all major decision making, reflecting little trust in foreign employees.

Global exporters produce products that seek to find the lowest common denominator in product appeal, so that as little customisation as possible has to be done locally. These homogeneous or 'global' products are primarily successful when they are of an extremely high quality, as service and support can pose a real challenge to the global exporter. Because of their highly integrated world business systems, they have little overlap of resources and, consequently, have high economies of scale. Global exporters are very patient, and prepared to take a long-term view of such investment decision as subsidising a start-up operation in a new country.

2. The multinational—the United States model

Most multinationals were once global exporters, and most global exporters will probably have to pass through a multinational phase.

Multinationalism usually begins with the creation of a domestic but nationwide sales and service organization in another nation initially marketing imported products followed soon after by the setting up of local manufacturing organizations. Research and development is often the last function to be moved out from the home country, though significant innovations can be rapidly transferred from headquarters to the rest of the world.

The multinational develops relatively homogeneous products or services for the world. Manufacturing is distributed around the world to exploit economies of scale and vault barriers to entry. By physically moving closer to customers and taking advantage of scale economies, the multinational is able to deliver fairly low-cost products to most customers.

In a multinational company, headquarters plays a strong role in setting strategies and policies and establishing standards. Sales and delivery channels tend to be regionally controlled with some level of autonomy from corporate headquarters, provided fairly rigid revenue and profit guidelines are met. This concern creates a bias toward the further development of home-country and major markets, since markets are often judged by profit-generating measures.

Multinationals, like global exporters, produce homogeneous products for world markets, while also producing tailored products for specific markets. Because they have a much broader geographic presence than global exporters, they acculturate better.

3. The multilocal—the European model

Once a company expands its frontiers beyond export, the management may sometimes decide to develop markets with a less strong, centralised approach and go to the other extreme, laissez-faire. This approach allows the management to focus on local customer expectations.

Customers increasingly want the customisation of some aspects of their products and the services they receive. The multilocal specialises in local customisation to meet local customer requirements. It is through customisation that companies add value to commodity goods. Local sales and delivery offer customised products.

The multilocal is focused on and responsive to its customers and flexible to local requirements. The balance of power lies with the national organisation. These strong national organisations operate as a set of independent, self-reliant and geographically dispersed units. While fostering independence and initiative, the sharing of management knowledge across boundaries is minimal, and such an approach forces unit managers to go through steep learning curves as they continuously reinvent knowledge on how to carry out the business.

The multilocal company tends to duplicate a large portion of the value chain in each country where it does business, and sacrifices economies of scale in an attempt to meet local market requirements.

The aggregate worldwide customer pays a high cost for this. The global customer has to deal with several separate operating units of the same company, and at times has to help sort out its account administration. In multilocal companies, there is often no assurance of consistency in company policy across borders with regard to price and quality.

Multilocals have to contend with high walls built around each country, as well as the strongest case of the 'not invented here' syndrome. On the other hand, multilocals have a strong advantage over other current forms in terms of cultural fit, often leading to high-value differentiated services.

The new business model

So, as we discussed above, a new business model has been created. One cannot find a single large manufacturing conglomerate in any developed country that does not have subsidiary or contract manufacturing facilities in other parts of the world.

There has been a steep worldwide rise in the number of foreign affiliates and in intra-firm trade. WTO, in its 1997 annual report, estimates that one-third of world trade takes place within transnational corporate networks, and that more than half the foreign affiliate exports of Japanese and American MNCs are conducted on an intra-firm basis. This greater interconnectedness implies dynamic growth and change. Developing economies can enjoy an accelerated transformation of their industrial, business and trading structures and environments. Even services which were traditionally localised and domestic-oriented have restructured to take advantage of economic liberalisation and to serve customers overseas.

The day-to-day management of widely dispersed production and service networks offers no problem. This ease of communication and movement of goods has also intensified competitive pressures. Companies are pushed to reap the benefits of the economies of geographical diversification. MNCs traverse the world in search of markets and profits. The result is the integration of value-added chains across the global economy, converting global inputs into outputs for global markets.

Whole industries no longer migrate, as ship building did from Europe to Asia in the 1970s. Because of the number of factors detailed above, manufacturing is becoming a genuinely international affair. Production of critical parts and the final assembly is done in rich countries by skilled workers, the simpler parts and the non-critical components are made elsewhere in the supply chain. Multinational companies are developing the skills to see what is best done where.

Indigenous technological capability

In tune with the rest of the world, our economy is moving up the value chain to produce high-tech and high quality goods and services. We therefore need to consciously develop our indigenous technological capabilities. Growth cannot be based on mere emulation and modification of technologies and ideas developed by others. We have reached the stage where we are competing head-on with developed nations and the ability to innovate is critical.

Having indigenous capabilities will enable us to capture much more of the high-end value in the production process. It will accelerate the process of internalising new technologies so that we are able to creatively apply and develop these further to create commercial solutions to meet market needs. At the same time, it will help ensure that our local companies remain relevant to the world economy and become value-adding strategic partners to MNCs operating in India.

Growing the external wing

All that I have been saying above can be summarised in a sentence. With our domestic constraints and a huge population with a limited purchasing power, Indian companies will need to learn to venture abroad to expand and ride on growth opportunities beyond our national boundaries.

✓ It should be pointed out here that hoardes of Indian companies did venture abroad in the late 1960s, with utterly disastrous results.

Disastrous because these ventures were spearheaded by only riff-raff firms with no domestic base and absolutely no organisational ability, plunging the nation into a small crisis. The lesson to be learnt here is that venturing abroad requires, first, a complete and careful assessment of your own organisational structure and strength. It is stupid to venture into setting up a project or a base overseas simply because 'my wife's brother has just passed his MBA and needs something to do'. I am personally aware of many Indian joint ventures which were set up in South-East Asia on this basis.

Of course, the next step is to carefully assess risk factors, including financial, economic and country risk factors. As the competition is intense, India companies going abroad require a strong financial position and ample resources to survive and thrive. Many overseas projects are huge, requiring large capital investment. Our smaller firms, on their own, may not be able to take full advantage of these opportunities due to their limited size, resources and capabilities.

What I am saying above, in simple words, is that you should first be a world-class company at home before thinking of venturing abroad.

Indigenous world-class companies

I have said above that there is already a growing trend among Indian companies, both local and partly foreign-owned, to have a global or regional emphasis. This expansion of local companies into regional and even global markets is helping build our external wing, and thus providing a firm foundation for India's growth.

For our firms to develop into world-class players, they must be prepared to recruit the best talent from around the world, and not necessarily expatriates. In most cases, people of Indian origin are doing superb work all over the world. Indeed, if our ambition is to build world-class companies with a significant presence around the world, the top management of these companies should take on a transnational complexion and ensure they possess an intimate knowledge of all the major world markets relevant to the particular industry. This is where the experience of people of Indian origin who have been working abroad comes in handy.

Of course, we should be prepared to pay competitive rates for international or domestic talents and, more important, nurture a risk-taking and entrepreneurial culture.

Many world-class companies have found that the principle of giving subsidiary companies the autonomy and responsibility for their own business and investment strategies has been key to their successful growth, and should be upheld. The parent firm's stewardship should extend to ensuring that the right people are in the right place and that there is sufficient funding for the firms to grow, especially internationally. Budding world-class companies in India should build on this role. They should oversee and monitor the strategic business thrusts of their subsidiaries and associated firms and improve the flow of information on business opportunities open to them.

Benchmarking for Indian companies

Typically, benchmarking against global practices comes into the picture when an Indian firm wants employees in far-flung locations. This calls for both empowerment and systems, and these firms are now increasingly looking for executives with transnational experience. People who would fit the bill are those who have either worked in different countries or at least in an environment of international best practices. These practices range from concepts such as measuring customer satisfaction and innovations to improving it to efficiency-enhancing methods on cutting costs and increasing speed, or simply to a more structured style of functioning such as having an agenda for a meeting, keeping to a scheduled time, and restraining from loose brainstorming.

My own experience is that such moves are mostly happening in Indian companies that have reached a certain size and now have a problem with future growth. These are the companies that are now retaining management consultants. They have the vision but not the competence to get there.

The challenge of driving this change for India Inc. is one of the charms for multinational hands, long used to working as small cogs in a wheel. Because the managerial base in most Indian companies is still in its infancy, Indian industry today provides an environment that a dynamic executive can redefine and recreate. The creativity employed can be a source of immense satisfaction.

An executive leaving an MNC and joining an Indian firm has several aspects that he needs to look into such as: Does the company have an open and free working style? Are its people a valued component? What is the level to which it runs on methods and systems? A negative factor is the influence of family members, particularly when they have authority without proportionate accountability or power without maturity which only comes after years of public dealing.

It should not matter how small the company is as long as its vision is clear and it has the wherewithal to get there. One has to see whether it is able to provide an assurance of being at an acceptable level of risk and of not being a gamble. It should not be whimsical or operate on a day-to-day basis.

For starters, it does take some getting used to working in the unstructured environment of most local firms after a multinational stint. There are no set ways of doing things, so you need to be both adaptable and assertive. This somewhat shapeless framework often relates both to day-to-day operations and strategic decisions. By contrast, in a multinational it is comparatively difficult to make a mistake. You are a small cog and there are numerous safeguards in the system.

Organisation culture is one fallout of management philosophy. Individual-driven to the core, employees in a large number of Indian companies confer an almost god-like status on promoters, whereas most multinationals foster a more casual and open atmosphere. There are always a number of people in Indian companies referred to as 'sirs' and no one would think of arguing with the promoters. Respect for elders is fine and is the basis of the success of most Japanese firms, but sometimes thoughts do need to be challenged. When companies hire professionals from other MNCs, the old hands do expect some changes anyway.

What remains unchanged is compulsions such as managing with a limited budget. Indian firms are very cost-conscious. There is never enough money to back a brand or a project to the hilt. Another difference that needs some getting used to is the little or no benefit derived from global learning in local companies. When launching a new business or product, vast amounts of data are normally just a phone call or an e-mail away in a multinational. An immense degree of resourcefulness is necessary in an Indian company, which, unlike a multinational, may have to depend upon an ad agency with overseas links or a branch office which may still be unable to come up with the information sought.

Conclusion

MNCs will remain an integral part of the India economy. They are world-class companies, bringing with them the best concepts, competence, connections and knowledge of world markets. We have to use this to develop our own pool of indigenous world-class companies to provide a major source of economic growth.

3
Some bottlenecks

To improve is to change. To be perfect is to change often.

Sir Winston Churchill

3.1 *Let's talk about shoddiness*

> *'I have the simplest of taste. I am easily satisfied with perfection'.*
>
> Oscar Wilde

Calling a spade a spade

Let me say straight off that of all the chapters in this book writing this particular one has, for me, been the most uncomfortable, or rather painful.

When I look at my nation and my people as others see us, I am not at all comfortable. Now, don't get me wrong. I am the last person with a holier-than-thou attitude. Certainly, when you read the dilemma I pose for you in last few paragraphs of this chapter, you will see that I see myself as no different from the rest of us.

My readers would have by now noticed an undertone of a message in this book. This comes, first, from my having spent most of my life living and working in many a poor, developing nation across the world, and second, from my habit of looking at ourselves through the eyes of others. Only yesterday, these nations were begging us for professionals and skilled people to help kickstart their economies. Today, many have overtaken us and, indeed, we are now going to them for help in building our infrastructure.

The message is that something is not right in the way we live and the way we work.

I have now retired and am setting up a new home in India. Coming here, I have found some remarks particularly infuriating. Remarks such as:

- Sir, we have found a good maid to work in your home. You will find her very good as she has been working for foreigners! Remarkable! Has working for foreigners made her superior?
- Sir, I will recommend this second-hand car. It was owned by a foreigner!
Remarkable again. Is an Indian-owned car assumed to be junk?

To me there is one thing that sticks out like a sore thumb, and I notice it, as I said, because I have a habit of looking at my nation from a different angle. I am talking about something we do not normally notice or talk about in India: our attitude towards shoddiness.

We may be shoddy or we may be neat and tidy. Why make an issue of it in this book? What has all this to do with exports?

Well, two things. First, I am looking for a connection between the overwhelming shoddiness of goods produced in India and our way of life. I feel it is possible that shoddiness has become a habit with us and is seriously damaging our export prospects. To us, 'quality' does not include 'finish'.

Second, it is my firm belief that firms that have a tradition of stringent quality control for all their products at all times exhibit better export performance than those that produce some items specially for export. To me a label saying 'Export Quality' is an advertisement that the rest of the goods produced are shoddy. Like a hotel advertising 'clean sheets and towels in the deluxe rooms'.

Doing something especially for a purpose, or doing it because you have been ordered to do it, is never as good as doing the same thing automatically, by habit.

- So, I am calling a spade a spade and am saying out loud that it is our attitude of accepting shoddiness as the norm that has lead to an immense damage to our economy in general and to our exports in particular. We are just not bothered by how things look.

Let me also make it clear that I am not only talking about how we do things in India. I have lived and worked with people of Indian origin all over the world. Well, they may have lived overseas for generations, but their attitudes, particularly towards shabbiness and shoddiness, remain the same. The point I am trying to make is that even if we see others right next door do things in a different way, we just ignore it. Remember, we are proud of the way foreigners use their cars and of how maids work in their homes!

Well, we may ignore it, but the world does not. I remember a news item in the press, sometime in December 1999, about Prince Charles commenting on the shoddy wiring in his bedroom. He said, 'It must have been an Indian contractor'. Of course, there was an uproar, but can anyone who has lived anywhere outside India honestly deny the truth of this remark? And of course, nobody can make this remark in India, as there is nobody else to compare us with.

True, there are flashes of elegance and good workmanship, which only go to prove the point. Making a special effort to do something, is not the same as doing it as a matter of habit, much like Aunt Connie's pallu (give me a minute and you will read all about it).

Let's go overseas first

Drive to Southall, the Indian conclave near London. I am not happy talking about this, but the shoddiness and shabbiness of the place hits you in the face as it is in stark contrast with the elegance next door. Nobody has to tell you that you have reached Southall. The very look of the Indian-owned shopfronts tells you that you are back home. The dirty and smudged glassfronts, showcases used for storage rather than for display, crude hand-scrawled signs for prices and announcements, unkempt and unshaven shopkeepers, and muddy floors all have a story to tell. Contrast this with the squeaky-clean shops run by the local whites, and, as I said, it hits you in the face.

This is true of Indian shopkeepers all over the world whether in the UK, the US, Singapore or Malaysia. Talk to the shopkeepers and you get their side of the story. They have to work 18 hours a day, 7 days per week. Of course, nobody tells them to work like this, but business is good and the more they work, the more money they make. They also have a point when they say that keeping their shops clean will not improve their sales. Their customers, invariably Indians, cannot be bothered by how the place looks!

Maintained by Ford? Wow!

I come to another example which also I am not too proud of.

A friend runs a tour agency in South India where he organises group tours, mostly for domestic tourists. A location that is rapidly increasing in popularity is Dakshin Chitra, about 50 km south of Chennai. A superb concept developed by the Madras Crafts Foundation, Dakshin Chitra depicts scenes from all the states of India and is very obviously the work of people who love India. I have been meeting Indians who have visited the place and they have had only good things to say about it.

For me, Dakshin Chitra was a very pleasant exception to the rule. The place was exceptionally well laid out and maintained. Now, however, the Ford Motor Co. has come into the picture and has begun sponsoring the maintenance of the place. Being a non-profit enterprise, I am sure this sponsorship has come in handy to the Madras Crafts people.

So, where is the sad part? Well, now when I talk to people who have been there, they have only one thing to say. Maintained by Ford! Wow! Of the ten sentences describing the place, nine will gush over the fantastic maintenance by Ford. I ask myself, why do we take it for granted that anything Ford will do will be superb? Is it because Ford is a foreign organisation? Is that all? What if the place was being maintained by a Bajaj, BPL, Godrej or Kirloskar? And in any case, why were Indian organisations not approached to sponsor the maintenance? Any reader can answer that. Indian firms are not interested in such activities and, in any case, would have done an awful job.

Without getting into an argument over this, I can repeat what I said above. Indians are just not bothered by how the place looks!

My aunt Connie

I would like to now press the rewind button and take the reader back to my childhood.

✓ Give me a minute and you will see that this is very much in context.

I was born and brought up in a very conservative and traditional part of Punjab, in a place called Hoshiarpur. In those days it was little more than a village and the main activity was agriculture and trading.

Right next door to the house we lived in was a large joint family mansion. I grew up with the son of the eldest brother in the family and we always treated both houses as home. In the mid-thirties, one of this friend's uncles went to the UK for education, married an English girl and brought her back home. Thenceforth, she lived in India all her life, going back to England only once. We called her Aunt Connie.

I grew up with her children and learnt a lot, not only from the way she adapted herself to the Indian way of life, but also from the things she did not accept. From a very young age, then, I was exposed to the contrast between the traditional Indian way of thinking and living and the western way. Since I have subsequently lived and worked in many poor developing nations, looking at the way other people live and work and comparing this to the way we do things has become a habit. I have learnt to look at ourselves from a very different angle.

✓ This contrast is now all the more evident because MNCs here are making dramatic changes to our business lives. I will discuss the impact this alien way of doing business is having on our traditional business houses. You will note that I use the word 'alien' and not 'western'. This is because a greater impact is being made by Japanese, Korean, Singaporean and now Malaysian firms that have set up shop here.

Now, back to my childhood, the first thing I noticed about Aunt Connie was that she could never keep her *pallu* on her head. In North India, it is a tradition for married women to keep their heads covered at all times when in public or in the presence of elders with the *pallu* of the sari or a *chunni*. Aunt Connie was English and being from a different world could never understand the need for doing this. She did so simply because she respected our customs, was told to do so and saw everyone doing so. The result was that even after having lived for 50 years in a small town in India, she was still clumsy when it came to covering her head. All the other married ladies did this effortlessly and gracefully. Though we children are all grown up now we still jokingly make fun of her.

✓ This is where, at a very young age, I realised the difference between just doing what you are told to and doing something spontaneously and naturally—'Like Aunt Connie's *pallu*'. I will give some more examples that are relevant to the context of this book.

I grew up noticing a lot of other things.

The family I am taking about lived in an old but huge house where the old folk, and all the married children each had a portion to themselves. It was a joint family and everybody had the same sort of beds, bedsheets, utensils and furniture. However, I noticed that Aunt Connie's area was always more cheerful. There was a place for everything and everything was in its place. All the tables and shelves had nice covers and on the walls and in the shelves were many small knick-knacks. The toothbrushes in the bathroom were in clean glasses. Everything was neat and the whole look was very pleasant. That was our favorite part of the house. We children loved spending time there. The rest of the house was like any other big family home—clean, but untidy and quite shabby.

I want it to be clearly understood that I do not mean that Aunt Connie was any more meticulous about cleanliness than, say, my mother and some of the other ladies in the big house. Indeed, the Indian ladies were far more meticulous in many things: the washing of hands before meals; bathing early in the morning in cold water even in winters; the kitchen utensils scrubbed scrupulously clean; all of this was a part of our rigorous up bringing. My mother, however, unlike Aunt Connie was concerned only with cleanliness and did not bother about elegance or how things looked.

✓ The point I am making is that clean is not the same thing as neat. And, neat and clean is quite different from aesthetically pleasing.

I distinctly remember the time when the whole house was being painted. The painters left ugly smudges all over the windowpanes and the woodwork when painting the walls and did a very casual job of cleaning up afterwards. Nobody bothered. Nobody except Aunt Connie. She was livid and shouted at the painters in colourful Punjabi. The result was that her portion of the house was exquisitely finished.

I am not talking of stray incidents. I am talking of a person who lived in the same house year after year and yet did things differently. The other ladies saw this but learnt nothing from her attitude to life. This is probably because we never really saw her as one of us. I do not mean anything even remotely offensive here. It is how we treat 'outsiders'. A Tamilian, in Punjab for generations and speaking the local language is never considered 'one of us'. There are many Punjabis and Marwaris who have been living in Tamil Nadu, Bengal and Assam for generations and the same is the case.

Let me go back to the point I was trying to make at the start of this chapter. I am intensely proud of our cultural and social traditions, and one of the traditions I am particularly proud of is our attitude towards simple living. All over India, our homes are clean but basic and simple to the point of being austere. Even the rich have almost spartan homes. But in modern life, this attitude is creating problems. By condoning the lack of finish and elegance in the design of products we use, so long as the item works, we are patronising shoddiness. I will illustrate this further, later on, with examples of my personal experiences in getting Indian industrial houses to produce quality items for export.

Working with or for aliens

One thing which I did not notice then but realise now is that as children we were always better behaved in Aunt Connie's portion of the house. We did not fight or shout and always spoke in softer tones almost as if we were not the same children. Come exam time, this was the favourite place for study. Same house, same people but somehow very much more peaceful, and immensely more conducive to mental work.

This did not apply only to the children. My friend's father was the eldest in the family and would go to all parts of the house to sit and talk. During summer, he always wore a *lungi* with no shirt, and was very fond of smoking *beedies* (small hand-made cigarettes popular in small towns and villages all over India). One peculiar thing I noticed was that he always wore a shirt when in Aunt Connie's rooms and never ever smoked! Thinking it over I realise now that elders and children alike would exhibit one type of personality when Aunt Connie was around and a completely different type when with the rest of the family.

The point I am trying to make here is that we subconsciously realised that Aunt Connie was an alien. Never mind that she had been a member of an Indian family all her married life and had admirably adapted to our way of life. She was an alien and we all became different people when she was around. I can give a number of examples of this happening in India all the time, and this is crucial when we look at the performance of MNCs in India.

Example: Go to any village and see how an uneducated villager behaves with a visiting social worker. The attitude is remarkably different if the visitor is European.

✓ I seek to establish that it is not simply that the MNCs in India are better organised or have brilliant managers. It is only that we become very different people when working for or with foreigners. Also, that we quickly revert to our set ways immediately afterwards.

Take the example I gave above of the maintenance sponsorship by Ford. I doubt whether any Europeans in the Ford organisation in India actually visited or supervised the work at Dakshin Chitra. The superb work was done by Indian executives. The same work would probably not have been done if the executives were working for an Indian organisation. Different management gurus will have different versions of why this is so, but I repeat the point that an Indian executive working for Ford is a very different person from the one he becomes as soon as he leaves Ford and joins an Indian organisation.

Similarly, if an Indian executive leaves Godrej, BPL or Dabur, and joins, say, Cadbury, one look at him after six months and you know he is not the same person. I have seen this happen again and again in the UK when Indian boys and girls leave their family grocery shops and start working for the next door white-owned supermarket. Their attitude towards neatness and tidyness undergoes a sudden and remarkable change.

Fussing over a label nobody sees

Let me tell you about one of my first experiences as a consultant to a Singapore-Chinese group of companies. You will see what the Indian attitude towards quality minus finish, or quality plus shoddiness is doing to our exports.

We were helping in the setting up of an automobile spare parts manufacturing facility to supply components to Bosch of Germany. Robert Bosch gmbh is known to be one of the most difficult buyers of components and their standards of quality control are legendary. Since the project was funded by the Commonwealth Fund for Technical Cooperation, which is a division of the Commonwealth Secretariat, London, we had to give priority to sourcing from Commonwealth countries.

My assignment was to locate a firm in India which could assemble indicator switches. The entire output was to be exported. Only the assembly of these parts was involved, but rigorous adherence to quality standards was a must. I located a fairly large firm in India which was manufacturing these switches besides a number of other more complicated items.

I came to India with a German engineer to see the plant and talk about technical aspects. The head office was a very impressive fully carpeted, air conditioned, glass and aluminum edifice. We met the technical people and were impressed with their knowledge. The firm had an excellent track record of sales to local automobile firms but had never exported.

Then we went to the factory. From the moment we entered, my German friend was unhappy about the all-pervading shabbiness of the factory. The walls were unpainted, the windows black with cobwebs, goods, materials and cartons were strewn all over the floor and the factory manager's room did not even have a decent chair to sit on.

We went around the production area and picked up some finished items at random. My German friend called me aside and showed me a dozen pieces. The items had a very poorly finished plastic casing. There was a rectangular marking at the bottom where a self-adhesive label detailing the technical specifications was fixed. None of the items had the label properly fixed in the space provided. Pure sloppiness. In come cases, the label was completely outside the space provided.

The management invited us for lunch to the Managing Director's (MD) house. It was a superb mansion and the MD proudly showed us into the very elegant lunch room. We mentioned the finish of the items and also the overall appearance of the factory and got a very logical response. The item is meant to be fixed inside the car, under the hood, where nobody will see it once it is fixed, he reasoned. Why, then, comment on the finish of the casing and the mere positioning of the label which, in any case, are not critical to the performance of the item? The item worked and there had been no complaints! He also assured us that if we wanted he could arrange to have the casing better finished and the labels properly fixed for an export order, as it would not cost anything extra. As regards the factory, again, why spend time and money on something which does not affect the quality of the product, he argued.

The MD made it clear that, to him, quality meant not being rejected by the customer. My German friend said:

✓ 'Indians care more for where they live rather than where they make their living.'

Question. If it does not cost extra, why not make a practice of providing products with a good finish? In the international market, particularly when dealing with the meticulous and quality-conscious Germans or Japanese, this is akin to suicide.

To cut a long story short, we never went back, and the business went to a firm in Malaysia. However, the story does not end there. I was in the same town recently after a gap of almost twenty years and happened to ask about the firm. I was told it had folded up since two MNCs had come on to the scene and taken away the entire market.

Patronising shoddiness

I have been asking myself a question. True, we are fond of simple living and do not particularly bother about how things look. But if we are asked to choose between an elegant-looking place and an ordinary or shabby one, how many of us would offer a premium for elegance?

For an answer, I remember being at the Sahar Airport at Bombay. Before one entered the departure area, there used to be a restaurant run by a local hotel group—not-very-clean, with a humdrum decor and fairly reasonable food. An NRI started a new restaurant in the same lounge, just a few feet away. This was a neat, clean, spanking new glass and aluminum place of the type one sees in the West. Though the menu and the prices were about the same, I found the old place full and the new place almost empty. The reason? Apparently, the new place looked expensive.

Well, it seems that far from paying a premium, we are intimidated by the mere elegant looks of a place. My experience in nearby countries such as Malaysia and Singapore suggests that customers will first try the more elegant place and only if they feel that it does not offer value for money will they go elsewhere. Firms fight on the basis of price, quality, service and elegance. Unlike in India, nowhere else would a car be bought if the showroom looked shabby. Price and the basic minimum quality are all that you need to fight in the marketplace. However, the entry of MNCs such as Kentucky Fried Chicken, McDonald's, Domino's and Wimpy's are changing the rules.

One last point before I make a few confessions. Nowadays, when a new car leaves the showroom, the interior is meant to be the last word in finish and elegance for that particular class of vehicle. But, before leaving the showroom, there is a requirement that the factory-installed polythene sheet cover be removed from the door panels and the seats. I have seen cars in India where the owners have insisted that these covers not be removed. After a couple of months, these thin polythene covers get discoloured and tear. They offer absolutely no protection, and are hot and uncomfortable to sit on and awful to look at, but they remain in place.

The overall look is unattractive and destroys the elegance that was designed into the interior. This is an example of actually creating and patronising shoddiness.

Time for a confession

Here is a dilemma for you:

A committee has been formed to help select the CEO of a 100 per cent export-oriented food-processing unit. You are a member.

I am a candidate. You are familiar with the work I have done all my life. I am eminently qualified for the job.

You also know that I have a great weakness for eating roadside snacks in India. Things like *Batata Wada, Panipuri* or *Phuchka, Pao Bhaji, Aloo tikki* and so on.

Would you select me?

Surely, I must be joking! What is the connection? I am eminently qualified for the job, so why worry about my eating habits? First, you hear my confession in full, and then decide.

I have a weakness for eating roadside snacks in India. All over the country there are roadside food hawkers selling all sorts of local snacks. In the North, we have a whole range of items like *Gol Gappe* (also called *Panipuri*) and *Chaat*. In the East, we have *Allu Kabuli*, *Jhal Muri* or *Chilla*, sold all over Calcutta. In Mumbai, you have *Pao*

Bhaji. This is an all-India phenomena. Smaller towns have special areas where the children are brought for an evening out particularly during the summer. Snacking at these roadside stalls is almost a family social occasion. I am at the head of this list and cannot count the number of times I have been to these places, especially with my children when they were growing up. The patrons of these stalls are drawn from all walks of life and all levels of society.

Now, there are three things to be noticed. First, this activity is particularly popular during the summer when India witnesses an acute water shortage. Second, it is a roadside, open-air activity where there are often no water taps nearby.

So, where does the hawker get the water needed for cleaning the utensils? True, the items are sometimes served in disposable cups made of dried leaves, but this is not always the case. Similarly, what about the washing of utensils in which the ingredients are mixed before serving? The fellow doing the serving uses bare hands, so where does he wash his hands? And, how often?

If you look behind the stall, there is a bucket or two of water, enough for the whole evening. And the hawker uses a dark grey towel to wipe the dishes after the so-called washing, using the same towel to wipe his hands. This towel was white a long long time ago.

Can anybody say that I am exaggerating? Is this not true in almost every town and city in India? The point is that I notice these things and I am sure I am not alone. And yet, nobody can stop me from patronising these very stalls.

Oh! I almost forgot. I had mentioned earlier that there were three things to be noticed. The third thing being that these stalls are almost always under large trees. And trees have birds!

So back to the dilemma.

If I am selected as the CEO of a large food processing unit, what if I find that a particular large batch was processed in a container which only looked clean, but was not properly washed and sterilised? Would I reject the whole batch and lose a lot of money—after having spent a lifetime eating at roadside places, in utensils that only looked clean?

Would you trust a person like me to head a sophisticated food-manufacturing unit where the stringent quality control procedures are meticulously laid down?

When we eat at these stalls or at the ubiquitous roadside *dhabas*, we are fully aware of the complete lack of hygiene or cleanliness. Yet we close our minds to these aspects and only see to it that the plate in front of us 'looks' clean before going on to enjoy the delicious food.

Handled without care

I will be talking about India losing a food manufacturing project in Chapter 6.4. I will explain that we lost the project partly because the overseas promoters visited the areas where the unskilled workers lived. They saw the surroundings in which these workers lived. If an entire life is lived in shabby and filthy surroundings, a certain attitude seeps into a person's mindset and this cannot be changed overnight.

We need to look at ourselves through the eyes of others, which is something we do not normally do in India. Our attitude towards the overwhelming shoddiness around us is bad enough. However, the environment in which our workers live is an equally important element in our efforts to unleash India on the highly competitive and increasingly sophisticated world market.

This is a serious problem that cannot be solved by businessmen alone.

3.2

The missing essentials:
moulds and tools

> The efficient supply of dies, tools, moulds, jigs and fixtures is the foundation of industrial production.
>
> The remarkable growth of the plastic toys industry in Hong Kong in the early 1960s is mainly due to an excellent tooling and machining infrastructure.
>
> I seek to highlight that inadequate production capacity in this sector is partly responsible for the dismal performance of many of India's export sectors. It is indeed ironic since there is no shortage of highly skilled tool room technicians who earn respect the world over.

Tooling and machining

'Tooling and Machining' covers the design and manufacture of special tools, dies, jigs, fixtures, gauges, special machines and precision machined parts. This is the lifeblood of our industrial production base.

Tooling is, in its simplest sense, any mechanical aid to mass production.

'Special' toolings, such as jigs, dies and moulds, are custom-designed production aids and are made to help in the manufacture of specific products, generally in quantity, and to desired levels of uniformity, accuracy, interchangeability and quality.

Machining involves the use of a wide variety of machine tools to cut or form material, usually metal, to precise shapes and dimensions.

The custom precision manufacturing industry and the tooling and machining industry is critical to our country's economic health as it makes possible the existence of virtually every other manufacturing industry.

The example of Hong Kong

The remarkable growth of the plastic toys industry in Hong Kong in the early 1960s is an example of how critical the tooling industry can be to the growth of an economy. With little government support for R&D and technological development, manufacturing firms in Hong Kong opted, at that time, not to enter technologically advanced sectors or products involving the early stage of new technology life cycles. Instead, they sought to achieve a cost competitive advantage in relatively mature, less capital-intensive sectors like watches, electronic toys and games. Hong Kong was able to corner the world market first, because they had an excellent tooling and machining infrastructure and, second, because of the Chinese attitude towards networking or Guanxi. I have discussed Guanxi in detail in Chapters 1.4 and 4.4, but it is the increasing sophistication of the tool-making industry in Hong Kong that is responsible for Hong Kong being at the top of the electronic toys and games manufacturing list.

Of late, firms in Hong Kong have developed sophisticated CAD/CAM design and electronic data interchange capabilities that allow them to process buyer requirements from anywhere in the world, quickly developing design specifications and then the finished tooling ready for production. This has enabled them to focus on niche markets involving quick fashion or specification changes or short product runs.

Status in India

In India, too, this industry is probably the most technologically advanced of all small manufacturing activities. There are, indeed, a huge number of mostly medium- and small-sized companies specialising in the design and production of moulds and tools. Some of these companies, particularly subsidiaries of large plastic goods or appliance manufacturers, use the full range of state-of-the-art machine tools and related equipment, ranging from small automatic lathes for miniature parts to enormous boring mills. There is widespread deployment of computer numerically controlled (CNC) machines and other computer aided design and manufacturing (CAD/CAM) techniques.

This industry supplies the necessary precision tooling and machining to the entire spectrum of vital industries such as the defence, automotive, aerospace, domestic appliances, business machines, electronics, agricultural implements, ordnance, transportation, environmental, construction equipment and nuclear industries. In point of fact, nearly every manufacturer does business some time or the other with the contract tooling and machining industry.

The problem

Manufacturers doing business with the contract tooling and machining industry will tell you horror stories of their dealings with the suppliers. First, it is difficult to find a good supplier, then there is the inordinately long delivery period and, after all that, there is absolutely no assurance that the delivery schedules will be observed. There is, indeed, an acute shortage of installed capacity for the production of all sorts of moulds and tools and India is increasingly relying on imported tools.

There is a contradiction here. On the one hand I am saying that this industry is probably the most technologically advanced of all small manufacturing activities in India. On the other, I am also saying that one cannot find a good supplier and that India is increasingly having to rely on imported tools.

Somebody has got to be joking! India short of capacity to make moulds? Indian tool room technicians are highly respected and keenly sought after all over the world as mould makers. So, what is the problem in our own country?

I am immediately reminded of Tata Precision Industries Ltd of Singapore. This firm is highly respected in its own field and is doing very well indeed in the intensely competitive high tech environment of Singapore. The question I want to ask myself is: how is it that this firm can make such a brilliant success of using design and manufacturing technology developed almost entirely by Indian engineers and technicians in Singapore, while back home we have to depend upon imports?

It is true that some of the big business houses in India, such as Godrej, Tata, Siemens, Bentex and Bright Bros have developed captive tool room facilities of a very high standard, enabling them to produce excellent quality goods. But here again, the demand far outstrips the supply and even these big houses have to import their requirements. To analyse the problem and possible solutions, let's look at a specific industry.

Toolings for plastics in India

It is a sad fact that very few independent tool rooms in India are geared towards designing and manufacturing state-of-the-art moulds for the fast-growing plastics industry in India. Some of the larger independent producers do have excellent equipment, but not the dynamic organisational infrastructure needed to take buyer requirements, quickly develop the design and have finished tooling ready for production. The major cause for this may be sought in the history of development of plastics in this country.

It was in the early 1950s that our entrepreneurs recognised the potential of plastics as a suitable material for mass production of household articles such as buckets, mugs, jugs, tumblers and plates. What they did was simply take samples from abroad and copy them. The moulds were crudely made, the consumers accepted the awful finish and nobody felt the need for any design and development. Moreover, the range of raw materials available was severely limited, the shapes were simple and the skill and technology called for was of a lower grade and could be satisfied with the expertise available in the country. Due to the abundance of cheap labour, productivity was not a compelling factor and hence the need for improving tooling techniques, or investment in research or the quest for excellence was considered superfluous or even wasteful.

Cheap manpower and the consumer attitude of accepting poorly finished items so long as the item served its purpose, made up for less efficient and low quality tooling.

Very unlike Hong Kong, India did not have a specialised mould-making industry. The plastics processors, who were mostly small entrepreneurs, approached small mechanical workshops nearby for moulds. These workshops learnt as they went along and some of them developed into bigger tool rooms but the experience gathered was repetitive, as they were busy doing more and more of the same thing. They had no time or interest in upgrading their designing or manufacturing technologies as a result of which the range of products remained limited.

Very unlike Hong Kong again, where the government neither helped nor hindered the plastic products industry, in India, the government policy considered it a low priority area and accorded it a step-motherly treatment. Plastics was a purely private sector affair and the import of machinery, tools, materials and technology was almost forbidden or, in the least, a tedious business. The few locally manufactured raw materials were enormously expensive and were of grades suitable only for simple, low quality products.

It will be no exaggeration to claim that the standard of plastics tooling, like all other types of tooling, remained stagnant from the early 1950s till the mid-1980s due to a vicious cycle of disincentives and abject neglect.

It is understood that plastics processors in other countries developed because their industrial consumers grew and prospered. In India, the consumer goods industry, which should have been a major customer of the plastics industry, was also a victim of both the restrictive policies of the government as well as of lethargic consumer attitudes. Because the available standards satisfied the requirements of the domestic market, related industries like alloy steel companies, processing machinery producers, steel manufacturers and toolmakers did not make any efforts in investing in research and development. The most glaring example is the automobile industry, which has provided a major impetus to raw material producers, machinery manufacturers, tool steel developers, toolmakers and plastics processors in developed countries. In India, car makers were busy leaping backwards.

It was only in the mid-1980s that technical articles with a degree of intricacy and sophistication calling for special skills in the design or fabrication of tools were produced in India. So also, the real growth of mould and tool design and production can be traced to this period.

Where are the skilled technicians?

Facilities for training skilled tool room technicians in India were always grossly inadequate because of the low priority this sector was accorded. Boys passing out of the large number of vocational institutes got themselves jobs as mechanics in machine shops and in maintenance departments of larger firms. These students saw very little incentive in spending years training as skilled tool room technicians because they got more or less the same jobs. It was a vicious circle. There were no large tool rooms as there was a shortage of skilled tool makers and vice versa.

So, enter some far-sighted industrialists in the mid-1960s. They saw the problem and instead of doing something about it themselves, they solved the problem in typical Indian fashion. They prevailed upon the government to create specialist facilities in the form of the Central Institute of Plastic Engineering (CIPET), the Central Institute of Tool Design (CITD), etc.

Again, in typical fashion, India asked for and got development aid from countries such as Germany, Switzerland and Denmark that had a tradition of excellent tool room technologies. These governments came forward and founded (and funded) tool rooms with state-of-the-art imported machinery. These institutions were designed to serve the dual purpose of providing high tech, advanced tooling as well as trained toolmakers. Indo German, Indo Swiss and Indo Danish tool rooms in various parts of the country do fulfil the projected aim, but they are grossly inadequate considering the huge needs of India's fast growing industry. Also, being government organisations, they suffer from the same maladies plaguing all other government institutions in terms of structure and policies. They are next to useless for the needs of the more sophisticated industrial consumers as they have, naturally, not been able to inspire any confidence as far as dependability of delivery and efficiency in work are concerned.

The toolmakers trained by these institutions are, no doubt, good but in view of the investment in terms of the numbers of years spent in training, the expectations are naturally high. The very small number turned out yearly look for opportunities overseas, secure government jobs or are absorbed by the larger industries in supervisory positions. So, back to square one. The ultimate tool making is handled by machinists.

There are, of course, certain organisations in India, such as Godrej, Tata, Siemens, Bright Bros etc., who have developed captive tool room facilities of a very high standard, enabling them to produce export quality goods, but this is strictly for their own use. They also train their own tooling technicians and pay them well so that small organisations can ill afford to tempt them. Therefore, the experience gained remains confined to these big organisations.

The small tool rooms

As I said above, it has become a vicious circle. The small tool rooms in India have no shortage of clients who require toolings of a very high standard and are willing to pay for it. But since tool rooms cannot find good, experienced toolmakers, they only do less demanding jobs. Their experience, skill and expertise remain limited.

The other aspect of tool rooms in India is that these are invariably owned by a skilled toolmaker and run as one man shows. This often means a poor organisational set-up. Even though some of these tool rooms are successful, have state-of-the-art machine tools and produce excellent moulds and dies, the organisation remains small and overworked, and the delivery schedules tend to get longer and more unreliable.

The expensive export of toolmakers

As I said above, the first priority for most of our skilled toolmakers is to find a job overseas. I have seen Indians working in tool rooms all over the world and earning respect for their hardwork and skill. India also exports computer technicians but the difference lies in the fact that the cost of training a computer expert is a small fraction of the cost of training a toolmaker. Computer education needs only a couple of years and the only equipment needed is, often, an old and outdated computer. Producing a good toolmaker requires years of training on very expensive, modern, up-to-date machine shop equipment.

3.3   *Product innovation*

The lack of innovativeness in Indian industry is one of the major hurdles as far as exports are concerned. I have also addressed this point in some detail in Chapter 1.3.

On the face of it, what I am saying may not be obvious. By lack of innovativeness I certainly do not mean that there is a shortage of clever, original ideas. Any visitor to India hears aplenty about our tradition of innovativeness. The visitor is told that our extremely restrictive import regime has made us learn to do without imported spare parts and equipment. Everywhere one goes one finds evidence of how we have somehow managed to get the job done. Now that we have left the restrictive regime behind us and have had a so-called liberalised economy for some time now, we find that this attitude of somehow getting the job done is still very much a part of us, becoming almost a habit.

'Short cuts' have almost become our definition of innovativeness. Go to a roadside mechanic and he will somehow get your old Buick going again by repairing the carburettor with a piece of string. Enter an Air-India aircraft and the first thing you notice is the use of sticky tape as the ubiquitous repair tool. Even the tape used is carelessly torn and slapped on shoddily. Is that what innovativeness means to us in modern India?

I seek to establish that this attitude of ours towards innovativeness is landing us in trouble. We are losing the export markets we already have to highly innovative producers of consumer goods.

To substantiate my claim that lack of innovativeness in our industry is one of the major hurdles for exports, we need to have some yardstick by which to measure the nature and extent of our innovativeness.

Let us look at the domestic environment first. I mentioned above that we have a tradition of innovativeness. However, it should be clear that innovativeness does not mean somehow managing to get a job done: repairing a carburettor with a piece of string or an aircraft lavatory door with sticky tape, for example. In the increasingly competitive domestic and export environment in India, with added pressures from multinationals, innovation clearly means not only the development of new products but also new ways of producing and marketing them, besides new ways of approaching and servicing domestic and overseas customers.

An academic point of view

Innovation is the industrial religion today. International business sees it as the key to increasing profits and market share. Governments automatically reach for it when trying to fix the economy.

What precisely constitutes innovation is hard to say, let alone measure. It is usually thought of as the creation of a better product, process or procedure. It could just as easily be the substitution of a cheaper material in an existing product, or a better way of marketing, distributing or supporting a product or service. Even commercial banks in India are trying out innovative schemes to attract deposits.

A few of our entrepreneurs are good practitioners of innovation, but they rarely stop to examine how they benefit from it. Most of them simply get on with the job of creating more value by exploiting some form of change which has produced results, be it in terms of technology, materials, prices, taxation, demographics or even geopolitics. They simply see a new demand being generated, find a new way of exploiting the opportunity, and that is it.

'The entrepreneur', said Jean-Baptiste Say, the French economist who coined the word around 1800, 'shifts economic resources out of an area of lower and into an area of higher productivity and greater yield.' Two centuries later, there are as many economists as there are theories about this most mysterious part of the wealth-creation process.

One way to describe innovation is to explain what it is not. A new business venture is strictly, well, a business venture and not an innovation. The husband and wife who open a coffee shop opposite a new office block may be gambling on their life savings, but they are not innovating. The Japanese electronics firm that launches a niftier video camera is merely making a bid to push competitors' goods off the shelves. The drug firm that makes a generic version of a block-buster ulcer pill is simply cashing in on the expiry of a rival's patents. These are business ventures, not innovations.

Innovations not only break the mould, they also yield far better returns than ordinary business ventures.

To appreciate the difference between opening yet another ham-burger joint and innovating in earnest, consider what McDonald's did. McDonald's created not simply a new product, but a whole new market category with a whole new marketing approach. It stand-ardised the product, designed entirely new cooking procedures and trained its people meticulously, thereby giving customers some-thing they had never had before—a high-quality hamburger, freshly delivered at the speed of just-in-time preparation in pleasant, hy-gienic surroundings and at a knockdown price. This was innovation of the highest order.

Who are these people who can make the leap from an idea to a new product or process that customers will queue up to buy? Two things set apart all organisations with a good record of innovation.

- They foster individuals who are internally driven. It is of little con-sequence whether they are motivated by money, power and fame, simply curiosity or the need for personal achievement
- They do not leave innovation to chance: they pursue it systemati-cally. They actively search for change, the root of all innovation, then carefully evaluate its potential for an economic or social return

In his book *Innovation and Entrepreneurship* published in 1985 Peter Drucker, one of the most venerable management gurus, lists seven sources of opportunity for organisations in search of innova-tion. Four can be found within the enterprise itself, or at least within the industry of which it forms a part and should, therefore, be rea-sonably obvious to insiders. The other three come from the outside world and should be apparent to anyone who takes the trouble to look. All seven are symptoms of change.

Listed in order of increasing difficulty and uncertainty, they are:

- The unexpected success that is gratefully received but rarely dis-sected to see why it occurred

- The incongruity between what actually happens and what was supposed to happen
- The inadequacy in an underlying process that is taken for granted
- The changes in industry or market structure that catch everyone by surprise
- The demographic changes caused by wars, political change and even superstition
- The changes in perception, mood and fashion brought on by the ups and downs of the economy
- The changes in awareness caused by new knowledge

In the context of the Indian economy, the irony is that officials, academics and even entrepreneurs pay far more attention to trying to exploit science-based discoveries. This is the riskiest form of innovation. It would be far easier to profit capitalising on unexpected success. If we did something that worked unexpectedly, we should study it, analyse it and develop it further. This is the easiest and quickest type of innovation.

> The Indian organisational immune system, which attempts to kill anything that is strange and new, can rarely be switched off.

I am convinced that innovation has more to do with the pragmatic search for opportunity rather than with romantic ideas or lonely pioneers pursuing their vision against all odds. There may be no single recipe for producing innovations to order, but there is a cookbook of sorts that is proving more useful all the time. Today, more than half of the world's economic growth is from industries that barely existed a decade ago. Such is the power of innovation.

Competing by innovating

Thriving in the marketplace of the new millennium will require a new and innovative relationship between supplier and buyer. Remember, products and services are largely commodities in the overseas customers' eyes. Products are not the future, services are. Almost any innovative product that India produces can be rapidly replicated elsewhere by those better organised. The only sustainable difference lies in the ability to wrap services around a product to create something innovative.

In short, creating a competitive advantage will need new solutions, new ideas, and new ways of working with customers. Having the best products or the most flexible pricing just gets you into the stadium for a quick look. It certainly does not get you onto the playing field anymore.

In trying to define innovativeness, I have tried to establish that, for us in India, innovation has become a critically important competitive tool. There was a time when learning how to get a license, learning how to prevent anybody else from getting one and sitting back and raking in the moola was all the innovation you needed. Thankfully, those days are gone. In our crowded marketplace, there is greater need for differentiation; in markets that tend to be stagnant there is pressure to create excitement. The development and launch of new products helps in both situations.

New product development

In the chapter on the export of toys, I addressed the problem of successfully developing and marketing an innovative product in India. This was in the world context.

In the domestic context too, unlike established companies in developed markets, Indian companies face a lot of hurdles when they decide to take up the challenge of new product development. I will seek to establish that our companies cannot do this as a routine, casual, let's-see-if-this-works exercise. They have to take it up as a strategy and as a new policy commitment.

I will go into this in some detail below. In short, the hurdles:

1. An environment of limited design skills and experience
2. Few qualified vendors, inappropriate engineering resources
3. Very limited financial and human resources
4. Lack of access to appropriate manpower
5. Design-based courses becoming increasingly inadequate in engineering institutions
6. Lack of a market orientation
7. Strong centralised control by business family heads
8. Few employees who combine the technical and managerial skills needed to take on the role of project managers for new product development projects

9. Functional chimneys without deep functional expertise, and resistance to change on numerous fronts all at once. The very structure of the managerial hierarchy becomes a bottleneck. People lower down feel choked and suffocated and those in the middle rungs cannot move in any direction.

Design-based courses and skills A major constraint faced by Indian companies is access to appropriate manpower. On the one hand, it is unfortunately true that the brain drain of qualified scientific and engineering personnel from India has been due to the lack of challenging and remunerative employment opportunities at home. On the other, the employment scenario has changed and most of the best brains and the best engineers today join the highly successful Indian software industry. This industry offers attractive job opportunities, often at international locations, with attractive monetary benefits. We have discussed this at some length in the chapter on India's software success. This sector is poised to grow further, and with the current media attention, is likely to continue to attract India's best engineers in the years ahead.

Design-based courses are, however, grossly inadequate in Indian engineering institutions. In fact, few Indian engineering institutions have courses which integrate design theory and practice and that require students to create working prototypes. Even in institutions where such facilities exist (as in the IITs), the deterioration of administrative systems has seen a decline in workshop facilities. As a result, some institutes have even given up the requirement of a design project in the final year, or relaxed the earlier requirement that the product designed 'should work'.

As a result, the few Indian companies which have their own programmes on product design and development are, today, forced to create in-house training using expertise sourced from within the country and abroad. This makes it much more expensive for a company to add a new product design and development division. It also creates a chicken and egg situation in that the few companies who want to enter the field do not find suitable people, while the people who are trained in the field cannot get jobs and have already moved elsewhere. This is a serious problem, particularly in the area of industrial design. While the Industrial Design Centre at IIT, Mumbai and the National Institute of Design at Ahmedabad do produce qualified industrial and product designers, the larger Indian companies experience difficulties in locating and placing them within their organisations so as to make the best use of them.

Even the large Indian business houses have few employees who combine the technical and managerial skills needed to take on the role of project managers for new product development projects. With authority in Indian companies depending mostly on seniority within the organisation hierarchy or in the family, rather than on skills and capabilities, it is very difficult to find employees who can take on the role of 'heavyweight' project managers even if the companies want to set up such project teams.

A related problem that has emerged is the finding of a common language between designers and the manufacturing and marketing departments. Engineers who have been at the shop floor never agree with managers in functions like marketing. Perhaps, like in many Japanese companies, Indian companies should consider requiring all engineers to start in the sales function before they go into technical roles.

Partly as a result of these problems, many industrial designers have set up independent design houses but have found that product design projects are few and far between.

Risk of developing new products

In a capital-scarce economy, the risk of developing new products has always seemed unnecessary because one can always import the technology under licensing agreements. This comes with the built-in advantage of access to a ready-made brand name and market.

There are many products manufactured in India that are governed by these agreements, but there are severe restrictions on the modification of these products. This not only kills any innovative spirit, but Indian companies also face difficulties in absorbing the imported technologies adequately. An additional headache is that, notwithstanding the liberalisation and the opening up of the economy, import restrictions make it difficult for companies to source particular components or the skills and capabilities needed to suit the imported technologies.

Only in India did protection kill innovation

Till the early 1990s, India had a highly protected economy. Within the economy as well, competition was restricted by a complex licensing system. So, most believe that it was 'not surprising then that levels of competition were low and that the need for product innovation was not felt by Indian companies'. I find this a silly line of thought. Perhaps the best example of this short-sighted approach was the Indian automobile industry. The two major players, Hindustan Motors and Premier Automobiles, made at best cosmetic changes to their cars over three decades.

I say this approach is silly because I compare it with what other nations have done. Having a protected market or a closed economy does not, by itself, lead to any killing of innovation. Almost every emerging economy has tried to protect its fledgling domestic producers. No domestic market has been more jealously and rigorously protected than Japan's, Korea's and also, to some extent Taiwan's. Elsewhere in this book, I have gone into the details of the various tariff and non tariff barriers that, until recently, have been in place making imports of finished products into these countries next to impossible. Yet, the same protective policy that is said to have destroyed Indian innovativeness has lead to the mind-boggling development in these countries.

Even earlier than that, in 1945, the US was the only industrialised nation untouched by the devastation of two World Wars. American business had absolutely no competition. The world was borrowing money from America to buy products from them and they could set whatever prices and standards they wished to. The American business houses, however, far from becoming complacent, used an incredible degree of innovativeness to consolidate the early start they got.

Where do we go from here?

Studies across the world on the competitive advantage of nations have shown that a historical emphasis on industrial innovation by a community has lead to the development of a critical mass of firms and associated ancillary units, eventually leading to the nation's long-term competitive advantage. Product development has been a neglected area in India for a long time to the detriment of our competitive advantage. Whatever little product development has taken place has been to counter situations where the Indian firm has been denied imported products or where the imported product was unsuitable for Indian conditions. More emphasis in product development has historically been placed on making modifications of existing products for Indian conditions rather than on creating entirely new products.

With little historical tradition of industrial innovation, especially in the creation of new products, Indian firms struggle to overcome a handicap. Research emphasis on new product development that addresses the concerns of Indian firms is therefore welcome from both the practical and industrial policy points of view. Such research in the Indian context may also provide a base to extend and test results obtained from studies conducted in industrially advanced countries.

We must not, however, make the mistake of thinking that the world is as competitive as it can get. This is only the beginning. Increasingly, domestic and overseas customers are demanding, and receiving, customised solutions tailored to their specific needs. Customers are individuals, with distinct needs, requirements and concerns. The generic customer is gone, and so are generic solutions and the 'one size fits all' product development and sales process. The best of all worlds is that in which we are versatile enough, as organisations and as individual business people, to match customer requirements with the right products and processes.

3.4   *Indians outside India*

A Malaysian lover of India

I remember going to the office of Dr P.P. Narayanan, the President of the Malaysian Union of Plantation Workers in Kuala Lumpur. Dr P.P. was a Malaysian of Indian origin, also called an ethnic Indian. While every inch a true Malaysian, he was also intensely proud of his Indian heritage. He had a wooden carving above his desk with a message engraved in golden letters which read:

> *Every Englishman abroad is an ambassador.*
> *Every Japanese, a salesman.*
> *Every Indian, a refugee.*

Dr P.P. would point to the large number of Europeans, Japanese and other expatriates currently working and living in counties like Malaysia. Each one of them, he said, was there as part of his nation's export effort. By contrast, every person from the Indian subcontinent, Indians, Bangladeshis, Pakistanis and Sri Lankans, was there to seek a livelihood which could not be obtained at home. He added that being proud of one's roots and singing praises of the glory that was India 500 years ago held little meaning when today its people were knocking on the doors of other nations for livelihood.

✓ When I mentioned this recently during a seminar it elicited a very strong response from two participants. How could I ignore the large number of India's IT experts who were earning a good name for the country? Nobody can say that they are refugees.

Well the youngsters of today can be forgiven for thinking like this as they have been inundated with India's IT success stories. These stories are recent and I am talking about a time more than 15 years ago when I saw this message, long before there was anything called IT. The message referred to a total of about 10 million people of Indian origin living outside India. I will be discussing this in some detail in this chapter.

Indians are everywhere

I need to define the scope of this chapter. The reader will notice that the title of this chapter is not NRIs or Overseas Indians. The reason is that when we talk of Indians living outside India, we invariably mean the NRIs in the US. Tell someone you had an Indian visitor from abroad, and you will invariably be asked which part of the US he was from! I have been living outside India for 30 years, but people here say that I should not call myself an NRI because I have only been in Malaysia.

Hardly a day goes by without some politician or the other 'going overseas to invite the NRIs'. For overseas, read mostly the US. The logic is that if the overseas Chinese can help build China, why can the NRIs not do the same for India?

I seek to establish that the contribution the overseas Chinese have made to the massive growth of the Chinese economy is in stark contrast to what overseas Indians have done and can do for India.

The overseas Chinese possess economic clout in many countries, and get goods produced in China for their own captive markets.

Indians have no captive markets anywhere and have nothing they can get specially made in India for themselves. Indeed, far from being of any help, overseas Indians have, albeit unwittingly, become a barrier to exports. The Eximbank publishes a blacklist warning against dealing with certain importers in other countries. These are mostly overseas Indians.

The term 'Indians living overseas' presents a complex picture and the subject needs to be addressed in some detail. I will be contrasting the attitude of these Indians with the attitude of the overseas Chinese, here as well as in Chapter 4.4 and 4.5.

In this chapter, I will talk about an entire spectrum of Indians living outside India. On the one hand are the people who left the nation even before it was called India, and went to places like Sri Lanka and South-East Asia and on the other are the recent emigrants, youngsters who go mainly to the US for education and stay back.

It is only recently that people living outside India have started meaning something to the motherland. Some excellent academic socio-economic studies are being carried out to find out who, where and what they are. One of the institutions at the forefront of this effort is the India International Centre (IIC) in Delhi. It has organised a number of seminars and conclaves on the Indian diaspora. This is also the subject of an ongoing research study by Dr Praksash Jain of Delhi's Jawaharlal Nehru University. Dr Jain has analysed major clusters of the Indian diaspora. I would refer the reader to Dr Jain's excellent publications on the subject.

The Indian diaspora

I need to explain what the unusual term, diaspora, means. The word has only recently come into common usage after people living outside India have, as I said, started meaning something to the motherland. It is a Greek word and originally referred to the forced dispersion of Jews among the Gentiles between the eighth and sixth centuries B.C. At that time, it described Greek and Armenian dispersion. Now, it is loosely used to describe any transnational community. So, Indian diaspora means Indians living outside India for whatever reason.

For the purpose of discussion, the Indian diaspora will be split into four classes. The following is an extract from Dr Jain's book *India and the Overseas Indians*. (pp. 6–7)

Overseas Indians

The term 'Overseas Indians' has different meanings in different contexts. It is generally employed to designate both people who hold an Indian passport and are working or temporarily living overseas, and people of Indian origin who have become citizens of the host country and have therefore attained a distinct political status in the country of their settlement.

For the purpose of this discussion, the term 'Overseas Indians' refers to people who left India some generations ago and have settled in the UK, the US and Canada as well as in Malaysia, Singapore, Fiji, East and South Africa and South America. These people are predominantly traders and small-time businessmen. This category also includes what is called free passage emigrants (resulting from the British Government's initiatives of transplanting some trading people), largely from Gujarat, who went to countries such as Kenya, Tanzania, Uganda and Zambia.

Non-resident Indians

The term NRI refers to recent migrants who are highly qualified and skilled, working mainly in the US and Canada as professionals.

In other words, Non-Resident Indians (NRIs) are those who have emigrated voluntarily during the post-independence period for an indefinite period. Despite their absence from India, many are Indian citizens as they continue to hold Indian passports. The status they enjoy in the country of their settlement thus is that of an alien. Many have become citizens of the host country but for all practical purposes they remain Indians, with their ties to the home country remaining strong.

It is this knowledge-based group, largely drawn from the 'privilegentsia' and based mostly in North America that is the focus of all our attention.

People of Indian origin

There is an altogether different category of the Indian community overseas. It represents a distinct phase in the history of Indian emigration. Most of these people emigrated as indentured labourers during the British colonial period under the assisted emigration scheme when the British took Indian labour to raise sugar plantations in countries such as South Africa, Mauritius, Trinidad, Jamaica, Guyana and Fiji and rubber plantations in Malaya. Unlike the NRIs, these people are now local citizens, well within the legal fabric of the country of their domicile and with full voting rights. As such, their links with India are not political but purely familial and sentimental. India is their ancestral and cultural home. They keep alive their linkage with India through emotional, not political, bonds and consider themselves not Indians but people of Indian descent.

Export of manpower

The export of unskilled and semi-skilled manpower to the Middle East is not relevant to this discussion. This group comprises workers in Saudi Arabia, UAE, Oman, Kuwait, Bahrain, Qatar and other West Asian countries.

Indians are called by different names in different countries. In East Africa, Uganda, Kenya and Tanzania they are called 'Asians', a term which clubs them with Pakistanis, Bangladeshis and Sri Lankans. However, this term, as used in East Africa, does not include Arabs or other people of West Asian origin.

In the North and South American countries, the term 'East Indians' is employed to mean all the people from Pakistan, Sri Lanka and Bangladesh and the descendants (predominantly Indians) of the South Asians who have migrated from the West Indies, Fiji, South Africa and East Africa. This is to differentiate them from the West Indians, i.e. the indigenous people of the West Indies.

How many of us are out there?

Well, nobody really knows. There is a considerable statistical bewilderment about the exact number of Indians of all categories living overseas. The usual difficulties encountered in any attempt to estimate their total population are many.

- I will point the reader to Srikant Dutt's very well researched paper titled 'India and the Overseas Indians', in *India Quarterly*, vol. 36, nos. 3 & 4, July–December 1980. Also, for whatever it is worth, to the then External Affairs Minister Mr. Narasimha Rao's written reply to a parliamentary question published in the *Lok Sabha Debates*, 7th series, Vol. 29, No. 10, 22 July 1980
- In some countries censuses are not taken regularly and the census figures are often 'adjusted'. As such, collecting a reliable cross-national data regarding overseas Indians is a difficult task.
- In several countries the Indian population is too small in number to be considered for separate enumeration
- In many others, they are classified under a monolithic category and computed with one or more minority groups

- There are no separate figures available for the total number of Indian descendants who migrated from, for example, the West Indies, South and East Africa, Fiji and Mauritius to Britain, Canada and the United States
- Above all, there is a high risk involved in relying on the Indian government's estimates

All these difficulties suggest that almost all population estimates of the number of Indians overseas are unreliable. It may come as a surprise to some that people of Indian origin are a majority in many countries and the single largest group in many others.

1. Mauritius (68 per cent)
2. Guyana (51 per cent)
3. Fiji (about 50 per cent): the single largest ethnic group
4. Surinam (37 per cent): again, the single largest ethnic group
5. Trinidad and Tobago is different from most other states in that all its peoples are minorities and the Indians make up the second largest group (40 per cent)
6. Indians' position is third or fourth in the population ranking in
   Malaysia (9 per cent)
   Singapore (6.4 per cent)
   Sri Lanka (5.5 per cent)
7. They also form an important group in French Guiana (12 per cent).

Money, money and money

After India's currency crises early on during the Narasimha Rao regime, Dr Manmohan Singh pointed the way to the NRIs as a source of salvation for India's foreign exchange problems. There was the success of the Resurgent India Bonds (RIBS), albeit at a high cost. This once again focused attention on Indians living abroad. There are a lot of us out there and by all accounts we are doing well for ourselves. So the mother country should have been accruing some benefit too!

Money has been coming in. Lots of it. Let's take a look of how the money is coming in, where from and in what form. Indians are following three broad routes to bring their dollars into India.

The first involves parking their savings in Indian banks. This is only because the government is offering very attractive rates of interest.

India needed foreign exchange in a hurry, offered fantastic rates of interest and provided exchange rate guarantees. So, Indians abroad pumped in their money.

There is, however, not an iota of loyalty in the whole process and the money is quickly pulled out when there is the slightest hint of a problem. Indians will simply take their money anywhere they get good returns. This is extremely volatile short-term money and is not good for the economy in the long run.

A lot of policy attention and incentives have been focused on these deposit schemes. There are now five such in operation. How much of these deposits are genuine savings of overseas Indians, how much is the money of local Indian businessmen turning NRIs for FERA and income tax purposes and how much is actually non-Indian money in NRI garb is anybody's guess. Such deposits have proved costly in the past. Their withdrawal triggered the financial crisis of 1991.

Deepak Nayyar, the noted economist, has estimated that between October 1990 and March 1992 there was a net outflow amounting to more than $2 billion of NRI deposits. In addition, the Reserve Bank suffered a loss of over $3 billion on these schemes in 1990–93 because it provided exchange rate guarantees. Even now, for some schemes the guarantee is provided by the central government, while the banks assume the exchange rate risks for others.

The second route is through actual investment: as equity in new projects, as portfolio investment and in real estate. NRI equity investment approvals since 1991 comprise a little over $ 3 billion, which is just 6 per cent of the total. This is only a tiny fraction of the total foreign investment and here again, all sorts of money could be coming in in the name of NRI investment.

A problem arises here. What is NRI investment actually? Say, a company called Eureka Enterprises, which has operations and branches in many countries, comes to India. If it is owned by Mr Raghu Nandan of the US, it is deemed an NRI company and a red carpet welcome will be laid and all sorts of incentives offered. But if it is owned by Mr John Smith it becomes an MNC, and our politicians and businessmen start getting agitated forgetting the fact that ownership can change hands overnight. What if Smith buys out the company from Nandan after it has been approved as an NRI project? Is the approval withdrawn? In both cases, the company is foreign-owned and the same set of laws should be applicable to both.

NRI money in the real estate market is a cause of headache for two reasons. First, the real estate market is a major outlet for 'black' money and the 'white' NRI money is a boon to money laundering operations. NRIs do not mind this as they get more value in rupees. Second, the dollar when converted into rupees turns into a lot of money in terms of value and so the prices NRIs are willing to pay for real estate in India are mind-boggling.

The third route is through annual remittances, which in 1998–99 may well have touched $15 billion. 50 to 60 per cent of this comes from Indians in the Middle East. This is not to be read as loyalty to the mother nation but simply in terms of support to the family back home. The same as a Bihari in Mumbai sending money to his family back home in Patna. The big spurt in official remittances came in 1993 and 1994, when India moved over to a market-determined exchange rate system and the incentives for the hawala route diminished substantially.

Here, the Indian workers in the Middle East are the true heroes. They have saved Kerala and some other parts of the country. Yet, institutions such as the government, airlines, banks and emigration, customs and immigration officials not only still find these workers easy prey but also treat them like second-class citizens. Their remittances, however, keep climbing, irrespective of the economic conditions at home and without any special incentives of any sort. They do not add to our debt and contribute to keeping our current account deficit within manageable limits. The use of remittances for consumption is good and to be welcomed. No attempt has been made to 'guide' them towards productive investment.

Our policy towards global Indians must change from chasing their money to leveraging and networking their professional skills. Indians abroad are distinguishing themselves in a large number of fields like science, engineering, medicine, management, economics, informatics, biotechnology, agriculture, finance and energy. This segment, which has the potential to transform and revitalise our educational, research, financial and manufacturing systems, has been largely ignored.

With increasing liberalisation, many Indians will possibly return to work in India. With a world-class patent system, India will be in a position to sell itself as an attractive R&D destination. Just imagine how many top-flight Indians would return if institutions like Bell Labs were to set up shop here.

The diaspora mindset also needs to change. Jagdish Bhagwati, one of the world's leading economists, had earlier proposed a 'brain drain' tax. A poor nation like India has subsidised the education of professional overseas Indians by at least Rs 100,000–150,000 million over the past three decades. This has to have ignited some spark of public service in our professional diaspora, some element of risk-taking, some sense of self-motivation and responsibility. Moreover, many of them belong to the privilegentsia and can do without inequitous sops like dual nationality.

Beware the overseas Indian

In a seminar organised by the the Export Credit Corporation of India which I attended, Mr G.M. Ganapathy, the DGM of the ECCI, spoke about the risk of dealing with overseas Indians. He said that the Export Credit Corporation of India had identified as many as 2000 'negative buyers' mostly from developed countries, who had a consistent track record of bad dealings with Indian exporters.

• Most of the negative buyers identified were traders of Indian origin settled in countries like the US, UK and Germany

He said that while steps had been taken to create an awareness among exporters in this regard and though the corporation did have details of bad buyers, they could not release the list as there were legal complications involved.

Since these rogue traders were Indians, they were fully aware of the weaknesses in the system. Exploitation was also easier because they were aware Indian exporters did not have recourse to legal action. The Indian exporter is often at the mercy of the buyer because of the very prevalent practice of under invoicing. While Indian exporters are forced to adopt a 'casual approach', their counterparts in other Asian countries are not under any such restraints. They are alerted by their watchdog bodies and do not deal with overseas Indians. The net result is that Indians as a body, both exporters and importers, lose out.

The overseas Chinese

We have had a good look at who the overseas Indians are and how they are participating in the economy of the mother country. Well, we can now contrast this with the overseas Chinese and what they are doing in China.

Before delving into the topic, I would like to mention that economic reforms started in China about 20 years ago. Since then, as per published United Nations data, it has received some $ 250 billion in foreign investment. About three-fourths of this is estimated to have come in from overseas Chinese, a vast prosperous community numbering about 55 million. The overseas Chinese presence is seen all over South-East and East Asia, in Taiwan, Hong Kong, Indo-China, Thailand, Singapore, Malaysia and Indonesia. Estimates say about two-thirds of Chinese mainland exports are from investments made by overseas Chinese to markets controlled by themselves. These investments are across all sectors: in manufacturing, service and infrastructure projects. These projects are in turn making a direct contribution to the growth of employment in mainland China.

If one goes by the massive amounts of money going into China, clearly, the overseas Chinese is richer and has greater investment surpluses than the overseas Indian. This is so because the Chinese possess massive economic clout and control large chunks of the Asian economy. Contrast this with the picture of Indians living overseas who are, largely speaking, either in the retail trade or are salaried employees or professionals. These Indians possess no economic clout and no real possibility of promoting any manufacturing, service or infrastructure project in India.

I also seek to establish that the emotional ties of the non-resident Chinese to the mother country are far more enduring, durable and deep than they are for the overseas Indian.

Hong Kong Chinese success story

To understand the success of the overseas Chinese, one needs to start with the story of Hong Kong. It was manufacturing that made Hong Kong's fortune. When more than one million refugees flooded over the border into Hong Kong in 1949 after the Communist victory in China's civil war, the British colonial authorities had to do something to keep them alive and Hong Kong afloat. Cheap land for the setting up of factories, and public housing, were the immediate answer. Helped by the networking talents of entrepreneurs who had fled from the mainland, the rescue and rehabilitation operation worked. By the early 1950s Hong Kong was supplying the world with T-shirts, plastic flowers and flip-flop sandals. The big industry was textiles, but handbags, toys, watches and shoes also poured out of tiny sweatshops for export to America and Europe.

Then the Chinese government took a historic decision which changed the fortunes of the entire overseas Chinese community. In 1978, it opened up some of its coastal regions, including the area bordering Hong Kong to foreign investors. Suddenly, Hong Kong's Chinese businessmen had a new supply of cheap labour and land for factory-building. Most of the light manufacturing that used to take place in Hong Kong crossed the border into China. Today, over five million mainland Chinese are employed in factories owned by Hong Kong businesses. Hong Kong now has $ 72 billion invested in China, nearly all of it in manufacturing. A lot of this money is overseas Chinese money routed via Hong Kong.

Two examples show what has been achieved by this leap across the border. Allen Wong runs Vtech, a Hong Kong company that has a large share of the world market for kiddies' computers and other electronic learning devices, and also makes cordless telephones. Its sales have grown from an annual $150 million ten years ago to over $800 million today. In 1987, when he found he could no get enough workers or cheap land in Hong Kong, Mr Wong moved production over the border into the Guangdong province. He now employs 22,000 Chinese women in two factories, most of them ferried in by bus from the Sichuan province deep inside China, because the wages the locals want are too high. The women get 500 yuan ($ 60) a month, in addition to board and lodging, compared with the HK$ 6,000 ($770) a month people get for similar work in Hong Kong. Mr Wong is now scouting for even cheaper labour in Thailand. Hong Kong is the conduit through which his exports move. The distance from the eventual market does not matter much to him because he has a close-knit network of agents, representatives and distributors all over the world.

Another company that crossed to the mainland is Johnson electric, which makes the tiny motors that go into such things as electric toothbrushes and CD players. The average Mercedes car, for example, has 80 such micromotors to open its sun-hood, adjust its mirrors and move its seats. Under Patrick Wang, whose father founded the business 39 years ago, Johnson has tripled in size in the past 10 years. It now has sales of HK$ 2.6 billion ($ 330 m) in 20 countries. It employs 13,000 people, most of them in Johnson Electric City, two huge factories 50 miles from Hong Kong in the Pearl River delta with its own dormitories, canteens and sports centres. In Hong Kong itself Johnson employs only 200 workers, mostly engineers designing new products. They work in teams and are in close touch with the customers. A car manufacturer, for instance, will want Johnson to come up with a little motor ideal for a particular function it has to perform in a given car. Mr Wang says that 10 years ago, customers asking for design changes were happy with a two-week response by telex. Today, they want an email within two hours.

Much of what began in Hong Kong and then moved over the border into mainland China is now having to think of migrating even farther afield. The continuing search for ever cheaper labour is not the only reason for this.

There are some disadvantages in selling things made in China through Hong Kong. Anybody exporting from China has to live with the risk that one day the Congress in Washington will take away China's most-favoured-nation trade status, which allows it easy access to the huge American market. Some manufacturers, therefore, have decided to move on from China, to set up at least some of their production units in countries where they can hope to disguise its Chinese origins.

Victor Fung is chairman both of the Hong Kong Trade Development Council and of the family firm of Li & Fung, a fine example of this new diaspora. Li & Fung is a spider's web of manufacturing operating out of 23 countries which includes not only various parts of South-East Asia but also Latin America, Eastern Europe, the Caribbean and Mauritius. Mr Fung explains how the system works. A foreign company will come to him with a modest product, a ball-point pen, for example, or a simple dress, and will ask him to find out where it can be made most cost effectively. Mr Fung's people then set out to find not only a source of cheap labour but also somewhere safe from trade restrictions on Chinese production. Take that simple dress. The yarn may be spun in Korea, the fabric woven in Taiwan, the zips bought from Japan and the garment part-finished in China before it passes through a final stitching factory in Indonesia. 'What we are doing is finding the best place for every operation', Mr Fung says. 'At the same time', he adds, 'we are lining up factors of production so that we can cut lead times from three months to five weeks.'

For all these companies the central functions of product development and engineering, the front end, as it were, of the manufacturing supply chain are in places like Hong Kong and Singapore. The back end, the marketing and distribution, is taken care of by closely associated firms all over the world. Although these are officially classified as 'service activities', they are really a part of manufacturing in the modern sense of the word.

PART TWO

How, What and Where to Export

We Indians are very well established as traders all over Africa, S.E. Asia, and Latin America. We are very good at selling anything for which there is a market. But please do not ask us to market anything.

An Indian businessman in Nairobi
talking to a trade delegation
from India, 1972

4

The mindset
of the competition

*If we are to unleash India on world markets, we must first
understand how the Asian Tigers unleashed their companies
on us. We must hit them with their own techniques.*

4.1
Contrasting routes to development

Indian and East Asian development models

In discussing the differences among the East Asian Newly Industrialised Economies (NIEs), and in contrasting these with India, I would like to highlight that it is not the business leaders alone who deserve credit. 'East Asian Miracles' (World Bank, 1993) discusses the various common facilitating roles played by the governments of these nations which include high investment in education, especially technical education, infrastructure development and the maintaining of macroeconomic stability. Indeed, these fundamental policies coupled with a strong bias towards export orientation represent the preconditions for the success of the more specific industrial policies adopted in these different countries.

I will draw on a huge amount of published data and analysis to derive some insights on how Taiwan, Korea and Hong Kong have successfully upgraded their manufacturing sectors while India has been left far behind.

All sorts of economic pundits blame India's government policies for its poor showing on the export front. In this chapter, I will be taking a hard look at the policies adopted by some of India's East Asian neighbours. I will seek to establish that though the policies are not all that different, it is the mindset of the business leaders that has made a remarkable difference.

I do not discuss Japan here as it is not an NIE. I will, however, discuss Japan separately in the following chapter. Japan is an example of how an intensely protective economy, placing enormous tariff and non-tariff barriers on imports, foreign investments and foreign participation, has grown at a mind-boggling pace. It is indeed ironical that the same sort of protective strategies are alleged to have destroyed the Indian economy.

Historically, India and the Asian NIEs have shared a common characteristic with many other developing countries in that they have all been rather late industrialising and entering the global economy. These countries have faced some common problems in terms of developing their export markets.

1. Distance: The main problem in developing high-tech industrial capability has been the distance of these nations from the lead user markets in North America, Europe and Japan.
2. Involvement: These nations are also far away from and disconnected to the leading sources of innovation in advanced countries.
3. Manpower Resources: It follows from the above that while all these nations may have ample manpower and a reasonable level of education, there is almost a complete absence of a trained and skilled workforce. It is a chicken and egg situation in terms of skilled manpower leading to industrial development and so on.

Despite these disadvantages, however, the Asian NIEs have managed to achieve significantly faster high-tech industrial growth over the last three decades, compared to other developing countries. In the process, they have rapidly overtaken India. A look at their manufacturing sector upgrading strategies shows the presence of common factors as also some approaches which have been distinctively different from one another.

Five routes to development

A number of academicians have looked at various development models and have studied the use of these by various nations. These studies are, well, academic, and the only conclusion I can draw from these is that 'what will work for you will not necessarily work for me'. Having said that, it is of course possible to look at the different routes taken by the Asian NIEs and see if there are any practical lessons for us.

The first route to a technological upgrading strategy is to borrow or copy technology and then develop it through R&D promotion at public research institutes. This is what Taiwan did.

The second route to manufacturing upgrading can be through deliberately promoting huge, high-tech conglomerates in the private sector and leaving it to them to spearhead export development, as in Korea.

The third route to manufacturing upgrading, as followed by Hong Kong, can be through encouraging relatively mature industries and product groups to move along the vertical value chain, towards marketing, logistics and technical support downstream and product innovation upstream.

The fourth route, the highly successful Singapore experiment, can be in terms of the government actively promoting MNC-induced technological growth.

The fifth route is that which forms the basic objective of India's industrialisation policy. This entails regulating the growth of a number of industries, in accordance with the development priorities of the government, by promoting a mixed economy and by reserving the further development of some industries exclusively for the public sector.

Let's look at Taiwan first

The first technological upgrading strategy I mentioned above is the one followed by Taiwan. This can be best described as one involving technology assimilation/transfer and cooperative R&D promotion through public research institutes. Among the NIEs, Taiwan has been the most successful in using public research institutes to promote the diffusion of industrially relevant technologies. For example, the Industrial Technology Research Institute (ITRI) has been widely credited with helping to create an advanced semi-conductor industry cluster in Taiwan through a well thought out and well executed strategy of assimilating foreign technology and transferring them to local enterprises through spin offs (see, e.g., Mathews (1995) and Lin (1994)). The successful execution of this strategy depended on a number of factors:

- Careful, long-term technology development planning
- Long-term vision
- Businesslike leadership at the helm of ITRI (Dr Morris Chang)
- An abundant supply of well trained engineers

- And last, but not the least, a significant presence of, and strong linkage with, competitive local electronics industries which provided significant markets and customer feedback

Besides such successful spin offs there are also many examples of public-research-institute-orchestrated R&D consortia in Taiwan. These have been promoted in the belief that the many small and medium enterprises in Taiwan would under invest in new technology development if left on their own. Over the last 15 years, it has been estimated that over 60 such R&D consortia have been established in various industrial sectors in Taiwan. Although the record of these R&D consortia in terms of eventual market commercialisation has been mixed, it is undeniable that there has been much faster diffusion of product technological capabilities among the participating firms as a result of these consortium programmes. As an example, the successful development of the notebook PC industry in Taiwan owes much to the ITRI-orchestrated development consortium.

Now, look at Korea

The second route to manufacturing upgrading can be described as one involving the deliberate promotion of huge business empires. These are high-tech conglomerate enterprises built on a sufficiently large scale. This has been the classic Korean *chaebol* model of expansion through horizontal diversification in product space and vertical integration in process space.

In the early stage of development of 'strategic' industries in Korea, the Korean government deliberately encouraged the growth of large scale *chaebols* as an instrument of bringing about economy of scale in capital intensive industries that were deemed 'strategic'. A variety of policy tools were used (see, e.g., Kim (1993)), including subsidised financing, protection of the domestic market, incentives for technological learning through capital goods import of turnkey projects and turning over failing state enterprises to the *chaebols*. Although there were notable failures as a result of this strategy, several other big *chaebols* like Samsung, LG, Hyundai and Daewoo did develop significant technological capabilities in a wide range of export oriented, capital intensive industries.

- Where Korea differed from other developing countries in promoting big business was in the discipline that the state exercised over these *chaebols* by penalising poor performances and rewarding only good ones.

This 'contest-based' approach (Amsden, 1989) enabled a number of high-performing *chaebols* to quickly establish large-scale production and marketing/distribution or R&D economies enabling them to compete successfully in several global industries like shipbuilding, automobile, consumer electronics, telecommunications equipment, and semiconductors. The large size of these *chaebols* enabled them to build global brands and distribution channels, and hence move quickly into a wide range of consumer products. Deep pockets have also enabled these *chaebols* to acquire technology capabilities rapidly by buying up established companies (recent examples include Maxtor, NCR microelectronics and AST).

However, the large size of the *chaebols* appear to be a source of disadvantage in industries such as software, biotechnology and specialty chemicals where scale economies are not important or less critical. Furthermore, indiscriminate and unrelated diversification has often led to over-extension and loss of strategic focus. This conglomeration trend has also been increasingly questioned as a result of political democratisation in recent years. Nevertheless, the basic idea of 'contest-based' resource allocation and the need to achieve a sufficient scale economy remain valid policy concerns for late industrialising economies seeking to make their presence felt in a wide range of capital intensive high-tech industries now dominated by advanced industrialised countries.

Hong Kong

The third route to manufacturing upgrading, typified by Hong Kong, can be described as one of promoting relatively mature industries and product groups, but emphasising the shift along the vertical value chain towards marketing, logistics and technical support downstream and product innovation upstream. With little government support for R&D and technological development, manufacturing firms in Hong Kong have opted not to enter technologically advanced sectors or products involving the early stages of new technology life cycles. Instead, they have sought to achieve cost competitive advantages in relatively mature, less capital-intensive sectors (e.g., textiles and garments, watches, electronic toys and games) by redistributing manufacturing operations to China and other low cost regions in South-East Asia.

At the same time, Hong Kong is moving upwards in the value chain by increasingly turning into the headquarters for product design, marketing, logistics management, technical support and accounting/administration. By focusing on niche markets involving fast fashion changes or short product runs and leveraging on their excellent communications and transport infrastructure, many Hong Kong manufacturers have developed core competencies in managing fast response, dispersed production networks. For example, in textile and garment making, Hong Kong firms have developed sophisticated CAD/CAM design and electronic data interchange capabilities that allow them to quickly turn buyer requirements into design specifications, which are then partitioned into job assignments to different subcontractors, often outside Hong Kong. In reality, this generic route involves the substantial deindustrialisation of Hong Kong itself, which retains, largely, the services-value-added stages of the manufacturing value chain.

Last, but not the least, Singapore

The industrial development strategy of Singapore can best be described as one emphasising government facilitation of MNC-induced technological learning. Through the Economic Development Board, the Singapore government has encouraged MNCs to bring in success waves of new technologies to their subsidiary operations in Singapore. Although some have criticised this MNC-led approach as stunting the growth of local firms, research evidence has shown that these MNC operations have spawned a large supporting industry in Singapore and induced substantial technological capability development among many local subcontracting and contract assembly firms (Wong, 1992, 1955b). Moreover, active innovative public assistance programmes such as

- the Local Industry Upgrading Programme (LIUP)
- programmes to promote the adoption of new information and automation technology by small and medium enterprises (SMEs)

- advanced technical manpower training programmes like INTECH
- and the early promotion of the ISO 9000 certification infra-structure

have been shown to have facilitated the technological and manage-ment learning process of these supporting industries. Many of these local supporting firms have pursued the process specialist route, and most have since internationalised their operations to nearby NIEs such as Malaysia and China, not only following the redistribu-tion of their customers to these countries, but diversifying into new buyer markets as well.

Regionalisation incentives provided by the government have facilitated these overseas ventures. Moreover, new innovative R&D incentives like the Research Incentives Scheme for Companies (RISC) have been introduced by the government to fund integrative process technology capability development efforts in these compa-nies, even though such efforts cannot be neatly packaged into spe-cific R&D projects. A smaller but increasing number of companies have also pursued the reverse product life cycle strategy, moving into new product R&D while leveraging their traditional strengths in low cost, high quality manufacturing.

An overall look

I have briefly described the different routes taken by Taiwan, Korea, Hong Kong and Singapore in upgrading industrial capability devel-opment before going on to discussing these techniques and strate-gies and comparing them with how things are done in India. In reality it should be recognised, of course, that as time has gone by and results of the experiments have started coming in, none of these countries have continued to pursue one route exclusively.

The Singapore government has, for example, in recent years also started to stress the need to develop high-tech firms of sufficient scale by setting up a government controlled group, Singapore Tech-nology Group, to spearhead entry into various high-tech industries (e.g., semiconductor wafer fabrication, chip design, aerospace repair and maintenance, systems software) where local entrepre-neurs had previously been found wanting. Many Singaporean firms have also adopted the upgrading route of Hong Kong by redistributing their manufacturing operations overseas and leveraging Singapore as their regional headquarter hub for product/process development, marketing, logistics and technical support.

The use of a public research institute to promote technology diffusion has also been used in Korea, particularly in the early years, as in the case of semiconductor technology acquisition through a public research institute like the Korea Institute of Economics and Technology (KIET) (which was later merged into the Economics and Technology Research Institute, ETRI) (Mathews, 1995). The considerably larger resources of the big *chaebols* meant that further direct government involvement in technology transfer was deemed unnecessary once the basic technology was diffused among companies such as Samsung, LG and Hyundai.

More recently, the Singapore Government has also started to promote R&D consortia as a means to hasten the technological capability development of local firms. Involvement with foreign firms or R&D institutions are particularly emphasised to facilitate technology transfers from advanced sources.

Contrast with India

Exports have accounted for only a small proportion of India's gross national product. The share of merchandise exports in the value of the GNP has ranged from about four per cent in 1960 to a little over seven per cent in 1998.

Very unlike the economies of the East Asian nations where exports have been the major thrust of planned development from the very beginning, in India, since planned development began, great efforts have been made to reduce the country's dependence on imports, with almost no emphasis on export promotion. The result of these efforts has been that foreign exchange has been in chronic short supply and India has encountered a series of balance of payments crises, each of which has required drastic remedies, with severe repercussions on the rest of the economy.

The basic objectives of India's industrialisation policy were charted out soon after Independence in the Industrial Policy Resolution of 1948.

- The growth of a number of industries was to be regulated in accordance with the development priorities of the government
- A mixed economy was envisaged
- The further development of certain industries was reserved exclusively for the public sector
- Small scale enterprise was to be encouraged
- The concentration of industrial ownership was to be prevented
- Industrial development was to promote balanced regional growth
- Research institutes were established and put under purely bureaucratic controls. Their contact with industry was carefully monitored to prevent misuse

It is useful to note at the outset that there were serious conflicts between these goals, and the formulation of industrial policy in subsequent periods has partly reflected the shifts in emphasis between overlapping objectives.

It is also useful to note that each of these objectives was incorporated into the routes taken by the Asian NIEs, with vastly different results.

With the advent of planning in 1950, these principles were incorporated in the Industries (Development and Regulation) Act of 1951, which created a tool for realising these goals in the form of industrial licensing. Lists or 'schedules' of certain industries (42 in number, initially) were drawn up indicating the sector in which their future development was to take place. Producers belonging to scheduled industries were required to procure a licence from the government before setting up any new industrial undertaking, substantially expanding existing ones or making any new products. Provisions for the statutory control over prices and distribution of certain commodities were conferred on the government in the same Act.

Thus the foundation of the 'License Raj' was laid.

The model was cast in terms of a closed economy and, although the shift towards heavy industry was not explicitly justified on the grounds of a foreign exchange constraint, there appears to have been an underlying assumption of a 'stagnant world demand' for India's exports.

- In other words, our planners were convinced that there could not be much of a demand for our exports!

Rapid expansion in the already massive non-productive, bureau-cratic controlled investments, in the first year of the Second Plan, lead to a sever balance of payments crisis. Thus 1957 also saw the first appearance, since development began, of a foreign exchange problem that was to become endemic to the economy. Together with the system of industrial controls set up for planning output tar-gets, therefore, import controls were introduced over all current transactions while other industrial controls were tightened at the same time.

Where do we go from here?

India should take a serious look at some of the relevant routes taken by the Asian NIEs I have just mentioned. I suggest that we try to see if there is anything in it for us.

1. Among the NIEs, Taiwan has been most successful in using pub-lic research institutes to promote the diffusion of industrially rele-vant technologies.
   Research institutes in India are only useful insofar as they convert highly theoretical academicians into practicing bureaucrats
2. Where Korea differed from other developing countries in pro-moting big business was in the discipline that the state exercised over *chaebols* by penalising poor performances and rewarding only good ones.
   ✓ Certainly, Korea differs from us in this respect. We already have an excellent system of rewarding our friends and cronies and penalising those who oppose us
   Nevertheless, the basic idea of 'contest-based' resource alloca-tion and the need to achieve a sufficient scale economy remain valid policy concerns for economies like Indias' seeking to enter a wide range of capital intensive high-tech industries now domi-nated by advanced industrialised countries.
3. A very important lesson for us lies in Hong Kong which has moved upwards from the manufacturing to the service sector and is now fast becoming the centre for product design, market-ing, logistics management, technical support and accounting plus administration. I explained earlier how Hong Kong firms

have developed sophisticated CAD/CAM design and electronic data interchange capabilities that allow them to quickly turn buyer requirements into design specifications.

✓ Here is food for thought for India's technocrats. An important point to be noted in this regard is that moving in this direction requires only private sector initiative without any government interference.

4. Singapore can best be described as government-facilitated MNC-induced technological learning.

✓ Though we are also moving in this direction, our initiatives here are seriously hampered by political interference and our apprehensions of what the MNCs may do to our economy. See Chapter 2.4 for a detailed discussion on this.

4.2 *Understanding the Japanese*

> *The secret of modern Japan consists in Japan's ability to make a family out of a modern corporation*
>
> Peter Drucker

The Japanese work ethic

I have had some unique opportunities of looking at and comparing the work ethics of engineers, technicians and mechanics of various nations. This is because as a member of supervisory teams sent in by multilateral agencies like the World Bank I have not only had people of various races as my colleagues, but have supervised the setting up of manufacturing projects where the technology and the equipment was supplied, installed and commissioned by various countries.

We have to come to terms with the fact that the fiercest challenge to our export effort comes from the East, from the Japanese and, to a lesser extent, the Koreans and Chinese. The challenge is not so much from the products they make. It is more from the ruthless efficiency of their large trading houses. They buy products made in Thailand and sell these in Kenya in such a way that Indian exporters to Kenya end up losing their markets. They are increasingly setting up offices in India and exporting Indian products, hitting our exporters right at home.

It is high time we made some efforts to understand the Japanese mindset and try to benefit from their networks. Indeed, there is a market for many of our products in Japan itself, if only we understand how to reach it.

I have been able to gain an impersonal and objective view of the working styles of people of various races as, being a part of a team, my role was purely supervisory and none of the professionals actually involved in the work were working for or took orders from the team. In other words, my perspective on the work attitudes of, say, the Japanese would be quite different from that of a person working as a subcontractor for a Japanese construction firm.

In this chapter I will be talking about the Japanese mindset. In a later chapter (7.2), I will be talking about the very difficult task of, maybe, selling to the Japanese.

I have been lucky to have had a unique insight into the Japanese way of thinking, further facilitated by a close friend, a person of Indian origin whose family was stranded in Japan during the war. He was born and educated in Japan and married a Japanese girl.

Working with the Japanese

Before going on to talk about how to deal with the Japanese, I will talk about some of my own experiences which will form the backdrop of what is to come later.

When a new factory is being set up, the overseas firm that supplies the equipment generally sends engineers and/or technicians to help install the machinery. There are a lot of jobs such as the plumbing, electrification and foundation laying which have to be carried out by local contractors as per specifications provided. It has been my experience in projects in Asia and Africa that people sent by European and Australian firms generally tell you what needs to be done or corrected but actually work only on the installation and commissioning aspects that require their specialised skills. They work with their own hands too, but only where needed. I have found that they do have a thorough knowledge of the working of the whole plant and can indeed be of help in various situations.

Indian engineers are far more hardworking and work well with the local contractors but have a very narrow spectrum of knowledge. A technician sent to commission and run a machine will generally be very good at running the machine but will be of no help in the installation of the electrical or the hydraulic system. He will openly make it clear that he is a machine operator only and cannot do any other job.

The Japanese are unique. They are involved in the proper functioning of the equipment as if their life depended on it. They seem to know the answers to every problem and get deeply involved in all aspects of the installation.

One point of contrast here is the paperwork the Japanese bring with them. It is far greater and far more detailed than what the others do, including a huge amount of reference sheets, charts and manuals. My experience of Indians shows that we tend not to have too much of paperwork.

A follow through of this is that the Japanese keep meticulous records. I have not seen anybody else, least of all the Indians, make a note of everything that happened. These records doubtless add to their knowledge when installing a similar machine in another location.

Personal experiences

The Japanese attitude towards self discipline never ceases to amaze me.

✓ You are on a visit to Japan and your hosts are walking you to your hotel at 3 A.M. after a night out in town. The streets are completely deserted but they never cross the street against the traffic light.
✓ I have seen a number of my Japanese friends come home from a long trip overseas and, instead of going straight home to their families, check into a hotel for sleeping off the jet lag in order to be fresh and ready for office the next day. They go home the following day.

Another example. I was in charge of setting up a project to manufacture super enameled copper wires in Malaysia. The plant was a second-hand Japanese one. There were two technicians sent to commission the plant which was designed for continuous non-stop operation. There were problems, however, and not even a single shift could initially be run.

I would pick up the technicians from their hotel at 6:30 A.M. and take them back in the evening. Gradually they got the plant running longer hours and one fine day I was told that they would try to run three shifts non-stop. I quickly made arrangements for the workers to reorganise themselves and waited for the technicians to go back to the hotel, but they kept on working. They had started work at 6:30 A.M. and it was only at about 3:00 A.M. that I was told they were ready to go back. I was thoroughly exhausted and after dropping them, I had hardly reached home when I got a call from the factory saying that the Japanese were already back at work! It seems they simply took a long hot shower, had something to eat and took a taxi back to work!

I have seen others working non-stop in emergencies but this was hardly an emergency! It was a routine plant start-up. In all my working life, I have not come across dedication of this sort.

The Japanese and the rest of us

The more I have worked with the Japanese, the more I have come to the realisation that the Japanese, and to some extent the Koreans, are different from the rest of the human race. In a given situation, there would be a lot of things common in the way a German or an American or an Australian would behave. People of every nation do possess their own distinctive characteristics but their commonalaties are highlighted when you compare them with the Japanese.

One of the outstanding characteristics of the Japanese is their intense nationalism. Everything Japanese is sacred to them. They are ruthless, for example, when it comes to maintaining the purity of their language. They have a dislike for most things foreign and a person buying, say, a foreign car would not be looked upon very kindly. Of all the countries I have lived and worked in, Japan is the only place where I have felt emotionally uncomfortable. The French and Germans are xenophobic too, but the Japanese are in a class by themselves.

HERE IS A SMALL DIVERSION FOR YOU:

1. How many languages in the world jealously maintain their purity by accepting foreign words but clearly identifying them as such?
2. How do these languages make sure that a foreign word remains marked out as such for centuries?

For the answers and some discussion turn to Appendix 3.

I wish to be clearly understood that I am not saying that the Japanese are a rude or offensive people. Far from it. They are an extremely polite people and their hospitality and cordiality is legendary. It is only their attitude towards things foreign that is under discussion.

Visiting Japan for the first time

Indians visiting Japan for the first time are, of course, not expected to know the finer details of Japanese attitude to life and work. It helps, however, if one has a reasonable idea of proper Japanese behaviour in order to be a gracious guest. I would have suggested that a visitor read up on Japan but I realise that most of what has been published is written by Americans for Americans. What will work for the Americans will, in most cases, not work for Indians as the Japanese simply do not behave similarly with both.

Having said that, it helps if visitors have some idea of the Japanese way of doing things. This demonstrates not only good manners, but also that you have made a sincere effort to get along with your Japanese associates. I would like to discuss some issues involving body language, politeness and social conduct.

- Contrary to what one reads in the American literature published, the Japanese respect personal space and do not like to be pushed around by other people
- If the Japanese suddenly go quiet during negotiations, it rarely means they are thinking very hard. It generally means that something said or done has displeased them
- Never extend your finger and point at a person while talking to him/her. This is considered accusatory, rude or hostile. Nod or speak with an open palm
- The meaning of laughter and smiles among Japanese is dependant on the situation. When the Japanese are nervous or embarrassed, they often smile or laugh nervously without the accompanying head bowing. This could be in response to an inconvenient request or to a sensitive issue brought up in conversation. Another possible reason for the laughter could be when someone nearby has done something silly
- Japanese set great store by being good listeners. They often complain that Indians pay too little attention in conversation and interrupt too often. Remember not to carry on talking on a subject when your host has interrupted you
- Japanese are taught to avoid direct eye contact which, they feel intrudes on the other's personal space
- When the Japanese yawn, cough or use a toothpick, they cover their mouths. It is essential that you do the same

- It is considered grossly impolite to point one's feet at another person or to use them to point out anything. The Japanese sit upright in chairs with both feet on the floor
- Good posture is important in Japan. Never slouch in public
- In some restaurants, men sit cross-legged on the floor. Women sit on their legs or tuck their legs to one side. Indians usually have no problems with this as we are used to sitting on the floor
- Blowing your nose or picking your nose in public is considered extremely rude
- In Japanese homes, shoes are removed at the entrance, but not the socks. Wear clean socks!
- The Japanese are very much like Indians in terms of body contact. They rarely hug in public. Lightly touching another person's arm or shoulder while speaking; as we often casually do in India, is a sign of familiarity and can be misunderstood for trying to be too persuasive. Avoid this
- Japanese executives normally introduce themselves by first mentioning the name of the company they work for and then their own names. Status in society is due to the company for which one works rather than the profession one is in. In other cultures the opposite is the case. If you do the same, they are impressed

Decision making in Japan:'Ringi'

A business visitor to Japan goes there for a purpose and expects some sort of a decision before he takes the flight home. If he goes there to buy something, he will come back with firm and detailed offers. But if he is there to sell or negotiate a deal, he will find that the managerial practice of decision making is considerably different from that anywhere else in the world. The Japanese call this unique technique of collective decision making, 'ringi'

A visitor in Japan with a new idea, a proposal or a suggestion for change is often frustrated by the blank looks he gets. No senior manager will interact with him to tell him whether the idea is good. This is mainly because the top management, very unlike the top bosses in India, does not feel that decision making is their sole monopoly. The managerial practice of decision making is built on the concept that change and new ideas should come primarily from below. Thus, lower-level employees prepare proposals for higher-level personnel. Supervisors, rather than simply accepting or rejecting suggestions, tactfully question proposals, make suggestions and encourage subordinates. If necessary, proposals are sent back to the initiator for more information.

Japanese management, then, believes in decision making by consensus; lower-level employees initiate the idea and submit it to the next level and so on until it reaches the desk of the top executive. If the proposal is approved, it is returned to the initiator for implementation. Although this decision-making process is time consuming, the implementation of the decision, because of the general consensus at various levels of management, is swift and does not require any additional 'selling'.

Japan is the world's greatest exporter. Looking at and understanding the Japanese mindset is useful for an Indian exporter wanting to export to Japan. But even this is not enough. For a true understanding and clear perception of what makes them tick, we need to take a quick look at various aspects of their social and cultural life and compare these with ours. Here there arises a problem. An Indian visitor to Japan can find hardly anything to read on the subject and the fellow Indian presence in Japan is at best minimal.

An important characteristic of Japanese decision making is the large amount of effort that goes into analysing and defining the question or the problem. There is an immense amount of communication before a decision is actually made. Top bosses in India have a habit of making decisions on the spur of the moment, based on gut feeling and even before fully understanding or defining the problem. In contrast, a Japanese management will make a decision only after a long discussion on the issue. There is open communication among people at different levels of the organisational hierarchy, a great deal of collaboration and a recognition of mutual dependence.

The Japanese are teaching the world a thing or two about how to run businesses. However, India cannot simply copy what they do and the way they do it as we do not think and behave like them. Also, we must realise that very few empirical studies exist on the subject and most of the available literature is in the form of opinions and perceptions of western management gurus.

✓ Their very attitude to life and work is different. Later on in this chapter, I will compare the Indian value systems with that of the Japanese. Therefore, if we are going to get anywhere dealing with and selling to the Japanese, we need to understand the basic points of difference and try to adapt our work ethic accordingly.

Indian and Japanese value systems

The very fact that Japanese culture and work environments are typically Japanese and Indian culture and work environments, Indian with a strong western influence, makes a comparison of Japanese and Indian value systems very interesting. Even though the two countries are Asian, their historical backgrounds, cultures and people are very different. The idea is to identify and appreciate these differences and to work towards developing strategies of dealing with the Japanese.

1. *Comparing Management Education Systems*   One does indeed realise that changes are called for in the Indian organisation system and work ethic. However, change cannot be expected to be initiated in the system only at or from the time of entry to a commercial organisation. It has to start much earlier, through the management education system.

Let us try to appreciate the sharp difference between the Japanese and Indian management education systems. In Japan, students basically use Japanese books which help them understand their own management styles and work environment; secondary to this is information about other management styles, mainly that of the U.S. The situation is just the reverse in India, where the education system is US and/or European-based in content and methodology. Very few education centres offer detailed studies or information about anything Indian. In short, in the Indian context, a truly Indian system has never been given the opportunity to emerge and grow.

2. *Comparing Childhood Influences*   The Japanese understand the power and benefit of being group-oriented very early in life. The ideal upheld is individual self-sacrifice and conformity with the group. If we take a closer look at the average Japanese and her/his beliefs, we find that the Japanese are taught to be socially correct

from early childhood. There is also an emphasis on building and maintaining relationships over long periods of time. The stress laid on being socially correct leads to respect for seniors and for the elderly. The relationship of sempai (senior) and cohai (junior) is further strengthened in the school and at university. Most activities at this stage are group activities. Seniors, after graduating from university, often assist their juniors during the most demanding of times in a Japanese student's life—job hunting.

What makes an Indian's situation different from that of a Japanese's? In India, too, there is an emphasis on the sanctity of social relationships. However, lessons of social correctness are received only at home. Outside the home, an individual fails to appreciate the advantages of social correctness because, for example, there are no constructive, meaningful and prominent senior–junior relationships visible in a student's life. There are very few activities where a student would be exposed to working in a group. Also, due to the huge population and the ever-increasing competition in every field of life, the average Indian cannot but be individualistic. When it comes to making a decision, an Indian normally takes an individualistic decision rather than conform to the wishes of the group.

3. *Comparing Company Politics*   In Indian organisations, there is an atmosphere of high internal competitiveness. There is also always the possibility of the status quo being disturbed for the least reason. This is what I would term internal politics. The lack of senior–junior relationships also means that there is no reason why an individual should not eye a senior's position once he/she feels he/she is capable enough. There are no sentiments attached in the relationship with the senior as in the case of the Japanese. Insensitivity or lack of concern towards others often leads to tensions avoidable in a group-oriented system like that of the Japanese. Thus, situations in Indian organisations are more volatile. This is further aggravated by the arrival of the new generation of educated, competitive, career-conscious managers proficient in the use of new technological tools. They are also aware of their rights as industrial workers. Being individualistic in approach, they do not shy away from demanding what they think is due to them.

Under similar circumstances, the Japanese would not demand their rights as it would be deemed socially incorrect behaviour. For an Indian, however, there is no way out. As most companies are not sensitive enough, individuals are forced to protect their interests and fight for their rights. Job security in organisations also becomes a right which, once ensured, acts as a *demotivator*. It is tragic but true that not all senior–junior relationships in Indian organisations are positive or conducive to work. More often than not, this relationship degenerates into manipulation and ingratiation.

4. *Comparing the Status of Engineers*   It is a fact that most organisations in India have a tendency to seek out management graduates and place them above engineers. In India, engineers are 'second-class citizens' in an organisation, comparatively poorly paid and neglected. In such an environment most engineers turn to management schools to ensure for themselves better living standards and a higher status in the organisation and in society. The Indian system produces managers who only believe in 'managing people' and not in 'assisting' them. Organisations in India have so far failed to give engineers the place due to them in the hierarchy. This has resulted in the deterioration and degradation of the technical base as engineers have either left the country or turned into managers.

This does not happen in Japan. An engineer is the most respected person in the organisation and in society. Managers as such are an invisible class. Everyone whose job it is to assist fellow workers is a manager. A detailed study in *Business Week*, Oct. 1994, found that the Japanese workforce is the smartest in the world. They have been masters of innovation, even though the West tends to see them as 'imitators', and still continue to be among the leaders. This is partly because of their investment in technicians and engineers. The success of Japan has been due to heavy investment in technical and vocational education and in courses in engineering. Only selected universities offer MBA courses and the investment in 'making' a manager is low.

Dealing with Japanese executives

Your first meeting as a business visitor in Japan will be with a number of executives who will all listen to and try and understand what you are looking for. They will then discuss matters among themselves and, if the firm allocates an executive to keep you company, you can consider the first battle won. You will often find that this executive has been allocated to you full time.

Our tendency from this point onwards would be to try and 'tackle' this executive and to win him over or, worse, pump him for inside information. This is a mistake. Though every overseas business visitor to India is guilty of this, and is successful in many cases as the Indian executive generally proves 'amenable,' a similar approach would just makes matters worse in Japan.

The other mistake is to expect the executive to try to impress you with his/her personal knowledge or personality. A Japanese executive is not even remotely interested in winning personal laurels in his dealings with you, unlike experiences I have had with some executives in India in similar circumstances. You will not even be told the status of the executive you are with.

Also, in dealing with executives you may find that there are no job descriptions and that there is freedom to rotate work amongst employees. This makes everyone capable of handling almost all types of jobs.

I have seen how, after work, office colleagues sometimes go out for a drink together. They often entertain overseas visitors this way. During such meetings, I have found it difficult to distinguish seniors from juniors. There is hardly any visible status consciousness and one is free to discuss anything. This helps keep organisational social relations intact and, in fact, helps bolster them. The superior is normally aware about subordinates' desires and expectations because of this regular interaction.

When a new entrant starts work in a Japanese organisation, the last thing on her/his mind would be to compete with a senior. Their gratefulness stops them from pursuing narrow individualistic goals. For them, social acceptance is of greater significance than individual achievement. Group recognition is the only reward they seek. They are fully committed to the group and to their organisation. Cooperativeness and devotion to the goals of the company count more in the Japanese context than individual ambition, drive and decisiveness. At the workplace, being group-oriented leads to cooperation and the suppression of individual competitiveness and ambition. Competitiveness in Japanese organisations is controlled and senior–junior relations, not easily disturbed. Some may view this as a drawback as it hinders, for example, the growth of talent. However, this system has provided Japanese organisations with discipline and stability resulting in their unbounded success in many areas of business.

4.3   *Understanding the Koreans*

A FANTASY

Let us imagine for a moment that we are in a large developing nation such as Africa.

- We find the local papers full of aggressive advertising by Indian companies for products such as automobiles, refrigerators and TV sets. We also find the most prestigious sports and TV events sponsored by Indian companies
- We are amazed to find that certain large Indian firms have had no problems capturing a substantial market share from decades-old, well-established and well-respected local firms

This is truly a fantasy. Substitute India for the African country, and Korea for India, and it is no longer a fantasy but a tragedy.

Korean firms have had no problems capturing markets from well-established Indian firms in sectors such as automobiles, white goods and electronics. Neither are the ruthlessly efficient *chaebols* facing any problems capturing India's export markets. They are exporting our products for their own benefit and on their own terms.

✓ To do something about it, we have to first understand their mindset. Until our people get a good grip on the emotional factors that control and motivate the Koreans, it will be difficult for us to anticipate their moves and work with them smoothly

---

A little historical background

The Koreans, an ethnically cohesive, linguistically united people, enjoyed over a thousand years as a unified, independent kingdom until the Japanese annexation of 1910. After Japan's defeat in the Second World War in 1945, Korea was divided into Soviet and US zones of occupation and then, in 1948, into two hostile republics. The north's invasion of the south in 1950 led to three years of war, in which the UN supported the south and China the north. The two sides were left glaring at each other across a ceasefire line not far from the 38th parallel, which marked the original US and Soviet zones.

South Korea made education a priority and owner-occupation by smallholders the basis of land tenure. In 1962 a military government, seeking an engine for growth in a country with few natural resources, initiated a strategy of export-oriented industrialisation. It depended on South Korea's one major asset: cheap but well-educated labour. The next quarter century was one barely interrupted boom, with GNP growth averaging 8.8 per cent a year. Positive agricultural policies helped maintain self-sufficiency in food grains, with the country seeing some of the world' highest rice yields. I have discussed at some length the strategies they used for economic development in Chapter 4.1.

✓ A point to be noted here is that, very much like what was done in India, Korea followed very rigid protectionist policies and all foreign investment was strictly forbidden untill recently. The Korean people have an inherent dislike of anything foreign, so a number of tariff and non-tariff barriers were placed on all imports, except for the much-needed raw materials. Till very recently, nobody could even sell a screwdriver to the Koreans

✓ The result of these was an enormous export thrust and the establishment of many world-class companies

✓ The results of similar protectionist policies in India was an unmitigated disaster

South Korea, at the start of the 1990s, was in a state of transition. In domestic politics, it was moving slowly from military dictatorship to a more democratic system. In international relations, erstwhile communist countries had moved towards recognising South Korea, and even North Korea had relaxed its hostility sufficiently to agree to 'talks about talks'. In economic terms, the question is not whether South Korea will leave its developing-country status behind and join the OECD, but when.

South Korea on the world market

Lending credence to the view that South Korea may well be the country to lead an Asian economic recovery, ratings agency Fitch-

IBC raised the country's debt rating from 'junk bond status' to one level behind 'investment status' in late 1998. Moody's and Standard and Poor also acclaimed the progress between South Korea and international bankers in developing a debt accord and they, too, are revising their ratings. The envoys sent out by Korea to the West to negotiate debt accords have obviously been successful in raising foreign investor confidence. Yet, as always in South Korea, the behaviour of the *chaebols*, the major Korean conglomerates that dominate Korean international business, will determine to a large extent the country's revival.

✓ Very unlike the larger Indian corporates, the major Korean conglomerates have concentrated on expansion rather than profit, assisted by a close relationship with the government

The Korean route to manufacturing upgrading has been by deliberately promoting huge, high-tech conglomerates in the private sector and to leave it to them to spearhead export development. These sufficiently large-scale, high-tech conglomerate enterprises have followed the classic Korean *chaebol* model of expansion through horizontal diversification in product space and vertical integration in process space. The top four are, Samsung, Hyundai, Daewoo and Lucky Goldstar, all with management portfolio strengths but exposed in the Asian currency crisis due to expansionary acquisitions that, in a climate of never-ending Asian growth, made sense not so long ago.

Attitude towards each other

Central to the growth of the *chaebols* is the Korean attitude of cooperating with each other. I have not been able to find any similar traditions in Indian folk or cultural literature where society demands mutual help or assistance. True, helping others is a good thing but nobody says it is mandatory.

There is a lot of published literature on Korean social-value systems, some of it because it has had such a profound influence on the nation's economic success. The literature, some of which I have mentioned in the bibliography, refers to the influence of three major sources, namely,

1. Confucian thought imported from China

2. the patriarchal system of large joint or extended families
3. the collective community system

First, the heritage of Confucian thought is still deeply rooted in the social values of Korean people. Confucianism emphasizes virtuous human character in terms of generosity (ren), righteousness (yi), etiquette (li), wisdom (zhi) and trust (xin). It also advises people to take the middle path (zhong yong) in dealing with tasks or problems, avoiding extreme measures.

In the folk culture of Korean communities, there were three kinds of what can be termed social or community cooperative customs: Kye, Dure and Pumatshi. Kye refers to the association for mutual help for ceremonial occasions such as marriage and funerals, or for financial needs, or just for friendly goodwill. The Kye is still widely practised, even in urban areas, especially among schoolmates, members of the same workplace and even among those with the same hobbies. Both Dure and Pumatshi are like manpower banks created through cooperative effort for serving mutual needs in farming activities.

The effect of such customs and folk culture has been to foster group unity and a cooperative spirit. Together with group orientation, the Koreans have traditionally been very conscious of such things as reputation and face-saving in terms of their social role and status in the community. A person is usually judged by his/her overall character or personality and not by his/her manifest ability and/or short-term achievements. This Confucian heritage is believed to influence the criteria for both the evaluation and recruitment of personnel in a business organisation.

How does all this matter to us?

✓ It has been my contention that it will not be possible for India to deal with and compete with the Koreans unless we understand their mindset and develop our strategies accordingly
✓ It should be remembered that the Koreans do their homework before coming and setting up base in India. They take pains to understand our mindset, and their business and managerial strategies in India are considerably different from those, say, in the Middle East

So back to the Korean mindset and what this has to do with their corporate scenario. It is true that there has always been the problem of nepotism, believed to have derived from the large, patriarchal family system. Korean society is characterised by this extended family system, where the majority of members live together, including grandparents and members of married brothers' families. The extended family system is patriarchal in that it emphasises the principles of strict hierarchical order and Confucian filial piety in father–son relationships.

However, the same tradition has resulted in the establishment of strong corporate entities or *chaebols* because in the patriarchal family system, children are expected to be obedient to their parents and pay them respect. In return, the father, as the chief of the family, is expected to be benevolent to family members by caring for their welfare. Thus, large patriarchal families are authoritarian, with a strict hierarchical orientation and, at the same time, a benevolent paternalism in organisational life. Because large families are traditionally cohesive and self-sufficient 'in-groups' with a common destiny, their social values and interpersonal relationships get translated into corporate loyalty and dedication.

Another aspect where the Indian and Korean people differ is in value orientation. While Indians are generally highly individualistic, Koreans are oriented to group or collective thinking. This is said to be attributable to the characteristics of their traditional rural communities. Like many other societies, Korea consisted of typical agrarian rural communities which were relatively closed and self-sufficient, requiring cooperative effort among community members for production, consumption as also for various social events.

A very important point to be noted about the Koreans, again in sharp contrast to Indians, is that they are very this-worldly in their thinking. Though they follow different religions, including Buddhism, one thing common to all Koreans is their wish to attain worldly success in this life rather than bliss in the afterlife. Having experienced conditions of destitution until recently, wealth and fame have become life-goals for many Koreans. They are materialistic in orientation with a strong motivation to achieve success here and now. This is immediately evident when one sees the ruthless and almost inhuman efficiency of their dealings resulting in a callous and often hostile attitude towards others. This is also a consequence of their emotion-centred mindset. The Koreans, therefore, demonstrate extraordinary goodwill, cooperation, and hospitality towards family, clan members and close friends, and, as I said, a callous, often hostile attitude towards all others.

Indian and Korean corporate cultures

I have talked above about the attitudes of the people and how this is reflected in the way business is done. Now, let me talk about corporate culture itself. I see important differences between Indian business houses and Korean ones.

First, corporate culture in India is highly individualistic. On the other hand, corporate culture in Korea is group-based or collectivistic with emphasis on order and harmony among group members. As a result, work preferences and evaluation systems in both countries vary sharply. While workers in India tend to prefer specific work assignments on an individual basis, and are evaluated and rewarded in terms of individual achievement, workers in Korea feel more comfortable with team-work assignments and a reward system based on seniority. Indian management in larger firms is task centred, with specialised division of labour being emphasised. In Korea, this is more person centred and is rooted in personal trust. In general, both managers and employees tend to regard the work organisation as an extension of the family.

Morality in Korea has traditionally been based on Confucian concepts of 'virtue' rather than on universal principles. Confucian relationships—the family, the clan, hometown ties, school ties, and company ties, generally in that order—come before everything else. In the western management style we follow in India, this is often considered irrational and unethical because it goes against the very foundation of rational behaviour by ignoring universal rules of conduct that transcend personal feelings and personal relations.

I come back to the mention I made earlier about the Korean way of respect for their seniors. Within companies, particularly among management and white-collar workers, seniority is generally equated with rank and authority, and demands strict conformity to a minutely prescribed protocol. Having said that, I find that Koreans are usually much more amenable to adopting western concepts than are the Japanese or Chinese, and one finds a much wider variety of management philosophies and techniques in Korea.

Since most Koreans still base their conduct on personal values and relationships rather than objective reasoning, employees expect companies to be paternalistic. It is a serious breach of social and business etiquette to put a young person in charge of older people and invariably causes endless problems.

Obviously there is some merit in the purely Korean way of conducting personal and business affairs, as evidenced by the number of Korean companies that are now among the world's leading enterprises. The challenge facing any enterprise wishing to deal with the Koreans is to achieve a balance between western and traditional Korean behavioural patterns—a merging of the best of the two systems.

Hints on doing business

I have discussed the Korean attitude which has resulted in the building of world-class companies. Let us now discuss doing business in Korea or, as is increasingly becoming the case, dealing with Korean firms here in India.

a) For the Koreans, very much like it is for Indians, business is a personal affair. The product, the profit and everything else takes a backseat to personal relations. The peoples of both these nations bend over backwards when dealing with a friend. If you do not or cannot establish good personal relations with a large network of people, it will either be difficult or impossible for you to do business with the Koreans.

b) Personal relations and contacts, combined with a high sense of honour and trust, are the primary foundations of Korean business ethics. Written contracts among Koreans are rare. Most business arrangements are based on verbal agreements. As a result of this system, Koreans spend a significant amount of time expanding and nurturing their personal contacts because their business depends on maintaining these relationships. Executives wanting to succeed with the Koreans must adapt to this system to a substantial degree.

c) It is essential that Indian business people programme this kind of activity (and expenditure) into the time frame of their plans and expectations. The more one tries to rush a decision or activity, particularly before the correct personal relationships have been established, the slower the process will be and the more likely the efforts are to fail.

d) I have talked to many Indian businessmen who believe that the right product and price is all they need to sell to or buy from any Korean company. This is a wrong assumption. You are not going to get anywhere in Korea until you establish the necessary human relations. This includes approaching the company in the 'correct manner,' meaning through an acceptable introduction and at the appropriate level.

e) In India, if you have the ear of the top man of a company, everything will be hunky-dory. This is the first mistake foreign business people make in their approach to doing business in Korea, believing that meeting the president of a company and getting the president's approval and cooperation means smooth sailing from then on. In most cases, the managers at the lower, middle, and upper rungs who actually run the company will resent being bypassed and will be less than cooperative, sometimes even to the extent of not allowing a foreign proposal to get off the ground.

f) It is all right to meet the president, but you must also meet and establish a satisfactory relationship with various managers, treating them with the same respect and concern that you extend to the president. This also applies to companies that are still in the hands of their founders who appear to be making all the decisions.

g) Because human relations are so important in doing business with Korean companies, it is vital that you keep yourself up to date on personnel and personal changes within companies. The character personality of a Korean company is as changeable as the ties and emotions of the people who make up the organization. It is therefore necessary to treat the relationship as a personal one, requiring regular maintenance.

h) To deal with a Korean company, it is essential to understand the personal relationships between managers at different levels, especially the relationships between individual managers and the directors or president. Personal ties such as kinship, marriage, belonging to the same school or sharing the same birthplace often take precedence over job seniority, rank or other factors and may have a significant influence on who actually runs a company and how it is run. A clear understanding of these ties is often necessary to identify the real decision maker in a Korean company. Getting all of this information may sound like a daunting task but it is really not so. Remember, the Koreans want to do business and they have departments to facilitate dealings with foreigners.

i) Although Koreans now readily sign contracts with foreign companies, the contracts are invariably interpreted personally rather than in the legal sense, making them no better than the personal relationship that exists between the two parties. If the relationship is not constantly renewed and reinforced, the contract becomes just a piece of paper. It is therefore very important for the Indian business owner doing business in Korea to be personally involved in all stages of the process of setting up the operation.

j) In dealing with the government, one must remember that bureaucrats in Korea are perhaps even more sensitive than usual to the social and business status of people who approach them. It is especially important that the foreign company dealing with them be aware of this. Sending in a young, lowly and inexperienced person is definitely not the way to go.

A very unusual point

I will now address a very unusual but important point to be noted by anybody wishing to deal with the Koreans. This concerns one of the most unusual aspects of Korea's clan-based society, and one that also plays a vital role in business and all other areas of life: people's names.

✓ Please remember that because of the special, almost mystical, role that names play in Korean society, Koreans are very sensitive about their names, and there are numerous taboos about using them.

Altogether there are more than 200 family names in Korea, but over half of all Koreans are named Kim, Lee, Pak or Choi. This situation apparently exists because Korea in the early days had only a few families whose names became imbued with a sacred quality and were assiduously maintained from one generation to the next. Confucianism incorporated the concept of revering one's ancestors, which further encouraged the maintenance of the family name and negated any inclination to adopt a new surname that would have no history and honour.

Another long-standing custom is for each Korean to have two given names, a personal one and the other, a generational one. This latter is chosen by the parents, grandparents or an onomasner, a professional name giver. A male generational name is given to the first son born in a family and a female generational name, to the first daughter. Thereafter, all additional sons and daughters in the family are given the same generational name. As the family branches out over generations, the generational name continues in the male and female lines so that eventually very distant relatives may have a common generational name that can be traced back to a remote ancestor. A great deal of thought goes into the selection of both personal and generational names and it is still common for parents to seek the help of onomasners. The object is to select a name that is appropriate for the child based on time of birth and the parents' expectations of the child.

As I said above, Koreans are very sensitive about their names, and there are numerous taboos associated with their use. Generally speaking, first names are used only by family members and close school friends. Many older Koreans are so sensitive about their personal names that they do not like to hear other people say them aloud. Korean women do not change their names when they marry.

To get around the extraordinary problem created by having many people named either Kim, Lee, Pak or Choi, the Koreans use titles connected with their profession, place of work and rank. In a large company with hundreds of managers named Lee, Kim, Pak and Choi, the distinguishing factors would be rank (supervisor, manager, general manager) and the section or division to which these managers belong. If there are two or more manager Lees in one section, they may be referred to as manager Lee of Production No. 1, manager Lee of Production No. 2, and so on.

On the personal front, Koreans also use the areas where they live to identify each other. Many of the most common names in Korea may be spelled in two or three different ways. Certain syllables of the Korean language are also pronounced differently by different people, making the names sound different, especially to foreign ears that are not totally sensitised to the variations in the language. This situation creates special problems for foreigners newly arrived in Korea. Not being aware of the seriousness of the situation, they frequently fail to remember the titles/ranks and sections or departments of people concerned and are therefore unable to identify which Lee, Choi, Pak or Kim they want to meet or talk to. Koreans who have been educated abroad or have had substantial experience with westerners in Korea have become accustomed to foreigners addressing them as Mr, Mrs, or Miss, and it is becoming more commonplace for them to use these western titles when addressing each other, especially when they do not know an individual's proper Korean title.

4.4 *Overseas Chinese business culture*

I have lived and worked with overseas Indians in many countries and have also worked with the overseas Chinese in South-East Asia. Nobody denies that the overseas Chinese have done far better than overseas Indians. Why is that so?

We have discussed overseas Indians in Chapter 3.4 and in this chapter, I am going to take a hard look at what makes the overseas Chinese tick and contrast it with how Indians behave under similar circumstances.

DEFINITIONS:

ETHNIC CHINESE: There are many nations like Malaysia, Indonesia, Thailand and the Philippines where the Chinese are in a minority and are working with other races. For the purpose of discussion I will use the term 'ethnic Chinese' to mean the people of Chinese origin who are citizens of these countries, with full voting rights. In addition, there are many Asian nations like Singapore and Taiwan which are predominantly Chinese.

ETHNIC INDIANS: Similarly, I will use the term 'ethnic Indians' to refer to people of Indian origin who are citizens of countries such as Malaysia, Singapore, Kenya and South Africa. I have already explained in Chapter 3.4 that the term NRI refers to a completely different category of Indians, not relevant to the discussion here.

The idea behind this chapter is to compare the behaviour of people living 'away from home'.

- The context is a continuation of what has been discussed in Chapter 3.4., that the ethnic Chinese have been responsible for the massive export growth of mainland China but that ethnic Indians have been able to do no such thing for India. Indeed, the Chinese are now making successful inroads into Indian domestic markets too.
- Another strong reason for my writing this is to explain why Indian visitors often get a cold response from the Chinese in South-East Asia when seeking appointments.

The Chinese diaspora

Many countries have produced travellers, but generally in a limited range of modes. Many settled, but the pattern has usually been one of colonisation or of annexing the new arm to the parent body. Then, if you were as disorganised as an ancient Greek city-state, the limb fell off of its own accord and, if you were as insensitive as Britain or as weak as Spain and Portugal, it wrenched itself free with a lot of pain.

The Chinese have also had such colonies. What is now south China was once alien ground. Like a lucky few, however, they have kept what they had won. Prosaically again, some of these peoples traded abroad. What was unprecedented was the sudden, huge efflux that began in the 19th century and led to their permanent settlement overseas in foreign states.

- Before, during and after the days of the British conquest, Indians also left in fairly large numbers and took abode in many lands. They were happy, however, to remain second-class citizens and made no conquests (see Chapter 3.4 for a detailed discussion on this).

The precursor wave of overseas travel and trade started during the era of the late Ming dynasty, in the form of Ming loyalists who settled all over what is now called Indo-China, Taiwan, etc. By no means was everyone who ventured across the waves running scared. A fair few seized the opportunity, managed to get additional foothold (in South-East Asia to begin with, further afield later on) and eventually built two homes, one in the adopted country and another in China. Younger brothers and cousins would be sent for to help set up and run the family business; successful merchants would travel home to marry, show off outrageously and bring back a bride; subsequent sons would be sent 'home' for a 'proper' education; all aspired eventually to be buried with their ancestors.

Today, the young and dynamic nation called Singapore, with an over 70 per cent ethnic Chinese population, owes much of its basic ideology to Chinese tradition. Confucianism is taught at schools.

Chinese business culture

Let us take a look at some aspects of Chinese business culture in contrast to the western (American) and Indian business cultures discussed earlier, and explore how the former is manifesting itself in entrepreneurship and in the management of businesses by the ethnic Chinese.

Remember, my discussion is limited to business aspects only and my intention is not to discriminate against or belittle other aspects of Indian culture. In these other aspects we are closer to the Chinese than to the West.

It is interesting to note that the Chinese business organisation has strongly retained its original basic character in spite of very open economies in nations where the overseas Chinese are in place, and in spite of potential influences by MNCs and transglobal connections. Most other Asian nations have deliberately been courting western technology since their independence.

Chinese management is, even in modern times, mostly a one man show: an autocratic boss assuming responsibility for all management functions. The Chinese manager is very 'boss-centred' but also intensely self-reliant. The proper word for a Chinese business organisation is 'personalised' or 'personified'. There are conventions as well as constraints set by the person at the centre of the organisation, the owner or his representative, and in this it differs strongly from the western management mode.

Autonomy, to become a boss, is the dominant driving force in Chinese entrepreneurship. But this driving force seems to be more vigorous and widespread in, say, Hong Kong than in Singapore. The former is fostering what may be called entrepreneurial capitalism while the latter is championing managerial capitalism.

Familism

Families are not only the bedrock of Chinese society, they are also the bedrock of Chinese business. A Chinese firm is almost always a family firm. Chinese tradition puts the rights of the group ahead of those of any individual. In Asian cultures, individuals have a very deep attachment and sense of belonging to ethnic groups, and the Chinese, very unlike the Indians, but like the Japanese, score very low in individualism.

One reason why the Chinese family system is so important is that it provides for security in an insecure world. For the Chinese who left their homeland (often forced out) and tried to settle abroad, the environments were not always easy or friendly. As a consequence, strong family self-interest is rampant in many of these societies. Perhaps not surprisingly, in Singapore, there are strong declarations by the government supporting the social responsibility of businessmen towards family.

Peter Drucker has said that 'the secret of modern Japan consists in Japan's ability to make a family out of a modern corporation.' The secret of Chinese management may well consist in the ability of the Chinese to convert the family into a modern corporation. Comparing Japanese and Chinese managements, we can also say that the Japanese style of management may best be described as 'head-office oriented' while the Chinese style of management may be characterised as 'grandpa oriented'. It should be noted that a 'family' may here include people from the same ethnic background and even birthplace. Kinship terms (like 'uncle' and 'aunt') are widely but loosely used in social interaction, even if not genealogically accurate. The overseas Chinese have built their strength on, among other factors, an unusual ethnic solidarity, even clannishness.

- HOW ABOUT EUROPEAN FAMILY BUSINESSES? Family-run businesses are, of course, not the monopoly of the Chinese. There are many studies which show that family businesses dominate the economies of many countries. Jonathan Boswell in his excellently researched book *The Rise and Decline of Small Firms* (1973) has said that the boards of nearly two out of three medium-sized British manufacturing enterprises (25–500 employees) were family dominated. He also estimated that 80 to 90 per cent of all Dutch businesses are family owned. Comparable findings have reported that family farm products accounted for two-thirds of the value of all farm products sold in the US. There are similar studies for rural agricultural and industrial enterprises in India.

There is, among the Chinese, a much stricter borderline between family and non-family (or non-ethnic) members both in attitude and behaviour. Also, growth in Chinese business is commonly carried out not by expanding the same firm (thereby possibly losing family control) but by mushrooming another family unit run by a relative.

For the new Chinese family member, starting a business is relatively easy. First, the former employer gives his/her blessings to the employee to strike out on his/her own and, indeed, often encourages and assists the employee financially. Second, businesspeople from within the ethnic network provide facilities and credit. In the language of Indonesia's former colonial power, Holland, the employee is furnished with a *catabelece* or a letter of introduction. In cultural terms, the *catabelece* is like a golden key—it opens doors locked to others. This sense of family loyalty and mutual responsibility is reflected in the fact that most shares of large Chinese Indonesian companies are owned only by the families of the Chinese Indonesian business magnates.

• I would contrast this with overseas Indian families whose businesses invariably split and are often destroyed when the patriarch dies as the children start fighting to break up the estate. Indian-owned businesses in South-East Asia are characterised by infighting and bickering. Not only businesses, even Indian political parties in these countries have been split many times.

Guanxi

This is a nice-sounding Mandarin word, pronounced exactly as it is written. It is very difficult to translate and can roughly mean 'relationships', 'common bonds,' or 'connections': almost a human version of the internet. The Chinese business environment can best be described as a series of interlocked networks. This is a key element of Chinese business. The distinctive feature of the overseas Chinese model has never been the individual firm but a network of them. This is Guanxi.

You need contacts everywhere in the business world, but if you magnify their importance many times, you will understand Guanxi. Hundreds of books have been written about Guanxi, but it takes a lifetime for a non-Chinese to master the concept. Every Chinese society in Asia is built around relationships and a unique sense of trust. In the West, it is business first and then trust and networking; in Asia, there is networking first and then business.

An important aspect of this networking is the mentality or the attitude of the people involved. All parties need to have the patience, motivation, training and tools for conflict resolution. How do we agree to disagree? How do we agree to solve our problems together? For example, do we agree to trust each other's intentions regarding the unwritten partnership, no matter the depth of the disagreement? Guanxi has to be in your blood or it will not work.

Guanxi is based on mutual obligation. In an extended family, members are mutually obligated to help one another. For instance, a wealthy member helps a poor one. Similarly, in business organisations, it is common for members of a family to use their family connections to try to obtain jobs or other benefits. The overseas Chinese have found that dialect, kinship or common origin in a clan or a village have placed them on a more sure footing of trust with regard to business deals conducted even at great distances. In fact, the overseas Chinese power rests on a sort of an underground network. Regional identity is important to a Chinese anywhere in the world.

All over Asia, there are small, intensely independent, family-owned firms working with each other. Independent family-owned firms specialising in different fields of design, manufacturing, marketing and financing build instant networks whenever an opportunity arises. This is typical of all overseas Chinese.

- An important reason for the failure of Indian firms is due to the fact that they are mostly small, independent units, working on their own and happy to remain small and isolated. Indians would rather not have growth if it required giving up or sharing absolute control. Though the Chinese businesses stay singularly apart, when an opportunity presents itself, they close ranks and cooperate.

Characteristics of ethnic Chinese

Most ethnic Chinese in Indonesia and Thailand live in urban areas and are involved in what can only loosely be called 'business.' This is not to say that they are all entrepreneurs. Indeed, one finds ethnic Chinese in all walks of life, namely as wage-earners, professionals, civil servants, army officers, etc. Nevertheless, it is important to realise that although this group makes up no more than 3 per cent of the total population in countries like Indonesia, it controls approximately

80 per cent of all private business. Their activities encompass almost every sector of the Indonesian economy. Wealthy Chinese Indonesian capitalists have for many years enjoyed the enthusiastic patronage of Indonesia's most powerful men and women.

✓ This is in contrast to Indians in countries like Malaysia and Singapore where they are about 12 per cent of the population but have no tangible control over any business. Even in countries like Fiji, where Indians constitute about 45 per cent of the population and are incharge of running the economy, they do not have any tangible control over it.

The size of a particular Chinese business can vary as much as the goods and services in which it trades. Individual concerns range from small family firms to corporate empires. For anybody intending to conduct business anywhere in the Asia Pacific, it is difficult to avoid this highly successful group. This is why it is essential to appreciate their distinctive business culture, an enormous advantage to those wanting to export to these nations.

For the Chinese, networking or Guanxi builds trust. This is a fundamental principle of conducting business with the ethnic Chinese community. A trustworthy associate will find it easier to obtain concessions. Moreover, the advantage of gaining the trust of a partner or associate is that investment capital can often be raised very easily and repaid after the enterprise is established.

I have seen that networking is very effective in Indonesia and Thailand. A network is often the spontaneous creation of an informal business group to seize an opportunity. This group centres its activities on mutual objectives and is formalised merely by a gentleman's agreement. There are many such groups operating within the Chinese community, frequently competing with each other in other activities.

• The important question is, how does the non-Chinese business-person gain access to these networks in these countries?

Network groups often use the services of a common, always Chinese, accounting firm, corporate lawyer or business consultant. There are many such professional firms in Indonesia and Thailand.

The boss of a particular company often organises this type of professional assistance. Each accounting firm, lawyer or consultant operates within several different networks at the same time. The assistance of these professional firms makes breaking into a network possible, and accelerates the building of mutual trust.

The importance of trust can be further seen in the fact that ethnic Chinese prefer to deal with reliable people rather than through formal business systems.

> ✓ A very important point to note is that a visiting Indian businessman often finds an impenetrable wall in front of him when seeking an appointment with ethnic Chinese in Malaysia and Singapore. This is because there were Indians before him who did not bother about the sort of a goodwill they were leaving behind. The Chinese talk to each other about such people and newcomers get booted out in the process.

Chinese management style

In a Chinese company, the formal organisational structure is often similar to the western model. However, it is the management practice which differs from similar models in the West. There appears to be a distribution of authority through various departmental managers with almost no clear delegation of authority. Instead, the 'system' is characterised by a 'one-person show'. For example, the managing director, who is usually the head of the family, gives commands, oversees and controls departmental managers without conforming to a formal management structure. Again, one reason for this is that the Chinese place their trust in people rather than in systems. This patriarchal approach is very common and is successful.

The manner in which the ethnic Chinese conduct business, while distinctive, is not as secretive as some believe. Business people use a simple principle: they are what I would call creative imitators. They readily adopt the successful methods of others and adapt them to their own requirements. They have a very sharp eye for good ideas and are not restricted by political dogma, philosophy or method. They are impressed by, and use, whatever method works best.

Never say never

Another way in which ethnic Chinese have been successful is that they almost never say they cannot do something. When asked whether they have the organisational or technical ability to provide a service or manufacture a specialised item they will always say 'yes'. This is despite the fact that they may not have the capacity to do so at that particular moment.

> ✓ This is true of Indian businessmen as well who think they can do anything. But herein lies the difference: While a businessman from the West may refuse to accept an offer on the rational grounds of his own limitations, the Indian businessman will make a commitment purely on bluster and then quietly walk out and make sure he is never seen again if things go seriously wrong.

For the ethnic Chinese, the failure to fulfil a commitment will cause him to 'lose face'. As this can almost be fatal, it enforces his or her own resolve to achieve success. I have seen many cases where a Chinese businessperson embraces the project as a personal challenge.

The ability to fulfil commitments is often tied up with the concept of 'credit worth'. Again, this is developed through a business network. This phenomenon encompasses an international 'brotherhood' of Chinese people, people from the same clan or dialect group. Membership is based on trust and reliability. If you can prove to your business associates that you have these qualities, then you are welcome into their network and they will see to it that you do not fail your commitments.

Another thing to remember is that the Chinese have the cultural capacity to meet any specification you want. This can be further illustrated with the following example:

In some countries in the West take-away fish and chips are very popular. One day a man went into a fish and chip shop and tried to place an order for something which was not on the menu. Ordinarily, the fish is fried in crumbs or batter but this order was for fish fried without crumbs or batter. The customer was unable to find a shop which could process this order as it was outside certain cultural and cognitive terms of reference. Apparently no one ordered fish like this. The order was not met perhaps because it was difficult to determine the price, or because extra work was involved, or because the store owner felt that the man did not know what he wanted. The Chinese businessperson, on the other hand, will gladly accept such an order. The same principle applies to everything the Chinese do. In the absence of formal procedure, anything is possible.

Relationship building

Business negotiations with the ethnic Chinese can be a lengthy process. It is common for all Chinese to invest a great deal of time in getting to know their business associates before they settle contracts, and it is considered culturally appropriate for most of these discussions to take place over dinner or late into the evening. Because of this, the best time to make an appointment to see the 'big boss' is after so-called office hours. Many business visitors fail to take advantage of the enormous business opportunities that exist in Asia because they tend to constrict their business dealing hours: they start and finish their business meetings according to strict, pre-determined timetables. Remember, if an agreement is not achieved within what you regard as a reasonable period of time, you should not try to end the meeting. Instead, be patient and keep going. You should continue with discussions until you get an invitation for dinner and then pitch for your case before, during and after dinner.

The Chinese are here too

In 1962, China took India by surprise when wave upon wave of its soldiers crossed the Himalayas, overran Indian outposts and moved through the hurriedly mobilised defense columns. Seemingly, India has not learnt any lessons from that because it has once again been surprised. Only this time the battle is being fought in the marketplace.

The Indian industry has been given a storm alert, caused by a five-fold increase in Chinese imports in the last six years. This time, the advance army of the Chinese invasion was made up of products like cigarette lighters, electrical components and toys. From attacking the low end of the Indian market in the early 1990s, the Chinese have now begun raising their sight.

✓ For Chinese, please read overseas Chinese, because it is mainly the overseas Chinese who have gone into China and set up superb manufacturing capacities using equipment and technology which is obsolete (and useless) elsewhere, but is excellently suited to the hoardes of low-skilled and low-wage Chinese workers.

The Chinese are knocking at India's gate with a range of consumer durables, the forerunner of which, Konka TV, is already on shop shelves. The products do not come with the brand aristocracy of American labels, or the marketing chutzpah of the Japanese but are capable of giving domestic producers goose pimples because of the ridiculously low levels at which they are priced.

The Chinese challenge is not just of the market-opening variety. It is very real. The value of China's export of electronic components to India shot up 15 times between 1993–94 and 1998–99. If you dismantle an Indian TV set, you'll see 'made in China' labels on dozens of parts. These labels are embedded not only in colour TVs but on the mouse being clicked on to write this, in the hard disc of the computer and within the compressor of the air conditioner.

The Chinese companies are obviously orchestrated on the one hand by the Chinese government which fully owns all the four new entrants to India except Konka, where its stake is 85 per cent (the rest of the equity being held by banks and private investors), and on the other by overseas Chinese entrepreneurs from countries such as Singapore and Taiwan who bring in the technology and carry away the output.

India has become a market of choice for the Chinese. India and the US are Konka's focus markets, because of India's trade liberalisation and steady economic growth. The consistent lowering of the tariff wall has made it possible for Chinese companies to bring in completely assembled colour TV sets or airconditioners and sell them in India after paying the requisite import duty.

China's globalisation efforts, sponsored by the overseas Chinese, have obviously resulted from the same cycle that Japan and South Korea had earlier gone through: domestic demand leading to a capacity expansion so large that only low cost subsidised export can save assembly lines from rusting. The only difference is that production capacities in China are large even by the standards of its Asian neighbours.

That should particularly worry Indian appliance makers, many of whom are now integrating vertically, making all components under one shed. Yet, their volumes are small and cannot match Chinese prices, even after customs duty has been paid. A typhoon is poised to rip through the Indian market.

4.5 *The Asian renaissance*

IS THE WORLD ONLY LIMITED TO THE US AND EUROPE?

All over India, I have met exporters and traders interested in exporting. They are invariably interested in only knowing what to export to the US and Europe. They never ask me how to export, what the problems are that one can expect or which the most attractive markets are given the circumstances, etc. They only want addresses of importers in the US and Europe and a list of items. If I want to talk about the huge potential we have of exporting to what is called the Asia-Pacific Rim countries, our friends quickly get bored and change the topic.

I will be addressing here in some detail the 'what, where and how' of exporting to the Asia-Pacific Rim nations. I think it will be a good idea to have an overall look at these nations and talk about how they have quickly made their presence felt on the world market: what many observers have called the Asian Renaissance.

The Asian network

A new collaboration is being forged in Asia for the first time. A new network of nations based purely on economic linkages is emerging: the Asian network. It is imbued with a spirit of working together for mutual economic gain. The catalyst is the free market.

Earlier these were discrete countries, each working on their own, divided by culture, language, political ideology, religious philosophies and, of course, geography. The new Asia, forged by economic integration, technology, especially telecommunications, travel and the mobility of people, is increasingly looking like one coherent region.

It is something like the early 1960s in Europe. At home people called themselves English, French or German, but when outside the region they began, for the first time, to call themselves Europeans. Similarly now, people throughout Asia are beginning to call themselves Asians.

There is a message in this. Business leaders in Asia already have a sense of the real importance of the event occurring today. The West, up to now preoccupied with its own well-being, is also waking up to what is going on in Asia today and realising how this is radically changing the world. The economic resurgence of Asia has been mainly driven by an aggressive global network of Chinese entrepreneurs and off-shore money, and is moving towards eclipsing the West.

The Asia-Pacific rim

An interesting term that the media has recently coined is the 'rise of the Asia-Pacific Rim'. As always, economic development plays a vital role in the shifting dominance of various geographic regions. The dominant role earlier was played by the Mediterranean countries. This shifted to the Atlantic region in the twentieth century. The end of the last millennium further shifted the focus to the Asia-Pacific Rim countries.

Though the geographic definition of the region called the Pacific Rim includes a vast area from the west coast of South America northwards and from Russia southwards to Australia, the term Asia-Pacific Rim is nowadays normally used to denote the Asian countries from Myanmar to Korea. India to the West and Japan to the East are not considered a part of this.

The shift in focus to the Asia-Pacific Rim is mostly due to the dynamic nature of economic development in these countries in recent years. It is expected that within a decade, the GNP of the Asia-Pacific Rim countries will be equal to that of Europe or the US. The region has diverse cultural and religious traditions. Though it is dominated by Japan at present, the region has already witnessed a shift in power within east Asia. The growth-rate in each of the four dragons (South Korea, Taiwan, Hong Kong and Singapore) has been five times more than that seen in the European countries during the Industrial Revolution. The four dragons have adopted the strategy of trying to beat Japan at its own game. They have been able to skip the industrialisation phase and make a direct, very robust entry into the information economy.

It was during the 1980s that four Asian countries, variously designated as the four dragons, four tigers and newly industrialising economies became the focus of attention and appreciation. These four countries were, as mentioned, South Korea, Hong Kong, Taiwan and Singapore. In a later chapter, we will be looking at the profiles of these countries to provide background information on their political natures and economic policies, particularly directed towards the inflow of foreign direct investments.

Despite their varied backgrounds, all of them had economies which were outwardly oriented. All the four economies developed due to their policy of export promotion. All of them started attracting industries due to low labour costs. Gradually, they have moved to active foreign-sales and product-market push and are now trying to develop their own brands in the international market.

- Hong Kong, as a British colony, has had laissez faire policies. The Sino-British agreement made Hong Kong a part of mainland China in 1997. Though Hong Kong is now fully a part of China, it is acting as a gateway to the giant dragon that is China through its trade and investment activities and has become an entrepot for China's economic interaction with the outside world. The market mechanism introduced by Deng Xiaoping in China in 1978 has facilitated cross-border trade
- South Korea (used, in this context, also as Korea) has substantially increased its per capita income during the last two decades. It has been under authoritarian regimes for the major part of the last three decades. However, it actively promoted exports first with labour intensive industries and later, heavy industries. The new President is trying to create a 'new Korea' by promoting conglomerates in order to become a member of the rich countries club. Till recently, Korea adopted very restrictive policies towards inward FDI but it now wants its enterprises to move outward and compete internationally.
- Singapore is an example of a city state which has exploited its geographic location and its highly disciplined, educated and skilled workforce to act as an entrepot to Asian countries, becoming, in the process, one of the wealthiest countries in the region. In spite of being under an authoritarian regime, the inflow of FDI into Singapore was actively encouraged. It followed, from

the very beginning, a 'world market' policy instead of an import substitution one, and has one of the most FDI-friendly policies in the region

- Taiwan is changing its economic structure by shifting from labour-intensive products to the production of high-value electronic items. Taiwan, like Korea, has been under authoritarian regimes and only recently has there been a movement towards a multi-party system of governance. It is also changing its policies towards inward FDI
- Other Asian countries like Malaysia, Thailand, Indonesia and the Philippines have joined to form the Association of South East Asian Nations (ASEAN) to focus on economic development

India has also started improving its relations with South-East Asian countries. In 1992, it became a sectoral partner of the ASEAN in areas like science, technology, tourism, trade and investment, and now has 54 joint ventures going with ASEAN countries.

The new multinationals

The budding, indigenous multinationals of these nations are becoming more proactive in their approach to international business. Most multinationals in South-East Asia are management and investment companies, not tied to specific products. Their procedure is to identify opportunities, recruit managers, borrow the money and then buy the technology through a joint venture.

The *chaebols* of South Korea, conglomerates which are now concentrating on a few areas in which to compete globally, are moving away from this initial stage to developing new products on their own or entering into global strategic alliances with other multinationals. Samsung's move in advanced computer workstations and the path-breaking designs of the new compact cars from Hyundai are examples of the change in position from being a recipient of technology to the forging of an alliance for development.

The Hong Kong multinationals are mostly engaged in trading activities. Many ethnic Chinese here have become tycoons in a short span of time and are expanding their business into mainland China and into other Asian countries. The dramatic growth of these enterprises has posed a threat to the established multinationals of other countries. While many multinationals were hesitant to enter China, enterprises from Hong Kong were in the forefront of investment here. It has also acted as a conduit for other foreign investments into China.

Taiwanese multinationals show a gradual, step by step approach from being OEM (original equipment manufacturers) suppliers to procuring licenses from others to then establishing their own manufacturing units overseas. They have used different strategic components in their internationalisation scheme such as technological innovations, a marketing and advertising approach, a global channels orientation and a regional focus.

The modernisation of Asia

The modernisation of Asia—economically, politically, and culturally—is by far the most important event taking place in the world today. The true force behind this modernisation is ruthless and immensely sophisticated, though secretive and so invisible to most. It is this force which is rapidly catapulting China into becoming the world's dominant economy. It is a decentralised, pan-Asian, increasingly global, and family- and education-oriented force. And most of all, fabulously rich. It is the phenomenon of the ethnic Chinese. There are 57 million of them, 53 million in Asia alone.

The ethnic Chinese are the new great economic power. Though this phenomenon has been around for centuries it is only now that the world is becoming aware of its extraordinary presence.

I have already discussed some aspects of the overseas Chinese particularly in terms of a contrast with the overseas Indians in Chapters 3.4 and 5.7., but if we need to look at the dynamics of Asia's extraordinary growth, it cannot be understood without a thorough examination of the ethnic Chinese who live outside the mainland. Arguably, they are the greatest entrepreneurs in the world. According to an assortment of estimates, the economy of the borderless ethnic Chinese is the third largest economy in the world, after the US and Japan.

The astonishing revelation of the tremendous economic power of the Chinese is not confined to public listed companies. It includes the less glamorous, small and midsize enterprises which together make up 96 per cent of all companies in the Asia Pacific Economic Cooperation (APEC) realm. According to Bustanil Ariffin, the former Indonesian minister who co-chaired the Pacific Business Forum in 1999, small and midsized Asian companies employ half of the workforce in most Asian countries and the Chinese own 90 per cent of these.

In the thriving new countries of Asia, the ethnic Chinese control a huge chunk of the wealth, far more than their numbers might suggest. According to Bustanil Ariffin:

- In Malaysia, they represent almost 30 per cent of the population and, at one time, accounted for 60 per cent of the economy. The New Economic Policy of the present government is addressing this imbalance and the hold of the Chinese on the economy is being sought to be checked
- In Indonesia, they are only 3.5 per cent of the population and account for 70 per cent of the economy
- In Thailand, they make up 10 per cent of the population and account for 80 per cent of the economy
- In the Philippines, they constitute two per cent of the population and account for 50–60 per cent of the economy

Some historians go so far as to say that till recent times, the economies in South-East Asia were in a sense leased to the ethnic Chinese, while the indigenous peoples concentrated on government.

The ethnic Chinese are not a nation-state, and the vocabulary and concept used to think about nation-states will not help us understand the phenomenon. The Chinese overseas are a network of networks. This is a new paradigm, a new formulation within the framework of the world's economy.

All the key players among the ethnic Chinese know each other. Though their businesses stay singularly apart, they work together when necessary. They are intensely competitive among themselves, and exclude outsiders, especially those not of the same family, village or clan. When a crisis arises or an opportunity presents itself, they will close ranks and cooperate. Chinese business boils down to people and contacts.

The family businesses of the Chinese overseas are networks, of companies, enterprises, clans and villages. These networks are in turn part of larger networks, something like the internet. The other general characteristic of both the internet and the ethnic Chinese network is that no one is in charge. It is the marketplace which is the deciding factor. Economic decisions involving China are driven purely by the dictates of the market and are guided strictly by the rates of return.

Individual ethnic Chinese networks of companies are completely decentralised from the whole, they are extraordinarily efficient parts. The Chinese function efficiently as individuals, in contrast to the Japanese who only excel collectively. This mode of operation makes the Chinese, and their enterprises, immensely nimble in the competitive global economy. They react speedily to changing conditions, especially to political vagaries.

Taiwan

Events in Hong Kong were not going to escape other people's notice. The Taiwanese have caught on well. Back in the 1950s, Taiwan was part of the region's plastic-flowers- and flip-flop-sandals-economy. Things moved on when state planning created a series of industrial parks along the island's coast, each designed for a particular type of industry—petrochemicals and plastics from imported raw materials, cement, steel, and so on. But the economy really started coming alive when the government gradually stopped interfering. The bureaucrats now no longer tried to pick winners, though they still provided cheap science parks and handy tax breaks.

Hence the blossoming of companies like Acer, a computer company which has its main factory in the Hsinchu science park, two hours down the road from the capital, Taipei. Acer is now the world's third-largest maker of personal computers. Its boss is Stan Shih, who started his business life selling ducks' eggs off a street stall. Until 1993, all Acer's computer motherboards, the basic circuitry, would be assembled in Taiwan. But then, with local wages approaching US$ 600 a month and local labour falling short, Acer had to ship in hundreds of Filipinos. It thereafter opened factories in Zhongshan in China's Guangdong province and in Subic Bay in the Philippines. Now it has added another, in Mexico, and has assembly plants in Malaysia, Singapore, Indonesia and Dubai. Acer also has assembly plants in Britain, France and Italy. These are expensive to run but they are physically close to the market, enabling the final product to be quickly adjusted to meet local requirements. Mr Shih has got the message about distributed manufacturing networks.

It took Acer nearly 20 years after its foundation in 1976 to move to offshore production. Other companies are doing it more swiftly. About ten years ago Kuo Feng Corporation and Shamrock Technology, among others, started making personal computer monitors in Taiwan. Now, as demand for them levels off and profit margins fade, their manufacture is already seen in Taiwan as a sunset industry. But the sun is not disappearing into the sea; it is just moving over the water into China, where costs are much lower. Both Kuo Feng and Shamrock plan to shift the bulk of their production to the mainland in the next 12 months.

5
A commonsense approach to exports

The Indian export effort is all topsy-turvy.

The people who should be exporting, our big business houses, are not bothered.

The people who are giving us an awful image, the self-employed, small-time, catalogue-carrying exporters, are going out in increasing numbers.

People who should not be allowed within miles of an overseas buyer, our babudom, are at the forefront of our export promotion effort.

First, make the world take us seriously

Topsy-turvy export effort.

I will seek to establish that one of the main reasons for our dismal performance in the export field is the level at which we have been conducting our export effort. The people who currently go out to sell, should not be, and the people who should be, do not.

✓ First, the people who should not be at the forefront: the hoardes of well meaning, self-employed but grossly unprepared small time traders carrying briefcases full of unrelated catalogues. These people, who make overseas trips to book orders, are giving us an awful image.
✓ Second, the people who should have been at the forefront of earning our foreign exchange, the larger business houses, are all inward looking and not taking any interest in this area.
✓ Third, the people who should not be within miles of an overseas buyer, our babudom, are at the forefront of our export promotion effort.

Let me first elucidate upon the last point from my personal experience. Our export promotion effort has hardly made a mark in the competitive global arena. I attended the SMAU Information and Communications Technology Fair at Milan, Italy, in October 1998, Europe's second largest in terms of visitors and volume of business transacted. The Indo-Italian Chamber of Commerce was invited to the fair and even promised free space. Not only did the delegation fail to make any noteworthy gains, it arrived late, came ill-equipped and, of course, had nothing significant to offer. This, despite the fact that Europe is a thrust area for Indian software exporters, especially after the formation of the European Union.

The Electronics and Computer Software Promotion Council (ECS), a commerce ministry sponsored body, was invited too. This body was babubom at its best. ECS accepted the invitation because its delegation was already going to Munich for the Systems '98 fair. With one fair following the other closely, the Munich fair closed on October 23, while the SMAU started a day before, the participants, mainly medium and small companies, found that they lacked the requisite infrastructure for both the exhibitions. The result: the Indian pavilion was bare on day one, boasted of less than half the total strength the next day and was totally geared only a day before the fair ended. The Indian displays were no match for those of other countries. And with reputable Indian names not part of the official delegation, and no one putting up stalls independently, it was not surprising that business inquiries were lukewarm. At the cocktail reception on the final evening, our officials said they were satisfied with what they had accomplished. This attitude is unlikely to take the domestic industry very far.

India was conspicuous by its absence at the same fair in 1999. Though the organisers invited the National Association of Software and Service Companies (NASSCOM), it couldn't turn up. I spoke to senior officials who said that they did not participate because the dates clashed with their annual general body meet and they did not wish to put up a poor show. The empty Indian pavilion on the fair grounds didn't send a very encouraging message.

The hosts too were disappointed at India's response. Even China came to the fair with an 18-member delegation. Trade fair enthusiasts say a delegation strength of at least 15–20 is needed at these fairs with a range of large-, medium- and small-scale players and a lot of gimmicks to attract attention. Then there's the issue of what India has to offer in the software fields. Going by global standards, not much. India has a strong foothold only in the customised single-client package market, which is a mere 20 per cent of the global market. The rest is the innovative multi-client product-and-packages market, where both risks and profitability are higher. India's share in this segment is a mere 0.01 per cent.

People who should export

If India has to consolidate its export business, it is the big business houses who have to lead the push. It is a tragedy that these business houses, who have the best brains and excellent managerial set-ups, still hanker after easy and immediate profit. They tend not to be interested in developing export markets either for themselves or for the nation. For the credo of the Indian firms, we only have to take a look at the issue of *Business Today* dated August 22, 1998 (p. 71). A detailed analysis of the export performance of 50 of the largest manufacturing companies, ranked as per their 1997–98 sales, shows that 'the majority of the country's largest corporations export so little, and the value of their imports so large that they are massive net negative exporters.'

50 of India's largest firms put together earn only Rs 800,000 million in foreign exchange, but spend a massive Rs 6,900,000 million every year. A drain of Rs 6,000,000 million in foreign exchange every year, perpetuated by the very people who should have been earning it. And, this drain is only increasing every year.

It is essential for larger firms in the well-organised and established private sector to take a leading interest in the field of exports. They must start thinking of going global as it is only these firms that can afford a long-term view and plan to have a stake in the goodwill being created. India must look to these firms, not to the government, for its deliverance. The first task for our export effort is to undo the damage that has been done to our goodwill.

What is wrong with the small exporter?

Well, I wish there was a simple answer. Actually, I wish there was an easy way to prevent the wrong sort of people from trying to export. I am talking about the non-traditional exports of engineering, innovative or consumer goods to non-traditional markets in the developing world. This is where the greatest potential for growth lies, and this is where well-meaning, self-employed, small-time traders booking overseas orders convey the image that India is not at all serious about doing business. Undoing this image and building a fresh image is our first task and, as I said above, it is only our larger business houses who have the means to do this.

There are countless small firms in India claiming to be exporters, listed as such in most export directories. In many cases, the phone number listed in their business cards is of the shop downstairs. These firms have a casual knee-jerk attitude towards exports.

The problem is worsened by the huge number of qualified export promotion specialists produced each year by institutions offering certificate and diploma courses in export management. Most of the institutions impart excellent training, and the students certainly get full value for money, but where is the market for these people? I have met many of them and they are, without exception, budding exporters. Somehow, the impression these youngsters have is that exporting is a far easier proposition than, say, a career in marketing.

A number of these budding exporters manage to make export promotion trips abroad. So, the same overseas buyer meets person after person who is unprepared, casual and non-businesslike. In the process, the very small number of genuine exporters get thrown out as well.

The real tragedy is that there is nothing that can be done to solve this problem. Forget the budding exporter, it is impossible to convince a small but seasoned businessman in say, Mumbai, not to waste his money by going on an order booking spree to a nearby country. He points to his successful track record of booking orders from places within the country as far afield as Chennai and Darjeeling. So, he collects a few random samples and catalogues of completely unrelated products and off he goes to foreign lands. That is the extent of his homework. I have had many such 'exporters' visit me when I was in Malaysia.

Small exporters ruining markets

Indian businessmen being impressive talkers, they do sometimes succeed in persuading overseas buyers to place small orders. Then, finding the complications in India overwhelming, and their resources inadequate, they write off the whole thing without a word to the poor buyer. At the end of the day, one is left with the trader listed as an exporter and the overseas buyer swearing never to deal with an Indian again.

What I have described above is tragically, not an exception but the rule. It is a sad fact that some of these small traders have multi-million dollar turnovers. In attitude towards professionalism, in terms of organisational structure and in their commitment towards earning long-term goodwill, however, they remain small-time traders. They are there only when the going is good. When the customer has a problem, the phone calls remain unanswered.

A market lost is a market lost

From my personal experience, I will analyse the example of two countries which could have been captive markets for India. Instead, we have worked very hard here to earn the quite undeserved reputation of being grossly unreliable people.

The two countries are Maldives and Kenya—vastly different nations with differing economies. The only thing common is the huge and untapped potential for low-technology exports.

Maldives, a small but very prosperous country only 45 minutes by air from Thiruvanathapuram, India, should have been a very attractive market for India. Their tourism industry has made them rich and they have no foreign exchange problems. Their consumption of consumer and hardware items is grossly out of proportion to their population of only 250,000. To my utter surprise, I saw the supermarket shelves full of items from all over the world, the bulk being from Malaysia including tinned food, tiles, toilet goods and tissue paper! I do not speak of hardware, engineering and electronic items from China, Japan or Europe as India cannot compete in these markets. However, India should have had an edge in fast moving consumer items of daily household need. But there was almost nothing from India except some low value added items like fruits and vegetables. There were very few manufactured goods and almost no fast moving consumer goods.

I felt that there was something seriously wrong here. The wage levels in Malaysia are four to ten times higher than those in India, as are the overheads, combined with which are the very much longer distances to export and service the market. So, how has such a situation come about? Before going into a discussion on this, let's first take a look at Kenya.

Unlike Maldives, which is a newly developed market, Kenya has traditionally been a good importer of low technology items from India mainly because the entire economy is in the hands of people of Indian origin. Recently, however, I found this market flooded with goods from, again, Malaysia and China.

Each trader in Kenya has a long list of horror stories of his dealings with Indian traders. The products we sell are OK and the prices competitive. What, then, is wrong? In the words of a dealer, 'importing from India is a prescription for hypertension.' None of India's large business houses have taken a direct interest in these markets or have a presence there. Representative offices of Korean and Singaporean firms, however, exist in the same city. They are there to handle any problem that may arise.

So, in both cases, it is the way we sell our products that makes the difference. The entire export effort is in the hands of the small-time traders I mentioned above. Products made by the business giants in India are purchased and exported by these small traders. The result is that buyers have always felt an increasing sense of frustration when dealing with India as against excellently organised firms from South-East Asia. The degree of professionalism these firms show is incredible, making the buyer feel secure and comfortable.

To give you a specific example, my host in Maldives was building an extension to his home and I went with him to select wall tiles and sanitary fittings. The shops had some very attractive products from India, of excellent quality and finish. What I found shocking was that my host did not want to even look at them though the prices were very attractive.

* The shopkeeper said that individual house owners did not like Indian products, though the quality was excellent. Only the very price-conscious contractors bought them. The reason was simple. If a few tiles got damaged after, say, two years, getting the same quality and shade would be impossible. The supplier from India would be a small agent and not the well-established manufacturer. If he bought Malaysian tiles, on the other hand, he would be buying directly from the manufacturer.

I could not believe my ears. When I came back to India, I looked up the exporters directory of the Federation of Indian Export Organisations. For anybody interested in importing from India, this directory is the master document.

I found a few entries for ceramic tiles and products, but they were all small firms dealing, besides, in a large range of unconnected items such as mushrooms, rice and vegetables. There was not a single well-known or established manufacturer.

I tried to test the problem in another context. In the first part of this book, I had discussed the problem of the export of toys. I had a friend of mine in Singapore contact the dozen or so firms listed under 'toy' and 'toys'. His was an enquiry concerning innovative wooden toys. There was no response.

First undo the bad image we have

Anybody interested in importing from India will find innumerable export directories and telephone yellow pages. Many of these are excellently prepared, but are overwhelmingly full of obviously small traders who claim to be able to export anything from handpumps to handicrafts. One understands that this cannot be helped as the publishers are not expected to go around checking the credentials of each and every applicant. So, a lot of well meaning but useless people get listed.

This, in turn, creates a problem for the prospective importer overseas. There are no Indian trading houses based in his country which he can contact, and he has no other means of getting any further information. He wades through whichever directory he can lay his hands on, writes twenty letters and gets no response. The importer gives up even before starting and goes off to another country.

- It is only the larger firm, committed to building long-term relationships, which will acknowledge enquiries promptly and follow up. In case the item is beyond its range it will, of course, refer the customer to someone who will be able to handle it. It is essential, in this way, that we undo the poor reputation we have earned.

It is essential that the large firms in India's well-organised and established private sector take a leading interest in the field of exports. This is easier said than done. To start thinking along these lines these firms have to cultivate a global mindset. Unfortunately, a large proportion of them do not even have a national mindset.

5.2 *Just get up and go*

Where does one go?

The basic reason for getting your firm to go global is to grow in the long term. For that, you must first decide on your target markets or regions. International markets can be segmented in numerous ways but for the purpose of this book and the convenience of discussion, I will address the issue of where to go by looking at three types of markets.

MATURE MARKETS. I would define a mature market as one with a forecast GDP growth rate of one to three per cent per year. The majority of the world's mature economies—the US, the countries of Western Europe, Australia—have already undergone significant industrialisation in the two preceding centuries. At present, most of these countries are well-developed, mature, industrial and consumer economies aiming to become technology- and information-based economies.

Typically, these economies have a well-developed infrastructure: government; health care; education; highways; a water system; telecommunications system; and industrial, retail, and consumer product sectors. Most of the economy is privately-owned, with capitalism (or a mixture of capitalism and varying degrees of socialism) and competition being the dominant economic ideologies.

As the domestic markets of these countries are mature, and because they have highly organised commercial sectors, they are increasingly marketing their products and services throughout the world to achieve growth. Mature and developed countries are seeking new locations with lower manufacturing costs and a well-developed industrial infrastructure to manufacture and re-export their products throughout the region. This is an excellent way for Indian firms to cash in on these economies.

This was the point I was addressing in the first few chapters of the book. I explained that often it is not the Indian firm that goes looking for the overseas market. One of the results of the massive globalisation, and the increasing maturity of the market in the developed world, is that your firm is likely to be contacted by a foreign customer, distributor or original equipment manufacturer. You have to learn to capitalise on this opportunity. They have obviously done their research and selected your firm for various geographical, technology or product attributes that you possess. They know more about you than you think. Don't bluff or play smart. And don't slam the door in their face even if you are unable to entertain their proposal. Keep channels open for future opportunities. These opportunities often enable small firms to leverage their research and development activities with the more advanced European and Asian firms.

DEVELOPING MARKETS are mainly countries which have achieved some degree of political stability and are working democracies of one kind or the other. These generally have a forecast GDP growth rate of four to six per cent or more per year. Consumers in these economies are beginning to have a high enough average disposable income and are now starting to develop brand preferences. Markets for products such as automobiles, cosmetics, various food brands, health and beauty aids and building materials for private housing are beginning to emerge. The governments of these countries are privatising sectors such as telecommunications and are investing capital in infrastructure improvements. These countries are now industrialising rapidly and so are a good market for the entire spectrum of industrial inputs.

EMERGING MARKETS are countries whose governments have stabilised only recently. One finds here that while most organisations or companies are publicly held and have been grossly mismanaged, there is a significant demand for industrial development of the very simple, low tech, labour intensive kind. Start-up capital is often not difficult and there are plenty of donor agencies working here for economic regeneration. These countries have been known historically for their cheap but untrained labour pool. Typically, these countries are attractive to three types of exporters from India.

- Manufacturers of products who can use local raw materials and cheap labour to sell locally and re-export their products throughout the region

- Developers of infrastructure projects
- Exporters of tough durable and very basic consumer goods, pharmaceuticals and vehicle spare parts, to meet the demand of a young, growing population. Invariably, these nations, as well as nations that have just come out of a long drawn civil or regional conflict, are an excellent market for anything to do with road transport, particularly for tyres and retreading material.

The early bird gets the worm

It is clear that if you do not capitalise on market opportunities in the diverse global market of today, your competition will. And, in the case of an Indian company, the competition may not just be another Indian company. Competing in the global marketplace means that the aggressive and better-organised firms will be ahead and, presently, this means the Korean, Japanese and Singapore Chinese firms. In developing and emerging growth markets, early market entry often translates into dominant market share. Once a local government has signed large infrastructure projects with your competitors and once consumers have switched their brand preferences from local brands to those marketed by your competitors, you will have a difficult time not only entering the market but also meeting the additional challenge of facing your competitors in global markets.

This can work in your favour too. If you are there early enough, and make your mark, you will benefit from this loyalty. In many respects, once established, international accounts often prove more loyal to brands. You see this in India too. Overseas suppliers have a more long-term relation with Indian customers than local ones.

Service, service and service

After making massive investments of time and money in winning markets, it is critically important to service international distributors, customers and affiliates. When you are competing in global markets, all you have is your reputation. While the world is a large place, you will be surprised how fast your reputation for products and services (either good or bad) can spill over into other countries within or outside of the region.

Most Indian manufacturers are already competing with multinationals on home turf. This experience should provide them with additional insight into the adaptation of products to international markets. Alternatively, this is the opportunity to compete against domestic competitors on their 'turf.'

In addition, when you are competing on a global basis, you can learn not only from other cultures but from global competitors selling in that country or local market. You can learn better ways of manufacturing, selling, distributing and servicing your products. This is a great opportunity to observe these methods and import them into your domestic operation.

Do as your customers do

It is important to focus your efforts in doing what your customers are doing. When your customers go global, you should follow them. In this day and age, your customers are more likely to be exporting their products or sourcing them from international markets. You must do the same. Or, you will find that you are losing your markets to people who are doing so. You could also gain a competitive edge by cultivating international contacts with scientists, researchers, marketers and so forth. More particularly, your global mindset should include:

1. A decision (and commitment) to sell your products in international markets.
2. A choice of one or two product lines that you believe has potential overseas.
3. A choice of an 'international champion' within your company, a person who is enthusiastic about taking charge of the operation.
4. A mental time-frame for your first export sale.
5. A mental picture of how you will service this business.
6. A decision not just to sell in the international market, but to be there.
7. Not wanting to look for agents or distributors in other developing countries and being determined to look for and work only with partners.

As I said earlier, you may sometimes be contacted by a foreign customer, and will be amazed by how much they know about you.

They have obviously done their research. The foreign firm has grown and reached the point where you are keen to do business with them mainly because they do their homework thoroughly. These business opportunities in turn enable small firms in India to also tap the benefits of these firms' research and development activities.

Clearly, the risk of going global will entail the expenditure of the precious, and probably limited, resources (human and capital) of your firm. Aside from the risk of the loss of capital, many firms are concerned about the risk of having their ideas, products and patents stolen or copied, with no legal recourse.

However, this risk is also prevalent in domestic markets, as there is no longer any such thing as a captive domestic market in this age of global competition. The race for global markets and for global competitiveness will only continue. While there is the risk that your foreign distributors/partners may not be able to reach their sales targets, the opposite is also a risk: that they will exceed their sales targets and you may not be able to fulfil their demand for your product!

Proceed step by step

Having determined a significant market demand and potential for your products and services in a country or a series of countries (a region), your next step would be to conduct in-depth research that will provide you with the following information:

1. Customer attitudes towards and preferences for your products or services.
2. Accurate market-sizing data, rural–urban breakdown demographics, mapping of distribution channels, and so forth.
3. Field product tests (feasibility studies). You need to know not only what products have succeeded in the market but, more importantly, what failed and why.
4. Studies regarding pricing.
5. A potential customer list.
6. Names of distributors, joint venture partners, strategic alliances, and so forth.

Having been in the business of gathering this type of information in developing countries for over three decades, I have found that published information on import and export statistics do not provide even a snapshot of the market opportunity in that particular country. So, the next step is getting out there and determining for yourself what the market opportunity is and how best to start cashing in.

The critical data and information is obtained purely through field research. Because this type of research is costly, it is important to first determine an approach to your global expansion efforts.

After you have selected your approach to globalisation, you should identify someone, either yourself or your top sales or marketing person, as your international marketing team leader. This person should be your champion for international growth. He should be sent abroad to meet with potential customers, representatives, agents, affiliates, and partners and should plan on spending at least one or two weeks there to gauge the total market potential for your products and services.

The only way to determine whether select countries are hot markets for your products or services is to go there yourself. You can maximise your travel budget if you plan trips on a regional basis. However, do not assume that countries within a particular region will have similar markets, customers, preferences, or a similar demand for your product. Also, be careful when granting an agent or distributor exclusive rights for a region. You could miss significant market opportunities on a country-by-country basis.

Your international champion should be able to standardise your sales presentation, yet adjust the sales pitch to the cultural nuances of each country. While your products and services in the domestic market may be mere commodities, they may possess a significant uniqueness in other countries. Moreover, you may be able to command premium prices for these products in developing and emerging growth countries. In some countries where high prices are expected (for example, Japan, Korea and Taiwan), a low price may even scare potential buyers off!

Your initial costs should comprise travel expenses, communications, literature and promotion materials, and so forth. You should avoid the expenses of leasing an office, hiring staff or negotiating formal joint ventures. All of this will be discussed in greater detail in the following chapter.

5.3 *Having a global mindset*

National mindset first, then global mindset

I have a friend in New Delhi who manufactures quality bathroom fittings, items such as taps, showers and soap holders. He has an extensive range of these chromium-plated brass fittings and is very careful about quality control. His brand is increasingly gaining respect and his business, growing. He has made a considerable investment of his time and money in making a number of trips to South-East Asia and Kenya. Indeed, he has been able to carve out a small foothold in some of the markets.

What I found surprising was that in India, his market was restricted to Delhi, Punjab, Haryana and UP, all within a radius of about 400 km. He has a small market in Madhya Pradesh and Rajasthan but has never sold anything in the South or in Mumbai. He makes no secret of the fact that he has never made an attempt to penetrate these markets.

He has all sorts of reasons which, considering his tight financial and manpower resources, do seem valid. His competitors in Mumbai and Chennai are based there and service the customers on a personal day to day basis. He will have to sell through agents and stockists and will face all sorts of problems requiring him to make frequent trips. It is clear that if he wants a reasonable degree of market penetration, he would need a long-term presence there. This does not, then, fit into his management strategy of maintaining absolute control over all operations. Very correctly, he also points out that firms in Mumbai and Chennai do not have much of a market in the north.

On the flip side, however, he thinks he will succeed in exporting to overseas markets when he does not even have the managerial set-up to handle markets in his own country. Every entrepreneur in India, like my friend, thinks exports are a breeze.

There are countless manufacturers who think global before thinking national. Every other manufacturer will tell you that he sells only in the immediate region and that 'we are also exporting.' Indeed, there are plenty of examples of some of these firms actually managing to get export orders. However, my experience of Indian exports to the developing nations I have worked in, is that it is always a short-term proposition, with exports fizzling out after a couple of deals. Invariably the problem lies in servicing the overseas customer. More importantly, one is leaving behind an unhappy customer swearing never to deal with India again.

First go global within your company

Let's now assume that you have decided to aggressively seek expansion into foreign markets. The text book approach of expanding overseas only after you have reached maturity in the domestic markets does not often work in a huge market like India. Indeed, one of the reasons for our dismal export performance is that there is always a lot to do in the domestic market.

There seems to be a bit of a contradiction here. I said above that before you develop a global mindset, it is a good idea to develop a strong national mindset. I said that it was going to be very difficult for well-established and respected firms, say, in the South, who are completely unknown in Delhi or Punjab, to start thinking global. The point was that they obviously do not have the organisation or the resources, and certainly not the mindset, to go national. If you look slightly below the surface of these firms, you will find an owner or a boss who decides on and does everything himself. He grows as an individual but his organisation does not. So, for a firm that wants to aggressively expand overseas, the managerial set-up has to be professional and senior executives must have decision-making leeway.

So, let's go back to assuming that you have decided to expand your business outside India, which means your business is professionally managed. While the thought of entering foreign markets is exciting, optimistic, and exhilarating, it is also overwhelming when you consider the size, complexity, and risk of expanding into global markets. Also, you should not approach global expansion as an alternative to your domestic business. Having a global mindset means realising that the need to go global lies at the heart of your business.

Within your firm, the biggest problem that you will face is internal: the inward-looking mindset of your owners/shareholders, management and staff. You will find people willing to take up an assignment overseas but when you tell them that you are not sending them to New York or London but to places like Nairobi or Dar Es Salaam, they will often lose interest and try to oppose the proposal. You will be asked/told that:

- We have limited resources
- We can barely handle our domestic business
- It's too risky
- We are not making enough money at home in our local markets
- How can we make a profit in foreign markets?
- It will take years for the international business to pay back
- We have never exported any of our products
- How do we go about this?
- Who in our company can/will handle this effort?

The timing of and commitment to globalisation are critical. There is never an optimum time. You have to make the expansion plans and follow them through. On the other hand, should the political and economic conditions of the countries selected change dramatically it would, of course, be prudent to delay your expansion efforts.

If you still have doubts, stay domestic until you're sure going global is a good decision. Companies with the highest rates of success in overseas markets are known to have cultivated 'global mindsets' from the very beginning. When you expand globally, you will do it because it is best for your company. If your firm is just getting started or in the process of becoming a regional company, you may need to concentrate your resources and capital. International expansion can fuel rapid growth that your firm cannot yet handle. The crunch need not only be financial. You also need trained, trusted people, besides the infrastructure within your organisation.

The global market place

The world is now rapidly becoming a global marketplace. Just about every aspect of our lives, from the food we eat, to transportation, energy, clothing, financial services, household goods and entertainment, is either sourced from or exported to other countries.

The new economy of the world today is dominated by inter-company trade and person-to-person communication. Countries no longer trade; people and businesses do. Networks strong in commercial and organisational infrastructure are at the core of the new global economy.

The cost of air and sea transportation has fallen significantly. Helped by rapid technological improvements in transportation and in information and communications networks, a new business model has been created. Big and small companies are pushing outward to reap the economies of geographical diversification. MNCs are traversing the world in search of markets and profits. They seek and cash in on the abundant resources and capabilities available in different countries. The result is a new entity called a 'production network.' Diverse production units in different countries network across the global economy, converting global inputs into outputs for global markets.

As the number of foreign affiliates rises, intra-firm trade is boosted. It is estimated that one-third of world trade takes place within transnational corporate networks, and more than half of the foreign affiliate exports of Japanese and American MNCs are conducted on an intra-firm basis.

Learn to make useful friends

Don't make the mistake of thinking that the world today is as competitive as it can get. This is only the beginning. Let's look ahead into this century by looking back 50 years. As I said when discussing our innovativeness, in 1945, the US was the only industrialised nation untouched by the devastation of the two World Wars. US business had no competition. The world was borrowing money from them to buy their products, and they could set their own prices and standards. However, they did not sit back and enjoy the monopolies they had, unlike India's big business houses in the heyday of the License Raj. US businesses went out and made alliances, set up subsidiaries, went into franchising in a big way and made sure the world remained their backyard.

Then came the Japanese, followed by the Koreans and the Taiwanese, who ruthlessly protected their home markets, but also went out and conquered the world. That was only the beginning, because we are now hearing of countries that were earlier never imagined as competition countries that were pejoratively labelled

'Third World' because it was thought they could never 'measure up': Mexico, the People's Republic of China, Malaysia, Thailand and Singapore.

What does this mean for you? What will your business be like when all these countries, powerful industrial forces, compete for your market share? They will be hungry for what you have. They will work long hours and, in the beginning, for less. They will exploit your competitive weakness just as the Japanese exploited the quality gap.

Most senior managers in India understand all too well that if their companies are not awake to the global challenge, they will be eaten alive by the competition. There is already a price competition in India's domestic markets. There will, in addition, be companies who will add better value than or innovate around you. Competitors will also lock you out of new customers through single-source relationships. These competitors might be next door or halfway around the world but, armed with a fax machine and a telephone, the global competitor will be talking and proposing to the customer whose workplace is only two blocks away from you!

The challenge in today's marketplace is to beat other products around the world in terms of innovation, price, quality, service, sales, marketing and responsiveness. But few companies have the expertise or a world-class leadership to address all these areas and come up with results. As such, it is prudent for Indian companies to team up with outsourcing or alliance partners in other countries that have the competencies and expertise they lack. It is only now that companies are discovering the power of teaming up with companies overseas for mutual performance advantages.

I am not, here, thinking about Indian firms setting up joint venture manufacturing operations with local partners in other developing countries. This was done in large numbers in the 1970s and 1980s with disastrous results. I am talking about networking with other firms elsewhere for an integrated marketing or manufacturing operation. The overseas Chinese are exceptionally good at this. The advantages are obvious. Companies choose the suppliers with the needed expertise and resources for a given venture or product line. The selected partners can then foster peer relationships. This form of business should not be confused with what is commonly done when firms form consortiums to bid for large projects: coming together for a market opportunity, dissolving when the opportunity ceases. What we are talking about is companies seeking a long-term presence in each other's territories without having to make the massive investment a branch office or a subsidiary would require.

It is clear that in the twenty-first century, companies in India will be operating in open-market situations, so those who are unable to adjust their operations to changing market conditions as fast as their competitors do will lose their market share, partners, investors and, possibly, employees. Remember, the competitor may not be an Indian company! Indian companies of the future should be able to quickly change their business processes and operations without putting undue strain on their resources. They must be able to redesign processes to support new market opportunities, supply chain partnerships, product characteristics, organisational change, or virtual operations. The only way of doing this is to forge cross-cultural alliances.

Cross-cultural competence

Why do homegrown MBAs succeed in some places and fail in others? It is largely because they fail to develop cross-cultural competence. For example, sensitivity to other cultures would entail understanding that Germans prefer facts, figures and logic to flowery presentations, or that time is elastic all over Africa, Thailand and Indonesia, or that it is not only India where people have a fatalistic view of things, leading to a relaxed worldview.

Cross-cultural competency is understanding other peoples' ways of thinking so as to anticipate likely cultural mines and come out unscathed. The importance of cross-cultural competence is obvious as is evident in the case of the $ 5 billion Euro Disneyland theme-park project in Paris where the American dream vision of a united workforce wearing Disney outfits and groomed the American way turned into a nightmare. The French way of thinking and their behavioural codes are vastly different from the American one. It took the organisation many years and millions of dollars to undo the damage.

Developing cross-cultural competency needs systematic planning and an organised effort. From selecting the right people, to garnering inputs, to supporting creativity to bridge the cross-cultural gap, the package does not come easy or cheap.

Is there a well-defined process for developing the cross-cultural competency of managers? Not really. At least, I have not found one. Instead, here are some basics. First, identify the target area. Then, find suitable people with the willingness to function in culturally diverse fields. Develop a cultural feasibility study identifying the real diversities at the target location, analyse the gaps likely to emerge and decide the cultural action plan to avoid booby traps. Next, identify a trainer with extensive overseas and business experience or engage a consultant. Provide inputs on the profile of the target country, cultural attitudes towards time, risk and decision making, communication and negotiation styles, employment issues, legal issues, issues surrounding hierarchy and formality and, of course, the country-specific manners and behavioural patterns. Additionally, provide a brief knowledge of the country's history, political structure, religion, geography and economy. Supplement the theoretical input with a visit, preferably in a group along with a mentor. Keep an account of interactions by videofilming and later analysing them. Make a list of people with international exposures and involve them in your cross-cultural orientation program.

A word of caution. Developing cross-cultural competence should be an ongoing activity in view of the rapid changes in demographic profile, values, ethics and a host of other factors. So, depending on the budget, size and other aspects of your organisation draw up a suitable plan and implement it. The rewards can be surprising.

Do not just think of going there, you must be there

Greater interconnectedness on the world business horizon implies dynamic growth and change. I will seek to establish how the last 15 years have seen the phenomenal growth of Japanese, Korean, and Singapore Chinese export houses. These are professional export houses who trade by 'being there' and have, in the process, changed the rules of the game. These firms now have an extensive network of branches in all the major cities in the world. They have conquered the developing world by having a presence all over Asia and in Africa, the West Indies and South America. Their strong organisational infrastructure is rapidly taking the market of non-traditional exports away from Indian export houses.

Sadly, even India's large export houses do not have any professionally-managed network outside of the country. Having a presence in another country does not necessarily translate into the expensive option of posting an executive there. As recently as the 1970s, it was only the very large corporations in the West that had the resources and capabilities to grow internationally and they did so primarily by establishing marketing offices or branch plants overseas. That is how a large number of multinational firms then made direct investments in other regions. Today, by contrast, new transportation and communication technologies allow even the smallest firms to build partnerships with foreign producers and entrepreneurs and to set up foreign bases to service distant markets.

In an earlier section we discussed at some length the negative goodwill generated because of the well-meaning but slipshod efforts of small-time traders: people who should *not* be spearheading India's export effort. I also mentioned that India's export effort has to be spearheaded by its larger corporations. It is only these firms who can pull the country out of the downward spiral of declining exports. Most foreign business development efforts in India today are a result of a casual or 'knee-jerk reaction' to what is reported in the press. One reads of business booming in countries such as Singapore, China, Korea, Malaysia and Thailand and of millions of companies and entrepreneurs transforming these traditional countries into economic powerhouses. So, how does one capitalise on these market opportunities in developed, developing, and emerging-growth countries?

Firms with a deep-rooted national mindset and firms with a strong presence in most parts of the country are the ones likely to be successful as professional export houses. Unlike the large multinational firm which would have a hefty budget for international market research, critical to market entry in foreign markets, a smaller firm would have limited financial and human resources and cannot afford to take significant risks in the global marketplace. This simply means that the nature and extent of homework small firms, like most Indian ones, must do before entering a new market is even more critical. The research must not only be on other markets and cultures but also on the driving forces behind these markets and cultures. We will talk about this in some detail in the following sections.

It is my contention that before you start developing a global mindset, you must have a strong national presence. I know many well-established and respected firms in South India who are completely unknown in Delhi or Punjab. It is pointless for these firms to start thinking global. They obviously do not have the organisation or the resources and certainly not the mindset to go global.

Let's assume you are a firm which has nationwide operations and a strong national presence. You may be a manufacturing, trading or services firm. If you are a large business house, you are probably all of these. The next step is deciding that you want a long-term interest in developing the export market. This can, or rather should, be a project by itself. So, you must start thinking of having a presence outside India. As I said, you cannot simply hire a suitable executive, set up an exports division, and go hunting for orders. You must determine to be a global player.

Remember, once you enter a foreign market with your products or services, you have to stay there. Companies that have entered a market, withdrawn, and then tried to enter again have not only had a very hard time establishing or regaining their market position but have also earned negative goodwill (the only exception being when a company is thrown out due to political considerations). International markets, particularly in the developing world, are like elephants: they do not forget anything. If you are not ready to make the kind of commitment necessary, you should rethink your globalisation efforts.

Of course, expanding globally is very risky. But if your firm is based in, say, Delhi, expanding domestically by having additional units in Hyderabad and Coimbatore is risky too! If you can manage this, you already have a proven national mindset, and you can certainly consider expanding your business into international markets.

My own experience in the developing world has shown that there are no short cuts or sure-fire formulae to globalising a firm. Along with courage, you must develop the stomach for international political risk and be willing to await long-term results. Going global entails immense amount of research and the burning of a lot of midnight oil in planning. With some cost-efficient preliminary market research, you should be able to develop a workable strategy.

Learn from successful nations

The spectacular results of international business competitiveness are evident in certain firms in the US, Europe and Japan. These three moved quickly away from simple foreign trade activities to foreign direct investments and then to establishing competitive links across continents. Their efforts in creating multinational firms have been outstandingly successful.

We will briefly discuss the various aspects of gaining, maintaining and sustaining competitive advantage. These are academic aspects and are taught in most business schools. While not making any claims as to the originality of what I say below, I will be detailing these points as they are crucial for any Indian firm evaluating the prospects of going global.

The following points detail how countries, management and organizational issues affect international business. If they are all investigated and implemented successfully, then executives can go about the business of creating a global business network for their firms.

First, how do international firms in these countries gain competitive advantage? Well, every nation is unique and has its own language, culture and history as well as economic and political systems. All of these, for example, make the US different from Mexico, France from Germany and Japan from Korea. CEOs of international firms direct their executives to seek information and feedback on hundreds of questions relating to a particular nation. What do they find in the country? Can they use their core skills to export to or invest in that country? And, will they be able to overcome the entry barriers raised by local firms in their home market? Only if the risks are acceptable, the skills transferable and the barriers surmountable does international business take place. Let's talk about this in some detail.

✓ Choosing market opportunities: As international business crosses national frontiers, executives must, perforce, deal with political, currency and cultural risks. Their task is to identify and avoid high-risk countries, find high-growth market segments in low-risk countries and capture significant market share in all mass-consumer markets of the world. Given that Japanese executives prefer a longer time horizon than do US executives for gaining market share and becoming profitable, the former see less risk and more opportunities than do the latter.
✓ Fitting core skills: Not every product, manufacturing system, marketing strategy and organisational technique can cross national boundaries with ease. While some countries show a great deal of

similarity in their ability to absorb new technologies and willingness to copy consumer preferences established elsewhere in the world, others do not. Given that customers worldwide prefer Japanese technology incorporated within an international (sometimes referred to as Western or American) lifestyle, executives across the globe must get new products out more quickly and commit themselves to foreign market development in all parts of the world.

✓ Overcoming barriers: Incumbent firms use their home market advantages (such as scale economies, learning curve and links with distributors) to keep out foreign contestants. The latter must overcome these entry barriers through new technologies, products, services and markets. Through a combination of technological competition and home-market protectionism, Japanese executives have emerged as active players in international business. This is a wholly new lens through which American and European business executives must learn to view international business.

Next, how do international firms maintain competitive advantage? Many manage entry into overseas markets only with a minimum level of difficulty. They learn to deal with the reality of domestic firms that have fully depreciated plants, strong links with local wholesalers and significant market share. For foreign competitors, their sunk costs are not depreciated, their forward pricing strategies rack up losses instead of profits and their local competitors do everything legally possible to keep them from gaining significant market share. Therefore, these foreign firms must find the least expensive offshore products, seek customers with the highest discretionary income and create valuable new products and services.

Let's look at these strategies:

✓ Sourcing: Executives look to source raw materials, parts and components and finished goods from the low-cost areas of the world. They want products with a high export-sales potential, meeting the technological and lifestyle expectations of customers abroad. Their task is to adapt international products to national, regional and local markets. In the past, US mass markets and high-class European products built strong market segments throughout the world. Today, products from Japan and other Asian countries are capturing market share with the expectation that Japanese executives have something to say about the long-term development of international business.

✓ Selecting customers: Executives seek to improve the demand quality by pursuing customers with high incomes, refined tastes and a preference for expensive goods. Executives seek goods from countries with, according to the customer, a good reputation. This country-of-origin affect is one of several cues that convinces customers of quality. Today, high-performance cars from Germany, and low-, medium-, and high-priced cars from Japan have excellent ratings, whereas cars from the US have fair to poor ratings. The key to long-term development of international business is to pitch products with the right price, quality and service to the most appropriate customer, niche and market segment irrespective of national boundaries or differences in language, culture and history.

✓ Creating value: Executives acquire brands, trademarks and other intellectual property to create value for their firms. They measure the actual movement of the branded products through the channel of distribution and develop promotional campaigns to enhance the movement of products from manufacturer to customer. Today, valuable American and European brands are for sale to those who have the cash namely, the Japanese, Koreans and other East Asians. The key to long-term development of international business is to create new brands, service marks and other forms of intellectual property so that value is enhanced for customers everywhere in the world.

Finally, how do international firms sustain competitive advantage? Information is the organisational lubricant and helps executives decide which and how many markets to enter, and at what pace to finance market expansion. To make an expansion strategy work requires the leveraging of capital, human resources and other assets, with an eye on the national difference details worldwide. More on this in the following paragraphs.

✓ Using Information: Organisations use production, marketing and financial information to determine how the management should go about its international business. Information is sometimes kept internally within the multinational firm whereas it is used, at other times, as the proverbial carrot to induce other firms to join in licensing deals and joint venture partnerships. Information is also used to scan markets and decide which of those are similar so that the cost of additional market penetration is not prohibitive.

✓ Positioning assets: After decisions concerning concentration versus diversification have been made, executives then position capital, human and other assets. All expansion strategies require executives to make a host of predictions about the chances for success in, for example, the sales response functions, industry growth rates, competitive lead times, spillover effects, costs of product and promotional adaptation, distribution expenses, costs of managerial control and the loss of revenue due to external constraints. The task of the executive is to leverage assets to outperform sales quotas so that the company can grow internationally.

✓ Understanding national differences: Information and data are of no use without executives who have a feel for the real local, regional and national differences among countries. Some of these are specific to one language or cultural group (e.g., the respect for the king and royal family among the Thais) while others transcend cultural groups and bind peoples into nations (e.g., the maple leaf of Canada or the stars and stripes of the US). Still others cut across nations and bind market segments worldwide (e.g., the Union Jack of Great Britain as a symbol of quality on Reebok running shoes). These competitive connections among countries help turn projections into international marketing plans that are then integrated into a worldwide corporate strategy for enhancing the firm's international business. Information about national differences is all-important and executives must know and utilise this.

Globalising the firm

Successful international business executives employ both global and local marketing strategies to increase competitive connections among countries. They also foster organisational learning about international business among subsidiaries, affiliates and branches. Moreover, these executives are often able to turn certain subsidiaries into sole-source firms, others into export platforms and still others into great international firms in their own right. That is the genius of international business.

5.4

Don't just go there, be there

Look at how others sell to India

I will seek to establish that the strategy most widely prevalent in India, of making overseas trips to book orders, has long been obsolete. Travelling salesmen do not come to India to sell anything. Most big and small trading houses exporting to India have a presence in the country. It is high time we learnt from them. Increasingly, the overseas customer is also no longer the small-time wholesaler or family trader. We are more and more likely to be dealing with large, well-managed and efficient organisations.

We have been discussing, in this book, ways and means of increasing our exports and I have repeatedly made the point that we should not simply make overseas trips to sell but try to have a long-term presence overseas.

✓ It has to be clearly understood that I am certainly not advocating the incurring of massive expenses in setting up offices abroad.

Well, setting up offices, yes, but incurring big expenses, no. Read on and I will make myself clear.

During the heyday of protectionism and the License Raj, a foreign company in India was considered an untouchable. But India was still importing a plenty. This was made possible by foreign companies coming to India and entering into sole-agency and distributorship arrangements. This suited them fine as they did not have to invest a penny in the business. The foreign firm was a well-organised entity and the Indian side was invariably managed by an individual who saw a chance to make some good money.

Post liberalisation, foreign companies are welcomed. These companies have set up their own trading offices in India. The local agents have become partners while the local firm has a foreign

name and a nominal paid-up capital. There is often no foreign partner based in India and the Indian partner puts up the money to run
the local day to day business. Overseas investment is made only if
and when the firm goes into manufacturing. So, at the end of the
day, it is a foreign trading company in India, run, financed and managed by Indians. The operative word here is 'financed.' Trading
firms are doing this the world over. I have seen the local offices of
Japanese, Korean and Singaporean trading companies in Kenya
and other African nations. The entire operation is rigidly remote-
controlled by the head office.

- The point I am making here is that these trading firms have developed a strategy of creating a highly profitable local presence all
  over the developing world at little cost to themselves.

No agents and no distributors, only partners

Customers everywhere today, even in small African and South
Pacific countries, display no loyalty. The world is their shopping
mall. There are no national boundaries, only the boundaries of price
and convenience.

The relationship between an overseas buyer and seller is changing as the world becomes more competitive. With a lot of similar
options available today, buyers make their decisions based on price
and convenience. The relationship is simply a *transaction*, an exchange of goods for money. The best kinds of transactions are short
and to the point. In a transaction relationship, customers want an
order taker and a price negotiator, not a salesperson.

To raise the bar and stay competitive in this new world, the more
sophisticated organisations have discarded traditional notions of
what drives the relationship between buyer and seller. Products in
themselves don't provide the competitive advantage. The expectation now is of value-added service. The new game is based on the
ability to help solve significant business problems for customers. If
you want to play, competitive advantage lies in helping your customers make money, save money or add value to their product. The
same applies if your customers are looking for a relationship that
can assist them with their quality or cost initiatives. If you're not

willing to play that game, to understand your customers' larger needs, you will be promptly passed over.

You can work with your export customers at any of the following levels.

Level 1: You are viewed as just another vendor. Contract negotiations are adversarial events. Your primary point of contact is usually limited to the department or individual requesting delivery of a package.

Level 2: You are viewed as a problem solver. Contract negotiations are collaborative efforts in which you and the customer make compromises and create options rather than engage in hard bargaining to achieve concessions. Your primary contact is at the middle-management or department-head level.

Level 3: You are viewed as a partner. Contract negotiations focus on structuring an alliance and sharing the gain generated from collaboration. Your primary contact is at the senior-management level.

The most complex and profitable relationship is that with the partner. Customers in a foreign country tend to be well established and committed to buying or selling for you over a long period of time, recognising that the business relationship extends beyond any individual product offering. As the buyer and seller grow more dependent on each other, it becomes harder for the customer to switch to another vendor and receive comparable value. It is difficult to see where one organisation ends and the other begins. When a partner is lost for any reason, restoring a similar relationship is difficult and likely to take a great deal of time and effort.

First, understand the other fellow

The implications for exporters in India are clear. Building competitive advantage solely around products and services isn't enough. Understanding your customer's business, strategies, market and financial situation is the new core competency.

Of course, no person or organisation is going to let you in the door easily or make you privy to their critical business issues, unless they trust you and are confident that you share their basic beliefs and values regarding business.

In three decades of dealing with business organisations all over the world, I have always made excellent progress by asking the right people the right questions in the right way. Take them out for a meal and let them tell you stories about their business. While nobody will disclose trade secrets or confidential stuff, when you sit down face-to-face with someone you may often discover what keeps the person up at night. In this way you will fairly soon amass a knowledge base that will help you understand what the world looks like through the eyes of your customers.

The objective is to view your overseas customer as a niche one, to be seen by your customer not just as a representative of a product or supplier organisation, but as a consultant and an expert in that business. From that deep understanding, large opportunities flow. When you can speak their language, understand their business, and understand what they are trying to accomplish, and when you can match that with an understanding of your business and what your company offers, opportunities that would have gone unnoticed will become obvious.

There is another important benefit to being a 'niche player.' People will work with you not because they understand what you offer but because they believe you understand them. Customers always prefer to work with those who understand their business and are focused on solving their critical business problems, not people who simply want to 'push products.'

Think of it this way. As a customer in a transactional environment, all I wanted was a product dropped off at the loading dock. Your values were not that important to me. Honesty and fair pricing were all that was expected. At a more evolved level of buyer–seller relationship that we are now talking of, much more is required. Both organisations and the individuals involved need a higher level of commitment to a partnership. The deeper and more interconnected the relationship, the more critical the role of trust and values. For example, if proprietary information is shared or products are developed in common, everyone needs to feel confident that the same information will not be shared with competitors.

These relationships are often akin to hiring a new employee rather than to working with a new vendor or a new customer. When an employee is hired there is an expectation that, at some level, he or she will share the core values regarding work, people and ethics that are expressed by the company and that are shared by other employees. A partnership requires the same level of disclosure, discourse and discovery.

Your customer knows all about you

In a world becoming more competitive everyday, every business faces the immediate threat of losing its differentiation in the eyes of its customers and becoming simply another vendor in the price and convenience transaction wars. Leading the list of causes is the fact that customers have more choices than ever before. Global competition, the commoditisation of products and services and the price wars are all good news for the customer. It is no longer a matter of choosing between a few players. There are now hundreds of choices available to the customer from all over the world and that trend is certain to continue.

Customers today also have the knowledge to use that choice. The relevant information is often on their fingertips. There are no longer any secrets; customers can learn all about your industry and your business without ever leaving their offices. Instant electronic access exists to annual reports and industry journals. Public companies are truly open and even schoolchildren can source information about the salaries of corporate officers and the stock owners of a company, or examine a dozen reports on the financial health of a company, all on the home computer. Information regarding your reputation and about how you treat other customers can flow in nanoseconds to other customers and prospects. We are in the information age, on the entry ramp to the information highway. Knowledge is power and customers are taking full advantage of it.

Ironically, selling organisations have helped create this highly informed and educated buying public to the point at which buyers are often better at buying than salespeople are at selling.

Who is involved?

The simple answer is: every part of the organisation. Partnering transforms the relationship from just a single or a few points of contact (salesperson to buyer) to multiple points of contact between organisations.

The ability to solve high-level business problems is the reason buyers and suppliers come together in partnerships. It used to be that products or price drove the relationship; the person who had the best product or the best price got the business. That is no longer a reliable rule. In today's highly competitive world, there are rarely competitive differences between suppliers; if there are distinguishable differences, they are short-lived.

The implications for salespeople as relationship managers for export activities are clear. In order to manage these new relationships, the 'partnership builders' will require a high degree of integrity and new competencies, like the ability to work at the highest levels of a customer organisation, the skills to facilitate groups and a deep understanding of organisational dynamics. Many customers prefer to work with low-cost providers; they will be commodity-type customers forever. But the emerging, sophisticated customers, the customers of world-class organisations, are looking for organisations and individuals with whom they can partner to do serious business because of the enormous rewards to be reaped.

The export division of your organisation has to be open and structured to receive and nurture partners. The Indian organisational immune system, which attempts to kill anything that is strange and new, has to be switched off in order to accept new relationships.

All the organisations in the partnership need to be in alignment, held together by efficient communication, a shared vision of what is possible, and shared goals. The top executives have to be in agreement and support the principles of the partnership.

How to start?

If you want to develop partnering relationships with export customers, where do you start? Which customers and which countries present the most logical and the best opportunities? The fact is that not every customer is ready for, or cares to be involved in, a partnership. There are customers who will simply always go for the lowest price, shopping amongst several bidders for every piece of business.

Understanding which customers are ready for a partnership is vital for a couple of reasons. First, working at a more complex business level with customers requires, as you may have already guessed, a lot of effort and time. Working at this level requires choosing the right opportunities and the right customers. It may also mean having to let go of customers who take up much of your time without producing appropriate results. Second, since you can't spend the same amount of time and energy on every customer in every country, you have to decide how best to use your resources. The key here is learning how to get as much done as possible with as little effort as possible. For example, this means trying to get introductions and locating common friends. This may also mean continuing to grow existing business, because it is much easier to do business with people who already know you than it is to go out and find new business. Finally, it is obvious that every customer is unique. Some customers buy price, others are more interested in a long-term relationship. Some are truly interested in strategy. But the point is that they are all different; they cannot be treated generically. A common business sin of the past was treating all customers as if they were exactly alike, presenting them with the same products, the same proposals, the same sales process.

Increasingly, customers are demanding, and receiving, customised solutions tailored to their specific needs. Customers are individuals, with distinct needs, requirements and concerns. The generic customer is gone and so are generic solutions and the 'one size fits all' sales process. The best of all worlds is that in which one is versatile enough—as an organisation and an individual business person—to match customer requirements with the right products and processes. The crucial, next part of a partnership is to envision clear milestones. Sometimes there is a tendency in the early part of the partnership to pull up the roots to see whether it's growing,which, of course, can kill the partnership. There needs to be discipline and agreement around indicators. Like a marriage, partnerships are created for long-term advantage and they often need time to flower and grow. Finally (just like in a marriage), all the parties need training and tools in conflict resolution. How do we agree to disagree? How do we agree to solve our problems together? For example, do we agree to trust each other's intentions regarding the partnership, no matter the depth of the disagreement?

As I said above, this is the era of mass customisation. Customers want solutions tailored explicitly to their situations. The question for many businesses now is not how large the market is for a product or service, but how one can adapt and customise products and services for the smallest markets, or that one industrial customer, and still make money.

In that light, customers are rarely interested in your organisation's definitions of service and quality; they have their own and they differ for every customer. A certain customer will expect just-in-time delivery, another, a defect rate lower than you've ever produced and yet another unique packaging that fits into his/her work-flow process, but has little to do with how packaging has always been done in the industry.

These customers are no longer bound by political or geographic boundaries; they can go wherever they want in order to get the quality and prices they require. Information technology makes it possible for consumers to shop around the world. Mix all this together, add new technologies, add political and social upheaval, and the result is massive, dislocating, structural change. This is the big picture. By almost every definition, we are at a turning point, moving toward a decisive change in how we do business and how we work together.

Most important: You must understand finance

You have to be practised at discussing finance, beyond the price and value of products and services. Driving business results requires a fundamental understanding of financial concepts, a certain fluency in the language of finance and the ability to read the vital signs and know what they mean. You need to understand, for example, what causes pretax profitability for your customer. This is the stuff that customers want to talk about, what gets their attention.

5.5 *Information sharing*

Making a habit of noting everything

Visiting Japan and Korea, I have noticed, time and again, that local executives will spend the whole day with you discussing business, do a late night on the town and yet have a full report ready on their tables the next morning. This will include details of everything discussed plus your eating and drinking preferences.

Customer relationships and customer information are too valuable to be the sole property of one salesperson. Too often, customer information is either not recorded or recorded in such a manner that it cannot be easily disseminated throughout the organisation, is not understood or is not 'stored' in a way that the organisation can easily access. When a particular salesperson leaves the organisation (or is sick or on vacation), the information becomes unavailable and with it, the customer.

Somehow, Indian executives are not in the habit of making notes immediately after the occasion. I have seen them visiting factories and projects overseas. They do not carry notebooks and invariably use the backs of visiting cards of the people they meet for any notes they wish to make.

You cannot find what you are not looking for

It is a sad fact that Indians, in general, are not very keen to seek information about and gain knowledge of overseas markets. If we do not seek it, we shall certainly not find it. We are not interested because we cannot see how this can improve our business.

Indian businessmen are bored when I talk about the political or the economic situation in a particular country. They only want to know what they can sell, to whom and where. In the words of an exporter who met me before going to Kenya, 'Don't bore me about life in Nairobi. Tell me who I should meet and what he wants. I will tackle him when I get there, I know what to do.'

Having said that, it is one thing to collect information, but quite another to manage it such that it becomes an essential productive tool. The notes that the Japanese, for example, bring back from their overseas trips quickly get converted to indexed, cross referenced and accessible databases. There is no way that even an insignificant bit of information about a customer's taste is lost.

Customers, now and in the future, are/will be more important and more demanding, and their issues too complex, for one salesperson to handle. The underlying truth is that individuals working by themselves—no matter how intelligent and experienced—simply do not/ will not have the answers or the breadth of knowledge to respond appropriately given such an environment. That is a broad generalisation, but it is becoming a reality for more and more industries.

Information and knowledge management

Knowing something, in today's world, is useless if not properly documented, organised and accessible, as mentioned above. I will now discuss the subject of knowledge management as applicable to all professionally-managed Indian companies. I have been saying all along that it is essential for India's large corporations to develop a global mindset. I have also been qualifying this to say that you must first have a national mindset. Growing into a national entity and then going global would require the capability to gather, leverage and use knowledge effectively. This includes an intimate knowledge of the markets, competitors, forecasts of economic conditions and growth prospects. This will become a major source of competitive advantage in businesses over the next few years not only for exports but even in the domestic market.

It is an area in which the rules of competition are being redefined. Acquired excellence in knowledge management creates new avenues for growth by allowing companies to fine-tune key capabilities to new businesses and markets. Effective knowledge-based companies can also develop a cost advantage by sharing operational improvement ideas more rapidly than their competitors.

If you are growing into a global, multiple-business company, you have higher stakes in this game. You have many more opportunities to learn directly about markets, competitors and best practices than the more focused regional players, but you also face a greater challenge to turn these insights into action because the difficulty of managing knowledge transfer increases exponentially with an organisation's size and complexity.

Managing the knowledge jungle

Knowledge is, of course, power. However, even if knowledge can be accumulated successfully, and this is a big if, it could end up being buried in mysterious places and be difficult to find without encountering a lot of bureaucracy or without expert searching skills. To be effective, business information and knowledge bases must be easy to use and comprehensive.

This implies that significant effort needs to be spent on archiving skills. Intelligent archiving is the key to success here. This means accurate indexing, clear availability and presentation of data and the ability to manipulate and use it quickly. Ideally, executives in Indian companies must have access to a searchable network of confidential information where they can easily find the solutions they need as per the demands of the business situation.

In the more developed world, knowledge management pioneers are learning the value of using corporate information services staff as guides and search assistants, as well as as advisors on knowledge classification. Direct end-user searching works best if the knowledge categories are very clearly defined or limited to a specific function.

With more complex cross-functional knowledge repositories, it becomes critical to consolidate access to all sources and provide a clear map of the different ways to obtain codified knowledge. There is nothing more disconcerting than searching a database for hours only to find that it was the wrong one or that you could have learned the answer by just talking to a colleague next door.

Knowledge data banks

Once more data is available and people see the value of acquiring and sharing it for the greater good, information systems should be set up to allow different units in a company to become part of a network, interactively learning and sharing their knowledge as well as monitoring their operational, corporate and supply chain goals. People should have the means to interact intelligently while using the data, and making decisions or working with others based on this data. It would be a case of stating the obvious to mention that one should have access to the right data at the right time in order to make better decisions.

As more Indian companies develop their knowledge management capabilities, some of the ground rules should become more clear. Success depends on a clear strategic logic for knowledge sharing, the choice of appropriate infrastructure (technical or non-technical) and an implementation approach that addresses the typical barriers: motivation to share knowledge, resources to capture and synthesise organizational learning and the ability to navigate the knowledge network to find the right people and data.

Too much or too little knowledge can both be dangerous. So, an optimum assessment of strategic objectives is a must. What are the key areas of knowledge required and how will they benefit the business? What are the concrete activities involved and how would improved knowledge gathering and transfer affect the speed, quality and cost for particular activities? How would better knowledge management, for example, speed up the preparation of a client offer, solve a technical problem more effectively or improve test procedures for a new product?

If the overall goals are clear, the next step is to decide on the appropriate channels for transferring knowledge. The answer varies by business, geographical scope and the type of knowledge to be tapped: Is the knowledge codifiable or contained in people's heads? Is it technical or general? Does it apply across all regions or only to some?

The solutions may vary from the information-technology-oriented (e.g., structured databases, electronic work groups) to the human-resources-oriented (e.g., personnel rotation, new team structures, new roles for exports, just-in-time training) and all points in between.

✓ It is important to realise that knowledge in business becomes out of date very quickly. So archives and databases are less important than quick access to experts or simply to people who have knowledge about your problem.

Pharmaceutical companies, for example, have a strong need to encourage access to documentation and test results across functions and projects. Personal interaction and explanation is still important but, increasingly, so is the ability to locate the right data rapidly and use it immediately.

If the objective is to give employees continuous access to expert knowledge in all areas, then a stronger knowledge infrastructure is needed. One solution is to dedicate people or systems to gather and index small pieces of knowledge, relate them to broader topics of interest and anticipate when others are going to need them and in what context. Most consulting firms, for example, have teams of practice experts and 'knowledge integrators' who extract useful insights from ongoing work and relate it to general practice know-how.

Making a start

Getting started is the trickiest problem. People are used to keeping knowledge gained to themselves. They need to be made to realise the potential benefits offered by a new, accessible knowledge base. This is not such a big problem as most people have already woken up to the potential resources available to them on something like the internet.

Knowledge management initiatives vary widely in scope and format. Many are low-tech, needing low investment, while others require a major organisational commitment. Here are some pointers:

1. You must think about adopting a phased approach, where you initially focus on those areas that will have a clear payoff and require putting into place only simple sharing mechanisms, like making it mandatory for all information on overseas and outstation visits to be recorded and cross indexed. Then build more permanent networks and infrastructure, as needed.
2. As the value of such a database starts getting recognised, think carefully about ways to make knowledge sharing easier for both the provider and user.
3. Only after first making sure of the feedback from senior executives, both as contributors to and users of the system, should you embark on broad-based cross-business knowledge sharing or make heavy infrastructural investment.

4. Repeatedly measure the success of the knowledge management effort in terms of its impact on your business, and continually look for ways to streamline your knowledge-sharing channels and improve their effectiveness in the future.

These approaches normally have a very low incremental cost and are easy for all to understand and adopt. They also help to demonstrate the value and highlight areas where bigger investments (e.g., in specialist expert recruitment or the setting up of permanent databases) would be worthwhile. In fact, before the computer age, some of the most effective knowledge management programmes in Japan, for example, have been in specific areas with low-tech approaches to knowledge transfer, and run on purely traditional lines.

The hurdles

The acid test, of course, lies in the implementation. There will be hurdles though they will vary from firm to firm. The most serious of these are: the propensity to hoard knowledge, the unwillingness to learn from others, the lack of incentives to share or learn and the low priority and resources accorded to knowledge gathering as opposed to the seemingly more urgent day to day business needs. People are simply not ready, willing or able to share knowledge.

There is also the very serious problem of staff mobility. I have met a number of Indian sales staff and executives on visits to other countries—superb personalities, friendly and very good at their jobs. But on talking to them you realise that they have no loyalty towards their firms and are only marking time. They often make no secret of the fact that, in their opinion, either the company is not doing well or they do not have much of a future in the company. These people bring back a lot of information which they jealously guard and consider their private property, to be used when they change jobs. This is tragic and a refection on how we run our businesses.

Indeed, there are people who are perfectly willing to transfer knowledge but don't have the time or the attitude to reflect on what could be valuable to others, and make an effort to codify or otherwise transfer it. Financial incentives are unlikely to help. Most people will still make the daily trade-off in favour of getting their day-today work done. Even where incentives do have an impact, they may tend to generate quantity rather than quality of input.

Creating the motivation

The crucial steps in the successful implementation of knowledge management initiatives are summed up in the following business school jargon, 'some of the key building blocks for a successful knowledge management programme are leadership and a strategic focus on systems and follow-up metrics' and also that 'some of the most critical issues are found within the "culture" and "support" areas, creating the motivation to share and use others' knowledge, and finding practical ways to leverage input and access to the knowledge network, whether it's people or databases.'

In simple language, we ask ourselves, is there visible senior management commitment to knowledge sharing as a critical goal of the business? Do the top bosses really want an executive to know what his colleague garnered from an outstation visit? Information, say, about the personal habits, weaknesses and preferences of an important customer? If so, an organisation then has to work its way downwards to see whether people are motivated to make their knowledge available to coworkers. And then, whether those coworkers are motivated to use it.

One solution to this problem is to make knowledge transfer a prominent criterion in the company's evaluation and compensation system, with high-profile rewards and recognition (not necessarily monetary) for significant contributions. The Koreans and the Japanese do this by default.

By far the strongest motivation for a firm having a national mindset and wanting to go global is the immense goodwill this can create. It is a very powerful way to emphasise knowledge transfer effectiveness to customers. As I said earlier, if the customer knows you know how to make full use of and value all the market information you get, you will get surprising feedbacks. And, your competition will be left wondering how you are ahead in in the race!

5.6 *On being posted overseas*

In modern life, being transferred from one place to another is a common enough occurrence. In particular, even before starting work, Army officers and government servants are mentally prepared to spend almost their entire working lives being shunted from one place to another. Taking a wider view, for more than a century, Indians have been leaving the country of their birth and availing of the option of settling down in foreign lands. This has sometimes been voluntary and sometimes not. I have discussed this migration in some detail in Chapters 3.4 and 4.3.

In the modern corporate world in India, however, being posted overseas is something not everyone is comfortable with. This was not always so. In the 1950s and the early 1960s, going abroad was reserved for either the ultra-rich or the uneducated illegal immigrant. Being sent abroad on an assignment or a posting was much prized at that time. Things have changed now and every family has someone living overseas. So, an executive posted to Malaysia or Kenya, for example often looks upon the assignment as a punishment, somewhat akin to what a Punjabi from Chandigarh may feel on being posted to Coimbatore! Often, therefore, the frame of mind an executive is in when he goes abroad is not conducive to his adjusting to the new environment.

> I have been stressing that our export effort will gain momentum if, and only if, instead of going there to sell, we make arrangements to be there. This assumes the need for some staff members to be located overseas. It is true that there are an immense number of corporate, financial, administrative and organisational aspects to setting up offices or representations abroad. These are discussed elsewhere in this book. In this chapter I will be talking about the personal aspects, instead. I have seen countless cases of Indians not being able to take what I call the 'relocation trauma' and ending up as nervous wrecks.
>
> I will be talking about what happens the first time you go overseas, not on a holiday, but to live, and how you should prepare yourself for it.

Please note that I am NOT talking about going to the US on an IT assignment. I will be talking about countries where life on the streets is very unsafe. I will also be talking about countries like Japan and Korea where you are made to feel uncomfortable merely because you are a foreigner.

I am reminded of a funny story I read somewhere. There was this fellow who died and went up to heaven. He found everything nice, cool and rosy, and had just started to enjoy himself when he was told that there had been a mistake and that he was not supposed to have died so soon. He was sent back to earth and lived for a few more years. When his time came and he returned to heaven he found that it was nothing like what he had seen the first time around. Everything now was just about OK. He asked a passing angel and was told, 'The last time you were here as a tourist. This time you are here to stay.'

Well, this is not so far from reality. I have seen people visit developing countries in Asia and Africa and enjoy themselves. However, they often develop problems once they come to stay for a prolonged period.

Relocation trauma

A milder term for the trauma an executive sometimes undergoes when suddenly exposed to alien environment is 'culture shock.' This, as I said above, is not something that people generally experience on a holiday. As soon as your boss calls you into the office and says, 'Hi! Subra, you have done such a great job selling to Kenya that we want you to go to Nairobi to set up our office there,' you find yourself in a tizzy! You need time to think about the implications, time to talk to your wife and maybe time to think of how you are going to get around this 'offer.'

I have seen this happen time and again, even to people who have repeatedly visited the countries they are being posted to. So the case of a technical or an administrative person who has never left home being asked to go overseas for the first time on a long term assignment is even more serious.

✓ For the purpose of discussion, we will ignore the trauma of a person being asked to leave his present environment and focus instead on the transition he has to make to live in country or a place different from the place of his origin. I will try, based on my experience, to provide as many pointers to make this transition easy and comfortable.

There are many books on the subject which look at the problem from a psychological angle and there is also a series of books that deals with culture shock in different countries. However while these books are a very good starting point, I feel that you will not really understand the message fully until you are actually in the country mingling with the locals.

This trauma or shock is part of the process of learning a new culture and can also be called 'cultural adaptation.' Of course, one's way of life may not be the norm in the new place. Common difficulties encountered, for example, are: not speaking the language, not knowing how to use bank teller machines, not knowing how to use the telephone and so forth. You may experience some discomfort before you are able to function well in a new setting. This discomfort is the 'culture shock' stage of the adaptation process. The main thing to remember is that this is a very normal process that nearly everyone goes through.

Cultural baggage

Just as you will bring with you to the new destination clothes and other personal items, you will also carry invisible 'cultural baggage' when you travel. That baggage is not as obvious as the items in your suitcases, but will play a major role in your adaptation abroad. Cultural baggage consists of the values that are important to you and the patterns of behaviour that are customary in your culture. The more you know about your personal values and how they are derived from your culture, the better prepared you will be to see and understand the cultural differences you will encounter abroad.

You have to understand and accept that there are differences and, sometimes, big differences between life at home and life in the new place. Differences in language, climate, religion, food and the educational system, and in how people make decisions, spend their leisure time, resolve conflicts and express their feelings and emotions. Body language such as the meaning of hand, face and body movements can often create confusion and emotional stress. Almost everyone has had to face such situations, albeit to varying degrees.

The book *Culture Shock Thailand* mentions that the Thai people are among the nicest people in the world. It explains a good deal about Thai culture and traditions and explains how Thais smile their way out of embarrassing situations and, more importantly, look down on those that don't. The book then lists a couple of interesting examples, which are close to the experiences I have had living in Thailand. If, for example, you are walking down a street and someone unintentionally throws dirty water over you from a doorway, you should look up and smile at the person that did this, showing your immediate forgiveness. This will help clear the air and the person will, most likely, go out of his way to call you in and help you clean up. Imagine this happening in Mumbai or Delhi! There would be a fight here, instead. Thais shy away from confrontation, and understanding this is one of the many aspects that would make your life with them comfortable.

The extent to which you will be affected is dependent upon how much past experience you have had with the culture you are interfacing with and the assistance that you will receive from your colleagues and associates. People are often diffident when it comes to speaking for fear of offending someone. Some other reactions you might experience are: feeling isolated or alone, sleeping too much or tiring easily, finding it difficult to sleep, suffering body pains such as a headache and, of course, wanting to return home.

Handling the shock

What should one do about it?

✓ First, remember that you may not be faced with it at all or not really to any degree of extreme.
✓ Second, you should know that even if you do face culture shock, it will most likely pass off with time. It is very rarely permanent.
✓ Third, understand that if you are being posted overseas, you will not be marooned on a desert island. There will be people around you. As I said above, the local people you will be working with are often there to help and encourage you.

Arrive at your destination with an open mind, looking forward to new experiences and ideas, and never mind if you make a mistake, remember, you are doing things based upon your own cultural experiences and are new to the differences. It helps if you bring some small things of comfort from India. For example, some good books in your own language, photos of your loved ones, a special food item or some special spices that would liven up the food. Before leaving home, learn to cook a few simple dishes. These things will greatly help you get through homesick or lonely moments. Almost every country has local Indians. Try to locate and establish contact with your ethnic group. This will give you a feeling of belonging and will reduce your feelings of loneliness and alienation. Try to set up a network of such contacts with whom you can exchange books, magazines, videos and disks from back home, and perhaps cook familiar food together. You will be able to discuss your reactions with them and swap experiences. You will also be able to talk about your home country and share your feelings about how living abroad affects you. In fact, it helps to generally acknowledge that you need links to your own culture so that you fell less cut off and alone.

One of the biggest causes of relocation shock is language. Remember this is equally bad if you are moving from one part of India to another. A Punjabi family moving to Tamil Nadu has the same problem. In each case, it will make a difference if you are able to learn a little of the new language before you leave. Try to meet people who speak the language in order to practice it. If you have free time, try to volunteer for community activities that will allow you to practice the language that you are learning. This will help you feel less stressed about the language and is also a way to prove useful at the same time. This small step will make your life a lot simpler and will ensure immediate respect when you arrive in the foreign country, not to mention the opening of many new doors. If you show an interest in the other person's language and culture, they will surely show an interest in you.

I always tell my Indian friends in new environments to try to socialise outside regular work patterns, and meet and befriend as many locals as they can. Somehow, I find that we do not make friends outside our immediate work circle, and that our social contacts remain within our own language group, not extending even to people from other parts of India. Without this, it is really not easy to develop any understanding of the place you are in.

Relocation and your company

If you are being relocated by your company try to find out a little about the living conditions in that country and the package that the company is offering you. My experience of Indian firms sending their staff overseas is that the firm itself has little idea of what sort of support the executive will need. Very few Indian firms have any sort of a presence outside India and we just do not have adequate experience about any of this. You will need to talk to your firm about the support they are prepared to give, including the budget, etc.

Questions you need to discuss with your firm:

✓ Will they supply you with temporary hotel accommodation or will you be allocated an apartment or house?
✓ Are you to be given a fixed housing allowance and asked to choose the accommodation yourself?
✓ Will the company pay the deposits that the landlord requires? This point is very critical as landlords in many countries like Indonesia can ask for two years' rent in advance!
✓ Will you be able to get local maids? Or, can you bring one from home? This point is critical in countries such as Singapore and Malaysia which have stringent regulations and steep deposits for importing domestic help.
✓ Will they provide you with a car?
✓ How many return trips will you have a year to India?
✓ What about family benefits? The cost of children's education can be prohibitive in many countries.
✓ How long is the posting for? Is it for a fixed term, flexible or performance related?
✓ Will the company pay for repatriation due to illness?
✓ Do they have limits as to the amount of household stuff and furniture that you can send over and, more importantly, bring back to India? Will they cover these charges? Do they have any restrictions in terms of how you send these things?
✓ Do they offer you medical and personal insurance suitable for the country you are travelling to?

Stages of relocation and re-entry trauma

I have met and lived with many an Indian executive posted overseas for the first time. Except for dangerous countries such as Nigeria and

Guyana and the emotionally uncomfortable ones such as Japan, which I will discuss below, I have identified roughly four stages of the relocation trauma. The last stage is what I call the re-entry stage, where one returns to India and has to fit in once again with the way things are done back home.

Of course, each person has their own way of reacting in each of the different stages. For some, particular stages may be longer and more difficult than others. Many factors contribute to the duration and effects of culture shock. For example, the individual's state of mental health, type of personality, previous experiences, socio-economic conditions, familiarity with the language, family and/or social support systems and level of education.

The first stage is the *incubation stage*. In this first stage, the new arrival may feel euphoric and pleased with all the new things encountered. I call this the 'tourist visa' stage, as everything is new and exciting.

Afterwards, the second stage, *the trauma stage* presents itself. A person in this stage may encounter difficult times and crises in daily life. For example, communication difficulties may occur making the person feel incompetent because he is not being understood. In this stage, there may be feelings of discontent, impatience, anger and sadness. This is bound to happen when a person is trying to adapt to a new culture that is very different from his culture of origin.

The third stage is *the belonging stage*, when one has already gained some understanding of the new culture. A new feeling of pleasure and good humour may be experienced. You may not feel as lost and will probably gain a sense of direction. This also initiates an evaluation of the old ways versus those of the new. You start real-ising that the new culture has good and bad things to offer. This is accompanied by a feeling of belonging.

The fourth stage is the stage that I call the *re-entry trauma* phase. This occurs when, after living overseas for some years, one returns to India. You will face difficulties, believe it or not, returning to India and the more the longer you stay away and the better the life you had abroad. People no longer seem to welcome you in quite the same way as before, probably because you start to judge India by the standards of the country you have just left. You tend to look at the way things are done at home in a different light. Your comment on things are not all appreciated and you are back where you started, in relocation trauma. Remember that you will need a similar period of readjustment before you can settle back in again. In the end, however, you will be the richer for your experience and will have a wider perspective on the diversity of human society.

Countries to avoid

Before accepting an assignment in any of the following countries, I would suggest that you think twice. And then, if you still decide to go, do think some more. Some of the countries are:

- West African nations such as Nigeria and Ghana
- Some of the Central African countries like Botswana and Mozambique
- Most North African nations such as Libya, Tunisia and Algeria
- South American nations like Surinam and Guyana
- The South Pacific countries from Papua New Guinea all the way east to Fiji

The main reason for avoiding these countries is the bad law and order situation. You can be waylaid and robbed, sometimes with considerable violence, on the streets in broad daylight. There is enough information available on the net and in the archives of leading newmagazines to help you prepare yourself in case you do decide to take a chance and accept an assignment in any of the above countries.

Moreover, these nations are very poor and do not offer any sort of a market for our goods. I have been to many of them and have met Indian traders and professionals (mainly accountants and medical doctors) living there. They claim they would like to continue to do so, no matter what the conditions. Indian traders and shopkeepers do stock and sell many items of Indian origin, but these have not been generally imported via official channels. So from the point of view of Indian export houses wanting a presence overseas, these nations do not offer a good starting point.

Some nations are uncomfortable

There are two nations, Korea and Japan, which are excellent markets for Indian goods and which are outstandingly successful by any consideration. They are at the top of the list for export houses wanting to sell to the competition via well-established local export houses. There will be more on these nations in the following chapters, but from the point of view of a person having to live there for some years, I can not think of other countries, which offer more difficult choices.

Japan is the second-largest economy in the world, and a lot of this is due to the fact that it is a resource poor island nation, an economy particularly tied to the 'global marketplace.' However, it still remains a remarkably insular nation, with the people being intensely nationalistic. Everything Japanese is sacred to them and everything and everybody non-Japanese, looked down upon. I have met many expatriates, European and Asian, in Japan who have stories to tell of empty seats on either side of them in an otherwise jampacked subway train or a full-house cinema hall, or of being openly stared at. This is humiliating. As I said, this is the shared experience of all non-Japanese living in Japan.

The government realises this somewhat awkward aspect of their culture, and the strain this puts on international relations. Even the smallest of Japanese towns have 'Internationalisation' offices that exist solely to inform and educate the populace on how to behave decently with foreigners. Though these programmes have had some impact, when it comes to foreigner-interaction, the daily stares and the sight of children running off in fright are simply accepted parts of life in Japan.

I have lived and worked in Japan for many months at a time and even I have not got used to the shockingly boring tea ceremonies, being served live, still-flopping-about fish with my dinner and being casually expected to strip naked and join my coworkers in a bath!

What I said above also holds true for Korea. Moreover, a person planning to stay in Japan, say for an extended period must also come to terms with the very uncomfortable accommodation all but the ultra-rich can afford. The rooms are so tiny that you need to come out of your room to spread your arms to put on a coat! And an attached bath or even a toilet is an unheard of luxury.

And, lastly...

Relocation trauma basically comes from a lack of understanding and built-up anxiety, and can be caused by the most minute things.

All in all, every expat has his or her bad days, and there are times when you just want to get onto that plane and fly back home. Here, it may be a good idea to allow yourself to feel a little sad about the things that you have left behind. A little homesickness is always a sign of the happy memories you have of the time spent with your family and friends back in India.

However, as time goes by, and with all the amazing discoveries you will make, the days of homesickness will be minimal. An expat assignment is also an opportunity for redefining one's life objectives. It is a great opportunity for leaning and acquiring new perspectives. Culture shock can also make one develop a better understanding of oneself and stimulate personal creativity.

6

Looking at some missed opportunities

Banking on traditional exports to traditional markets is a recipe for disaster.

6.1
The euphoria over India's software success

First, some plain-speaking

I am selecting my words carefully and would like it understood that the remarks in this section are born of my conviction that,

- for Indians in India as well as in the US, nowhere is the difference between what has been achieved and what could have been achieved greater than in the fields of computer software
- India's efforts at computerising the nation are benefiting the Asian Tigers, because we import from them all our hardware needs. We are nowhere on the hardware map.

In writing this chapter, I have been faced with two problems. First, the software scene is changing everyday and second, I do understand that the subject is a somewhat sensitive one for certain people. I have been overwhelmed in the last few years by the collective euphoria over India's huge success in the software field. Both Indians in the software industry in the US and software companies in India, I have been told, are glowing examples of what the country is capable of. Indeed, at $1,750 million (97–98 figures), software exports represent a major source of foreign exchange for the country, with an astonishing growth of 677 per cent in five years.

So, in presenting the fairly extensive facts and figures I have on the subject, I would like my motives in presenting these, as in writing this book, to be clearly understood.

✓ Unless we take a hard look at ourselves, we are not going to do anything about what needs to be done.

Statistics do indeed tell a story but not, often, the whole one. The question we need to address here is whether, in due course of time, India will be left behind in the information-technology revolution?

286 Unleashing India on World Markets

We have the potential and the people. All that is missing is the will and the attitude to organise ourselves. I will give my twopenny worth of comments on this.

Indians in Malaysia and Singapore

Based in Malaysia, I had a slightly different perception of what was really happening. I was looking at India from the outside and was able to evaluate the performance of people of Indian origin in the newly emerging fields of electronic manufacture in South-East Asia. What I found sharply contrasted with what people in India were talking about. In Malaysia and Singapore, people of Indian origin make up about 12 to 15 per cent of the population and have always earned respect as professionals, doctors, lawyers and accountants. However, local Indians have not done as well in the new high-tech fields of computers and electronics.

- I need to explain here that by local Indian, I mean local citizens of Indian origin. Their families migrated many generations ago and they themselves have been born and brought up in Malaysia. It is a moot point that one should not compare Indians in South-East Asia with Indians back home. This may hold true for Indians born and brought up in distant countries like Fiji and the West Indies but Indians in Malaysia, for example, are in no way different from the people in India either in their habits, attitudes or culture.

Malaysia and Singapore have played host to a large number of high technology companies which came in and set up manufacturing facilities. These firms hired locals and trained them for all levels of operations. In a very short span of time, these multinationals had locals manning all levels of operations. Starting from scratch 20 years ago, today, more than a million people are estimated to be employed in these two countries, directly or indirectly, in the computer and electronic sectors. For me, the amazing thing is that almost all these people are Chinese or belong to races other than Indians. Indians are few and far between, and only at the lower levels. There are hardly any Indians at top managerial, executive or technical levels.

I have also seen the mind-boggling speed with which local Chinese entrepreneurs have set up all sorts of high-tech, world-class, ancillary units to manufacture components, sub-assemblies and consumables to feed these multinationals. Here again, there is not a single local Indian entrepreneur who has set up any such sort of operation.

So, I got to wondering how it was that in South-East Asia, Indians in competition with the Chinese and other races, come out tops in most professions like law, medicine and accountancy, but are a complete disaster in computer software and hardware fields? How does one explain the unmitigated success the same Indians are supposed to be enjoying back home and in the US?

First, I want to take a close look at what exactly, as an Indian, I am supposed to be feeling proud of.

- ✓ True, India's highly qualified and brilliant software professionals are earning fantastic salaries in the US
- ✓ Also true, everybody in the software business in India is earning huge profits, and so is considered a great success
- ✓ Plus, some of India's more enterprising professionals have made an outstanding mark in the software world in the US

Traditionally, many of India's young people have gone to the West for higher education and stayed back. But the salaries they earned and the success they achieved is not a patch on what our youngsters in the computer field are now earning. Am I to deduce from this that we have suddenly become outstandingly clever? I know of many Indian brilliant architects, mechanical, electrical and civil engineers in the UK and US who are stuck in poor paying jobs, and are thinking of giving up their professions and taking up computer courses! To single out recent Indian achievements in the computer field in the US for unmitigated praise is an insult to the equally if not very much more clever people who are in other fields in the US or, those who have stayed back in India and are not earning these salaries.

For the second point, I would like to mention an example of an Indian firm I hold in very high regard. A purely Indian firm with a foreign sounding name, Larsen & Toubro (L&T). This firm has many excellently-managed divisions and has done path-breaking work in a number of engineering fields both in India and abroad. Any Indian should be rightly proud of this firm. This firm also has a software unit. The profits of this unit are vastly better than those of the other units, so it is only the achievements of this unit that are highlighted.

This, again, is an insult to the superior executives in other divisions who work under backbreaking competitive conditions.

It is merely a facet of modern technology that while the entire Indian economy is working in intensely competitive conditions and getting its remuneration in rupees, those in software in India are working under American conditions and getting paid in dollars. Let us not forget that in India, where a university professor takes home a mere Rs 15,000 or so every month, software firms are able to offer newly qualified youngsters salaries of approximately Rs 30,000 to Rs 40,000 per month. These salaries were, till recently, beyond anybody's wildest dreams. However, on the flip side, this is less than US$ 11,000 per year. Where will you find people in Taiwan, Korea and Hong Kong willing to work for this meagre amount? It is no wonder, therefore, that our software firms do not have much competition from the East. I will address this point in greater detail later on to show that our software firms take up jobs that are unprofitable for anybody else.

Third, this generation has, indeed, made its mark in the US software world. However, this is nothing new. For generations, Indians have been making their mark overseas in almost every field. An important point to be noted here is that Indians do well only where individual effort and performance counts. All through this book, I have emphasised the fact that we are a nation of brilliant, hardworking but intensely individualistic people. We do not work well with each other and do not succeed in areas where group effort and organisation building is essential. So, it is only as individuals that we have been creating a flutter, from winning Nobel prizes to selling Hotmail to Microsoft for US$ 400 million! This, no doubt, brings the nation immense pride and credit. But it does not generate foreign exchange or any jobs for our people.

I know both successful Indian and Chinese entrepreneurs in the Silicon Valley, and I can fully appreciate and understand the common American saying that 'Indians are better educated and cleverer but the Chinese are more successful.' Indian entrepreneurs always talk about their firms in the first person singular. It is always about what 'I did' and who 'I am.' Sadly, their staff are aware of it too. The Chinese on the other hand talk about the people who work for them. They take immense pride in being able to attract and keep the best. It is a very common experience in the Silicon Valley (and elsewhere in the high-tech world) to see successful Chinese entre-preneurs as community leaders and role models for subsequent generations of Chinese entrepreneurs.

The real test, of course, lies in the nature and extent of interest Indians overseas show in building organisations and helping fellow Indians. It is a sad fact that the only job prospects India's middle- and senior-level computer professionals in the US have is being employed by non-Indians.

Why only software?

I am going to make an important, albeit debatable, point here.

* India has no shortage of capable and qualified people happy to work for salaries which are very low by world standards. Thus the software firms are making a killing. The point is, why is this only the case in software? What about other industries? Far lower cost inputs have been available to all our industrial and commercial sectors. Why are we not internationally competitive in other fields?

Status of the Indian software industry

As I said earlier, nowhere is the difference between what has been achieved and what could have been achieved greater than in the fields of computer hardware and software. Almost all our hardware needs are imported. The reasons for this will be clear when we take a look at our presence in the Silicon Valley later on in this chapter.

There is a mass movement of qualified engineers into the Indian software industry. The number of people qualifying as computer professionals is increasing rapidly and is far greater than those for any other technical professional field. This might suggest that inno-vative product development activity in the software industry is grow-ing at a rapid pace. However, it is not so. The majority of India's computer professionals are involved in work for which they are grossly overqualified.

A 1992 survey sponsored by the World Bank, for example, found that US and European companies ranked India as the top choice for onsite and offshore software development, ahead of other low-wage locations such as Mexico, China, Hungary and the Philippines. The use of the English language for education and business, and a familiarity with Unix-based systems were important factors, as was the presence of a large numbers of Indian engineers in US companies.

During 1999, much work in India was focused on addressing the Y2K problem—work that generated significant exports but no new intellectual property. For example, the time difference made it possible for programmers in India to log on to customer computers in the US once they had left office for the day to perform relatively routine testing, coding or programming tasks.

Body shopping

Body shopping was the market entry strategy for most Indian software firms. It can be defined very broadly to include the sourcing of skills in India to meet overseas demand. Here, however, I am using the narrower definition, which refers to the practice of offering programming services at a customer site (in the US, mainly) on the basis of 'time and material' contracts where billing is directly proportional to the number of programmer hours contracted. In the early 1990s, this was almost all India did by way of software exports. Even now, this accounts for a major share by value of Indian software exports.

The wages of qualified software programmers and systems analysts are approximately ten times lower in India, and the fully loaded cost (wages, the firm's overheads and the incidental costs of providing the service) of an engineer is 35–40 per cent what it is in the US.

Given the size of the wage gap, the world embraced India's brilliant and hardworking, but low-salaried, engineers, software programmers and systems analysts which our so-called software firms exported. The providing of services has been a natural transition for these companies from body shopping. However, for a number of reasons, Indian software firms have concentrated their efforts on the lower end of the spectrum, of providing information technology and software services rather than on developing products. Software services enable Indian companies to be highly profitable very quickly and with relatively low risks. The Indian software industry has boomed in recent years, but most of the growth is still driven by low-value-added services. Throughout the 1980s and early 1990s, India was confined almost exclusively to the low-value segments of data entry and medical transcription, with software production being confined to coding, testing and maintenance.

Social network and community support

As recently as the 1970s, only very large corporations in the US had the resources and capabilities to grow internationally, and they did so primarily by establishing marketing offices or branch plants overseas. Today, by contrast, new transportation and communication technologies allow even the smallest of firms to build partnerships with foreign producers to tap overseas expertise and markets, and for cost-savings. Start-ups in Silicon Valley today are often global actors from the day they begin operations. Here again, Indians face a hurdle. Taiwanese and other people of Chinese origin raise capital from their own communities. Indians cannot as the social network for such community support is missing.

One of the main constraints to the upgrading of the Indian software industry is the inhospitable entrepreneurship climate. India has also, until now, lacked a venture capital industry. However, the main problem associated with developing products is the lack of adequate functional expertise. As I mentioned above, Indian software firms, after gaining a competitive advantage based merely on labour costs, have felt the need to move to greater value addition. They have tried to make attempts to convert their experiences of developing customer-specific packages into more generic products. While in the former they have had strong support and help from their customers, developing generic products is a different challenge altogether. The lack of domain expertise within the software industry has made this transition difficult, aside from other issues such as capturing user needs for generic products and marketing the products effectively.

- It must be clearly understood that the most scarce of resources in this new environment is the ability to locate oneself quickly and to manage complex business relationships across cultural and linguistic boundaries. This is particularly a challenge in high-technology industries in which products, markets and technologies

are continually being redefined and where product cycles rou-
tinely last a matter of months
- In sharp contrast to the Chinese, the Indians in the Silicon Valley
do not want to act as foreign partners, associates or representatives for Indian companies

A cheer for the Asians in the Silicon Valley

When local technologists claim that 'Silicon Valley is built on ICs'
they refer not to integrated circuits but to Indian and Chinese engineers. One reads glowing accounts in the American press of the
contribution of Asian immigrants to the growth of the Silicon Valley.
These are delightedly reproduced and quoted by the Indian press.
At different times, the achievements of Indian technologists, entrepreneurs or executives is highlighted.

The American press is now of the view that far from stealing
American jobs as some politicians and lobbyists claim, Silicon Valley's Asian immigrants are an invaluable component of the high
technology industry which drives the growth in California and the
nation at large. In 1999, the Public Policy Institute of California published a 150-page, in-depth study by Dr AnnaLee Saxenian. This
study, 'Silicon valley's new immigrant entrepreneurs' is available
in the public domain and the full text can be downloaded from
www.ppic.org

Rather than a 'brain drain' from the supplier countries, Dr Saxenian
sees the emergence of a 'brain circulation' as immigrants return to
their home countries to take advantage of promising opportunities
or play a key role in building markets in their native countries based
in California itself. Saxenian suggests that there is a healthy flow of
financial and intellectual capital between Asia and California and
that this flow has made a major contribution to technological innovation and to the economic expansion of the state.

The argument that immigrants displace native workers needs to
be balanced by evidence that foreign-born scientists and engineers
are generating new jobs and wealth for the state economy. Nor is it
valid to assume that skilled immigrants will stay permanently in the
US as they frequently did in the past. In the case of some Asian countries, the 'brain drain' may be giving way to an accelerating process
of 'brain circulation' as immigrants who have studied and worked in

the US increasingly return to their home countries to take advantage of opportunities there. Even those immigrants who choose to remain in the US are playing a growing role in linking domestic technology businesses to those in their countries of origin.

Increasingly, Silicon Valley's new immigrant entrepreneurs are building far-reaching professional and business ties to regions in Asia. They are uniquely positioned because their language skills and technical and cultural know-how allow them to function effectively both in the business culture of their home countries as well as in Silicon Valley.

Table 1
Silicon Valley Workers, 1990

	Total Workforce		High-Technology Workforce		Scientists and Engineers in High-Technology Workforce	
	Nos.	%	Nos.	%	Nos.	%
Total	1,806,233	100	274,335	100	57,495	100
Of which: Asian born	205,603	11	50,608	18	12,237	21
Other foreign	241,360	13	31,233	11	6,261	11

Source: U.S. census 1990 PUMS. Quoted by The Public Policy Institute of California.

The presence of large numbers of Chinese and Indian engineers in Silicon Valley is a recent phenomenon, mirroring the changes in US immigration legislation, but there is a disproportionate representation of Chinese and Indian engineers in Silicon Valley's technology workforce. This reflects broader national trends: foreign-born engineers and computer scientists in the US are significantly more likely to come from India or Taiwan than from other Asian and South American nations.

The glass ceiling

Indian and Chinese skilled immigrants account for at least one-third of the engineering workforce in many of the region's technology firms and they are increasingly visible as entrepreneurs and investors. However, it is indeed unfortunate that one finds plenty of fully documented evidence of the existence of a glass ceiling here (cf. Fernandez (1998), Tang (1993)). The US Department of Labor defines the glass ceiling as comprising 'those artificial barriers based on attitudinal or organizational bias that prevent qualified individuals from advancing upward in their organizations to management level positions.'

The predominance of Asians in technical and engineering as opposed to managerial occupations is also reflected in the composition of the management teams of Silicon Valley companies. The CorpTech Directory lists the names and titles of all executives in public technology firms in the region. This data shows Chinese and Indians in significantly greater numbers in R&D than in other functions such as finance, marketing or sales. Many Asian engineers I know say they feel as if they are seen as 'good work horses, and not race horses' or 'good technicians, rather than managers.'

Dr. Saxenian has tried to gauge ethnic entrepreneurship in Silicon Valley by identifying businesses whose CEOs have Chinese and Indian surnames in a Dun & Bradstreet database of technology firms started after 1980. She feels that 'these numbers may still understate the scale of immigrant entrepreneurship in the region because firms started by Chinese or Indians with non-Asian CEOs are not counted. Our interviews suggest that this has frequently been the case in Silicon Valley, where venture capital financing has often been tied to the requirement that non-Asian senior executives be hired. This seems a more likely source of bias than the opposite scenario, i.e., firms started by non-Asians that hire a Chinese or Indian CEO.'

How do Indians compare with the Taiwanese?

✓ Taiwan is a nation of 20 million people: a fraction of our size.
✓ Lack of fluency in English is a major handicap for the Taiwanese. Mandarin is the sole medium of instruction. English is taught only in some schools and only after high school. The Taiwanese have to attend special English language classes before coming to the US. They have serious problems reading and understanding technical stuff. In contrast, most Indians are fluent in the language.
✓ The racial prejudices that Indians face on arrival in the US are nothing compared to what the Chinese have to face. It is very

difficult for a student or a single person to rent accommodation in a good neighborhood. Nobody wants a Chinese moving in next door. Chinese families also face an uphill task purchasing a home.
✓ Indians have been a part of the professional scene in the US for generations. Indian doctors, accountants and engineers are to be found all over the US, so a newcomer from India is not really coming to a strange land. By contrast, a Chinese is entering an almost hostile environment.

Considering the above, Indians should have been way ahead in numbers in the Silicon Valley. However, they are not.

Table 2
Number of immigrants, Indian, Chinese and White, to Silicon Valley
High-Technology Industries, by Year

	1980–89	1970–79	Before 1970
Indian	4,367	1,963	803
Chinese	7,921	5,697	2,491
White	7,553	6,136	10,143

Source: US census 1990 PUMS. Quoted by The Public Policy Institute of California.

This information, quoted from one of the most reliable of sources, is indeed amazing. In spite of the hurdles mentioned above, the Chinese have been immigrating in much greater numbers. However, the following two tables are even more disturbing. The Chinese have not only been coming in greater numbers, they are also deriving greater benefit from the American system of education, and are mostly better employed than Indians. Considering it is one-fiftieth our size, Taiwan had more doctoral candidates in engineering in the US in the 1980s than did any other country (Johnson, 1998).

Please see also:
Bouvier, Leon F. and David Simcox (May 1995). 'Foreign Born Professionals in the United States.' *Population and Environment*. Vol. 16, No. 5.
Ong, Paul, Lucie Cheng, and Leslie Evans (1992). 'Migration of Highly Educated Asians and Global Dynamics.' *Asian and Pacific Migration Journal*. Vol. 1, No. 3–4.
Kanjanapan, Wilawar, (Spring 1995). 'The Immigration of Asian Professionals to the United States: 1988–1990.' *International Migration Review*. Vol. 29, No. 1, pp. 7–32.

Table 3
Education of Indians, Chinese and Whites in Silicon Valley
High-Technology Industries, 1990

	Indian		Chinese		White	
	Nos.	%	Nos.	%	Nos.	%
M.S./Ph.D.	4,043	55	7,612	40	34,468	18
B.S.	1,581	22	5,883	31	59,861	31
School graduate	600	8	1,002	5	23,488	12
< High school	279	4	1,170	6	9,319	5
Total:	7295	100	19218	100	91217	100

Source: U.S. census 1990 PUMS. Quoted by The Public Policy Institute of California.

The Chinese are simply better organised and this is reflected in all spheres of activity. The National Taiwan University Alumni Association in the Silicon Valley has 1,500 members in the bay area and Chiao-Tung, 1,000. These alumni associations are extremely active and serve as important sources of trusted personal and business contacts among the Taiwanese engineering community in Silicon Valley. Indeed, the Indian Institutes of Technology (IITs), India's elite engineering institutions, also appear to have played a comparable role among Indian immigrants in Silicon Valley, but to a much reduced extent.

As the Chinese immigrant community grew during the 1970s and 1980s, they responded to the sense of professional and social exclusion by collective organisation. They often found one another socially first, coming together to celebrate holidays and family events with others who spoke the same language and shared a similar cultural background. Over time, they used these social networks for business purposes, creating professional associations to provide resources and support structures within their own communities. The institutions they created have mirrored those created in an earlier generation by native engineers in the region.

This contrasts sharply with the arm's-length behaviour of Indians in the US, towards each other in general and newcomers in particular. It is a rare Indian student or job hunter who finds any sort of a social or community support, except from immediate family members who happen to be there.

The networks Silicon Valley's Chinese immigrant entrepreneurs are building are not simply local. They have far-reaching professional and business ties to regions in Asia. They are uniquely positioned because their language skills and technical and cultural know-how allow them to function effectively in the business culture of many Asian countries. A transnational community of Chinese, primarily Taiwanese, engineers has thus fostered a two-way flow of capital, skill and information between California and the overseas Chinese people in countries such as Taiwan, Malaysia, Singapore and Thailand. In this process, Silicon-Valley-based entrepreneurs have benefited from the significant flows of capital that these immigrants coordinate, as well as from the privileged access they provide to Asian markets and the region's flexible, state-of-the-art semiconductor and personal computer manufacturing capabilities.

To a certain extent, Silicon Valley's Indian engineers have also played a similar role, linking technology businesses in Silicon Valley with India's highly skilled software programming and design talent. But this role has been a less involved one, the attitude being 'I want to help you, and can tell you what to do, how to do it and give you all the contacts, but leave me out of it. I am not ready to make big investments in India yet.'

It cannot be denied that most overseas Indians (NRIs) feel out of place in India. NRIs often face resentment when they return to India—a resentment that is not unrelated to our long-standing hostility towards foreign corporations. In contrast to the close collaboration between Taiwan's policymakers and their US-based engineers, there has been almost no communication between India's Silicon Valley engineering community and its policymakers, even those concerned directly with technology policy. Young engineers in India prefer to work for multinationals because they not only pay better, but are seen as a ticket to Silicon Valley. Of course, there are some US-educated Indians who do return. Overall, however, the 'braindrain' of skilled workers to the US continues unabated.

The statistics that follow are for firms started by Chinese or Indians between 1980 and 1998, and which have a CEO with an Indian or a Chinese surname. It has been discussed earlier that these numbers may understate the scale of immigrant entrepreneurship in the region because firms started by Chinese or Indians with non-Asian CEOs are not included in the count. It seems that this has frequently been the case in Silicon Valley, where venture capital financing has often been tied to the requirement that non-Asian senior executives be hired.

Table 4

1998 Sales and Employment Figures of Silicon Valley High-technology Firms Led by a Chinese or Indian CEO

	No. of Firms	Total Sales $ million.	Total Employment	Average sale per employee
Indian	774	3,588	16,598	$ 216,110
Chinese	2,001	13,237	41,684	$ 317,555

Note: The average sale per employee of all technology firms in the Dun & Bradstreet database, 1998, for Silicon Valley is: $ 242,105

Source: Dun & Bradstreet database, 1998. Quoted by The Public Policy Institute of California.

Table 5

Chinese- and Indian-run Companies as a Share of the Total Silicon Valley High-technology Start-ups, 1980–1998

	1980–1984		1985–1989		1990–1994		1995–1998	
	Nos.	%	Nos.	%	Nos.	%	Nos.	%
Indian	47	3	90	4	252	7	385	9
Chinese	121	9	347	15	724	19	809	20
White	1,181	88	1,827	81	2,787	74	2,869	71

Source: Dun & Bradstreet database, 1998. Quoted by The Public Policy Institute of California.

These data indicate that the rate of Chinese and Indian entrepreneurship in Silicon Valley has increased significantly over time and that their businesses are creating wealth and a large number of jobs in the region. The Chinese and Indians were at the helm of 13 per cent of Silicon Valley's technology companies between 1980 and 1984, but were running 29 per cent of the region's high-technology companies started between 1995 and 1998. In the case of the Chinese, their significantly larger growth has been fuelled both by the emergence of role models and of supportive networks within their ethnic communities in the region, as well as by growing ties to Asian markets and sources of capital and manufacturing capabilities.

Chinese and Indian firms remain small relative to the technology sector as a whole, with an average of 21 employees per firm compared to 37 employees per firm for all firms. Although these immigrant-run firms employ fewer people, the Chinese-run firms have sales of $ 317,555 per employee, better than the national average of $ 242,105 per employee. The Indian-run firms show poor productivity, and have sales of only $ 216,110 per employee.

Organise and win

A point to be noted is that while many emerging economies suffered financial crises and a recession in the late 1990s, the US economy boomed. As a result, the income gap between the rich and poor countries has, of course, widened. Over the next decade or so, the information-technology revolution is going to add to this gap as this is widely seen as being the main driver of growth. Since the rich economies, notably the US, have a vast lead in this field, does this necessarily mean that it will inevitably cause the gap to widen further?

This, however, need not prevent emerging economies like India from growing at an even faster pace. It is easier to catch up than to be an economic leader. The West would have to devise new technologies, and devise ways of optimising the use of existing ones, the more to maintain their rapid growth. In poorer countries, these technologies can be used at a relatively lower cost. Here, innovation is less important: growth can be achieved by buying the developed world's technology. In less developed economies, growth is generated not only by increased inputs of capital and low cost labour but by a more efficient use of these inputs. The lone-ranger attitude of a highly individual style of ownership and management will have to be abandoned in favour of larger, well organised, cohesive entities.

Where does India go from here?

India has plenty of entrepreneurs in the Silicon Valley who are acknowledged to be brilliant. And very very rich. Surely, these people realise that every nation grows by and though the performance and contributions of its citizens. No nation wants charity from its people, but it is not outsiders who will come and lay the foundation for its development!

There is massive evidence in the Silicon Valley of how the Chinese, in spite of serious handicaps, have attained admirable successes, for themselves and for their people back home. A closely-knit community of Taiwanese returnees from the US, and its US-based engineers and entrepreneurs, have become the bridge between Silicon Valley and their homeland. This transnational community has accelerated the upgrading of Taiwan's technological infrastructure by transferring technical know-how and organisational models as well as by forging closer ties with Silicon Valley. It is admirable that management practices in Taiwan (and in other South-East Asian countries) are now more like those of Silicon Valley than like that of the traditional Chinese family-firm model that dominated older industries. As a result, Taiwan is now the world's largest producer of notebook computers and a range of related PC components including motherboards, monitors, scanners, power supplies and keyboards. In addition, Taiwan's semiconductor and integrated circuit manufacturing capabilities are now on par with leading Japanese and US producers; and its flexible and efficient networks of specialised small- and medium-sized enterprises coordinate the diverse components of this sophisticated infrastructure.

The growing integration of the technological communities of Silicon Valley and Taiwan offers substantial benefits to entrepreneurs in both economies. Silicon Valley remains the centre of new product definition and design and the development of leading-edge technologies, whereas Taiwan offers world-class manufacturing, flexible development and integration, and access to key customers and markets in China and South-East Asia.

Unlike the Taiwanese immigrants who have increasingly returned home to start businesses or work in established companies, it is indeed a tragedy that the Indians in the US tend to look down upon India and everything Indian. Far from choosing to return and live and work permanently in India, they do not wish to have anything to do with their home country. Indeed, there are a number of Indian entrepreneurs who have become successful by subcontracting their hardware requirements from Taiwan.

The result is that the Indian software industry is dominated by a small number of large export-oriented domestic and foreign corporations that have minimal ties with each other, local entrepreneurs or the Indian engineering community in Silicon Valley. These companies have been so profitable playing the wage gap that they have had few incentives to address the higher value-added segments of the market or to nurture entrepreneurial companies that might do so. As a result, most economic relations between Silicon Valley and regions like Bangalore are still conducted primarily by individuals within large US or Indian corporations.

6.2   *Export of construction services*

Look East for work ethic

I remember I was in Malaysia in 1981 when the present Prime Minister of Malaysia, Dr Mahathir Mohammad, assumed office. At that time, one of the world's most prestigious construction projects, the Penang Bridge, linking the island of Penang to the mainland in the northern part of the country, was up for bidding. The design and paperwork were complete. Tenders had been called for and the construction contracts were to be given out as separate packages. Many world-class firms formed consortia and bid for the various packages.

A leading Indian construction firm had joined hands with a leading French firm to bid for some of the work. Advance teams of engineers, administrators and financial experts had been camping in Malaysia for months in advance preparing the groundwork for the bids. The Indians were among them. This was the time of the construction boom in the Gulf when Indian firms were flush with funds and were able to afford the substantial expenditure involved.

A short list of eleven consortia was made which included the Indians. A few days later, the short list was cut down to three and only Japanese and Korean firms featured on it. Dr Mahathir Mohammad had just launched his 'look east' campaign and he was openly saying that he wanted to use this massive project to bring into Malaysia a new work culture. He pointed out that the project would bring in thousands of skilled and supervisory staff into Malaysia and he wanted the Malaysians to work side by side and learn from the best. He did not much care for the easygoing work style of the western firms and was particularly critical of the Indians' work style. Though he did not name names, he pointed to the work ethic of Indian firms in the Gulf, which were mainly involved in subcontracting and doing the more labour intensive, routine, low technology jobs. Dr Mohammad very specifically mentioned the behaviour of contractors and workers in the Gulf and said he was going to be careful Malaysians did not acquire these habits. It is also true that a number of Malaysian engineers who visited India at the invitation of the Indian firm were shown the very crude and shoddy finish of our roads and bridges. It is also tragic but true that a number of Indian engineers and technicians were then recruited by the Koreans and the Japanese and did a superb job.

On the flip side, a very strong point in favour of the Koreans was that they had demonstrated learning the finer point of construction technology from the Americans during the Vietnam war. The Americans then needed a lot of roads and bridges built all over Indo China and Thailand. They wanted a good job done and done fast, and were prepared to pay for it. Korean construction firms seized the opportunity, learnt the technology and the methodology and rapidly became world-class contractors themselves.

✓ Many Indian construction firms also had ample opportunity to work with the world's best in the Gulf. Indian firms however, did not benefit from this. Instead the engineers and the technicians of these firms got better jobs with other firms and most are no longer in India.

Penang bridge has been built as per schedule and so have a large number of superhighways all over Malaysia. The work was mostly done by Korean and Japanese firms in joint ventures with Malaysian firms. The Malaysians have learnt the tricks of the trade and today are world-class contractors in their own right. Today, it is the Malaysian firms who are in India building highways and bridges.

Indian construction industry

✓ Note 1: The word 'construction' can include many activities. When reading the following, please remember that I am talking of construction projects in terms of building, say, highrise appartment blocks, residential complexes, holiday resorts, highways, bridges, airports, harbours, railways and other types of infrastructural facilities. The ambit I have defined includes civil engineering and architectural services.

✓ Note 2: I am NOT talking of mechanical, electrical and chemical engineering projects, turnkey installations, design and consultancy and supply contracts.

India has everything it needs to be a major player in the field of world construction.

- Look at our history. We have been blessed with a rich cultural heritage of traditional craftsmanship. Our ancestors have left behind a veritable treasure house of a number of structures of exquisite workmanship. This heritage of architectural and artistic skills should, by itself, have been a constant source of inspiration for our construction companies to reach greater heights in their professional accomplishments
- Today's architects, engineers and technicians are the descendants of these same accomplished craftsmen. Coupled with this, we have some of the best brains in the world. So, we should have been well ahead of everybody in sophisticated technology combined with traditional architectural styles
- Indian companies have been engaged in overseas construction projects for many years and have worked side by side with some of the best in the world. We should have acquired, by now, adequate expertise and capabilities in all fields of construction

Yet, we have been left scraping the bottom of the barrel of the world construction markets as an Exim Bank annual report shows. The highlights of Project Exports, as revealed by the Exim Bank analysis, were (I am ignoring the rupee value of the contracts as the Indian currency has been depreciating consistently during this period and the dollar value of the contracts are not available for comparison. In any case, we got only five contracts for actual construction work, so the values are negligible):

- 63 contracts were secured during 1998–99 as compared to 60 in 1997–98. This represents an increase of 5 per cent
- The success ratio, measured as a percentage of contracts secured to bids submitted, was 41 per cent. This was the same as the previous year
- Out of the bids submitted during 1998–99, almost one-third were for projects funded by multilateral agencies like the World Bank, African Development Bank, Asian Development Bank, Overseas Economic Co-operation Fund (OECF) and Japan and Kuwait Fund for Economic Development. Out of the 34 bids India made,

only nine contracts were secured under multilaterally funded projects overseas

- Out of the contracts secured during 1998–99, five were for construction projects, 23 for turnkey projects, 21 for supply contracts and 14 contracts for consultancy services
- The top six countries in terms of the number of contracts secured during 1998–99 were Kenya (10), UAE (7), Bhutan (5), Bangladesh (4), Oman (4) and Saudi Arabia (4)

Major contracts secured included oil drilling services in the UAE, a turnkey cement plant in Bangladesh, transmission projects in Tunisia and Lebanon, a telecom network in Zimbabwe and a HVAC plant in Hong Kong.

Well, this is the sum of Indias efforts in terms of exporting construction skills. India's markets are other Third World countries and the projects bid for are the routine, run-of-the-mill sort where elements of price and technology are all that matter. We are nowhere on the scene when it comes to building prestigious or sophisticated projects such as luxury hotels, resorts, upmarket housing and important institutional buildings.

Maldives is a country next door to India where millions of dollars are being spent on building and renovating high-class luxury resorts. The architects and designers are European, but the construction contracts are increasingly going to Malaysian and Singaporean firms.

India has no share of this market.

An important aspect of the South-East Asian firms is that they have strong organisational and managerial setups. They can make investments in the projects they participate in, while Indian firms want to merely be contractors or subcontractors. Indian firms are even happy with mere supply contracts.

Tiny Singapore

Singapore's efforts in enlarging its external economy is based on an intensive regionalisation programme. Singapore-based enterprises, which include local companies and multinational enterprises, have the strong institutional backing of the Economic Development Board (EDB). As per the annual reports available on their site on the net, in 1995, the EDB facilitated a total of 381 regional projects by 187 local enterprises and 123 MNCs. The number of companies set up abroad grew from 3,540 in 1993 to 4,128 in 1994. The contribution of overseas operations to the value added of the Singaporean economy amounted to 12 per cent: a remarkable figure for a nation of less than 3 million people.

Assistance in various forms is available from the Singaporean government in order to encourage local construction companies to tap the international contracting market and export their services. Way back in the early 1970s, the authorities concerned had already seriously thought about exporting Singapore's construction expertise overseas. The Ministry of National Development Holdings, together with the Urban Redevelopment Authority, set up Indeco Pte Ltd to make available to countries in the region the expertise and know-how developed by Singaporean professionals in the areas of public housing, urban renewal, town and city planning, and industrial estate and other infrastructural development. Indeco was to act as a vehicle agency to spearhead the export drive and to farm out successful overseas contracts to various Singaporean subcontractors.

In early 1986, the Trade Development Board (TDB) set up an on-line information retrieval service to provide crucial advance information to local businessmen, and in the process help them clinch deals.

✓ By assessing the 'Scan-a-Bid' database, the TDB can furnish the latest information on consulting, contracting and supply opportunities for Third World country development projects *long before tenders are called for.*

In 1987, the Construction Industry Development Board (CIDB) introduced the Tenders Estimating Data Services (TEDS) to provide Singaporeans submitting tenders with a means of gauging the prevailing wage levels and prices of important construction materials in other countries. TEDS enables companies to assess the quotations submitted by indigenous subcontractors or suppliers for particular overseas projects. Tender prices can then be computed and the risks evaluated. As a coordinator, the CIDB also helps promote the exchange of cost information between local construction companies. In conjunction with the TDB, the CIDB has organised overseas missions for the construction industry in order to identify export opportunities in foreign countries.

Launched in 1987, the APPECS (Attachment of Public Service Professionals for the Export of Construction Services) scheme was designed to enable government employees and professionals to be attached to private firms so as to help them compete for and carry out overseas projects. This scheme scored some success in the early years but it is seldom used nowadays, as private companies have accumulated enough experience.

A unified agency, the Singapore Contractors Association, has been very useful in upgrading the capabilities of local construction firms. Merging small companies to form larger entities is an excellent option for pooling resources so as to face international competition more effectively.

A point to be noted here is that the underlining reason for the outstanding success of the Singaporean Chinese companies is their attitude towards working with each other, the sharing of knowledge and information and networking to gain competitive advantage overseas. Without this attitude, the government could have done nothing.

By contrast, Indian firms have awfully managed trade associations where the only thing one is assured of is the infighting.

Finish and the work environment

One of the major barriers to India's export effort in the construction field is the fact that bringing prospective overseas clients to see the work any large Indian construction firm may have done in India is often an unmitigated disaster.

The clients already know that India possesses state-of-the-art technology and some of the world's best engineers. But when the client comes here and sees the way work is done here, the colossal mess that is made of the surroundings and the crude, slipshod finish given to otherwise excellent structures, he quickly takes the next flight out to nearby Malaysia.

Let me cite an example here. In the recent past, many nations have built mass rapid transit systems for their big cities. Very near India, Bangkok, Kuala Lumpur and Singapore have quickly completed a mixture of elevated and underground systems. Travelling to these cities one is amazed at how efficiently the job has been done, without almost any mess being caused on the roads. The neighbouring residential and office areas have remained remarkably unaffected by the massive projects.

In contrast, in India, be it an extension to one's garage, a new multistorey building or a flyover, the mess the work creates and leaves behind is always phenomenal. A possible reason for this may be that, as in many western countries, it is mandatory in Malaysia and Singapore for the construction contract to include an undertaking by the contractor to ensure that the road immediately in front of the site remains free of dust, mud and debris. One can see the tyres of the lorries leaving the site being carefully hosed down and cleaned. No lorries are allowed to be offloaded on the roadside even for a few hours. It is made clear to private householders building extensions, etc. that even a brick on the road in front will attract heavy fines. I have heard an inspector tell a house-owner that a public road is no place to store his bricks. If there is no other space, he should store them in his bedroom!

People in India have lived and worked under very different environments and overseas clients realise that it is not possible for these workers, supervisors and managers to change overnight.

Where do we go from here?

The Indian construction industry has developed over the last 50 years, but it is yet to mature fully. It has certainly contributed to the economic development and capital formation of our economy. For the industry to continue to grow and prosper further, it would have to undergo some strategic restructuring with respect to management methods, technological applications, human resource development and international contracting.

After more than 50 years of nationhood and development, local firms have indeed mastered the art sufficiently to be able to bid for international construction and engineering projects. Though they may be disadvantaged by the size and financial manoeuvrability of established companies in developed countries, they can still capitalise on their local knowledge and cultural familiarity with regional economies to establish joint ventures or partnerships with foreign enterprises.

Another reason to look to regional and international markets for business and sustainability is that the growth in domestic construction activities is dwindling. Furthermore, competition among construction firms is getting tougher. There is a steady deterioration in the profit margins of most construction projects. This is exacerbated by the increase in the number of construction firms that are able to handle jobs of large contract values. The increase in the pool of qualified firms comes from multinational firms in India and local firms who have managed to upgrade themselves through the years.

Even in industrialised economies, a number of conditions have provided the stimuli for change in the techniques used to manage engineering and construction projects. The dwindling volume of domestic and overseas construction projects (especially in the Middle East), without a commensurate reduction in the number of firms bidding for such contracts, has created a 'buyers' market'. Clients have begun to demand buildings of increasing complexity. The widespread diffusion of Information Technology (IT) and the need for greater environmental control have led to increased sophistication in building services. Private sector clients are demanding better performances by imposing more stringent contract conditions.

Large penalties are being imposed on contracts that have failed to be completed on time, creating a highly competitive environment. Increased project complexity and fragmentation due to the rise of subcontracting, together with greater technical sophistication, has led to a growth in the number of specialist trades in developed countries. The sourcing of building materials, components and equipment from a growing international market has added to the complexity of managing large projects.

In the international market, traditional methods of contracting are slowly giving way to alternative forms. The most distinctive point about traditional contracting is the division between the design and construction stages. This separation often leads to long project timeframes and has been a major factor in the shift to alternative forms of contracting. Traditional contracting methods also often lead to the design of unbuildable details, a problem that hinders the construction process.

New methods of contracting include a management contract, a management fee, construction management, project management, and a design/build contract. These have been adopted by cutting-edge innovative firms in the industry. Each involves the contractor in a slightly different role in relation to planning, pricing and managing the construction project. This proliferation of new forms is an indicator of the industry's state of flux.

The move away from traditional methods of contracting has had a profound impact on skills and employment, but some firms have also attempted to innovate through the use of new technologies.

The market

Entering an unknown area may invite more risks, but an Indian construction company with a true entrepreneurial spirit should not be afraid to take on new challenges for more lucrative returns. Risks exist everywhere and can be even higher in the domestic market. A way of reducing risk when operating in an unfamiliar environment is to form strategic alliances with local partners who know the market better. Such partnerships will enable you to penetrate the market via a consortium of experienced contractors, helping you win contracts by capitalising on individual expertise and competitive advantage.

Several factors favour the campaign of India's construction companies in terms of venturing and expanding their businesses abroad. The Asia-Pacific region is considered to be the growth region for the next century as it includes many developing countries, NIEs and emerging economies poised to take off. As such, these nations will offer tremendous business opportunities in infrastructural development and construction, in particular. The concurrent rise in the demand for construction goods and services follows the course of national integration, industrialisation and urbanisation.

International agencies such as the World Bank and the Asian Development Bank have estimated that the buoyant growth in Asia will incur infrastructural development expenditures of US$ 300 to 500 billion for the next five to 10 years. In Asia alone, development expenditures will amount to US$ 20 to 30 billion per year.

Economic reforms and the deregulation of the Chinese economy have also generated tremendous opportunities for India's construction firms. China has opened its doors to foreign investors and requires massive investments in infrastructure, buildings, civil engineering, and private and commercial projects to support its economic development initiatives.

For large construction projects, there is much purchasing to be done. The supplies, in most cases, will come from all over the world. There is immense scope here for the secondary export of India's highly competitive building material and industrial supplies.

6.3 *Export of wooden furniture*

India has plenty of first-class timber and it has a centuries old tradition of first-class woodworking craftsmanship yet. it does not export. It is the Indian businessman of today who is third class.

I am quoting a friend of mine here, a buyer of huge quantities of wooden furniture for an American wholesaler. He buys mainly from Thailand and Malaysia and came to India at my suggestion to see if he could buy anything from us.

We found three shocking things.

First, India has grossly mismanaged its huge forest wealth and is now forced to import timber.

Second, far from exporting furniture, we are importing completely built-up wooden furniture, mainly from Malaysia.

Third, large business houses have completely ignored this sector. There are only small, poorly organised, manual operations run all over the country, making what can only be called cheap furniture for the immediate market.

Note: Malaysia's furniture exports of over Rs 300,000 million (Appendix 6) clearly show that this is not a sector for riff-raff furniture makers and that India's big business houses should seriously consider making an entry.

A quick look at the furniture industry worldwide

The furniture industry has many international trade publications, and all the furniture exporting countries have their trade promotion councils which churn out a huge mass of data and statistics on the world trade in wooden furniture. As per estimates prepared by the leading international trade journal *Furniture Today* in their January 1999 issue, the international trade of furniture and parts has grown by over 220 per cent in the 10 years between 1988 and 1997. This growth has been generally facilitated by economic conditions, increasing household formations in developed countries and the aggressive export marketing by the furniture industry in Asia.

An examination of export trends and markets reveals three major trading blocks for furniture—Europe, North America and Asia. Import and export trends into and out of these trading regions are distinct and for Indian export houses wishing to venture into this field, offer insight into the future trade of furniture products.

While the US is the single largest market for furniture products of all prices, an examination of the three trading blocks for furniture reveals that Europe is the largest trading block. This is of no interest to an Indian exporter as the majority of trade carried out here is between European trading partners. Approximately 80 per cent of furniture and parts imported into OECD-Europe is from other European trading partners. Italy and Germany are leading exporting countries in Europe.

North America is the next largest trading block in terms of the value of total imports. This region is a net importer of furniture and parts, with the import/export ratio remaining at an average of 1.80. Trade of furniture in North America is multilateral, with several major trading partners in both Europe and Asia.

Asia is the third and smallest distinct trading block, but the fastest growing. This region exports more than twice the value of furniture and parts imported. Japan is the major importing country in Asia, importing over 70 per cent of the value of furniture imported into the region, mostly from other Asian trading partners. Taiwan has been the leading exporter of furniture in this region. However, the growth in exports from Taiwan has slowed dramatically while exports from the ASEAN countries have grown due to a strongly developing furniture industry and more aggressive marketing. Exports from this region to OECD countries grew by almost 200 per cent between 1989 and 1998, led by Malaysia and Indonesia.

An examination of wooden household furniture import and consumption trends in the US reveals that imported furniture has a significant place in US consumer homes. Approximately 30 per cent of the wooden household furniture consumption is satisfied by imported products, much of which is sold under the brand names of US manufacturers or large store chains. Many manufacturers have found it advantageous to fill out their product lines with imports that cannot be manufactured in their plants at a profit. Imports have maintained a 25–30 per cent share of the US furniture consumption since 1985 and will probably remain at this level unless exchange rates change drastically.

An examination of wooden household furniture imports by major regions of the world reveals that more than 50 per cent is shipped from Asia. Only imports from Europe have shown a decline since 1989.

As a quick summary, the US import of furniture as estimated by *Furniture Today* in its January 1999 issue is:

CANADA	21.6%
CHINA	14.7%
TAIWAN	14.4%
MALAYSIA	11.5%
INDONESIA	8.1%
THE PHILIPPINES	7.7%
THAILAND	7.6%
ITALY	5.5%
MEXICO	8.2%
INDIA	????

There have been several changes in the list of leading wooden furniture exporting countries to the US. In 1989, Taiwan was the undisputed leader, followed by Italy, Canada, the Philippines and Yugoslavia. These five accounted for 62 per cent of all US wooden furniture imports in 1989. Malaysia has, since then, rapidly risen to be the fourth largest exporter of wooden furniture to the US. This position was achieved by trippling exports to the US through an aggressive furniture export and market strategy.

Although Taiwan's exports of wooden household furniture to the US has dropped, its indirect exports have increased. The Taiwanese wooden furniture industry has moved offshore to strategically capture cost savings in labour and obtain access to raw materials. Countries like Thailand that have shown a marked increase in exports to the US have also seen an increase in direct foreign investment by Taiwanese furniture producers in terms of furniture manufacturing capacity.

In this chapter, we will be taking a close look at the furniture industry in Asia in general and in Thailand and Malaysia in particular. I am sure the interested reader would be able to draw some important lessons from this. Let's start with India first.

Personal experiences

After living and working in many developing countries for over 30 years, I retired and came back home some years ago. I have built a home in the South, near Chennai. My architect said I had two choices as far as the furniture I needed was concerned, either to get custom-designed items built by local carpenters, which would be very expensive, or, to buy readymade furniture from Delhi. He advised me against going to Bangalore or Mumbai as I would not get any value for money there.

I went to Delhi and visited almost all the large furniture showrooms. The first thing that struck me was the extremely disorganised nature of the operations. Nowhere was the owner available and nobody else would talk to me. In some of the showrooms, a junior salesperson would walk around with me but I had to wait to talk to the boss regarding any changes and alterations I wanted made.

I went around the showrooms and saw the fairly large range they had on display. In the end, I selected a few items, though with certain changes and modifications. I also chose the colour and quality of the fabric I wanted. I was surprised that nobody took any detailed notes of all this. The owner briefly scribbled on a slip of paper. They sheepishly explained that the less records there are the less the bother with the tax man. I was amazed at the immense reliance on memory and was very apprehensive of what would eventually be delivered.

I was expected to pay an advance, and in cash, before delivery, but I could check the consignment before it left the workshop. I was in the South so an inspection was not convenient and I was forced to rely on the owner's loud proclamations of quality consciousness and his apparently long list of satisfied customers all over the country.

The other thing that struck me as odd was the complete lack of coordination with the other services that were needed to pack and transport the furniture to my home 4000 km away. I am so used to the Chinese style of networking or Guanxi which I spoke about in Chapters 4.4 and 4.5, where many different firms come together and work as one, that I found this very annoying. I was clearly told that I could only be introduced to packers and transporters, and that it was up to me to check their credentials and negotiate prices and terms. The furniture factory made it amply clear that it would bear no responsibility as far as the delivery was concerned.

Once I had paid the money, the headache began. I had to make frequent trips to Delhi to deal with all the different firms, and as expected, what I ultimately got was quite different from what I had ordered. The packing was slipshod and awful and it seems the consignment was transshipped twice on the way, causing a lot of damage. I had clearly negotiated for a full truck load travelling directly to my home. On complaining, the furniture shop owner very firmly refuted my point, saying they had made and sent exactly what I ordered, and that the rest was not their problem.

All of this notwithstanding, the most amazing thing was that all the furniture showrooms I visited were making huge claims for having an all-India market and even for regularly exporting all over the world.

One last but important point.

✓ As I said above, I have lived for many years in other developing nations and have got used to their very hospitable and personal style of doing business. Though furniture manufacturers could see that I was an important outstation customer doing the rounds of the market evaluating options, nobody tried to develop or strike up a personal, friendly relationship. Beyond the routine cup of tea or soft drink, nobody, for example, invited me for a meal. This is in sharp contrast to the treatment overseas buyers expect as routine in other Asian countries where the deal is always closed over a drink and a meal.

What I have stated is not a stray example. Later on, I found out that there were much bigger and better furniture makers in places like Mumbai and Bangalore, but nobody with the organisation or the interest to cater to a larger all-India market. Many living in small-town India face the same problems I did when it comes to buying furniture. There are some large firms who undertake to supply, pack and ship the goods to you, but this is on a one off basis and so the price tag is often unacceptable.

This being the case, there is not the remotest possibility of India gaining any sort of a foothold in the export market. As I have repeatedly said in this book, the days when one could sell exfactory on the basis of price and quality alone are gone. Indian firms today would hardly withstand the microscopic analysis overseas buyers would put their set-ups to.

Hand-made furniture

Let's take the case of hand-carved furniture. The current sources of hand-made furniture are India, Thailand, Mallacca in Malaysia and Bali in Indonesia.

India is not on the world map though Indian craftsmen were, in an earlier age, known the world over for their work. Their descendents have mostly been put into a stranglehold by middlemen money-lenders. Moreover, the profession is no longer remunerative resulting in the next generation moving away from the trade.

The stuff sold under the name of hand-carved furniture in North India in places like Saharanpur is mainly junk. In the South, one can still find furniture of a fairly good quality, but the supply is extremely limited, the craftsmen easily sell what they make and the output is booked many months in advance by domestic customers. So, nobody, really, is interested in exports.

There is a huge market for high-class furnishings and fittings right next door. Maldives spends millions of dollars on building and renovating luxury resorts. Almost everything is imported from Malaysia or Europe. India has no share of this market simply because, apart from random unorganised approaches, no efforts have been made to cultivate the world-class architects and designers who select the suppliers.

India only has travelling salesmen. Nobody will buy expensive furnishings from them.

If one goes to Thailand, Mallacca or Bali, the craftsmen are all ethnic locals but the traders are all of Chinese origin. The Chinese have

318 Unleashing India on World Markets

a remarkable talent for networking among the different services needed and an overseas buyer will first get invited to a dinner and the quote, negotiated over drinks. The quote will even include customs clearing in his home country and the goods, delivered to his doorstep.

Let's look at Malaysia

I quote from a press release of the Malaysia Timber Council reported in the Malaysian press in April 1998.

> Today, Malaysia is the world's largest producer of rubberwood furniture. Of the total furniture export turnover in 1996, the wooden furniture sector accounted for more than 85 per cent, of which 90 per cent is rubberwood furniture. Exports for the period January to October 1997 reached US$ 555 million, representing a 17 per cent increase over the same period in 1996. The distribution of wood furniture was concentrated to the United States, Japan and re-exports via Singapore. USA alone took 38.5 per cent of exports or US$ 207 million, recording an increase over January-October 1996 level. While Japan eased buying by 3 per cent to US$ 101 million, Singapore purchased 16.9 per cent more, raising exports there to US$ 54 million. Demand from Australia and United Kingdom was stronger with exports of US$ 24 million and US$ 22 million, respectively. Efforts are also being taken by the Malaysian furniture industry to further diversify their markets around the world, particularly, in Europe, Asia-Pacific region, Middle East and other new emerging markets.

> In order to gain a large share of the world furniture market, especially in the middle- and upper-end segment, Malaysian furniture manufacturers are investing a lot of effort in improving quality standards and productivity through the employment of higher technology in furniture engineering. The Malaysian furniture industry is spreading its wings and looking to new markets instead of relying heavily on its traditional markets, the US and Japan.

> A ploy shared by some furniture manufacturers I know is to target non-traditional markets for their products, such as Eastern Europe, Africa and Latin America through market diversification and niche marketing. They feel this will help the industry stay ahead of its competition.

Joint ventures are also seen as a strategy to offset rising raw material and production costs, particularly in the manufacture of components and sub-assemblies for the final product in Malaysia. Some furniture manufacturers are involved in joint ventures in countries such as Myanmar, Indonesia and China.

The Taiwan success story

The wood product industry in Taiwan is similar to its counterpart in the US in many ways. Like in the US, most furniture manufacturers in Taiwan are always on the lookout for more skilled labour and for new and appropriate equipment. This is because they are under pressure to maintain short lead times while manufacturing to Japanese, European and American standards. Also, like a lot of American manufacturers, Taiwan has found ways to work around these pressures and remain competitive.

Taiwan mainly attracts buyers from the US with its exotic Asian softwoods and veneers while being able to keep finished product prices low because it has lower labour and manufacturing costs than its US counterparts. Though standard wages in Taiwan are the fourth-highest in Asia, they're still much lower than US wages.

A colleague on a World Bank assignment came from a family who owned a very large furniture business in Taiwan. The 40-year-old family business involved manufacturing artificial jewellery for low-to mid-range retailers in the US. The product was popular, but seasonal, selling well only around Christmas. In the past few years, therefore, the firm has branched out by manufacturing mostly high-end residential furniture, particularly large cupboards and computer desks which are sold by major US retailers.

The 80,000-square-foot plant is vertically integrated by default. It would outsource parts during the busy season, but most of its former suppliers have since left Taiwan in search of cheaper labour in other Asian and African countries. The family was then left with no choice but to perform every aspect of production in-house. A lot of the plant's space is used for stockpiling raw material, because most items are imported and one cannot rely entirely on delivery schedules. This is the only way the plant can make sure it has enough on hand to process all sorts of orders which invariably have short lead times.

The plant produces an average of 6,000 parts every day and has been asked to take on more work, but won't. Though importers are anxious, the company cannot find the labour needed to expand. The plant receives an ample number of offers from overseas importers, but that doesn't mean it signs every one of them. The company has placed itself in a position where it can afford to be selective. The challenges it faces when choosing clients include ascertaining their distance from the US market and their credit worth. To find dependable customers, the firm uses its invaluable network of American Chinese firms and spends a lot on research.

It is an immense advantage that the company doesn't have to spend time and money designing new product lines. As a reputable and dependable exporter, it has acquired a number of importer clients. All of its importers provide designs for the products to be manufactured. That gives them more money and time to secure the appropriate materials and labour.

Now on to Thailand

Thailand is a market I know very well as I have implemented a number of manufacturing projects there. Producers in Thailand have geared themselves to producing furniture items that nobody else likes to, such as those with many parts. Sometimes, the making of one container requires the moulding of 60–70,000 pieces. Thailand produces a small amount of panel items and the full range of rubberwood furniture items. In this case, 'full range' refers to virtually any item the customer may demand, from a shoe rack to a buffet and hutch cabinet, all superbly designed and finished.

I know some American buyers who prefer Thailand to almost any other country because of the close networking relations or Guanxi the local Chinese display in working with each other. If somebody can't produce something according to the client's requirements, the business is passed on to a friend who can. I have seen competitors join hands instantly and put up a united front for a big buyer. In the end, the buyer gets troublefree supplies and the seller, better prices. I have attended business meetings where everybody is from a different firm. They fight each other and then go out for dinner together. If on a trip to the US, someone brings back an order too many, other factories get into the act. The point to be noted is that the other factories do not work as anonymous subcontractors. The customers know each of them and benefit by direct dealings.

This is very unlike in India where suppliers specialise in cutting each other's throat and, often losing the customer in the process.

While Thailand is doing well with furniture orders others may not choose to process, the industry is far from passive in its management modes and operations. In the area of product design and quality control, I saw a friend proudly demonstrate a bookcase, which due to carefully placed hinges, has sides and shelves that fold inwards to produce a flat item. This is not only excellent for packaging, the design means that the bookshelf requires no assembly and makes moving house easy too. My friend said, 'We really engineer our products—even the packaging. Where we put 800 pieces of an item in a container, we now fit 1000. We want assembly to be easy. Rubberwood furniture doesn't have to be cheap.' Always look around and learn from others, he encourages. Unlike some manufacturers, he is open to having visitors to his factory and is not concerned about others benefiting from his ideas.

Entering the US market has proven highly fortuitous for the Thais. Before the economic crisis, the majority of Thai furniture manufacturers focused solely on supplying high-end furniture to the Japanese market. For many, when the crisis hit Japan, this resulted in them having to shut shop. Others were forced to rapidly identify new markets, the US being a popular choice.

I will show later on in this chapter that switching to the US requires a complete change of attitude. Getting a foothold in Japan is very very tough. It could take a long while and there will be endless formalities before one gets the first order, but one can easily sell a chair for, say, $ 30. By contrast, it is easier to get into the US market but you will get, maybe, $ 15 for the same chair.

Although Thailand does produce large volumes, the manufacturers produce furniture to orders only and have the flexibility to change from one item to another quickly and with ease. Even small orders for, say, one container of an item is not a problem for them. Given the market today, it's not a good idea to mass produce any one item.

Thailand is also lucky with its supply of timber. About 30 years ago, the Chinese Malaysians came to the southern part of Thailand to invest in rubber plantations. These are non-depleting rubberwood sources, and are still supplying the industry.

The US market

Furniture demand in the US has traditionally been led by the housing industry. Demand for furniture products is directly related to new housing construction which in turn is effected by long-term mortgage lending rates. During downturns in new housing construction, declines in furniture consumption have been moderated by a general increase in repair and remodeling activities and the resale of existing housing.

The average size of new homes built in the US has generally been increasing. Most of these have three or more bedrooms. Today's home usually has both a formal area for receiving visitors and entertaining and an informal area for the family called a family room.

As the size and use of houses in the US change, so will the type of furniture that consumers demand. For example, today's modern family does not have time to take a long extended vacation, preferring 'mini' vacations over a three or four day period instead. Since so much time is spent at home, they view their home as a retreat and emphasise features that help them relax. One of these features is the family room containing an entertainment centre built to house consumer electronics and be the design focus of the room. Demand for home entertainment centres are growing significantly, with many US furniture manufacturers adding sophisticated home centre products at each new showing.

Another growing trend and feature of US houses is the 'home office.' Advances in computer and communication technologies have now made 'telecommuting' a reality and many companies are allowing employees to work from home at least on a part-time basis. This is particularly true in metropolitan areas with heavy traffic and long commutes. Telecommuting in these areas has proven to increase worker productivity. In addition, with the downsizing of many major US corporations, laid-off professional workers are opting to go into business for themselves and contracting their services even to companies they formerly worked for. Consumers with home offices want furniture to be functional and match furniture styles in the rest of the house. Typical office furniture does not perform this dual role so a new market has emerged which is small but growing.

There have only been a few changes over a 10-year period or so in the type of furniture products that have been produced in the US. One of the most significant changes has been in the amount of ready to assemble furniture. This type of furniture is assembled by the consumer at home. US manufacturers have achieved an advantage in this market by installing highly productive manufacturing lines and by maintaining a price advantage on a low profit margin product. Today, producers are trying to upscale a typically low price product by including wood veneers and solid wood trims and mouldings.

The home theatre market is still just a small segment, but it is growing at a rate of 10–12 per cent every year. Factory shipments are valued at an estimated $ 170–180 million. Consumer electronics is a growing industry, typically supported by upper income consumers under 50 years of age. In the future, home theatres will be part of a media room which will accommodate computers, entertainment electronics, home security systems, etc. Furniture systems will be designed to integrate electronics into our lives and hide the wires. The media room will evolve from today's standard living room, be less formal, and accommodate a changing lifestyle that will depend on computers and electronics to entertain and conduct business from home.

The latest trends in consumer goods include casual elegance, large-scale bedroom pieces, youth furniture and casual dining. The furniture trade forecasts the following trends for the US furniture market.

- In bedroom furniture, large statement beds with similarly scaled night stands, dressers and armoires
- Increasing market for youth bedroom furniture
- Increase in casual dining furniture and round dining tables
- Decrease in demand for china closets
- Expanding sales for mid-priced home theatre walls
- Demand for multi-functional armoires which accommodate televisions for the bedroom
- Stylist home office furniture at moderate prices
- A home that helps people relax and escape the stress of the workplace with furnishings with a casual style but elegant features.

The Japanese market

Japan is the largest wooden furniture importing country in Asia. Japan's population is roughly half that of the US and its consumers have a reputation for demanding high quality products. However, this may be changing due to both economic and social trends in Japan. Following a severe economic crisis in 1989 and the recent appreciation of the Yen against major foreign currencies, Japanese corporations have been forced to effect a reduction in their workforce for the first time in many decades. As a result of economic uncertainty and the increasing cost of products, many Japanese consumers have become value conscious. This has created an expanded market for mid-priced furniture products and imported furniture. Major furniture manufacturers in Japan are also looking to increase value by sourcing furniture parts and products overseas.

According to the International Development Association of the Furniture Industry of Japan (IDAFIJ), the Japanese furniture market was worth about US$ 20 billion in 1995, including both domestic products and imports. Although imported furniture products account for only an estimated seven per cent of the market share at the retail level, it is up substantially since 1987 when imports made up only two to three per cent of the market share. Overall, the market encompasses an extremely wide variety of items, from classic to modern styles, traditional and contemporary Japanese to western styles and from niche to conventional types. As housing itself has come to blend western and Japanese elements, a similar western–Japanese eclecticism has appeared in furniture. Traditional Japanese furniture now constitutes only a limited part of the market. At the same time, western-style furniture has to be redesigned to suit the physique and lifestyle of the average Japanese.

The purchase of furniture in Japan today is also changing significantly. During the years of economic growth, the main sources of demand for furniture were new housing and newlyweds. Again, as per the estimates of IDAFIJ, sales of 'wedding outfit sets,' consisting of wardrobes and cabinets, are down due to the trend towards built-in closets. Another consideration in the demand for wooden furniture is the marriage rate in Japan. The wedding season created a large special market for furniture as a high-priced 'wedding set' was traditionally given away at this time. This consisted of a Japanese dresser, a chest of drawers and a western-style wardrobe. However, a decline in marriages in the late 1980s and a preference among newlyweds for choosing furniture which is better suited to modern lifestyles and housing has led to a decline in the demand for traditional wedding furniture. The 1990s has seen an increase in the number of weddings as the children of the baby boomer generation reach marriageable age.

Living room furniture is increasingly being sold individually, rather than as entire sets. Consumers are starting to mix and match furniture to suit their taste. Sofas used to be mainly of the standard type with leather upholstery but now have shifted to being separate corner sets. In corner sofas, fabric upholstery is becoming more important and styles and designs, more casual.

In the dining room, the trend is towards larger furniture. In the past, the dining room and kitchen were connected as, for example, in public housing apartments. Dining room sets accordingly tended to be relatively small. Today, apartments are built with somewhat larger living spaces, with the dining room combined with the living room rather than with the kitchen. The demand, then, is mainly for relatively low tables and chairs in slightly larger, longer lasting sets. Traditional cupboards no longer sell well and the consumer now wants built-in cabinets and system kitchen units.

Only about 50 per cent of all Japanese homes currently have beds, but lifestyles are changing from the traditional tatami (straw mat) rooms to western-style ones. The generation raised on bunk beds is now becoming the consumer mainstream, increasing the demand for single and twin beds.

In the home study, most people previously used office-style desks and chairs. Today, the demand for wooden, high-quality products is on the rise. This reflects a tendency to view study furniture as interior decor or as a status symbol. Other trends include the brisk sale of fashionable sundry items such as curtains, carpets, cushions and candlestands. These items are selling well and have resulted in furniture companies expanding into these lines of products.

Storage units which fit into the wall are becoming popular. Chests, too, are being purchased as interior decor and tend to be sophisticated items with price tags to match.

Many of the newer houses in Japan have adopted western styling, although many still retain one traditional tatami room. Because of this trend towards western-styled housing, there has been an increase in the use of legged and closet-type furniture. Today's new home owner in Japan tends to be more value conscious than the home owner of a decade ago. These consumers are creating an expanded market for mid-priced casual furniture products. Many prefer to buy just what they need immediately. This creates a potential market in the future for higher-priced replacement products when consumers wish to upgrade their living environment. Many of these upgrades are expected to be for reception rooms and living rooms in the western tradition.

As per IDAFIJ estimates, almost 75 per cent of wooden furniture imported into Japan today comes from other Asian countries. Imports have grown from 38.3 billion yen in 1989 to an estimated 78.5 billion yen in 1995. This tremendous growth has been facilitated by the aggressive development of furniture manufacturing by ASEAN countries, particularly Thailand, Indonesia and Malaysia.

South-East Asian suppliers have shifted from components to finished furniture products along with the upgrading of product lines. The increasing demand and acceptance of these products by Japanese consumers has been attributed to quality improvements by the industry. Japanese consumers in the past have been extremely demanding of high quality furniture finish, often requiring the same finish on both the top and underside of tables and chairs. However, there is a growing trend among Japanese consumers to trade these high standards and expectations for reasonably priced products that offer reasonable quality. This trend is likely to benefit exporters from all regions.

There are several lifestyle trends occurring in Japan that affect furniture preference and purchase. Because of the small size of their dwellings, many Japanese need expanded storage space. Therefore, there is an increasing demand for wall storage furniture that makes better use of interior space. In addition, many Japanese families prefer western-styled tables for dining activities. They use this table for a variety of purposes other than for serving meals. The dining table is often the physical centre of family life in young families and as such, should have the finish to withstand excessive use.

Just like consumers in the US, Japanese consumers want to create a retreat in their homes from the busy outside world. Harmony in terms of room styling and design are important, especially in small living spaces. Consumers in Japan have a sophisticated taste in furniture and a keen eye for interior design and colour coordination. The general trend is towards natural wooden furniture and simple styling.

Japanese consumers have a traditional attachment to wood and an appreciation for the beauty of wood grain. They prefer quarter sawn as opposed to flat sawn wood and tend to dislike the presence of knots in the surface of furniture. However, today, there is quite a diversity of furniture styles, as mirrored in the Tokyo Furniture Show, with US country styles, traditional Japanese lacquered furniture, knotty pine children's furniture and sophisticated Italian designs existing side by side. Diversity in the furniture demand in Japan is growing and should benefit furniture imports.

The market for India

Globally, the furniture industry is undergoing a transition as there are a number of producers in Asia who can quickly adapt to changes in raw materials, processes and products. This means that new and improved products of consistent quality are being introduced at increasingly shorter intervals and being offered at competitive prices.

Indian furniture manufacturers must also do the same to stay competitive. One way to stay ahead of competition is to pay attention to design. It is important to have a range of unique Indian designs which, when coupled with modern manufacturing and a good marketing strategy, can be sold at high prices. The use of India's indigenous forest species together with some unique processes in terms of technology can give rise to a well designed product.

6.4   *Making simple items for export*

It is my contention that India has thousands of simple products which are very competitive in price and quality, but which it is not able to export because the commercial infrastructure is missing. I dealt with this problem in Chapters 1.1 and 1.2. In this chapter, I will illustrate this further using a specific example where a major buyer went away from India in spite of being offered low prices, mainly because he found the export infrastructure in complete disarray. This particular buyer was interested in a simple food item. His comments on our attitude to cleanliness in daily life are relevant to the context of this book.

An inside story

In supermarkets in the US, one finds superbly produced cans of simple coconut water. The quality, the design and packing are superb. This item has been promoted as a natural health drink and sells very well. Thailand exports container loads of it every month with other items like coconut milk not only to the US but to all the developed nations of the West. Coconut water is no longer an ethnic drink popular only with Asians. The whole world is drinking it and Thailand is the main beneficiary.

So, why Thailand? Why not India? Do we not have a huge surplus of coconuts? Why not indeed. I was involved in the setting up of the project in Thailand and I will tell you the inside story.

The idea was actually born in India. I have an American friend who is married to a lady from India. They were travelling in rural India on a holiday when he had a little tummy upset and was advised to drink the roadside coconut water. He fell in love with the drink and I could not stop him talking about the possibility of canning it for the US market.

He had a fair bit of money to invest and came to India again specifically to prepare an initial feasibility study. The objective was simple: to get the stuff made not only as per the rigorous American standards but to also meet the more meticulous standards of many supermarket chains.

The first thing we realised on coming back to India was that there would be no problems sourcing the raw materials, the suitably printed cans and the packing materials for our initial target of exporting one container load per month. However, we could not find a suitable manufacturing facility for an output of this magnitude. A new unit needed to be set up and we were faced with the problem of finding an entrepreneur willing to make the large investment envisaged for an untested product market.

My friend was keen to take on a major share as an investor, but here we faced our first hurdle. He was an American and could not invest in such a project. His wife, being a person of Indian origin was welcome to invest, though she was an American citizen. She merely had to execute a power of attorney in favour of her husband. This is when my friend first thought of alternative locations such as Thailand and the Philippines. He decided to do a survey there also before finally making up his mind.

To cut a long story short, the Philippines were rejected early on for various reasons and the project went to Thailand.

✓ India lost this excellent project. I will tell you why. There is a big lesson in this for us.

On commercial considerations alone, the project should have been in India. The supply and transport of coconuts, the availability of cans, the cost of the inputs and the export infrastructure in the southern state of Kerala were highly competitive. Thailand was about 40 per cent more expensive. Problems of red tape etc. did not arise as the promoters never came to the stage of actually making an application in India. Thailand won the project hands down merely at the feasibility stage. I will spell out what happened. We lost the project mainly because of the attitude of our businessmen towards exports.

The attitude of Indian businessmen

My friend made it clear that though he was keen to invest, he did not want to live in India and run the project. The main problem that arose then was to find an entrepreneur or a businessman who would be the main investor and would promote, implement and manage the entire project. A number of rich individuals and small,

> The way the businessmen in India spoke to us was perfectly normal and natural. They spoke to us as they would to prospective customers from other parts of India, though with some reservations as Indians have a tendency not to waste time on long-term export inquiries. It was no different from the way businessmen in most developing nations speak to overseas visitors.
>
> But if one looks at this from the point of view of an overseas buyer, the response one gets in India is lukewarm and disorganised. This by itself should not be a barrier, but the visitor then goes next door to Thailand and Malaysia, gets an enthusiastic and highly organised response and never comes back.

one-man-show type of firms showed initial interest. None of the larger, well managed business houses, however, seemed interested in the project. We spoke to a few such firms in Mumbai and Chennai. They liked the idea and promised to look into it and let us know! This stands out in stark contrast to what we found in Thailand, which I will mention shortly.

During the initial survey in India, we met a number of entrepreneurs, businessmen, suppliers and subcontractors. While we were looking for firms to take up the project, we were also looking for quotations, terms of service and the organisational details of the suppliers. These were some of the outstanding characteristics of our talks with the Indian people.

1. We were well received and enjoyed the hospitality of some very nice people. However, everybody we met, be it the plantation owner or the transporter, wanted us to deal only through him, leaving him to deal with people down the line. Each clearly wanted to be the boss. The person talking to us as, say, the main entrepreneur, did not want us talking to the suppliers and subcontractors. He would ask us to tell him what we wanted and to then allow him do it for us.

No problem here. This is common.

2. When we insisted on talking to everybody, each person made it clear that he was willing to talk only about his own aspect of the deal. One coconut supplier, for example, made it clear that he wanted the sole contract for the supply of coconuts to the factory, another, that he would not have anything to do with the transporter we selected. The latter, of course, refused to introduce us to his candidate for the job.

No problem here either. This is also common.

3. A very unpleasant aspect of the talks we held was that everybody stressed that his business ethics were better than those of the others in his line of work. It seemed as if the entire PR effort of the businessmen we met was to run others down.
4. The attitude of the large number of trade associations, government bodies, entrepreneurs, businessmen, suppliers and subcontractors we met was also the same. We were very well received and promised all sorts of help, but it was clear that it was our project and we were expected to set it up and run it. Everybody knew by this time that we were also considering Thailand and nobody was in the least bothered that India could potentially lose the project.

Handled without care

✓ I said above that we lost the project because of the attitude of our businessmen towards exports. This is not the whole truth.

At first, I could not comprehend why my friend wanted to visit the areas where most of the people who would work in the proposed factory, the unskilled workers, lived. When I asked him, he said that the way we work has a lot to do with how and where we live. Working in a factory and doing something for a purpose or doing it because you have been ordered to do it is never as good as doing the same thing automatically, by habit. If a person is not clean and fastidious in his everyday life, he cannot be depended upon to produce, say, quality food products. If an entire life is lived in shabby and filthy surroundings, a certain attitude seeps into a person's mindset and this cannot be changed overnight.

He said something which initially sounded very rude (and crude) but which made a lot of sense.

✓ He asked me if I would eat in a restaurant where I knew that the cook did not always wash his hands after using the toilet! Never mind careful supervision by the owner, he said, a habit is a habit.

This is to look at ourselves through the eyes of others, which is something we do not normally do or talk about in India. Our attitude towards the environment in which our workers live is an important element in this, a serious problem that cannot be solved by businessmen alone.

I have seen a number of studies carried out by the National Institute of Nutrition in Hyderabad on the massive contamination of everyday food items by bacteria. Most of these have been published in bulletins of the Indian Council of Medical Research. One such study was reported in the *India Today* issue of Sept 4, 2000. The studies make it abundantly clear that contamination can be controlled if simple hygienic measures like washing hands with soap and water can be implemented all along the food chain from collection to processing and packaging. However, this is all often a part of the unorganised backyard sector, making it difficult to monitor. As I said above, this is not a problem which can be addressed by businessmen alone.

Thailand

There was one outstanding, and very reassuring, characteristic of our talks in Thailand. We spoke to a single, cohesive group of people, each of whom spoke for everyone else. The response was nothing if not enthusiastic.

Our first point of contact was a large coconut plantation near Hadyai, in the South. We were directed to meet the owners in Bangkok and the person there fixed an appointment for us. We went to Bangkok and met the owner who was of Chinese origin. He gave us a patient hearing, took us out to lunch, asked a lot of casual questions and suggested we meet again in three days' time. When we turned up at their office, we were surprised to find about a dozen people from different organisations, all of Chinese origin. There were three competing plantation owners, two aluminium can manufacturers, and, of course, the transport contractors, the shipping agents and the food technologists! They had already run a check on my friend's credentials via their contacts in the US! We could see that everybody had businesses that stayed singularly apart, but which instantly formed a network and worked together when the opportunity presented itself.

It was immensely reassuring talking to a cohesive body which spoke in one voice. Our discussions went like a charm because everybody connected with the proposal was in there, participating and cooperating, even people who were obviously competitors. We spoke directly to everybody and got data, offers, and terms and conditions right across the table. We could see that the prices they were going to charge for the canned drinks were much higher than those in India but we did not care. We were at least sure of getting what we wanted.

The bottomline is that we ended up with a firm proposal from the group, with the outline of the corporate structure of the new firm to be set up. We did not have to run from pillar to post, like we were doing in India, trying to put together a workable proposal. Sitting in Bangkok, we were even assured of the involvement of a Chinese firm in the US which would handle the American side of the clearing.

We did not have the foggiest notion as to who the shareholders of the new firm would be. A person was nominated as the CEO and thenceforth we dealt with one person only, though we were free to call any of the constituents and check on anything. The project is now doing very well indeed and is exporting a few container loads every month to many countries. Walk into any supermarket in the West and pick a can of coconut water—you will see that it is made in Thailand.

✓ GUANXI: In many places in this book, I have spoken about this art of networking, or Guanxi, the Chinese concept of networking or the integration of an entire spectrum of activities. The trick lies in the networking of disparate capacities, in how small specialist firms integrate their talents and management expertise.

Networking is not subcontracting

The above example also illustrates the sharp contrast between networking and subcontracting. The Indian firms were trying to subcontract: the transporter wanted to be the principal contractor, the boss; the truck owner, the subcontractor, who would, in turn, subcontract the handling to a labour contractor.

In networking, there is often no boss. An important aspect of networking is the mentality or the attitude of the people involved. All the parties need patience, motivation, and the training and tools in conflict resolution. Of course, there will be problems, both big and small. Customers will be upset with you for what someone else has done. It helps if the customer is aware of the composition of the instant consortium and is working directly with the components.

Networking is not simply teamwork

Teamwork is as essential to the success of an Indian enterprise venturing into the export market as is networking. Maybe even more so. Networking people or teams is how India will start making its mark on world markets. Teams are where the relationships must be created and where problem solving will take place. Networking is the stage where the teams go out to conquer the world.

The future of doing business with important customers will require that we discard the old model of the small-time businessman or salesperson and replace it with a diverse, committed group of people working closely together. Some of those people will be entrepreneurs, businessmen, suppliers and subcontractors while others will be product specialists and executives. Some may not even be in the same company. They will be united by the overriding mission of working together to meet the needs of an overseas customer.

The story does not end here

I spoke above of a simple food item. There are hundreds of other very simple, but highly innovative, plastic and wooden products currently being sold in the US and all over the West. These are cheap, well designed, elegant and very popular and include plastic toys, soft toys, games, kitchen utility and garden items, hobby and craft items, and so on.

In the West, the market for these items is growing exponentially. The reason is the increasing spending power of consumers. People want to live better, children expect better toys and householders, better utility items in the kitchen. This has created a massive new opportunity. Coupled with the shortage of skilled workers like carpenters and masons, people find that they have to do everything themselves. So, the above list gets enlarged to include items catering to the 'Do it yourself' trade, which is another growing market segment.

Much of these items are widely advertised and sold all over the West. Almost all are 'Made in China.' For 'Made in China,' read either

'Made in Hong Kong,' which is also China, or made in China by the overseas Chinese.

India has not been able to make and export such simple items, has no share of this fantastic market and is not likely to have it either. It is not that we do not have the technology. We are producing a number of far more complex and sophisticated plastic products, mostly without any foreign technical inputs, at prices comparable with world prices. So what is wrong? The reasons are very complex, but one of the main reasons is our attitude towards quality and finish. For a further discussion on this, please take a trip back to Chapter 3.1.

We are talking about a completely new range of immensely profitable products which did not exist a decade ago. These are all quick-turnover, high-volume, and low-lifecycle-cost items. The western market has a voracious appetite for these items which come and go in a matter of months, sell in huge numbers and cost very little. There is a new item on the market every day.

6.5   *Export of festivals*

> *'Any festival, be it religious, social or cultural,*
> *is to be considered an export activity if it*
> *brings in planeloads of tourists,*
> *and will be promoted as such.'*

This was a senior Thai bureaucrat talking to delegates attending the Pacific Area Travel Association (PATA) meeting in Thailand. The year was 1970. He was emphasising his government's newly formed policy that these festivals would not be seen simply as a tourist promotion activity, but would be given the additional thrust of export promotion.

The results of this very aggressive and original approach to export promotion are to be seen today when Thailand is jampacked with tourists at festival time. And there are numerous festivals throughout the year.

It is common knowledge that many emerging economies are promoting festivals as major tourist draws. Flights and hotels are booked months in advance. I will illustrate this in some detail here.

I will also discuss the unfortunate fact that travel agents in the West actually discourage tourists from coming to India during its festive seasons. The incoming flights may be full, but these are only overseas Indians visiting relatives in India and not tourists.

Festivals and feasts

Before going on to discuss how to attract tourists to come to India's festivals or, in other words, how to sell India's festivals as an export activity, I need to explain what type of festivals I am talking about.

- Purely religious festivals focus on the rituals of the holy days of a particular faith and mean the participation of the followers of the particular faith or creed. These, by definition, cannot, and should not, be promoted as a tourist attraction. There are many religious festivals in India that draw people from well outside the particular faith, sometimes from all over the world, but these people are devotees. There is no question of any sort of a promotional effort and so these are outside the scope of discussion here

- There are other religious festivals which have evolved into cultural celebrations. Examples are Durga Puja in Bengal and the Ganapati festival in Maharashtra. These involve outpourings of respect and devotion with carefully planned and merged cultural programmes, rejoicing and/or high revelry. These are established by custom and tradition and sponsored by various cultural groups, organisations or local residents' associations. Such secular celebrations can well be a part of a promotional effort to attract tourists and it will be my effort to illustrate how this has been very successfully done in many nations

- Festivals are also held on the public honouring of outstanding people, the commemoration of important historical or cultural events or the recreation of cherished folkways. In some parts of the world, however, particularly in Latin America and southern Europe, traditional secular festivities follow the attendance of religious services. An example is the Mardi Gras festivities which I will talk about later

- Then, there are a number of purely cultural festivals such as the Khajuraho Dance Festival in Madhaya Pradesh. Dance, music, art and theatre festivals are popular throughout the world and have been promoted as major tourist attractions

- The festivals of many ethnic and national groups are credited with the preservation of unique customs, folk tales, costumes and culinary skills. Communal feasts, as occasions for eating, drinking and merrymaking, have a long recorded history, going back to early Greece. The most famous contemporary eating and drinking festivity is the Oktoberfest, which has been held in Germany annually since October 17, 1810, the wedding day of the future King Louis I of Bavaria. It is an autumn festival celebrating the best in beer, food and entertainment

- There exist an infinite variety of harvest festivals, not only in India but even in the developed world. Harvest and thanksgiving festivals are an inheritance from the ages when agriculture was the primary livelihood. Among the most attractive are the British harvest-home festivals, where parish churches are decorated with flowers, fruits and vegetables in early autumn, and harvest suppers climax a happy event. Exhibitions of flowers are among the most beautiful of harvest festivals. Outstanding is the international Floralies held throughout the summer every five years since about 1837 in Ghent, Belgium. The festival traces its origins to the Roman Floralia, a spring rite honouring the goddess Flora. These festivals offer an authentic taste and flavour of the rural environment and are enjoyed immensely by tourists. It is, unfortunately, only in India that nothing is done to cash in on this potential

The origin of communal celebration is a matter of conjecture. Folklorists believe that the first festivals arose because of the anxieties of early peoples who did not understand the forces of nature and wished to placate them. General agreement exists that the most ancient festivals and feasts were associated with planting and harvest times or with the honouring of ancestors. These have continued in various parts of the world as secular festivals, with some religious overtones, into modern times.

Secular festivals and feasts have many uses and values beyond the public enjoyment of a celebration. In prehistoric societies, festivals provided an opportunity for elders to pass on folk knowledge and the meaning of tribal lore to younger generations. Festivals celebrating the founding of a nation or the date of withdrawal of foreign invaders from its borders bind citizens in a unity that transcends personal concerns. Modern festivals and feasts centring on the customs of national or ethnic groups enrich understanding of their heritage. Contemporary festivals related to regional developments aid the local economy by attracting visitors to a historical pageant, also fulfiling an informal educational function.

The timing of seasonal festivals is determined by the solar and lunar calendars and by the cycle of the seasons. The Chinese New Year, set by the lunar calendar, and celebrated for an entire month beginning in late January or February, is a time of family gatherings, gaiety, parades and theatrical performances. Many other kinds of seasonal festivals are celebrated, ranging from the Quebec Winter Carnival, usually held in February, to Beach Day (December 8), marking the beginning of the beach season in Uruguay. Historic customs are often perpetuated in seasonal festivals. An example is Homstrom (February 3), an old Swiss festival, exulting in the end of winter with the burning of straw people as symbols of the end of Old Man Winter. The most famous of seasonal festivities, set by the Church calendar, but secular in tone, are the pre-Lenten carnivals of Europe and Latin America, and the Mardi Gras.

Thai Songkran and our Holi

A few years ago, I was in Singapore and needed to go to a place called Hatyai in southern Thailand for a seminar. Hatyai is an important tourist destination, connected by flights from Singapore. I found, to my dismay, that all flights were full and that even the waiting list had been closed. My agent also told me that there was no possibility of getting a hotel room as this was the time of Songkran, the Thai new year.

I made the trip by road and arranged to put up with a friend at the University. Once there, I saw how the Thais had converted the traditional new year celebration in mid-April, which lasts three days, into a major tourist draw.

A point to note: It should be remembered that Songkran is not like the North Indian 'Shangrand' or 'Makar Sankaranti' or what the Brahmins in the South call Shankaranti. The Thai festival marks the new year and falls in mid April. The Indian ones mean 'transition' and mark the transition of the sun from the house of Cancer to that of Capricorn, and fall in the middle of January.

The Thai festival of Songkran is somewhat similar to our celebration of Holi in North India in origin, tradition and concept. Thailand is Buddhist and a lot of its traditions are Indian in origin. This festival roughly coincides with the Punjabi new year, which is also celebrated around the middle of April.

The similarities, however, end very quickly. During Songkran, the whole nation puts on a festive mantle. The main attraction is the spraying of perfumed water on each other. Being sprayed on and getting drenched is considered auspicious. I found cars, vans and pick-up trucks on the street full of families spraying water on everybody. Old and infirm people were sitting on chairs in these vans with spray pumps in hand. The water was clean and perfumed. If you are on the street and get sprayed, you gracefully fold your hands and say thanks. Something like our *namaste*, but far more respectful. Foreigners smile and wave. In the evenings, there is a carnival atmosphere. There are street marches, bands and floats in the larger cities, immensely enjoyable roadside concerts of all sorts and country fairs. Everywhere one goes, one encounters fun and merrymaking.

The Thais have realised the tourist potential of this festival. Starting from the local chambers of commerce to their overseas tourist offices, they have aggressively promoted not only this but many other similar cultural and social festivals all over the world. The result is hoardes of tourists and immense commercial and economic benefit.

Now contrast this with our Holi. Ancient literature tells us that Holi is an important Hindu spring festival and, in northern and western India, a harvest festival. It is celebrated on the full-moon day in the Hindu month of Phalguna (February-March) with a great deal of boisterousness and colour. On this day, the usual restrictions of colour, caste, creed and age are cast aside in the spirit of fun and merrymaking. Holi is also a time of goodwill, when people pay off or forgive debts, patch up quarrels and wish each other good luck.

The celebration of Holi today is nothing of the sort. I can say, without the fear of contradiction, that Holi is one of the nastiest festivals we have in India. The youth of today compete with each other in thinking of the foulest stuff to spray or rub on others. People of other religions and those in mourning are made special targets for the misery it causes them. Even in households today, the colours used are textile dyes which leave the skin coloured for days after the festival.

I do not know how many of my readers are aware of it, but most travel agents ask their clients to avoid India during Holi.

Durga Puja and Ganapati festivals

Like many other festivals in India, both the Puja celebrations in Bengal and the Ganapati festival in Maharashtra are powerful social events which mobilise entire communities. The religious fervour, the social participation and the wholesome family fun cannot be easily captured in words. Both festivals have things in common. They showcase India's rich culture including its talent in art, music, dance and drama. Both are excellently organised by hundreds of private set-ups and funded by local residents. The immense commercial and economic benefits that accrue mainly go to local traders who merely sit back and enjoy the results without actually promoting anything.

It is impossible for any foreigner visiting India at that time not to be overwhelmed by the ambience. Tourists who are lucky to be a part of it often come back again and again. But it remains a sad fact that far from promoting this immense opportunity, travel agents overseas warn non-Indians against visiting India at this time, because of the inevitable crowds, traffic jams and the general breakdown of public services. Moreover, there has been no effort by any chambers of commerce or citizens group to get any sort of an organisation or system together so that, for instance, one is aware of who is performing where and at what time.

Mardi Gras

Mardi Gras (French, 'fat Tuesday'), is the pre-Lenten festival celebrated in Roman Catholic countries and communities. In a strict sense, the last three days of Shrovetide are celebrated by the French as Mardi Gras. This a time of preparation immediately before Ash Wednesday and the start of the fast of Lent. It is thus the last opportunity for merrymaking and indulgence in food and drink. In practice, Mardi Gras is generally celebrated for a full week before Lent. It is marked by spectacular parades featuring floats, pageants, elaborate costumes, masked balls and dancing in the streets.

The most famous modern Mardi Gras festivities are those held in New Orleans, Louisiana, and in Rio de Janeiro, Brazil, but many small countries of the West Indies have also taken to celebrating this, making it a tourist draw.

It is said that the one week festival of Mardi Gras has transformed the entire economy of the city of Rio de Janeiro, a large city in southeastern Brazil. During the weeks that precede the carnival, the city receives thousands of tourists. Events include spontaneous street dancing with popular bands (marching bands comprising brass and percussion instruments), formal carnival balls catering to nearly every income level, and several days of Sambadrome parades where the best samba schools compete in marathon musical and dance presentations along a specially designed street where thousands of spectators gather to watch the events unfold. Tourism and entertainment have been made the key aspects of the city's economic life and the city is the nation's top tourist attraction for both Brazilians and foreigners.

Internationally, Rio is still the nation's best-known city. Though the city is set amidst stunning natural beauty between the mountains and the sea, it is also one of Brazil's most troubled with an exceptionally high crime rate. The shanty towns which house approximately 20 per cent of the city's residents are dangerous, unsanitary and lacking in basic services such as water, sewerage and, to a lesser extent, electricity. Police corruption is widespread. Environmental pollution is a problem, and the waters of Guanabara Bay are considered too polluted for safe bathing.

The point I am trying to make is that it is not always the best cities that bring in the money-spending tourists. People come for fun and the Mardi Gras carnival offers it in plenty. Its success would not have been possible but for the immense organisational and promotional effort. Detailed literature on the happenings at the carnival, list of hotels and incidental travel facilities are made available to travel agents all over the world months in advance.

We too have our carnivals

I have explained above how the carnival in a very unpleasant city like Rio is a huge success and a moneyspinner while 'carnivals' in India generate mostly negative publicity. This is in spite of the fact that:

- Indian festivals are clean, wholesome, family affairs. The one in Rio is brimming with sex and naughtiness
- Indian streets and cities are far safer than those in Brazil
- Brazil is very expensive. A holiday in India is not even a fraction of the cost

There are hoardes of people out there who do not like to go to places like Rio. Are we interested in getting them to India?

Khajuraho? Where is that?

One of the greatest dance festivals in India is the Khajuraho dance festival. Very few people are aware of that. What is commonly known is that Khajuraho, Madhya Pradesh, is merely a village where the world-famous Khajuraho Temples are the main attraction. This is a group of ancient temples that contain some of the finest examples of religious art in India. Khajuraho was once the capital of the Chandella dynasty and a considerable city. The 80 temples of Khajuraho, of which 22 are still standing, were built between A.D. 950 and 1050. The complex is divided into three main groups. The Eastern Group includes Jain temples within a walled enclosure and Hindu buildings. The Southern Group, south of the Jain temples, consists of two temples. The Western Group, the largest assemblage of buildings at Khajuraho, is surrounded by gardens and includes the Kandariya Mahadev temple, which contains a great colonnaded hall. This is the largest and most elaborately decorated temple in the entire complex. It rises in seven stages of lavish carvings, many of which portray animals, deities, warriors and dancers, some engaged in sexual activities that probably symbolise the religious ideas of Tantrism.

Khajuraho, now a village, was abandoned in the early 18th century and the temple sites were not cleared of vegetation and excavated until after they were discovered by the British colonial authorities in 1838.

India's tourist offices and, through them, travel agents all over the world have and can provide ample information on Khajuraho, its temples and the carvings. But one finds almost nothing on the annual dance festival.

By contrast, even in India, one can easily get all sorts of information on:

- The annual summer Salzburg festival of music in Austria
- The spectacular Aloha festival pageantry in October and November in Hawaii
- The annual Edinburgh Festival in Scotland, which showcases British drama, comedy and literature, as well as welcoming performers from overseas
- Various film, art, dance, children's, and theatrical festivals which crowd the calendars of many nations

Tourism in India

Tourism is one of the most neglected sectors in the country today in spite of the fact that it is an important foreign exchange earner. This is probably because of the following widespread misconceptions regarding tourism at different political levels.

- It is not an economic activity, but an elite 'five-star' activity
- It benefits only the rich
- Only the big cities benefit
- It brings to bear the wrong sort of influence on our youth
- Tourists indulge in undesirable activities

Now, contrast this with what the World Tourism Organisation, a U.N. body, lays down as the objectives of tourism:

- Poverty alleviation by employment generation
- Advancement of women
- Employment of both skilled and unskilled people without supplanting to urban areas
- Sustainable development by preserving the environment
- Preservation of heritage

Politicians in India are wary of tourists indulging in drinking and nudity, etc. on beaches. Well, right next door to India is a very conservative Muslim country, Maldives. It is outstandingly successful as a tourist destination in spite of the fact that liquor is strictly banned and any lewd exposure on the beach results in the tourist being expelled in an unpleasant manner.

Even countries like Iraq have pitched themselves as vacation spots with slogans such as 'From Nebuchadnezzar to Saddam Hussein, 2,400 years of peace and prosperity.' Not that tourists need much encouragement. The Antarctic last year received 15,000 holiday makers, five times as many as in 1991. Latin America and Eastern Europe are coming aboard too. Tourism thrives wherever politics allows it to, and politics has recently caused many barriers to fall. One of the fastest-growing destinations of the past few years has been South Africa, which in 1996 had 6.5 million visitors, well over three times as many as in 1990. Singapore and Malaysia get about 7 million arrivals. As against this, we have been aiming for years at an elusive target of 2.5 million arrivals out of which half are NRIs and from neighbouring countries. Why this dismal picture?

Although the Government of India opened a tourism office in New York as early as 1952, it is still considered a fringe activity, and the budget allocation of both the central and state governments is poor. This does not mean that the government alone should do everything, but it should provide a sufficient stimulus to the private sector. There are Tourism Boards even in developed countries. At present, a big chunk of the central government budget is set aside for the 18 foreign offices abroad. It is no doubt true that the foreign offices of the tourism ministry ought to function with greater efficiency, with performance auditing and monitoring, and well-trained personnel drawn from different sources including the open market. However, the time has also come for states such as Rajasthan and Kerala to open their own offices abroad because they have succeeded in attracting foreign tourists in large numbers.

Apart from the creating of a proper surface transport infrastructure, an important adjunct of tourism is the civil aviation policy. Bali has become an important tourist attraction through its promotion of direct tourist charters from developed countries. Visa on arrival is also freely allowed. The meaningless insistence upon reciprocal arrangements should be given up. We may not be interested in going to Ulan Bator, but they may be interested in coming to India, and this should be facilitated.

The set of people who still feel that tourism is an undesirable activity for a hypocritically moralistic country should change their mindset. Undesirable activities should, of course, be eschewed by proper policing. If these conceptual problems at different levels are resolved, tourism could well be the industry of the twenty-first century for India.

7
Selling to the competition

Japanese and western management styles are 95 per cent the same. They only differ in all the important aspects.

Peter Drucker

7.1   *Selling to the Koreans*

> I seek to stress a little known fact that, for Indian businessmen, South Korea should have been one of the easiest nations to trade with.
>
> One must remember two things. First, the brutal and ruthless colonisation of the nation by Japan and second, in recent times, the open support to North Korea by the Chinese. The Koreans intensely dislike the Japanese and the Chinese. The average man on the street, however, has a soft corner for India, in no small measure due to the all-pervading presence of Buddhism.
>
> The tragedy is that we, in India, have eyes only for the West. Far from India having any sort of a presence in Korea, it is instead the larger Korean firms who have come here and set up shop, even succeeding at exporting Indian products.
>
> In Chapter 4.3, we looked at the Korean mindset, in this chapter we explore ways of trading with them.

The East is not all the same

Indian business houses would do well to remember that not all Asians are alike. On talking to Indian exporters and executives in large firms, one gets the distinct impression that anything east of the Andamans is lumped together as one type of a market. Moreover, everybody is of the firm opinion that these are all great nations to import from, not to export to.

This translates into the way we approach business opportunities, and therein lies the tragedy.

When it comes to importing, most nations are interchangeable. If you have the money, anybody will sell you what you need. You do not need to be particularly clever! But it is a different story when you want to export. You will suddenly realise that the successful Asians, the Koreans, the Japanese and the Chinese, are not interchangeable. Even the Chinese in Malaysia are different from those in Taiwan. A strategy for one market will never fit into another. This is not like in Europe, where dealing with the Germans is not all that different from dealing with the Swiss. Or, for that matter, like in America, where dealing with those in the US or in Canada is much the same.

India's business people are more familiar with the business mores of the US and Europe than with those of the East. The cultural differences of doing business in Europe and Korea are often subtle, but they are reflected in everyday business activities and may also affect negotiations and contracts between Indian and Korean enterprises. Since the cultural differences are deeply rooted in tradition they are, of course, not easily changed. Different cultures and their phenomena cannot simply be judged as being 'good' or 'bad'. It is not possible to do justice to an attitude determined by a particular culture by measuring it with the yardstick of another culture. It is critically important to understand the thought pattern and actions of a business partner from a different culture if you are planning on a long-term relationship. It is a challenge that offers not only commercial success but is also a personally enriching experience.

We have a particular tendency to club Korea and Japan together. They do have more in common than that which they share with other nations, but the differences between the two nations are vast. Historically, the nations have been adversaries, and it would be wise to remember this point. The Japanese tend to be reserved; by comparison, you will be surprised at how assertive and outspoken the Koreans are. In some respects, they are eager to prove to the outside world that they, and not the Japanese, are the preferred business partners in Asia. The flip side of this is that this eagerness often makes it difficult for a Korean business partner to admit to any difficulties at hand. Remember this in your business negotiations.

Korea is nearer than you think

The world is being swept by a wave of internationalisation and a revolution in telecommunications. These trends are notable in both economically advanced and developing nations. To repeat a cliché, the world is becoming smaller. As a result, many of the difficulties that were once a hallmark of cross-cultural exchange are fast becoming relics of a more insular past. However, although businesspeople from different cultures are becoming increasingly knowledgeable about and familiar with each other's customs and business practices, the application of such knowledge is often superficial. In many cases, the very familiarity of a custom or mannerism merely serves to mask the underlying deep-seated differences.

I have said in Chapter 4.3 that a Korean organisation engaged in business in India knows a lot more about India than do Indian business people about Korea. This is unfortunate and has as much to do with business attitudes in India as with our tendency to do only cursory homework. Korean firms come to India to stay. We go there only to visit.

✓ Another point to note here, which I will address at some length later on, is our attitude towards gathering information. We tend to spend time and effort only on collecting the basic and essential information. The Koreans follow the Japanese in being obsessive information gatherers.

For India's exports to Korea to improve, this has to change. All that I can aim to do in this short chapter is get our exporters to start thinking in a new direction. There is a flood of information available on the net and more which can be accessed through Korean trade organisations in India.

The Indian businessperson working to gain a foothold in Korea faces two major problems with regard to Korean business customs:

✓ How to go about making an initial approach to a Korean company
✓ And, how to maintain and develop a business relationship once it has been established

I will try my best to offer advice and suggestions based on my experience of dealing with the Koreans.

An important way of preparing oneself for business in Korea is to develop an outlook that takes into account the relatively long-term outlook of the Korean businesspeople. Their primary goal is to build a lasting framework within which business transactions can take place. They do not seek short-term gains or relationships. In view of this, sincerity and commitment may well be the most important and effective platform from which an Indian company can start conducting business in Korea. As in most cultures, relationship building is crucial to successful business relationships. To that end, it is important to convince your contacts in Korea that you are not there for just the current visit. Make it clear that you will initially keep visiting and then, maybe, set up a base. It is a good idea to have a business objective which includes other Asia Pacific nations, so that it is easier to make continued trips back to South Korea. Your continued presence will solidify business relationships, especially if they come under strain.

It is also essential, though not easy, to be aware of the current political situation there. This is because, unlike in Singapore, Taiwan and Hong Kong, business and politics are closely tied together, with the government having significant influence over the private sector. Business conditions can change dramatically if a high-ranking bureaucrat is replaced. As a result, it is wise to know what kind of relationship your South Korean business partner has with key government officials. A lot of information is available in economic and financial newsmagazines, both Indian and foreign. However, the best way of gathering information is through friends in Korea, which pretty much boils down to your social and personal skills.

Similar policies different results

Before going on to discuss what India can do in Korea and how to go about doing it, it would help to compare the economic policies of India and Korea immediately after independence. Both followed strongly protectionist policies resulting in the growth of highly incompetent business environments which thrived on corruption and kickbacks. Business empires grew, to the great detriment of the nation.

In Korea, Japanese rule was cruel, ruthless and brutal. There were no Korean-owned enterprises. All industrial activity was subsequently devastated by the long-drawn-out war with the North. The development of big business enterprises began in 1962 with the export-driven policies of the first Five Year Plan. Korea too followed highly xenophobic inward-looking policies, cutting off all sorts of foreign investment and participation in the economy.

Very unlike what happened in India, these policies and the intensely nationalistic mentality of the Korean businesspeople have lead to South Korea becoming an industrial giant capable of undertaking practically all aspects of high-technology production. Over the past forty years, its economic growth has been among the fastest in the world. South Korea has overcome many obstacles to transform itself from a subsistence agrarian economy into an industrialising nation. Considering the fact that the Japanese left the nation with almost nothing, and coupled with the devastation wrought by the prolonged Korean War, these achievements are indeed impressive.

✓ It would pay us well to note that it is the Koreans who are on the world map today and who are successfully doing business in India, rather than the other way around, though the British left us with a massive and well-organised infrastructure, and despite the fact that India has had no devastating wars.

The dynamism of South Korea is beyond doubt and with some political skill the country should go far. An overwhelmingly urban community, with a falling and ageing rural population, it is now moving towards an open economy. A point of interest for India, which I will address, is that the more South Korea exports goods such as cars and consumer electronics, the more will it need raw materials, components and semi-manufactured goods. Ordinary South Koreans are likely to demand a much greater allocation of resources for the social sector; its highly-educated workforce will be able to generate the financial surpluses to satisfy their demands, and the market for simpler consumer goods will grow. The export-led growth was initially dominated by labour-intensive manufacturing especially textiles, clothing and footwear. Agriculture was protected from market forces to maintain self-sufficiency in food. In recent times, the growth has been in motor vehicles, aerospace, computers, advanced materials, nuclear power and financial services. Government R&D spending continues to double in real terms every five years.

On the flip side, it is true that Asia's more nationalistic countries have had to swallow some of their pride in the late 1990s as a result of the currency crisis and the difficult economic situation. In particular, Korea has had to launch labour, industry and banking reforms that run against the grain of more traditional values. In the process, foreigners are perceived to be either a cause of Korea's problems or of taking advantage of its difficulties to profit at the expense of the country. Nationalism can thus be fuelled, creating resentment and problems further down the road. Other, more positive scenarios are, however, also possible. At this time, there seems to be more local resentment being directed against the large Korean companies rather than against foreign companies and banks. These feelings could help to facilitate industrial restructuring even in the face of strong resistance from the *chaebol*, which might try to use nationalistic arguments to defend their positions. If the reforms being undertaken result in a more open environment in a way that foreign companies are perceived to be contributing to Korea's recovery and promoting general living standards, dealing with the current crisis could actually help to discourage the more xenophobic forms of nationalism for which Korea has developed a reputation.

Avoid cold contacts

By cold contact, I mean the act of writing or introducing oneself to someone directly, such as saying, 'I am here from India and I saw your firm in the yellow pages, so can I come and see you?' This is a strict no-no. It is essential to have somebody who knows you and can vouch for your bona fides write or introduce you to them first. You could then meet them after having made an appointment. Even better, approach a Korean firm in your country, introduce yourself and your firm, and present an outline of what you are interested in while seeking their assistance. This should be the procedure followed when you want to sell to them. Buying from them is a different story altogether.

Indian firms are used to cold contacts. We are accustomed to approaching western firms this way and visitors to India call to introduce themselves all the time. It will help to understand why we do and accept this and why the Koreans do not.

If you are a businessman, say, in Nairobi or in Kuala Lumpur, wanting to trade with India, you will be well advised to avoid discussing your plans or seeking advice from any Indian firm there as you will lose your idea and will have to unnecessarily channel everything through them. Dealing directly with almost no intermediaries is the best option.

This practice is not confined to the Indians. It is also an important difference between the way European and Japanese enterprises make their first contact. Probably because of the high esteem for self-reliance, the usual practice in Europe is also to be self-reliant and highly secretive when making contacts or when conducting searches. This has a serious impact on doing business, and on gathering information. The Koreans, like the Japanese do not work like this.

Korea now follows the practice which has existed in Japan since the Meiji era. This is the tradition of dispatching overseas missions (*kaigai chosadan*) for the collection of information. Instead of researching the relevant questions on one's own, voluminous questionnaires are first sent to an overseas (or outstation) industrial association, institute or enterprise. The mission then visits the institutions oversees and collects the answers which are carefully archived and studied on returning home. This involves certain costs, and the information is freely available to other Japanese organisations but remains confidential for outsiders.

In my view, this method is an expression of the high esteem for comprehensive information gathering and sharing in Japanese (and Korean) enterprises. This is the starting point for their own product development and business activities. I think this attitude is one of the important reasons for their success. There is a dilution of this in the modern times with Japanese firms competing with each other, but you will still find it very difficult to find another supplier or customer if you have a problem with a particular Japanese firm. You will be amazed at the amount of commercial information that is shared between Japanese and Korean firms.

European (and Indian) enterprises, on the other hand, have only themselves to blame for the disadvantages they suffer for not being as thorough in information gathering and sharing as the Japanese.

The size of the contracts

This is about the contracts you will be negotiating and signing. The traditional high esteem for the written word in Europe (and in India) is reflected, for instance, in the elaborate business correspondence. Not only is there a lot of talk in meetings and negotiations, but secretaries are also made to draw up long minutes of meetings and letters of confirmation. We strive to put the progress of our business in exact words in order to keep going.

Korean enterprises, on the other hand, are not especially fond of correspondence. Compared to European business letters, Korean letters tend to be brief and, in the European view, not sufficiently detailed. Sometimes, differences in these details of communication may cause problems in business relationships. I have repeatedly experienced this while doing business in Korea.

- Indians draw out long and detailed contracts but as a habit do not take down extensive notes. Koreans fill notebook after notebook of everything they see: your factory layout, your office set-up, and even your eating habits and drink preferences. Everything goes on record in the head office and is there for all to use. There is a very interesting story I mentioned in an earlier chapter where the Korean habit of making extensive notes resulted in the Indian team being grossly embarrassed.

In Europe and the US, contracts as a principle are put down in writing, and are minutely and expensively drafted. In this way one tries to foresee and provide for all conceivable problems of the contractual relationship in advance.

Korean and Japanese contracts are not always put in writing. Even if they are, they are often only of a summary nature. All the discussions and negotiations are in the notes the executives take and this is far more detailed and precise than anything that can be put in a contract. In Europe and in India such summary contracts will be of little use. Sometimes there is the impression that Korean enterprises do not readily enter into written contracts because they want to retain their freedom of action and flexibility in the future. According to traditional Korean thinking, a good personal relationship between the parties, reinforced by moral obligations, is more important than a written contract.

In order to avoid failure when trying to enter into contact with a Korean company, Europeans now employ a personal intermediary. Because of the high esteem for personal relationships as also the group relations between enterprises in Korea, this procedure is effective. In Europe, where the principle of personal independence is predominant, go-betweens are generally not required and you can establish contact directly.

In business relations in Korea, people try to establish personal relationships through generous hospitality and presents. Though such practices are not unknown in the West, they are much less developed. Europeans, like Indians, tend to preserve their independence and restrict business relations to the business area alone.

Points to note

- You must be prepared for the fact that, unlike meetings in Japan, which usually involve a group of people, your meetings in South Korea will most likely be with one person
- Do not book meetings during July and August, which are the peak vacation months
- Most meetings can be conducted in English because it is the most widely used foreign language in South Korea. It is almost always easy to find people who are comfortable with the language
- Expect to be entertained, most likely over dinner. Use chopsticks. If you are able to use them, your hosts will be impressed. If you cannot, ask to be shown how. This will delight your hosts. Expect the dinner to be a fun affair
- Don't be misled by the Koreans' seeming western orientation; their cultural values are very strong
- Don't rush into negotiations. Take your time. Establish a friendly relationship at the first meeting itself
- Do not forcefully say no. Find a tactful way to get your point across
- Trustworthiness and character are very important to Koreans. They will sometimes be silent in a meeting in order to examine your credibility
- Pay attention to age, rank, the way the person's name is printed on the visiting card and the way others talk to him. These are very important
- Be humble in your approach. Don't boast about yourself or your company's status or achievements
- If problems arise in your business dealings with South Koreans, don't expect an immediate solution. They will take time to carefully explain the problem to their management. The managers will then, over time study the notebooks of the various executives who participated in the meetings
- Never mark any document with red ink as, for Koreans, this is a symbol of bad luck or death. Koreans who are familiar with Indian traditions are aware of the fact that this is an auspicious colour for us
- Never gift a handkerchief; it symbolises suffering in the Korean worldview

- Women are not generally active in business in South Korea. They are, however, powerful behind the scenes, in the home and in the family
- Greetings: Korean men greet each other with a slight bow and sometimes a handshake, similar to the Japanese style of greeting. Indicate respect by bending from the waist and supporting your right forearm with your left hand while giving out your card
- Introductions: The Korean family name (surname) is listed first, for example, Kim Hyong Sim would be Mr Kim. Sim would be the first name; do not use it until invited to do so. Koreans are very sensitive about the use of the first name.
- Appointments: Punctuality is expected from foreigners, however the Koreans themselves might be 30 minutes late
- Negotiating: A respectful rapport between individuals is vital. Don't try and be 'chummy'. Find out who is negotiating for the other side, and match the rank of the persons represented. Status matters to the Koreans
- Triangles have negative connotations—do not use them in your presentations
- Entertaining: Refill your neighbour's cup and soy sauce bowl when empty; expect the same. If you do not want more, do not empty your glass.

For specific data and information please refer to Appendix 5.

7.2 *Selling to the Japanese*

Doing the impossible

The most difficult nation to sell to is undoubtedly Japan. The Japanese consumer, till very recently, had an intense dislike for anything non-Japanese, including foreign words in the Japanese language (see Chapter 4.2 and Appendix 3). They export just about everything to almost the whole world but buy only what they must, and that too, mainly raw materials.

Their ruthless export orientation has created an enormous trade imbalance with many nations including with the most powerful one, the US. The Americans have been shouting themselves hoarse over this issue for ages, to no effect. Japan may have lost the World War to America but they have been winning ever since. Take the grossly lopsided situation of cars. Japan simply does not want to buy American cars or spare parts. What the Americans do not seem to realise is that a Japanese with an American car would be looked down upon socially. I remember I was in Geneva in early June 1996. Mickey Kantor, the US trade representative, was ready to strike. Come midnight he would smite 13 Japanese luxury-car models with tariffs of 100 per cent, effectively cutting them out of the US market. Hardly half a day was left on the clock when a deal was struck. Bill Clinton hailed the deal as a 'major step forward for free trade' and claimed that the deal was 'specific' and 'measurable'. According to the Americans, the Japanese offered to deregulate their market for replacement car parts and repairs. American car makers were promised better access to Japanese car dealerships: by the end of 1996, Mr Kantor was told, American cars would be sold in 200 dealerships in Japan; by 2000, that number would rise to 1,000. Mr Kantor, like many American trade warriors before him, quietly laid down his shinai without striking a blow.

So, did the US get what it wanted? Most certainly not. The US was curiously naïve in the deal and, in any case, it had no redress if its expectations were not met. One of the items in the deal was a

I seek to establish that Japan is at the same time the most difficult and promising market for Indians to sell to. Considerations of price and quality do not come into the picture if they do not wish to buy. Yet, to keep their industries competitive, they are scouring the world for cheaper inputs of raw materials, components and offshore manufacturing.

And, more importantly, they believe in long-term relations. It may take time to get in, but once in, you are in for life.

promise by the Japanese Ministry of International Trade and Industry (MITI) to write to Japanese dealers 'affirming their freedom' to sell foreign cars. This is like Advaniji writing to Lalooji affirming his freedom to turn honest!

This sugar coating did little to stop the tactics that some Japanese car makers used to keep their dealers loyal. The Japanese government said that it would 'increase support' for its anti-trust authorities and 'take into account' American suggestions for better enforcement of its competition law. Well, again, that was no big deal. Japanese car makers were already planning to shift production abroad in response to the strong yen.

There are many more such juicy tales of Japanese perfidy. Take Eastman Kodak, the world's largest maker of photographic film. Outside Japan, Kodak has more than half the share of the world's film market. But in Japan it has a puny nine per cent. The reason? Kodak says that in the late 1960s and early 1970s Fuji, Japan's largest film maker, gained control of the four largest distributors of film and Kodak was squeezed out. Distributors and retailers are still kept in check by 'secret, discriminatory and remarkably progressive' rebates for selling Fuji film. Of course, that contravenes Japan's own anti-monopoly law; but the antitrust authorities have taken no action. The result is that Fuji has a share of about 70 per cent of the market.

However, as time has gone on, there is considerable evidence that Japanese attitudes are changing, and that markets can be cracked open. I will deal with this later on in this chapter. The foreign share of the car market is still small, but it is climbing. Japan, however, imports fewer cars than does the US or the European Union and has a distinct comparative advantage in car making.

A peek at the past

If one wants to export to Japan, one has to first understand the Japanese mindset. I have discussed this at some length in Chapter 4.2. It
would also help if one has an idea of the nature of Japanese society,
and the way it is organised. So, let's take a quick peek at its past.

The Japanese, as I mentioned, have an intense dislike for anything
non-Japanese. This has not always been so. They avidly imported
the ideas of Confucius from China; and Buddhism from India.

For a variety of reasons, Japan has preserved into the late twentieth century a kind of society that has largely vanished from the rest
of the world. The past has gone on for very long. The native religion
of the Japanese people, Shintoism, has always put great value on
the loyalty that members of a family owe each other. So do the ideas
of Confucius, and the Japanese soon Shintoised the non-family-
minded Buddhism too. All this provided a powerful underpinning
for the rules of feudal loyalty that took root in Japan, as in other
countries, during the time when warrior leaders took command of
and protected their peasant followers. The difference is that Japan,
unlike those other countries, kept the feudal idea alive right up to
the middle of the nineteenth century by cutting itself off from the
world for 250 years until Commodore Perry's warships sailed into
Tokyo Bay in 1853. Neither the 'first opening' of Japan, which followed Perry's bang on the door, nor the 'second opening', the post-
1945 American occupation, quite managed to remove this deeply
rooted way of life. The result is a Japan which, in the way its government and much of its economy is organised, still has a strangely
archaic look.

The country is a loose collection of semi-autonomous but intensely
nationalistic groups, each of which is held together by a powerful
sense of communal loyalty but which also grants a great deal of
authority to the man at the top. It is a very clannish set-up. The
clannishnesss explains, among other things, why the Japanese still
feel a far keener commitment than most other people to their workplace: be it their car-making company, their investment bank or
their government ministry. This loyalty gives each such organisation
great strength. But it also, as a consequence, makes the decision-
making process horribly slow. Each institution has to work out its
own laborious internal consensus, and then those institutions

whose interests overlap have to sit down together and hammer out a multisided compromise. It always took a long while for medieval barons to agree upon a new policy; so too with the baronial structures of today's Japan.

Hit them with their own techniques

Few dispute that the Japanese have performed an economic miracle since World War II. In a relatively short time, they have achieved global market leadership in industries thought to be dominated by impregnable giants from the West. The Japanese today lead the world in the automobile, motorcycle, watch, camera, optical instrument, steel, shipbuilding, piano, zipper, radio, television, video recorder and hand calculator industries, among others. Japanese firms are currently moving into the number two position in the computer and construction equipment industries and are making strong inroads in the chemical, pharmaceutical and machine-tool industries.

Many theories have been offered to explain Japan's global success. Some point to their unique business practices, such as lifetime employment, quality circles, consensus management and just-in-time delivery. Others point to the participative supportive role of government policies and subsidies, the existence of powerful trading companies and businesses' easy access to bank financing. Still others view Japan's success as being based on low wage rates and unfair dumping policies.

> It is my contention that we should learn from the Japanese how to sell to them, exactly as the Japanese who went to the US to study marketing and returned home understanding its principles better than many US companies did. The Japanese learnt how to select a market, enter it in the right way, build their market share and protect their leadership position against competitors' attacks.

One of the main keys to Japan's performance is its skill in marketing-strategy formulation and implementation.

✓ The situation of Japanese government and private companies working together to identify attractive global markets is indeed a unique one. The Japanese favour industries that require high skills and a high labour intensity, and only small quantities of natural resources: these include the consumer electronic, camera, watch, motorcycle and pharmaceutical industries. They prefer product markets that are in a state of technological evolution, and they look for industries where the market leaders are complacent or under financed.

The large trading houses make huge investments in sending study teams into a target country to spend several months evaluating the market and figuring out a strategy. The teams search for niche markets that are not being satisfied by current offerings. Sometimes they establish their beachhead with a low-price stripped-down version of a product, sometimes with a product exhibiting higher quality or new features or designs. The Japanese proceed to line up a good distribution channel in order to provide efficient service to their customers. A key characteristic of their entry strategy is to build market share rather than early profits. The Japanese are patient capitalists who are willing to wait a long time before realising their profits.

Once Japanese firms gain a market foothold, they direct their energies towards expanding their market share. They rely on product-development and market-development strategies. They spot new opportunities through market segmentation, and sequence market development across a number of countries, pushing towards building a network of world markets and production locations.

At last, Japan too is changing

The above discussion has focused on the centuries-old inward-looking traditions of Japan. The attitude of the Japanese consumer is, however, gradually changing.

A recent and important development in the Japanese market has been the massive exposure of the consumer to what is happening in the rest of the world and, at the same time, a substantial rise both in the consumer's average income and in his awareness of price and value. This growing demand for more variety and at lower prices is significantly altering the convoluted and inefficient domestic distribution system that has long caused difficulties for Indian companies attempting to sell in Japan.

The market for items such as the simple, but highly innovative, plastic and wooden products currently being sold in the US and all over the West is growing exponentially. The reason is the increasing spending power of the consumer. This has created a massive new opportunity. Added to this is the change in traditional Japanese living arrangements, with the growing popularity of single living and the emergence of a substantial group of double income married couples without children. These changes are creating new market segments that, in many cases, western companies are already quite familiar with.

A word of caution here. Despite these trends, however, there remain social, demographic, religious, economic and cultural differences that can have a profound impact on a product's success or failure.

An Indian exporter must make sure that his product is suitable for or adaptable to the Japanese consumer and never automatically assume that its merits are obvious. Certain products are becoming more westernised in line with lifestyle changes of the kind referred to previously. An example is refrigerators, which are becoming more spacious as working wives abandon the traditional daily visits to the grocer in favour of once a week trips to the supermarket. Other products, however, remain uniquely Japanese, and for this reason establishing a flexible approach to product development and marketing that caters to Japan's own set of cultural criteria is of utmost importance.

Aspects of business etiquette

The following are some pointers for Indian businessmen visiting Japan for business discussions. I have already addressed various aspects of preparing for a business visit to Japan in Chapter 4.2. These are some additional points of a personal nature.

1. SINCERITY AND RESPECT. When meeting Japanese businesspeople, Indian visitors can easily do the first thing the Japanese expect from a visitor: show sincerity and respect. We are used to this in our everyday life in India but, a word of caution. We are accustomed to showing respect mainly to elders and superiors. In Japan, you will need to learn to show genuine respect even to people much younger than you. Also, as I said earlier, the Japanese do not appreciate the extreme informality of the American back-slapping style of meeting people.

2. BOWING AND HANDSHAKING. Although the accepted form of greeting between the Japanese is to bow from the waist down with arms pressed to the side, most Japanese with international experience will not expect this immediately from a foreigner. Quite often, they will initiate a handshake instead. However, there are still some Japanese regions which are unfamiliar with handshakes and are uncomfortable with any sort of physical contact. Remember, the Japanese consider themselves to be a superior race and dislike contact with other races. If the situation is unclear, you should wait for the Japanese to offer a hand or to bow and react accordingly. You should never, repeat never, offer a handshake to a lady.

3. Amongst themselves, subordinates will bow deeply, their superiors not so. You may be able to judge the relative status of Japanese associates by observing the depths of their bows. If you are unfamiliar with bowing and are in a situation where you need to bow, pay more attention to the sincerity of your effort than to matching the depth of the other party's bow. A shallow bow is fine if done sincerely.

4. BUSINESS CARDS. The Japanese consider business cards a serious tool for establishing business contacts. These should never be taken casually or overlooked. Failure to present a card at a meeting can indicate to the Japanese that you are unaware of proper business etiquette or that you are exhibiting only a casual, fleeting interest. Cards supply key information, and without one you risk being forgotten. You should always have an ample supply of business cards printed in English on one side and in Japanese on the other. A business card should include your name, your company's name and a position title that will give the Japanese an idea of your relative status within the company.

   When Japanese individuals normally introduce themselves, they first mention the name of the company they work for and then their own name. Status in society is due to the company for which one works rather than the profession one is in. In most other cultures, the opposite is the case.

5. Time and again, I have seen Indian visitors offer cards where the printed phone number, for example, is struck off and corrected

by hand. Worse, the correction is often done in front of the host. This is stupid as it advertises the fact that the visitor has not given ample importance to the trip. Large hotels in Japan accustomed to dealing with foreign visitors can have business cards printed for you in a few hours. Count on needing at least a hundred cards for a one-week visit.

6. The proper procedure for exchanging business cards is to give and receive cards with both hands. Or, better still, hold the card by the corners between the thumb and finger of your right hand and support your right elbow with your left hand. When presenting your card, hold it so that the name faces the recipient. When you receive a card, do not pocket it immediately, but take a few moments to study the card and what it says. The card represents the person who presents it and should be given the respect he is due. You will see that the Japanese do the same.

7. In negotiation, arranging the business cards that you have received in the order in which your Japanese counterparts are seated will help you to identify the current speaker. Of course, you will want to keep the cards together with notes of the meeting.

8. LETTERS OF INTRODUCTION. At your first meting with representatives of a Japanese company, presenting letters of introduction from well-known business leaders, overseas Japanese, or former government officials who have dealt with Japan is an excellent way of showing both that you are a person of high standing and that you mean business. The Japanese are very concerned about social standing and anything you can do to enhance their regard for you is a plus. Be careful, however, not to appear arrogant or haughty, as Japanese morality condemns such behaviour.

9. PRESENTING YOUR BUSINESS. It is important to present your business properly early on in the relationship. In meetings with middle-level executives and technicians, you will need to explain the reasons for your trip and the details of your business fully if you want the relationship to progress. Japanese are an orderly, thorough people, and the way in which you present yourself is the most important element to business success at this stage of the relationship. You must be knowledgeable about every detail of your business and be able to display this knowledge in a manner that is at once concise and detailed. Most importantly, your presentation should not neglect the individuals to whom you are

speaking. Take their personalities and manners into account throughout your presentation.

10. MATERIALS AND INFORMATION. Before you make a presentation, you should prepare materials and information that will help explain your position. You may want to give a presentation kit to each member of the Japanese delegation, with as much of the material as possible in Japanese. These kits can also be sent to the Japanese company a few days before the meeting. A kit should contain:

   • A brochure introducing your company
   • An overview of your company that includes the company's name and address, the names and titles of its top executives, a list of its products and a short history
   • A short biography of yourself and of the top executives
   • Information demonstrating that your company's product or service is innovative, different and better than that of the competition

Materials presented in Japanese should be written or translated by a Japanese, and the Japanese text checked by a third person fluent in both Japanese and English. Poorly written Japanese will be an embarrassment to your company.

Help for Indian companies

Indian companies seeking to enter the Japanese market now have access to many services designed specifically to facilitate market entry. By using these services, companies can, in theory, obtain all sorts of information and assistance.

The main avenue of assistance is the JETRO (Japan External Trade Organization). You may also directly contact one of the newest sources of support for foreign business people in Japan, the network of Business Support Centers operated by JETRO in Tokyo, Osaka, Nagoya, Yokohama, Kobe and Fukuoka.

Assistance is also available from the Japanese trade office nearest to where you are located. These offices are listed in the phone books of all the metropolitan cities of India. You can ask them for the nearest JETRO office or representative. You can also access the net for information. JETRO has an immense amount of information for overseas business visitors on their websites.

You will find these organisations of immense help if you want to buy anything from Japan. However, if you are interested in exporting, this is not going to help.

✓ The Japanese are in the market to buy but they will not wait around for you to go selling to them. They have their own trading firms all over the world, efficiently on the lookout for the products and services Japan needs.

When you call a Japanese organisation asking for export trade information, you are already branded as someone not to be taken seriously. People who are keen to do business do not go around asking for addresses. I have made it repeatedly clear that the only way the Japanese will deal with you is through a Japanese trading house or through an Indian organisation they are already dealing with. So, the first step is to introduce yourself to someone already in business with Japan at your location. You can start by giving them information about yourself which they will check and verify. If they then come back and suggest a meeting, you have crossed the first barrier. If you have a product or a service which is competitive enough to be of their interest they will, most likely, have heard about you and make the first contact.

When you call JETRO you will be asked a lot of questions about yourself and what you are interested in and why, before they give you the name and phone number of a person to contact. Remember they exist to help Japan export. Remember also that the Japanese government trade offices, like the trade representations of all foreign missions in India, get a huge number of calls from people seeking all sorts of information. Only a tiny fraction of these are genuine business calls. The rest are mostly from people who are thinking of a holiday and are, at the same time, interested in exploring the possibility of exporting. For specific data and information please refer to Appendix 4.

7.3   *Selling to Thailand and Malaysia*

If someone were to ask me to name the region where there is the greatest gap between what India has achieved in terms of export trade and what it easily could have achieved, I would quickly name these South-East Asian nations.

Our potential for trade with these nations is indeed tremendous and we have tapped not even a small fraction of it. There is a considerable population here of people of Indian origin. Many of them are outstandingly successful as traders, professionals and also as politicians, and could have been a major asset in our marketing efforts. But alas, they are grossly disorganised and have no clout whatsoever.

For us to succeed in these nations, we have to understand, and make friends and deal with the people who control the trade: the local Chinese.

The message I have for my fellow Indians wanting to establish an export foothold in these highly successful nations is to avoid appointing local Indians as your selling agents.

- I have addressed, in general terms in Chapter 3.4, the matter of overseas Indians and NRIs and explained how they have unwittingly become a major barrier to our export effort

- In this chapter, I will discuss some specific issues concerning the Indian diaspora in Malaysia and Thailand. I will also discuss the relevant aspects of the economies of these nations

- I will then look at the mindset of the local Chinese in some detail because they are crucial to our exports to the region. I will put forward some ideas on how best to deal with them

- Please note that I have not included Singapore in this chapter, even though there are a number of Indian (and Pakistani and Bangladeshi) trading houses there, some more successful than others. The nature and extent of interest Singapore-based Indian trading houses are taking in India's export effort, and the contribution they are making to our economy is a subject I would rather avoid commenting upon. In saying this, I have already said a lot

368 Unleashing India on World Markets

I have spent a major part of my life living and working in Thailand, Malaysia and Singapore. So, based on my personal observations, I am going to make certain statements which, on the face of it, may not sound nice. But, if we have to do business and succeed, niceties play no part.

It is the local Chinese who have a firm grip on the retail and wholesale distribution networks in this region. They work very well with each other and jealously protect the interests of other Chinese, so it takes a Chinese to sell to a Chinese. I have discussed this point in great detail in Chapters 4.4 and 4.5. Appointing a local Indian to sell to the invariable Chinese customers is not only silly but a recipe for disaster. The same goes for setting up a local organisation in joint venture with only local Indians. By all means, have them to look after your interests, but have the Chinese with you too as they are the ones who will deliver the goods.

Here I wish to also add that local Indians in Malaysia, Thailand, etc. make excellent friends and even generous investors. Remember, I was one of them! They are, however, simply not suitable for importing and marketing industrial or engineering products. There are plenty of well-meaning rich and successful accountants, doctors or lawyers who are keen to do business with their ancestral homeland, but they are not the type of people one should join hands with to penetrate the stranglehold of the Chinese traders. The Indian traders there are merely petty traders.

The Malaysians

Cultures have been meeting and mixing in what was known as Malaya since the very beginning of its history. More than fifteen hundred years ago a Malay kingdom in Bujang Valley welcomed traders from China and India. With the arrival of gold and silks, Buddhism and Hinduism too came to Malaysia. Arab traders also arrived in Malacca by and by, and brought with them the principles and practices of Islam. By the time the Portuguese arrived in Malaysia, the empire that they encountered was more cosmopolitan than their own. Malaysia is a cultural mosaic and several of these cultures have had a lasting influence on the country. Chief among these is the ancient Malay culture and the cultures of Malaysia's two most prominent trading partners throughout history—China and India.

The Malays are Malaysia's largest ethnic group, accounting for over half the population. With the oldest indigenous peoples they form a group called bumiputra, which translates as 'sons of the soil.' All Malays are Muslims, though Islam here has a more moderate and progressive face. Traditional Malay culture always centred around the kampung, or village, though the present government has policies of urbanisation in place to help bring the Malays into the mainstream of national life.

The Chinese traded with Malaysia for centuries, then settled in large numbers during the nineteenth century when word of riches in the Nanyang, or 'South Seas,' spread across China. Though perhaps a stereotype, the Chinese have always been regarded as the foundation of Malaysia's economy, having succeeded in most enterprises. When they first arrived, however, the Chinese often worked at the most grueling jobs, including tin mining and railway construction. Most Chinese retain strong ties to their ancestral homeland. Today, they form about 35 per cent of the population.

Indians have been visiting Malaya for over 2,000 years, but did not settle en masse until the nineteenth century. Most came from South India, fleeing a poor economy. Arriving in Malaya, many worked as rubber tappers, while others worked on building the railway and the roads. Some of those who were a little educated worked as junior administrators and small-time businessmen. Today about 10 per cent of Malaysia is Indian, and Indian culture, intact with its exquisite Hindu temples, cuisine and colourful garments, is visible throughout the land. I can say without risk of contradiction that one gets a better iddli dossai in the Chettiar restaurants of Kuala Lumpur than in Chennai.

An example of Malaysia's extraordinary cultural exchange is the Malay wedding ceremony, which incorporates elements of the Hindu traditions of southern India—the bride and groom dress in gorgeous brocades, sit in state and feed each other yellow rice with hands painted with henna. The Muslims have adapted the Chinese custom of giving little red packets of money at festivals to their own needy; the packets given on Muslim holidays are green and have Arab writing on them. You can go from a Malaysian kampung to a rubber plantation worked by Indians to Penang's Chinese kongsi and feel you've travelled through three nations. But in cities like Kuala Lumpur, you'll find everyone in a grand melange.

Though Indians lived and still continue to live under conditions of appalling poverty in many places of the world where they were first taken as indentured labour, a number of remarkable transformations have been effected in Malaysia over two or three generations. Through sheer perseverance, labour and thrift, and, most significantly, by a calculated withdrawal into their culture in which they found forces of sustenance, some Indians have successfully laboured to give their children and grandchildren better economic futures. These children, in turn, have been able to make a mark in professional fields such as medicine, law and accountancy. This was just as true in South Africa, Kenya and Uganda, as it was in Malaysia.

Malaysian Indians have always kept a low profile in Malaysia. These migrant workers, the majority of them Tamils from south India, have got used to being forgotten in official discourse, which focuses mainly on the two largest groups: the politically dominant ethnic Malays, who make up about half the population, and the better organised and economically better off ethnic Chinese. Indian professionals do have a visible presence on the social circuit but have no impact on the corporate or political world. There is far too much divisiveness amongst them for any such impact.

The larger Indian trading houses are confined to mostly the textile trade and there too have been losing ground to the better organised Chinese. Invariably, as the children are educated and become professionals, the family business which was organised as a one-man-show dies out.

✓ In short, business in Malaysia is dominated by the ethnic Chinese, and government, by ethnic Malays. Only the professional, legal and educational community has partial Indian representation.

The Malaysian economy

Malaysia is a diverse tropical country which, until independence in 1957, served its colonial powers as an excellent source of supply of such raw materials as palm oil, tin, coconut, copper and rubber. All of that is changing as Malaysia's leaders implement economic development plans geared to the twenty-first century, and take the country rapidly into the arena of high-tech manufacturing and the services.

Indian companies wishing to take advantage of this dynamic and growing market must understand the foundation of Malaysian society, which happens to be Islam. The majority of Malaysians are Muslims. However, Malaysia has also maintained a steadfast campaign against fundamentalist Muslim extremism of the type often witnessed in the Middle East.

Another characteristic of Malaysian business is the government's active involvement through legislation, regulation and planning. But an activist government does not necessarily mean hostility to business. The government wants foreign businesses to succeed as long as the Malaysian people and business sectors do as well. Government controls have been enacted to promote Malaysian business while attracting the necessary foreign investment. Malaysia is a country which has not forgotten its colonial past, when resources were developed to benefit foreigners.

Growth demands infrastructure, which in Malaysia is translating into such massive projects as the new Kuala Lumpur International Airport, the mass rapid transit system, and new hotels, factories and offices that will house multimedia companies there to take advantage of the new IT era. And with public works come more opportunities. Big construction companies from Japan and Korea may get the huge contracts, but this will also create many niche opportunities for smaller subcontractors in countries like India. (For more on this refer to Chapter 6.2). These, in turn, will mean new markets for food, medical equipment, financial services, electronics, and manufactured goods and services. The IT era alone is opening up markets across the board, resulting in great opportunities for dynamic companies with concrete plans and an understanding of the market.

✓ In Malaysia, everywhere one turns, one finds an emphasis on quality as a way of life. This has had a major impact on the economy of the country.

Malaysia also aspires to becoming the regional hub for quality medical treatment and research. It hopes to do this by attracting experienced doctors and technologies, expanding the existing number of hospitals and improving their quality, and using government support to connect state-of-the-art medical technology and hospital centres. Malaysia is therefore looking to create joint ventures with companies that can facilitate new technologies.

Opportunities also exist for businesses that provide products and services for the petroleum, automobile and white goods sectors. Malaysia has substantial production capacity in these sectors, all of which is primarily export oriented.

The racial equation

If you happen to spend time in Malaysia working with the local people, you will come away impressed. Cultural and ethnic diversity have not torn the country apart. Rather, the Malaysian government has succeeded in linking material progress to cultural tolerance. It's a lesson that many developed countries would appreciate.

Malaysia is the product of its history and, as in the US, race has played a significant role in it. In particular, the bumiputra laws are a tangible expression of racial tension between the ethnic Malays and the prosperous Chinese Malays. These laws mandate the preferential treatment of the ethnic Malay people. There are, moreover, extensive laws that require bumiputra ownership of at least 30 per cent of most economic activity. Quotas also exist for ethnic Malay students attending universities and determining bumiputra employment levels in companies. These laws have been successfully implemented to ensure ethnic Malay participation in business; their existence has played a crucial role in making possible Malaysia's prosperity, and large, successful bumiputra businesses are now flourishing. But even though a peaceful coexistence has evolved, the local Chinese still control large pieces of the Malaysian economy.

✓ It should be noted that though the Chinese share of the cake has come down in percentage terms, the Chinese are happy as the size of the cake has increased and their share of it has thereby increased enormously. The Indians have not been able to organise themselves commercially, their businesses remain petty trading outfits and they have no share of this enlarged cake.

Malaysians are outgoing, friendly people and will do business with people they get to know, like and respect. You must build personal relationships to succeed. It is difficult to establish any such equation through fax. You must schedule many trips to Malaysia in order to develop your business relationships.

Although the Malaysian government is creating many new opportunities for foreign firms, business in Malaysia, especially big business, operates more smoothly when a company forms a joint venture with or takes on a local partner. In years previous, there was a great emphasis on bumiputra relationships. While the laws have been modified, bumiputra businesspeople are powerful and well established in the business community. As in any international market, a powerful local partner can greatly assist business growth. Moreover, with a local partner, a business can better identify and react to the specifics of the local marketplace, avoiding cultural errors.

Let's take a look at Thailand

Thailand alone, in the entire South-East Asian region was able to avoid colonisation, a success which owes something to its famous national pragmatism. Its kings have been modernisers ever since the nineteenth century. In 1932, the monarchy gracefully accepted an end to absolutism when the military demanded it. A succession of military strongmen held sway for most of the next four decades, accommodating and cooperating with, in turn, the British, French, Japanese and Americans. An unprecedented popular explosion in 1973 introduced Thailand to democracy, but the military intervened again and a sort of semi-democracy has since prevailed.

The pillars of the system remain the monarchy, the army, the bureaucracy and the political parties; but the balance has changed. Reverence for the king has been the only constant, ensuring that his rare political interventions are decisive. The military has been less obtrusive but has always threatened to intervene.

✓ The point to be noted here is that Thailand has almost never had a strong or stable government, yet has been economically very successful and able to make its mark on world trade. We, in India, have enjoyed relative stability but the results on the economic front have been disappointing.

Well into the 1960s, Thailand's wealth rested on growing rice and exporting the surplus. The Vietnam war brought in the Americans. They poured in money and helped develop Thailand's infrastructure. The Thais took advantage of this to diversify into export crops, and the local Chinese used the development of this infrastructure to establish a manufacturing base. By the mid-1980s, this had helped Thailand become a favourite South-East Asian location for offshore manufacturing. Manufacturing has contributed more to the GDP than agriculture since 1984. Textiles overtook rice in the export figures in 1985.

For all their recent successes, the Thais are handicapped in their attempt to emulate South Korea in a similar dash for growth. The main problem is that all economic activity remains focused on the kingdom's traditional hub, Bangkok, and the central plain. With a population of eight million, the Bangkok metropolis is 40 times larger than the next largest Thai city. Its clogged port and overloaded telephone and road systems are symptomatic of an infrastructure pushed beyond its limits by rapid growth. New investment and the dispersion of economic activity have become urgent priorities that will test the capacity, and ultimately the stability, of Thailand's political system.

Rice, the mainstay of the domestic economy and the chief export, still covers half the planted area, alongside newer crops like rubber, oil palm, maize, sugar and tapioca. Other valuable commodity exports are tin and timber.

Manufacturing is now largely confined to the following:

1. Consumer goods mainly for the domestic and regional market.
2. Excellent quality processed food items for export. I have discussed in Chapter 6.5, how a prospective investor in the export-oriented coconut-based industry chose Thailand against India. This still leaves the doors open for Indian businessmen to provide for niche food items or food processing equipment and generate substantial market gains.
3. Labour-intensive export industries such as textiles, electronics, shoes and toys, a boom fuelled by foreign investment. Thailand is a leading producer worldwide of cement, ceramic tiles, sanitary ware, bearings, printed circuit boards, computer assemblies, hard drives and varied agro-industrial products.
4. Gem trading and the cutting of gem stones, in which it is a world leader.

A major advantage for Thailand is that the business is mostly in the hands of the local Chinese. Their networking with fellow

Chinese in other Asian and American markets allows local producers to easily expand into international markets.

The problem however lies, as I said earlier, with the grossly inadequate infrastructure which is a constraint for further growth, and the
education system, particularly the inadequate teaching in the English medium, which has resulted in the country not being able to
cope with the expanding demand for skilled labour.

For Indian companies, Thailand is a ready market for the export of
medical products, instrumentation, information technology products,
infrastructure products and services, telecommunication hardware
and consumer goods. Opportunities abound for Indian companies
whose products or services meet the needs of the computer and/or
electronic industries. This includes everything from end-product
manufacturing to software and all products or services falling
between the two.

✓ However, any Indian businessman wishing to enter these fields
   would do well to remember that these trades are all in the hands
   of the local Chinese.

The Chinese in Thailand

Despite making up only 10 per cent of the national population of
about 60 million, the Chinese in Thailand wield significant control
over the private sector. They control four of the five largest banks in
Thailand, which handle 50 per cent of Thailand's GDP. Thailand's
largest bank, the Bangkok Bank, is also the largest in South-East
Asia.

The Chinese in Thailand are estimated to own at least 50 per cent
of all investments in the banking and finance sector, and 90 per cent
of all investments in the manufacturing and commercial sectors.
These are impressive figures considering that most Chinese were
driven by poverty from their homeland to find a better life in
Thailand.

That the Chinese make up 10 per cent of the population is only an
approximate figure at best. The Chinese have been in Thailand a
long time and have assimilated successfully into Thai culture. In
fact, there are not many Thais today who do not have some Chinese
blood. In the same vein, there are not many Chinese Thais today
who can trace no Thai lineage. The Thais have coexisted with the

overseas Chinese in remarkable harmony. Instead of attempting to replace the Chinese in the economic or political arenas, the Thai Government realised that it would be more practical and beneficial for the nation as a whole to initiate cooperation with the Chinese in developing the Thai economy.

The Thai-Chinese subscribe fully to mainstream Thai values. Most of them, particularly those of the third generation or so, now consider themselves Thai. They speak perfect Thai, eat Thai food and compete to obtain an education in the best Thai universities.

The Thai-Chinese, however, maintain Chinese religions and traditions. Alongside Buddha idols, they may have pictures of Chinese gods and ancestors in their homes. They usually ask for time off during the Chinese New Year (around mid-February) and will eat only vegetarian food during the Vegetarian Festival in October. To some extent, the rest of Thailand joins in these celebrations, particularly the Chinese New Year. You will see a lot of the department stores decorated in red, the Chinese colour for celebration and prosperity.

Some Thai-Chinese may use a Chinese name at home and speak a Chinese dialect with their parents. The attitude of some Thai-Chinese to work is also different from that of the indigenous Thais. They have high respect for education and lay emphasis on entrepreneurship, flexibility and hard work. Most dream of owning their own business one day.

Indians in Thailand

Though Indian culture has been a part of the Thai landscape for centuries, one finds that Indians are often misunderstood and sometimes disliked and resented. It is true that the official religion of Thailand is Buddhism, the local script is based on Pali, the Sanskrit script, the former capital was named Ayudhya and the present king is King Rama 4. Nevertheless, the Thais understand little of the group of people who have been living among them for years. However, the Thais are not to be blamed for this as it is the Indians who live in airtight compartments and do not make any effort to be noticed.

Like in Malaysia, where the Indian community is predominantly Tamil, the spectrum of Indian communities in Thailand is also not too broad. There are Punjabis (Sikhs, Hindus and Muslims), who mostly run flourishing textile businesses. Many have branched into other business areas such as manufacturing, real estate or fast food. Their offspring have entered professions such as medicine and finance or work for the government. The other large community is from Uttar Pradesh, and these people mostly work as watchmen in factories and warehouses, and are part involved in time trade as petty moneylenders.

Traces of Indian cultural influence abound in Thai history. There are records going back to about A.D. 1350, when King Uthong is said to have invited Brahmins from Varanasi to institute religious ceremonies, which are still performed today. History records that in the early centuries of the last millennium, trade and travel to Siam, as it was known then, and to other areas in South-East Asia flourished amongst seafarers from Chola and Kalinga. There are records of elephants being exported from Siam to Hindustan, which in turn exported to Siam cloth, gold, silver and gemstones. Scholars, skilled craftsmen, monks and priests often accompanied traders, and it was through trade routes that religion, political systems, astrology and other Indian influences were brought into Thailand. Some Chinese annals indicate that the first Thai Kingdom, Nanchao, used an alphabet of Indian origin and identified itself with India rather than with China. The peculiar thing about the Thai language is that it is a tonal language like the Chinese, but is written in a script of Sanskrit or Pali origin.

In the present times, like in nearby Malaysia, the Indians have been able to maintain their own cultural heritage. But that has not quite worked to their advantage. It is characteristic of Indians in Thailand, like overseas Indians in many countries, to keep to themselves and not assimilate with other cultures. There is divisiveness and disunity even amongst themselves. Take a small community like the Sikhs. There are three distinct sects of them, each with their own places of worship. Each, therefore, remains in a watertight compartment. Indians, thus, rarely indulge in any social or cultural exchange. The businesses owned by them, therefore, remain small and isolated.

✓ So, as I said earlier, if one is keen to do business in Thailand, it is as important to deal with the Chinese as it is to avoid the local Indians.

Hints for personal behaviour

- Always be prompt for meetings, even though your contact may not be. The meeting will invariably be at the office of your contact or in a restaurant
- The traffic in Bangkok is among the worst in the world. Always, therefore, allow an hour or two extra for traffic
- Always reconfirm meetings at least a day in advance; cancellations are common
- It is considered an honour to have the last piece of food on a plate. When offered the last bit, it is polite to first refuse and offer the bit to your host instead. When offered again, accept it
- Dress conservatively. Ties are essential but suits are not. Light cotton or polyester safari suits are fine. Remember, Thailand is hot and humid for a large part of the year, though you are likely to be in comfortable air conditioning most of the time
- A western handshake is acceptable between men. The Thai people have the equivalent of our folded hand 'namaste', though more gracefully done. Thai businesspeople will be impressed if you know how to do this, easily learnt if you observe them closely
- Never walk between two people standing and talking to each other. Bow low and pass through
- Address people by titles such as Mr, Mrs, and so forth. Titles are very important to Thais. Most Thai businesspeople are Chinese, but in Thailand it is essential to have a Thai name if one is a citizen. So you will often find people with two names, one for use in Thailand and the other outside. Chinese names are written with the surname first
- Remove your shoes on entering a home or a Buddhist temple, and avoid stepping on the temple doorsill when entering
- Never ever criticise the monarchy, even in private
- There are many cultural issues that pertain both to Thai business and to the general behaviour of the Thai people. It is a frequent occurrence for the foreign businessperson or tourist to offend the Thai cultural belief system without knowing why. Such would be the case, for example, in displaying anger. No matter the reason (and I would venture to say that anyone who tries to organise a business in Thailand will have his or her patience tested), do not appear angry. Thais interpret the expression of anger as a lack of

self-control, and it could seriously affect personal or business relationships. Keep your cool. Displaying your anger will only make a frustrating situation worse. It is far wiser to practice 'polite persistence' in order to make your point. This accepted method of dealing with disagreement will also allow for more fruitful discussions in the future. The local people make a serious effort to mask their feelings, but if you watch closely you will often see them squeezing the hell out of their chair arm rests!

* Be aware of gesture taboos. These include touching or passing an object over another person's head, pointing the sole of your foot at another person, stamping your feet or touching a person with your foot. Don't cross your legs while seated or place your arm over the back of a chair in which another person is seated
* Thais consider the head the most sacred part of the body and the feet, the least

How to make the Chinese your friends

What I am going to say here will hold good for Chinese business-people everywhere. I have already addressed this point in Chapters 4.4 and 4.5, but I would like to highlight here some points which should be taken note of particularly in dealing with the Chinese in Malaysia and Thailand.

As with most Asians, where ritual and personal relationships are a vital part of the smooth functioning of society, Chinese business-people do not rush into discussion or negotiations as people from the West are wont to do. The Chinese will want to get acquainted before they do business. They will also want to extend their hospitality to demonstrate their respect and their own appreciation of the finer things in life (eating and drinking), as also to soften their visitor up. There is usually a lot of small talk during the first day of business, when the Chinese counterpart will try to learn as much as possible about the visitor and his goals. That evening during the welcoming banquet, they will learn more, for it is in such casual situations that the foreign businessperson is most likely to reveal himself.

The Chinese have a highly structured style of negotiating that goes well beyond the usual western practices. For example, the Chinese often make use of the shame technique to gain an advantage, i.e. making the adversary feel ashamed about something and thus give way. They will also typically try to make the opposite side feel responsible for any problems or errors that might have occurred. Knowing that people from the West as well as Indians tend to be very impatient, they use this to their advantage, using go-slow tactics to encourage the opposite side to give away more than planned.

I have met many experienced businesspeople from Europe and elsewhere who say the Chinese resort to a variety of tactics to get what they want, including using the visitors' lack of knowledge about the local market, threatening to take their business elsewhere, and so on. The Chinese are past masters of the 'bad cop–good cop' technique of negotiating and interrogating, and they use this strategy in almost every situation imaginable, personal as well as business. By sustaining this kind of psychological pressure, adversaries, especially if they are inexperienced with this approach, generally tend to develop a paranoid personality.

At the same time—and unlike the Japanese—the Chinese can be very direct and blunt in their dealings with foreigners. While claiming to operate on the principle of equality and mutual benefit, they will often point out that what may be fair to the foreigner has nothing to do with the circumstances in Malaysia or Thailand. But, as in Japan, the Chinese do not see the contract as the end of negotiation and the beginning of wholehearted cooperation. For them, it is just the beginning of a relationship that will naturally change from one day to the next and will have to be reevaluated and renegotiated on an ongoing basis. Until very recently, one of the main challenges facing foreign businesspeople negotiating or doing business with the Chinese in these countries was getting reliable information, business or political, about the local market.

It is an unwritten law and an indication of how effectively the Chinese work together that all Chinese avoid providing the non-Chinese with information regarding their society, associations or business networks, regardless of how trivial this information may be. This makes it confusing and difficult for foreigners and the non-Chinese in the country to function well in any capacity.

This problem has been significantly addressed by the current regime in Malaysia at the highest official level, but has not been fully accepted in Thailand, where it is still a major handicap.

The Chinese are also masters at placing newcomers under obligation by employing an effusive, costly hospitality and further weakening their position by the use of psychological ploys. Foreigners with little or no cross-cultural experience tend to interpret Chinese attitudes and behaviour in their own cultural terms, even when they know better.

There is also always the strong preset notion that Chinese behavior is irrational and wrong. Remember they have their own code of ethics which may often be in sharp contrast to ours. So, in any dealings with the Chinese, though difficult, it is vital that we keep in mind that, from the Chinese viewpoint, we may be the ones who are off base.

The Chinese are also influenced not only by intense feelings regarding their own social systems but their cultural ways as well, and these invariably play a role in their business relationships with foreigners. Their feelings often take precedence over what foreigners regard as common sense or what we call a 'good deal'. Contrary to appearances, however, the Chinese are actually more compatible with Indians form India than they are with local Indians in Malaysia, Thailand etc. or with most other Asian and African nationalities. The Chinese believe that Indians are more trustworthy and respectful than, say, the Bangladeshis or the Pakistanis. It is certainly true that most Asians are impressed by the incredible ancient history of India and the arts and crafts of its civilization, and tend to demonstrate this in their behaviour.

Appendix 1:
India's competitiveness

Answers to the Questions in chapter 2.1

1. Of the 45 nations analysed in 1980, where do you think India stood?

   Number 25 from the top
   ✓ Number 38 from the top
   Number 40 from the top
   Number 44 from the top

2. Of the 49 nations analysed in 1999, where do you think India stood?

   Number 25 from the top
   Number 40 from the top
   ✓ Number 43 from the top
   Number 48 from the top

   We have gone down from the 38th to a measly 43rd position but are still sixth from the bottom.

3. India's share of the world trade in 1950 was?

   22.82%
   5.68%
   ✓ 1.91%
   0.88 %

4. In 1998, India's share in the world trade was?

   22.82%
   5.68%

✓ 0.07%
0.01%

The World Competitiveness Yearbook (WCY) is the world's most renowned study on the competitiveness of nations. It assesses and ranks how a nation's environment sustains the competitiveness of its firms.

The WCY measures and compares how countries are doing in providing firms with a climate that sustains their domestic and global competitiveness. The WCY analyses and ranks nations using 290 criteria. There is an extract of the criteria in Appendix 2.

The International Institute for Management Development (IMD), which publishes the WCY, uses two types of data: 2/3 are hard data—economic and other statistics that come from international, regional, national and other organisations; and 1/3, survey data—statistics about competitiveness that are compiled from the WCY Annual Executive Opinion Survey. It is essential to use these two types of data so as to capture both competitiveness as it is measured (hard data) and as it is perceived (survey data).

It is important for us in India to know who uses the WCY.

1. The business community, to assess national environments. In an open and global world, location is very important for companies. They need to reassess or choose new locations all the time. The WCY is used as a key input in their decision making.
2. The government community, to benchmark its policy success and to see how other nations perform.
3. The academic world, to understand and analyse how nations (not only enterprises) compete in world markets. Most business schools use WCY information in their executive development programmes.

Appendix 2:
Criteria for world competitiveness

Discussion on points raised in Appendix 1 and in Chapter 2.1

World Competitiveness Yearbook

This is the Competitiveness Criteria used in the yearbook.

Domestic economy

Gross domestic product (GDP) computed at current prices and exchange rates, according to purchasing power parity, and also on a local currency at constant prices basis
Parallel (black-market, barter, unrecorded) economy
Gross domestic savings (residents + non-residents) as a percentage of the GDP
Customer sophistication
Economic sector performance
Cost of living
Adaptiveness of private companies, government companies and the Government
Adapting quickly to changes in the economic cycle

Internationalisation

Current account balance
Export of goods and services

Import of goods and services
Exchange rate
Foreign direct investments
National protectionism
Investment protection schemes
Immigration laws
Openness
Globalisation
Image of the country abroad

National debt

Government expenditure
Fiscal policies
State efficiency
State involvement
Justice and security

Finance

Cost of capital
Availability of capital
Stock market dynamism
Banking sector efficiency

Infrastructure

Basic
Technological
Business, office rent, labour regulations, telephone lines
International telephone costs
Health
Energy self-sufficiency
Environment

Management

Productivity
Labour costs

Size of companies
Number of Fortune 500 companies
Management efficiency
Corporate culture

Science and technology

R&D expenditures
R&D personnel
Technology management
Scientific environment
Intellectual property

People

Population characteristics
Labour force characteristics
Employment
Unemployment
Educational infrastructure
Urban population: percentage of total population
Income distribution
Attitudes and values
Alcohol and drug abuse
Flexibility and adaptability

Appendix 3:
Japanese nationalism

A note on the concept of loan words in the Japanese language (ref: Chapter 4.2)

The Japanese language is the only language in the world which, while accepting and assimilating foreign words, keeps them clearly marked. To the best of my knowledge, there is no other language in the world that has such a term as 'loan words.' There are a number of foreign or 'loan' words in common use in the Japanese language but they have been cleverly identified as such. A foreign word in the Japanese language remains a foreign word even after 400 years because it is written differently.

The Japanese alphabet has two scripts, Hiragana and Katakana, though it works with the same alphabet and the same sounds. Up until the fifth century, Japan had no writing system. They therefore imported the very complex Chinese picture writing script which is called Kanji. This was inconvenient for the Japanese to use in everyday writing, so they simplified the characters and took the structure of the alphabet from Sanskrit into what is now Hiragana and Katakana, together called Kana. Unlike Kanji which is picture writing, the Kana is a phonetic alphabet. In Kanji, each character represents a complete word or sometimes a few words, but a Kana character represents a single syllable of a word, like in the Roman script.

The Chinese-style Kanji characters are still used to write many words in academic Japanese. The Kana, Hiragana and Katakana, are simpler symbols that stand for sounds. The Hiragana characters are written in a curving, flowing style. The Katakana are more angular characters. Hiragana works in exactly the same way as Katakana, except that the characters are written differently, and that Hiragana is used to write native Japanese words and word endings. Katakana is used for writing foreign-derived words, words adapted into Japanese from English or other European languages, as well as from Sanskrit which came in via Buddhism.

An example: The Roman equivalent of this is the sentence 'my son bought his new OOTOBAI in BURAJIRO'. The whole sentence would be in Hiragana except the words 'motorbike' and 'Brazil' which would be in Katakana. The Japanese have taken and modified the words but they are clearly marked out as foreign words.

There are some exceptions, however. Sometimes, again to create a 'special effect,' a writer will use Hiragana to write a loan word which should have been written in Katakana.

Appendix 4:
Items Japan would like to import

Note 1: As a member of an export promotion team for some African
nations, I visited Japan and South Korea some years ago. This was
a World Bank funded visit so we got a lot of official handouts. One
such note, extracted and edited for the readers, is given below.
This indicates a list of what Japan is in the market to import. We
got a similar list in Korea.

Note 2: An updated version of this list should be freely available
with the local offices of the Japan External Trade Organisation.

In November 1991, Japan's Ministry of International Trade and
Industry (MITI) established the Business Global Partnership with 40
of Japan's automobile, electronics, machinery, steel, nonferrous
metal, chemical and trading companies. These 40 firms together
annually import US$ 120 million in goods, amounting to 51 per cent
of Japan's imports. These companies, along with another 160 companies in key industries (for example, machine tools, manufacturing equipment and glass) are expected to draw up and implement
voluntary import plans. Targets for import expansion include parts,
components and capital goods. Foreign firms offering competitive
pricing and quality service can take advantage of lucrative prospects ranging from advanced ceramic components and industrial
plastics to refrigeration equipment, commercial art, cosmetics and
sporting goods. The following sectors are considered to be the best
prospects for foreign companies exporting to Japan.

Refrigeration equipment

Despite the recession, the demand for refrigeration equipment has been increasing in line with the high volume of building construction and orders for new residential housing supplies. Industry analysts predict that shipments of refrigeration equipment will only grow. Import items currently in demand are commercial refrigeration equipment, ice-making machines, freezers, pre-fabricated refrigeration and cold storage units, refrigerating display cases (freshness control equipment) and refrigeration units for transportation systems.

Interior and commercial art

A softening in prices at the high end of the art market has allowed amateur collectors to enter the lower end of the market. Japanese households are showing more interest in prints, posters, photographs and other forms of commercial art that can be used for interior decoration. For most of these purchasers, the primary criterion in selection is personal taste; only a small number buy art for investment purposes.

Retailers and other commercial entities are seeking high-quality art to decorate their facilities. Corporations are purchasing art to enliven the workplace environment, as well as to enhance corporate public relations through the contribution of art works for social and philanthropic purposes. Over the next several years, the projected annual growth for interior and commercial art in Japan is a healthy 50 per cent.

Herbal cosmetics and toiletries

Japanese consumers are extremely receptive to herbal cosmetics imported from Europe and the US. While European, particularly French, cosmetics have long been admired, Indian cosmetics are increasingly beginning to be well regarded among Japanese consumers. As price-consciousness continues to spread, opportunities improve for intermediate-priced Indian herbal cosmetics.

In general, though, the Japanese cosmetics market is a mature one, in which consumers are willing to pay high prices for high-quality products. Women under the age of 40 make up over 40 per cent of cosmetics purchases, with the greatest number of purchases being made by women in their 20s. Environmentally sound products, time-saving cosmetics for working women and products specially designed for women over 40 offer the greatest sales potential. Promising items include perfumes and body fragrances, hair care products, natural foundations, eye makeup, lipsticks and skin care products.

Advanced ceramics components

Advanced ceramics components are used in fields ranging from electronics, energy, aviation and space to medical and marine equipment. By the year 2000, the Japanese market for advanced ceramic components is expected to reach US$ 40 billion, approximately five times the present volume.

This market for advanced ceramics, in particular for electronic applications, is expected to grow rapidly. Opportunities for foreign exporters can be found in the electromagnetic components industry, which includes such products as integrated circuit (IC) substrates, semiconductors, magnetic materials, capacitors, piezoelectric elements and insulators.

Office and institutional furniture

Metal furniture accounts for 80 to 85 per cent of the office furniture market in Japan. The development of office automation equipment introduces an additional prospect for growth in the office and institutional furniture market.

The office furniture market in Japan began to expand after MITI announced the Proposal on Promotion of New Offices in 1986. According to the proposal, the new offices are intended to be more comfortable and functional so that employers and employees can be more creative and productive. A local trade journal recently reported that the new offices account for five to 10 per cent of the total offices in Japan. These offices need furniture that can accommodate office automation equipment, office systems furniture, panels and partitions, ergonomic chairs and desks for workstations.

According to industry sources, the Japanese office and institutional furniture market has not yet reached maturity, and the potential for growth looks strong.

Laboratory scientific instruments

Japan's relatively high level of spending on science teaching in schools, on R&D and on capital investment in quality control manufacturing continues to support a comparatively high growth rate for laboratory scientific instruments. Many foreign suppliers have already established themselves in this market in Japan. Industry sources project that the Japanese market for laboratory scientific instruments will grow at an average rate of three to six per cent during the next two years, depending on the speed of economic recovery. Glass equipment and general laboratory glassware represent two leading areas of opportunity for Indian exporters.

Sporting goods

There are almost no tariffs, import quotas or regulations in the Japanese sporting goods market, which has grown by six per cent annually for the last several years. Factors driving this growth include increased resort development, an increase in leisure time and the development of new lightweight materials. Japan produces and exports the upper end of sporting goods but imports the lower end sports products. The growing popularity of golf, skiing and other outdoor recreational activities promise a lucrative market for Indian exporters of the lower end of sporting goods and equipment.

Fifteen extra prospects for exporting to Japan

- air conditioning equipment
- aircraft and parts
- apparel
- computer and peripherals
- computer software
- diamonds and diamond jewellery
- herbal drugs and pharmaceuticals
- electronic components

- giftware
- basic industrial chemicals
- industrial process control
- pollution control equipment
- printing and graphic arts equipment
- seafood
- security and safety equipment

Appendix 5:
Items Korea would like to import

I visited South Korea like I did Japan some years ago on a World Bank funded visit. Following from that is a list of what Korea is in the market to import. An updated version of this list should be freely available with the local offices of the Korean Trade Missions in India.

Many foreign products are widely known in the South Korean market. Foreign firms offering competitive pricing and quality service can take advantage of lucrative prospects, ranging from automotive parts and communications products to videos and cosmetics. Demand is particularly strong for advanced machinery and electronics equipment. The following section describes the most attractive opportunities for exporting to Korea.

Computer Software

As computerisation progresses in almost all sectors of the economy, the demand for software is rising. Although South Korea is capable of developing its own applications software, much of the systems software is imported. A foreign supplier's willingness to modify software to meet the specific needs of Korean consumers will greatly enhance sales prospects.

Some hot items:

- application development tools
- applications systems software
- business software

- computer-aided design (CAD) systems
- database management systems
- military simulation systems
- networking systems
- operating systems
- programming languages
- systems and utility software

CAD/CAM Systems

Widespread growth of computer-aided design and computer-aided manufacturing (CAD/CAM) systems is expected in South Korea's electronics, aerospace, automotive, shipbuilding and machinery industries. CAD/CAM systems have already become a critical element in automated design and manufacturing. Foreign sales of CAD/CAM equipment in Korea are likely to expand, with projected imports reaching US$ 230 million.

The CAD/CAM systems supplied to Korea have generally used IBM, VAX, or Hewlett-Packard central processing units (CPUs). Recently, systems based on such engineering workstations as Micro Vax, Sun Micro and HP/Apollo platforms have become available. Technological developments in both computer hardware and software have substantially reduced the price of CAD/CAM systems and increased their user friendliness. The CAD/CAM market in personal computers has far surpassed that for the mid-range and large CAD/CAM systems. However, the general trend is now shifting away from microcomputer-based CAD systems (first introduced to Korea in 1987) towards systems based on engineering workstations. Demand for three-dimensional CAD systems in the architecture, shipbuilding and automobile industries has been increasing rapidly.

Refrigeration equipment

Applications for commercial refrigeration equipment include those from the food, medical and pharmaceutical industries. South Korea's imports of air conditioners and refrigerators have continued to rise sharply.

The domestic market for refrigeration equipment is also likely to grow due to an increased demand for processed food. Korean consumers are showing a preference for large refrigerators with energy-saving features. Rotary compressors, room air conditioners and heat pumps present additional opportunities for Indian exporters.

VCDs/DVDs

VCDs and DVDs in the English language are in great demand in South Korea. These are some popular items:

- cartoons for children
- documentaries
- English-language instruction programmes
- entertainment movies
- hobby and travel programmes
- music videos

Spare parts for household consumer goods

The South Korean electrical appliance market was first opened to foreign competition in 1989. Since then, foreign exports of home appliances to Korea have been increasing, and some foreign brands manufacturing washing machines, dryers, dishwashers, cooking ranges and refrigerators have acquired strong market positions. Given the growing demand in Korea for products that utilise advanced technologies, the market for foreign exporters of home appliances is expected to remain attractive, leading to an increasing demand for spare parts.

Machine tools and metal working equipment

The demand for advanced machine tools and metal-working equipment has increased remarkably. Local machine tool manufacturers are focusing on domestic research and development mainly for numerically controlled machine tools. But the demand for the lower end of the less sophisticated machine tools for vocational schools is considerable and is anticipated to increase.

Pulp and paper processing equipment

The South Korean paper manufacturing industry has grown steadily over the past three decades, and domestic demand for paper products has risen rapidly since the mid-1980s. The import market is expected to continue expanding. Demand is particularly strong for equipment used in the production of printing paper, toilet paper and newsprint. Rising exports of liner board and corrugated medium paper will, in turn, increase import demand for production equipment.

Cosmetics and toiletries

Foreign investment in South Korea's cosmetics industry was opened to foreign wholesalers in July 1991 and is expected to be opened to foreign retailers in 1994. Although foreign suppliers are still trying to establish themselves in this market, continued import liberalisation and diversification of sales channels will be the most important factors affecting future sales opportunities. Foreign imports, particularly of herbal cosmetics and preparations, are expected to increase by at least 30 per cent a year over the next few years.

10 extra prospects for exporting to Korea

- advanced materials
- aircraft and parts
- building products
- business equipment (non-computer)
- chemical production machinery
- herbal drugs and pharmaceuticals
- electrical power systems
- wood, rattan and metal furniture
- printing and graphic equipment
- pumps, valves and compressors

Appendix 6:
Malaysian furniture exports

Source: Malaysian Timber Industry Board (MTIB)

- Note: One Malaysian dollar (RM) was approximately Indian Rupees 10/- in mid 2000.

Country	Exports in RM Millions 1998	Percentage Change Over 1997
Australia	115.89	45
Belgium	14.40	19.1
Brunei	16.47	50.2
Canada	54.14	78.5
China	7.02	11.8
Denmark	2.37	1.9
France	14.41	82.4
Germany	16.33	19
Hong Kong	68.23	25.7
Ireland	27.75	61.5
Italy	2.45	117.4
Japan	465.59	-0.7
Kuwait	16.98	71.4
The Netherlands	18.46	38.2
New Zealand	21.90	53.4
The Philippines	14.04	149
Saudi Arabia	39.01	77.2
Singapore	256.56	18.9
South Africa	4.49	231.3
South Korea	64.31	6.5

Spain	1.97	−0.7
Sri Lanka	1.76	65.3
Sweden	10.43	19.3
Taiwan	55.77	21.3
Thailand	1.68	31.5
UAE	51.70	99
UK	106.95	39.8
USA	970.26	17.8
Vietnam	8.14	10.5
Others	72.77	72.4
Grand Total	2531.02	21.2

In Indian Rupees, this represents an export of Rs 2531 crores.

Bibliography

Amsden, A. (1989). *Asia's Next Giant: South Korea and Late Industrialisation*. Oxford: Oxford University Press.

Barro, Robert (1991). 'Economic Growth in a Cross Section of Countries.' *Quarterly Journal of Economics*. Vol. 106, pp. 407–44.

Barro, Robert and Sala-I-Martin Xavier (1995). *Economic Growth*. n.p.

Basant, R., P. Chandra and L.K. Mytelka (1988). 'Strategic partnering in Telecom Software: Northern Telecom's Technology Network in India.' Working Paper No 98–07–01. Ahmedabad: Indian Institute of Management.

Bhagwati, J.N. (1964). 'On the Underinvoicing of Imports.' Bulletin of the Oxford University Institute of Statistics, November, 1974.

Bhagwati, J.N. and P. Desai (1970). *India: Planning for Industrialisations*. New Delhi: Oxford University Press.

Bhagwati, J.N., A. Krueger and C. Wibulswadsi (1974). 'Capital Flight from LDCs: A Statistical Analysis.' Bhagwati (1974).

Bhole, L.M. (1955). 'The Indian Capital Markets at Cross-Roads.' Vikalpa, 20. pp. 29–41.

Boswell, Jonathan (1973). *The Rise and Decline of Small Firms*. London: Harper and Row.

Brennig, R.J. 'Silver in Seventeenth Century Surat: Monetary Circulation and the Price Revolution in Mughal India,' in J.F. Richards ed.

Business Korea: A Practical Guide to Understanding South Korean Business.

Carr, C. (1990). *Britain's Competitiveness*. London: Routledge

Chen, E.K.Y. (1979). *Hyper-Growth in Asian Economies: A Comparative Study of Hong Kong, Japan, Korea, Singapore and Taiwan*. London.

Cheng, Lim Keak (1985). *Social Change and the Chinese in Singapore*. Singapore: Singapore University Press.

Chia, Siow Yue (1989). 'The Character and Progress of Industrialisation.' K.S. Sandhu and P. Wheatley eds. *Management of Success*. Institute of Southeast Asian Studies. pp. 250–279.

Chiu, S., K.C. Ho and T.L. Lui (1997). *City States in the Global Economy*. Boulder, Colorado: Westview.

Chong, Grace (1992). 'The Chinese Clan Association in Singapore: Survival or Demise?' Unpublished Academic Exercise. National University of Singapore: Dept. of Sociology, Faculty of Arts and Social Sciences.

Coe, D. and D. Snower (1997). 'Policy Complementaries: The case for fundamental Labour Market Reform.' IMF Staff Paper. Vol. 44, No. 1.

Coe, D., E. Helpman and A. Hoffmaister (1995). 'North-South R&D Spillovers.' NBER Working Paper 5048.

Committee on the Third Shift (1986). Report of Findings. Singapore: National Productivity Board.

Das Gupta, A. (1982). 'Indian Merchants and the Trade in the Indian Ocean.' T. Raychaudhari and I. Habib eds. *The Cambridge Economic History of India*. Delhi. pp. 412–13

Dheer, S. and B. Viard (1955). 'Tata Consultancy Services: Globalisation of Software Services.' Stanford Business School Case Study.

Dicken, Peter (1986). *Global Shift: Industrial Change in a Turbulent World*. London: Harper and Row.

Doing Business in Korea (Bk&Csst). Sri Intl, Ice Inc.

Doing Business With Korea (Global Business Series). Paul A. Leppert.

Dollar, David (1992). 'Outward Oriented Economies Really do Grow More Rapidly: Evidence from 95 LDCs, 1976–1985.' *Economic Development and Cultural Change*. Vol. 40, pp. 523–44.

Drucker, Peter (1985). *Innovation and Enterprise*. Reprint (1991). Delhi: Affiliated East West Press.

'Electronics Industry in Malaysia and Singapore.' Occasional Papers in Women's Studies. University of Michigan: Women's Studies Program.

Economic and Political Weekly (EPW) (1997). 'Economic Reforms and Institutions.' May 17–24.

EPW (1998). 'Structure, Organisational Behaviour and Technical Efficiency', Journal of Economic Behaviour and Organisation. Vol. 34, pp. 419–34.

EPW (1999b). 'Internal Reforms and Increased Internationalisation: The Transition to Competition in India'.

EPW (1967). 'Fiscal Policies, the Faking of Foreign Trade Declarations, and the Balance of Payments', Bulletin of the Oxford University Institute of Statistics, February; also reprinted in Bhagwati (1974).

EPW (1974). 'Illegal Transactions in International Trade—Theory and Measurement'. North-Holland Publishing Company.

Evans, P (1995). *Embedded Autonomy: States and Industrial Transformation*. Princeton: Princeton University Press.

Fei, J.C.H. (1983). 'Evolution of Growth Policies of NICs in a Historical and Typological Perspective.' Paper presented during conference on Patterns of Growth and Structural Change in Asia's Newly Industrialising Countries (NICs)

Fernandez, Marilyn (1998). 'Asian Indian Americans in the Bay Area and the Glass Ceiling.' *Sociological Perspectives*. Vol. 42, No. 1, pp. 119–49.

Frankel, J.A. and D. Romer (1966). 'Trade and Growth: An Empirical Investigation.' NBER Working Paper 5476.

Friedman, M. and R. Friedman (1980). *Free to Choose: A Personal Statement*. New York: Harcourt Brace Jovanovich.

Froebel, F., J. Heinrichs and O. Kreye (1980). *The New International Division of Labour*. Cambridge: Cambridge University Press.

Fryer, John (1909). *A New Account of East India and Persia being Nine Year's Travels, 1672–81*. Ed. W. Crooke. I. Hakluyt Society, p. 301.

'Fundamental Labour Market Reform.' IMF Staff Paper. Vol. 44, No. 1.

Gamer, R. (1972). *The Politics of Urban Development*. Ithaca, N.Y.: Cornell University Press.

Ghemawat, P. and M. Patibandla (1997). 'India's Exports Since the Reforms: Three Detailed Case Studies.' Harvard Business School. Mimeo. November.

Grossman, G. and E. Helpman (1992). *Innovation and Growth in the Global Economy*. Cambridge: MIT Press.

Guha, K. (1999). 'India's Online Meritocracy.' *Financial Times*. October 25.

Guide to Key Words That Express How the Koreans Think, Communicate, and Be. H. Terpstra, De.Nederlanders inVoor-Indie, Amsterdam, 1947, p. 78.

Heeks, R. (1996). *India's Software Industry*. New Delhi: Sage Publications.

Heeks, R. (1998). 'The Uneven Profile of Indian Software Exports.' Working Paper No. 3. University of Manchester: Department of Informatics.

Ho, K.C. and B.H. Chua (1995). 'Cultural, Social and Leisure Activities in Singapore Census of Population 1990.' Monograph No. 3. Singapore: Department of Statistics.

Huff, W.G. (1994). *The Economic Growth of Singapore: Trade and Development in The Twentieth Century*. Cambridge: Cambridge University Press.

IMD (various years). *World Competitiveness Report*. Geneva, Switzerland

Industrial Strategy for Global Competitiveness of Korean Industries. Seoul: Korea Economic Research Institute. pp. 130–59.

Innovation Systems: A Comparative Analysis. New York: Oxford University Press. pp. 384–413.

International Business Handbook. Republic of Korea.

Ito, T. (n.d.). *Bonuses, Overtime and Employment: Korea and Japan*. No.1391.

Jain, Prakash (1980). 'Indian Diaspora.' *Indian Quaterly*. Delhi. Vol. 36, Nos. 3 and 4. July–December.

Jain, Prakash (1989). *India and Overseas Indians*. Delhi: Kalinga Press.

Johnson, C. (1981). 'Introduction: The Taiwan Model.' J. Hsiung et al. (eds). *Contemporary Republic of China: The Taiwan Experience*. New York: Praeger and the American Association for Chinese Studies.

Johnson, C. (1982). *MITI and the Japanese Miracle: The Growth of Industrial Policy 1925–1975*. Stanford, CA: Standford University Press.

Johnson, Jean M. (November 1998). *Statistical Profiles of Foreign Doctoral Recipients in Science and Engineering: Plans to Stay in the United States*. Arlington, VA: National Science Foundation, Division of Science Resources Studies, NSF 99–304.

Kim, J.I. and L.J. Lau (1994). 'The Sources of Economic Growth in the East Asian Newly Industrialised Countries.' *Journal of the Japanese and International Economies*. Vol. 8, pp. 235–27.

Kim, J.I. and L.J. Lau (1996). 'The Sources of Asian Pacific Economic Growth.' *Canadian Journal of Economics*. Vol. 29, Special Issue, pp. S448–54.

Kim, L.S. (1993). 'National System of Industrial Innovation: Dynamics of Capability Building in Korea.' R.R. Nelson ed. pp. 357–83.

Knack, S. and P. Keefer (1995). *Institutions and Economic Performance: Empirical Tests Using Alternative Measures of Institutions*. New York: Association of Economics and Politics.

Korea Business: The Portable Encyclopedia for Doing Business with Korea.

Korea, South Investment & Business Guide Vol 1. Emerging Markets Investment.

Korean Enterprise: The Quest for Globalization. Gerardo R. Ungson, et al.

Korean Etiquette and Ethics in Business. Boye Lafayette de Mente.

Krugman, P. (1994a). 'Competitiveness: A Dangerous Obsession.' *Foreign Affairs*. March/April, pp. 28–44.

Krugman, P. (1994b). 'The Myth of the Asian Miracle.' *Foreign Affairs*. Vol. 73, No. 6.

Krugman, P. (1996). 'A Country is not a Company.' *Harvard Business Review*. January–February, pp. 40–51.

Lall, S. (1992). 'Technological Capabilities and Industrialisation.' *World Development*. Vol. 20, No. 2, pp. 165–86.

Lee, James (1993). 'Information Technology and International Competitiveness in Consulting and Engineering Design Services: Perception of Firms from the United States.' *Information Technology and International Competitiveness: The case of construction services*. New York: United Nations.

Lee, Poh Ping (1978). *Chinese Society in Nineteenth Century* Singapore, Kuala Lumpur, Malaysia: Oxford University Press.

Leon F. Bouvier and David Simcox, 'Foreign Born Professionals in the United States.' *Population and Environment*. Vol. 16, No. 5, May 1995;

Lin, O.C.C. (1994). 'Development and Transfer of Industrial Technology in Taiwan.'

Low, L., M.H. Toh, T.W. Soon, K.Y. Tan and H. Hughes (1993). *Challenge and Response: Thirty Years of the Economic Development Board*. Singapore: Times Academic Press.

Lucas, R.E. (1988). 'On the Mechanics of Economic Development.' *Journal of Monetary Economics*. Vol. 22, pp. 3–32.

MacKie-Mason, J.K. and H.R. Varian (1994). 'Some Economics of the Internet.' Department of Economics, University of Michigan.

Mandelslo, J.A. *The Voyage and Travels of J. Albertoe Mandelslo*. Tr. John Davis. (1931). London.

Mankiw, G., D. Romer and D. Weil (1922). 'A Contribution to the Empirics of Economic Growth.' *Quarterly Journal of Economics*. Vol. 107, pp. 407–37.

Marjit, S. and A. Raychudhuri (1997). *India's Exports: An Analytical Study*. New Delhi: Oxford University Press.

Mason, E. et al. (1980). *The Economic and Social Modernisation of the Republic of Korea*. Harvard University Press.

Mathews, J.A. (1995). *High Technology Industrialisation in East Asia: The Case of The Semiconductor Industry in Taiwan and Korea*. Taipei: Chung-Hua Institution For Economic Research.

Metals in the later Medieval and early Modern World. Durham, 1982. pp. 482.8.

Migdal, J.S. (1988). *Strong Societies and Weak States*. Princeton, N.J.: Princeton University Press.

Mirza, H. (1986). *Multinationals and the Growth of Singapore Economy*. Andover: Croom Helm.

Munnell, Alicia H. (1992). 'Infrastructural Investment and Economic Growth.' *Journal of Economic Perspective*. Vol. 6, No. 4, pp. 189–198.

National Science and Technology Plan: Towards 2000 and Beyond (1996). Singapore: National Science & Technology Board (NSTB).

Nelson, R.R. ed. (1993). *National Innovation Systems: A Comparative Analysis*. New York: Oxford University Press.

Nelson, W.J. R.R. and E.N. Wolff eds. *Convergence of Productivity: Cross National Studies and Historical Evidence*. New York: Oxford University Press.

OECD (1994). *Manufacturing Performance: A Scoreboard of Indicators*. Paris: OECD.

OECD (1996). *Technology, Productivity and Job Creation*. Paris: OECD

OECD (1997a). *Information Technology Outlook 1997*. Paris: OECD.

OECD (1997b). *Industrial Competitiveness: Benchmarking Business Environment in The Global Economy*. Paris: OECD.

OECD (1997c). *Science, Technology and Industry Scoreboard of Indicators*. Paris: OECD.

Panchmukhi, P.R. (1978). *Trade Policies in India: A Quantitative Analysis*. Delhi: Concept Publishing Company.

Pang, Eng Fong and L. Lim (1977). *The Electronics Industry in Singapore*. Singapore: Economic Research Centre.

Pang, Eng Fong and Augustine Tan (1981). 'Employment and Export-led Industrialisation: The Experience of Singapore.' R. Amjad ed. *The Development of Labour Intensive Industry in ASEAN Countries*.

Patibandla, M. (1996). 'International Trade and Long-Term Economic Growth.' *Economic and Political Weekly*. Vol. 31, No. 27, pp. 3121–128. November 30.

Patibandla, M. and P. Chandra (1998). 'Organisational Practices and Employee Performance.' *Journal of Economic Behaviour and Organisation*.

Patrick, H. (1977). 'The Future of the Japanese Economy: Output and Labour Productivity.' *Journal of Japanese Studies*.

Paul Ong, Lucie Cheng, and Leslie Evans (1992). 'Migration of Highly Educated Asians and Global Dynamics.' *Asian and Pacific Migration Journal*. Vol. 1, No. 3–4.

Peterson, Paul (1981). *City Limits*. Chicago: University of Chicago Press.

Pires, T. (1949). *The Suma Oriental of Tome Pires*. Ed. and tr. A. Cortesao. Hakluyt Society.

Porter, M. (1980). *Competitive Strategy: Techniques for Analysing Industries and Competitors*. New York: The Free Press.

Porter, M. (1990). *The Competitive Advantage of Nations*. New York: The Free Press.

Raychaudhari, T. 'The Mughal Empire.' *Cambridge Economic History of India*, I. p. 185.

'R.O.C.' Lin, O.C.C. et al. eds. *Development and Transfer of Industrial Technology*. Elsevier. pp. 1–30.

Rebelo, S. (1991). 'Long Run Policy Analysis and Long Run Growth.' *Journal of Political Economy*. Vol. 99, pp. 500–21.

Richards J.F. ed. *The Imperial Monetary System of Mughal India*. Oxford University Press.

Richter, H.V. (1970). 'Problems of Assessing Unrecorded Trade.' *Bulletin of Indonesian Economic Studies*. March. Also reprinted in Bhagwati (1974).

Robert C. Kelly (Editor) Country Review, Korea, South 1998/1999.

Rodan, G. (1989). *The Political Economy of Singapore's Industrialisation*. London: Macmillan.

Roomer, P. (1986). 'Increasing Returns and Long-Run Growth.' *Journal of Political Economy*. Vol. 94, pp. 1002–37.

S. Arasaratnam (1987). 'Portuguese and the Indian Ocean in the Seventeenth Century.' Ashin Das Gupta and M.N. Pearson eds. *India and the Indian Ocean. 1500–1800.*: Oxford University Press. p. 108.

Sachs, Jeffrey and Andrew M. Warner (1995). 'Economic Reform and the Process of Global Integration.' Brookings Papers on Economic Activity.

Sarel, M. (1996). *Growth and Productivities in Asean Economics*: International Monetary Fund (IMF) Economic Issues, No. 1.

Sarkar, P. (1994). 'India's Balance of Payments and Exchange Rate Behaviour Since 1971: A New Approach.' *Economic and Political Weekly*. January 1–8.

Sassen, S. (1991). *The Global City*. Princeton: Princeton University Press.

Sassen, S. (1995). 'Urban Impacts of Economic Globalisation.' J. Brotchie et al. eds. *Cities in Competition*. Melbourne: Longman Australia.

Sen, P. (1986). 'The 1966 Devaluation in India: A Reappraisal.' *Economic and Political Weekly*. July 26.

Shaikh Sikandar ibn Muihammad (1611). *Mirat-i-Sikandari* Tr. Edward Clive Bayley. 1895. London. Refers to Surat and Rander.

Shapiro, C. and H.R. Varian (1999). *Information Rules*. Cambridge: Harvard Business School Press.

Singapore, Department of Statistics (1995). *The Extent and Pattern of Foreign Investment*.

Sinkin, C.G.F. (1970). 'Indonesia's Unrecorded Trade.' *Bulletin of Indonesian Economic Studies*. March. Also reprinted in Bhagwati (1974).

Solow, R.M. (1956). 'A Contribution to the Theory of Economic Growth.' *Quarterly Journal of Economics*. Vol. 70, pp. 65–94.

Stiglitz, J. et al. (1989). *The Economic Role of the State*. Oxford: Basil Blackwell.

Studies of International Development (FASID), November 1997.

Subramanian, C.R. (1992). *India and the Computer*. New Delhi: Oxford University Press.

Swan, T.W. (1956). 'Economic Growth and Capital Accumulation.' *Economic Record*. Vol. 36, pp. 51–66.

Tang, Joyce (1993). 'The Career Attainment of Caucasian and Asian Engineers.' *Sociological Quarterly*. Vol. 34, No. 3, pp. 467–496.

Tarabusi, C.C. (1997). 'Technology and Employment: The Role of Organisational Change and Learning.' *Science Technology Industry Review*. OECD. Vol. 20, pp. 89–119.

Task Force on Job Hopping (1988). *Report of the Task Force on Job Hopping*. Singapore: National Productivity Board.

The Dutch Vereenigde Oost-Indische Campagnie set up a factory at Surat in 1617.

The French Compagnie des Indes Orientales established its first Indian factory in 1668 at Surat.

The Global Competitiveness Report (1997). Geneva, Switzerland: World Economic Forum (WEF).

The Korea Super Job Catalog. James F. Haddon.

The World Competitiveness Yearbook 1997. Lausanne, Switzerland: International Institute for Management Development (IMD).

Toh, M.H. and L. Low (1992). Total Factory Productivity in Singapore: Some Myths and Issues. Mimeo.

UNIDO (1997). *Industrial Development Global Report 1996*. Oxford University Press.

Union Bank of Switzerland (1996). 'The Asian Economic Miracle.' *UBS International Finance*. Issue No. 29. Autumn.

United Nations (1993). *Information Technology and International Competitiveness: The Case of the Construction Services Industry*. New York: United Nations Conference on Trade and Development (UNCTAD).

Varian, H.R. (1998) *Markets for Information Goods*. Berkeley: University of California.

Wade, R. (1991) *Governing the Market—Economic Theory and the Role of Government in East Asian Industrialisation*. Princeton: Princeton University Press.

White, G. (1988). *Development States in East Asia*. London: Macmillan.

Wilawan Kanjanapan. 'The Immigration of Asian Professionals to the United States: 1988–1990.' *International Migration Review*. Vol. 29, No. 1, Spring 1995, pp. 7–32.

Williamson, O.E. (1985). *The Economic Institutions of Capitalism*. New York: Free Press.

Winston, G.C. (1969). 'Overinvoicing, Under-utilisation, and Distorted Industrial Growth.' *Pakistan Development Review*. Summer 1969.

Wong, Chow Ming (1990). 'The Singapore Chinese Chamber of Commerce 1906–1942.' Unpublished Academic Exercise. National University of Singapore: Dept. of History, Faculty of Arts and Social Sciences.

Wong, P.K. (1955a). 'Competing in the Global Electronics Industry: A Comparative Study of the Innovation Networks of Singapore and Taiwan.' *Journal of Industry*.

Wong, P.K. (1955b). 'Technology Transfer and Development Inducement by Foreign MNCs: The Experience of Singapore.' K.Y. Jeong and M.H. Kwack eds.

Wong, P.K. (1955c). *National Innovation System: The Case of Singapore*. Seoul: Science and Technology Policy Institute.

Wong, P.K. (1992). 'Technological Development Through Subcontracting Linkages: Evidence from Singapore.' *Scandinavian International Business Review*. Vol. 1 No. 3.

Wong, P.K. (1994). 'Singapore's Technology Strategy.' D.F. Simon ed. *The Emerging Technological Trajectory of the Pacific Rim*. N.Y.

World Bank (1993). *The East Asian Miracles: Economic Growth and Public Policy*. Oxford: Oxford University Press.

Young, A. (1993). 'A Tale of Two Cities: Factor Accumulation and Technical Change in Hong Kong and Singapore.' NBER Macroeconomics.

Young, A. (1995). 'The Tyranny of Numbers: Confronting the Statistical Realities of the East Asian Growth Experience.' *Quarterly Journal of Economics*. Vol. 110, pp. 641–80.

Index

About the Author

Raghu Nandan is one of the founding Directors of Specialised Projects International (UK) Ltd and is now based in Pondicherry. He has worked as a consultant and sometimes as the initial chief executive in as many as 24 developing nations on industrial development projects, including those funded by the World Bank and the Commonwealth Fund for Technical Cooperation of the Commonwealth Secretariat, London. He is a visiting faculty for professional courses in several universities in Thailand, Malaysia and Singapore. Raghu Nandan can be contacted at spiukltd@hotmail.com.